A Survey of Paramattha Dhammas

Sujin Boriharnwanaket
Translator Nina van Gorkom

2020

First edition published in 2006
Second edition published in 2020 by
Zolag
www.zolag.co.uk

ISBN 9781897633373

British Library Cataloguing in Publication Data
A CIP record for this book is available from the British Library

Contents

1

Preface

"A Survey of Paramattha Dhammas" is a masterwork, written by Acharn[1] Sujin Boriharnwanaket with great patience and a sense of urgency to help others understand reality. The whole book, in which she explains with great detail citta (consciousness), cetasika (mental factors), and rūpa (physical phenomena), radiates abundant mettā, loving-kindness. Time and again it is stressed that theoretical understanding, only knowing realities by name, is not sufficient, although it can be a foundation for direct knowledge. The real purpose of the study of the Dhamma is seeing that this very moment is dhamma, non-self. All realities, dhammas, have to be known now, when they occur, so that the wrong view of self can be eradicated.

Acharn Sujin is a wise friend in the Dhamma who untiringly explains the practice leading to the direct experience of realities. She has been explaining the Dhamma for over forty years and her lectures are broadcasted daily all over Thailand; they can also be heard in Cambodia, Laos and Malaysia. In recognition of her teaching, the venerable

[1] Acharn in Thai means teacher. The Pāli term is āchariya.

monks at Mahāmakut Buddhist University presented Acharn Sujin with an honorary degree in 2002. This book is based on her lectures.

The whole book points to the truth of anattā, non-self. The clinging to the concept of self is very subtle and intricate and therefore difficult to notice. We are inclined to cling to an idea of a self who develops paññā, understanding, but from the beginning we ought to remember that there is no self who can direct the arising of sati, awareness, and paññā. Sati and paññā are sobhana cetasikas (beautiful mental factors), which arise when the appropriate conditions are there, and then they perform their functions. Clinging to sati and paññā will be counteractive to their development. The right conditions for sati and paññā are listening to the Dhamma as it is explained by the right friend in the Dhamma, and wise consideration of it.

There are detailed explanations about cittas that arise in a process or series, with the purpose of showing that citta is only a conditioned element that is beyond control, and not self. The reader may wonder where in the scriptures he can find explanations about processes of citta. Acharn Sujin has a profound understanding of the whole Tipiṭaka, the Commentaries and sub-commentaries, and she used these texts as her sources. The "Path of Discrimination" ("Paṭisambhidāmagga" of the Khuddaka Nikāya)[2] and the "Conditional Relations" ("Paṭṭhāna")[3] deal with the processes of cittas. Many details have been given in the "Visuddhimagga"[4] and the "Expositor" ("Aṭṭhasālinī")[5], which are entirely based on canonical tradition. Also, the "Manual of Abhidhamma" ("Abhidhammattha Saṅgaha") and the sub-commentary, the "Abhidhammattha-vibhāvinī-ṭīka", which are also derived from canonical tradition, deal with the processes of citta.

The reader may wonder why so many details have been given about the different planes of existence where there can be birth. In the scriptures, especially in the "Jātakas" we shall come across the names of

---

[2]See "Treatise on Knowledge", Ch XVII, Behaviour, Cariya.

[3]See "Feeling Triplet", Investigation Chapter, under Proximity and Repetition, where also the process of enlightenment is dealt with. One has to remember that mind-element, mano-dhātu, includes the adverting-consciousness and the receiving-consciousness, and that mind-consciousness-element includes all cittas other than those included in mind-element and the sense-cognitions.

[4]Ch XIV, 96 and following, in the translation by Ven. Nyāṇamoli.

[5]"The Expositor", Introductory Discourse, §§3-4.

these planes. Knowing about them helps us to see the intricacy of the causes that bring their appropriate results.

Many details about the development of samatha and the jhānacittas have been given with the purpose of pointing out that only the right cause can bring the right result. Samatha has to be developed with kusala citta accompanied by paññā and if that is not the case, there is wrong concentration with lobha, attachment, instead of right concentration. If someone sits and tries to concentrate without any understanding, there is wrong concentration. People may erroneously take for jhāna what is only lobha, and therefore, it is explained that many conditions are necessary for the attainment of jhāna and how difficult this is.

In the development of vipassanā, insight, paññā is developed in stages. The book explains about these different stages of insight knowledge in detail, in order to show that the development of paññā is an extremely long process.[6] One may read the "Visuddhimagga" (Ch XVIII-XXI) or the "Path of Discrimination" (Treatise on Knowledge, Ch V-XI) about the stages of insight with wrong understanding. Or, one may erroneously believe that these stages are reached by thinking of nāma, mental phenomena, and rūpa, physical phenomena; by thinking of impermanence, dukkha and anattā. However, all stages, from the first stage on until enlightenment, are realized by direct understanding of nāma and rūpa. No matter what stage paññā has reached, the objects of paññā are the characteristics of nāma and rūpa as they naturally appear at this very moment. Acharn Sujin stresses this many times, because the practice of the Dhamma should be entirely in conformity with the Tipiṭaka.

With my deepest appreciation of Acharn Sujin's inspiring guidance, I offer the translation of this book to the English speaking reader.

The part of this book on Concepts[7] has been printed separately under the sponsorship of Robert Kirkpatrick, whose efforts I greatly appreciate.

---

[6] Cira kāla bhāvanā, a development that takes a long time. Cira means long, and kāla means time.

[7] "Realities and Concepts. The Buddha's explanation of the world", Bangkok; DSSF.

I have divided the sections of this book into chapters, each with its own heading, in order to make the text more easily accessible. The footnotes to the text are, for the greater part, from my hand. I added them to help the reader who is not familiar with some terms and ideas in the text.

The last section of this book, the appendices to citta, cetasika and rūpa, written by Acharn Sujin, are essential for the understanding of all chapters.

The quotations from the suttas in English are mostly taken from the editions of the Pāli Text Society.

May this book, fundamental for all who study the Dhamma, inspire the reader to carefully consider the realities explained here, and to develop understanding of them.

Nina van Gorkom

Part I

General Introduction

2

The Scriptures and their Commentaries

The word of the Buddha, the Dhamma and the Vinaya as taught by him, consists of nine divisions, which are Sutta, Geyya, Veyyākaraṇa, Gāthā, Udāna, Itivuttaka, Jātaka, Abbhuta and Vedalla.[1]

1. Sutta[2] includes all Discourses, such as the Mangala sutta (Good Discourse, "Minor Readings", V), and also the Vinaya Piṭaka[3] and the "Niddesa".

[1] See "The Expositor", "Atthasālinī", Introductory Discourse, 26. The teachings as compiled (not yet written) literature are thus enumerated in the scriptures as nine divisions, for example in the "Middle Length Sayings" I, no. 22.

[2] The Pāli term sutta means that which is heard. The word of the Buddha which has been heard.

[3] The three Piṭaka, or Tipiṭaka, are the three divisions of the teachings, namely: the Vinaya, Suttanta and Abhidhamma. When the teachings are classified as nine divisions, the Vinaya is in a section of the Sutta. The "Atthasālinī" mentions the "Sutta-Vibhaṅga" and "Parivāra" in the section on Sutta, which belong to the Vinaya.

2. Geyya includes all suttas with verses (gāthā), such as the Sagāthā-vagga of the "Saṃyutta Nikāya", or "Kindred Sayings" (I).

3. Veyyākaraṇa, or "Exposition", includes the Abhidhamma Piṭaka, the suttas without verses and the words of the Buddha that are not included in the other eight divisions.

4. Gāthā or "Verses" include the "Dhammapada", "Theragāthā", "Therīgāthā" ("Psalms of the Brothers and Sisters") and those parts of the "Sutta-Nipāta" not called Sutta and entirely in verse.

5. Udāna or "Verses of Uplift" include eighty-two suttas connected with verses recited by the Buddha, inspired by knowledge and joy.

6. Itivuttaka or "As it was said" includes one hundred ten suttas[4] beginning with "Thus it was said by the Blessed One" (in Pāli: "Vuttaṃ h'etaṃ Bhagavatā").

7. Jātaka or Birth Stories include five hundred fifty stories of the past lives of the Buddha and his disciples, beginning with the Apaṇṇaka Jātaka.

8. Abbhuta, "Marvellous," includes suttas connected with wonderful and marvellous things (dhammas with extraordinary qualities, which are amazing).

9. Vedalla includes suttas with questions and answers that have as result understanding and delight, such as the Cullavedalla sutta.

The word of the Buddha consists of eighty-four thousand units of text. The venerable Ānanda learnt eighty-two thousand units of text from the Exalted One, and two thousand units of text from the bhikkhus, mainly from the venerable Sāriputta. Each theme is one unit of text. Thus, the sutta containing one theme is one unit of text. Where there are questions and answers, each question forms one unit of text and each answer forms one unit of text.

When the scriptures are classified as the Tipiṭaka, they are classified as threefold, namely: the Vinaya, the Suttanta and the Abhidhamma.

[4] In the "Atthasālinī", the counting is one hundred and twelve.

The Vinaya Piṭaka or "Books of Discipline" consist of five Books, namely:

- "Mahāvibhaṅga"
- "Bhikkhunīvibhaṅga"
- "Mahāvagga"
- "Cullavagga"
- "Parivāra"[5]

The commentary that explains the Vinaya is the "Samantapāsādikā".[6]

The Suttanta Piṭaka, or Discourses, consists of five Nikāyas,[7] namely, "Dīgha Nikāya" or "Dialogues of the Buddha,"[8] "Majjhima Nikāya" or "Middle Length Sayings,"[9] "Saṃyutta Nikāya" or "Kindred Sayings,"[10] "Aṅguttara Nikāya" or "Gradual Sayings,"[11] "Khuddaka Nikāya" or "The Minor Collection."[12]

The "Dīgha Nikāya" is a collection of long dialogues (dīgha means long), consisting of thirty-four suttas. This collection is divided into three sections (in Pāli: vagga):[13]

- Sīla-kkhandha-vagga (sīla means morality and khandha means group);
- Mahā-vagga (mahā means great);

[5]The PTS has edited and translated the entire Vinaya Piṭaka as "The Book of the Discipline": "Suttavibhaṅga" comprising "Mahāvibhaṅga" and "Bhikkhunīvibhaṅga" (Vol. I-III), "Mahā-vagga" (Vol. IV), "Cullavagga" (Vol.V) and "Parivāra" (Vol.VI).

[6]The Introduction to the Vinaya, the "Bāhiranidāna", has been translated as 'The Inception of Discipline and the Vinaya Nidāna', P.T.S.

[7]Nikāya means body or collection.

[8]I am giving the English titles, as used in the translations of the P.T.S. "The Dialogues of the Buddha" have been edited in three volumes.

[9]Edited in three volumes.

[10]Edited in five volumes.

[11]Edited in five volumes.

[12]This collection consisting of sixteen parts has been edited in different volumes, but not all of them have been translated into English.

[13]These sections are in the Pāli text but not in the English edition.

- Pāṭika-vagga (called after the first sutta; Pāṭika is a proper name).

The commentary to this collection is the "Sumaṅgalavilāsinī".

The "Majjhima Nikāya" is a collection of suttas of medium length (majjhima means middle), and it consists of one hundred fifty-two suttas. It is divided into three parts, which are called in Pāli "paṇṇāsa," meaning fifty. The first two parts consist of fifty suttas each and the third part of fifty-two suttas. They are called:

- Mūla-paṇṇāsa (mūla means root), consisting of five sections of ten suttas;
- Majjhima-paṇṇāsa, consisting of five sections of ten suttas;
- Upari-paṇṇāsa (upari means above or later), consisting of five sections, of which four have ten suttas and the fifth has twelve suttas.

The commentary to this collection is the "Papañcasūdanī".

The "Saṃyutta Nikāya" is a group of suttas (saṃyutta means joined, connected) divided into five main divisions, namely:

- Sagāthā-vagga (gāthā means verse, with verses), with eleven sections;
- Nidāna-vagga (nidāna means origin or cause), consisting of nine sections;
- Khandha-vagga (dealing with the five khandhas), consisting of thirteen sections;
- Saḷāyatana-vagga (saḷāyatana is the sixfold āyatana or sense spheres), consisting of ten sections;
- Mahā-vagga (great chapter), consisting of twelve sections.

The commentary to this collection is the "Sāratthappakāsinī".

The "Aṅguttara Nikāya" consists of suttas grouped according to the numbers of Dhamma subjects or points dealt with. They are arranged in order, from one to eleven. Thus, there are eleven "nipāta," or sections in all. "Book of the Ones" consists of suttas dealing with one kind of subject, and so on up to the Book of the Elevens. Summarizing them, they are:

- Eka-nipāta (eka means one), Book of the Ones;
- Duka-nipāta (duka, from dve, two, meaning pair), Book of the Twos;
- Tika-nipāta, Book of the Threes;
- Catuka-nipāta, Book of the Fours;
- Pañcaka-nipāta, Book of the Fives;
- Chaka-nipāta, Book of the Sixes;
- Sattaka-nipāta, Book of the Sevens;
- Aṭṭhaka-nipāta, Book of the Eights;
- Navaka-nipāta, Book of the Nines;
- Dasaka-nipāta, Book of the Tens;
- Ekādasaka-nipāta, Book of the Elevens.

The commentary to the "Aṅguttara Nikāya" is the "Manorathapūranī".

Apart from these four Nikāyas, there is the "Khuddaka Nikāya", which contains the word of the Buddha. This consists of the following books:

- "Khuddakapāṭha" or "Minor Readings";[14]
- "Dhammapada" (pada means word or phrase);[15]
- "Udāna" or "Verses of Uplift";
- "Itivuttaka" or "As it was said";
- "Suttanipāta" or "The Group of Discourses";
- "Vimānavatthu" or "Stories of the Mansions" (in "Minor Anthologies IV");

[14] Translated into English and edited by the P.T.S. in one volume together with the translation of its commentary "The Illustrator of Ultimate Meaning."

[15] There are several English translations of this text.

- "Petavatthu" or "Stories of the Departed" (in "Minor Anthologies IV");
- "Theragāthā" or "Psalms of the Brethren";
- "Therīgāthā" or "Psalms of the Sisters";
- "Jātaka" or "Stories of the Buddha's Former Births" (in three volumes by P.T.S.);
- "Mahā-Niddesa" (niddesa means descriptive exposition);
- "Cūḷa-Niddesa" (cūḷa or culla means small);[16]
- "Paṭisambhidāmagga" or "The Path of Discrimination";
- "Apadāna" (life histories);[17]
- "Buddhavaṃsa" or "Chronicle of the Buddhas" (in "Minor Anthologies III");
- "Cariyāpiṭaka" or "Basket of Conduct" (in "Minor Anthologies III").

The commentaries to these collections of the "Khuddaka Nikāya" are the following:

- The "Paramatthajotikā", which is the commentary to the "Khuddakapātha" and the "Suttanipāta";[18]
- "Dhammapadaṭṭhakathā" or "Buddhist Legends" (in three volumes by the P.T.S.), which is the commentary to the "Dhammapada";

[16]The "Mahā-Niddesa" and the "Cūḷa-Niddesa" have not been translated into English.

[17]This has not been translated into English.

[18]The commentary to the "Khuddakapātha" has been translated into English as I mentioned, but the commentary to the "Sutta Nipāta" has not been translated.

- The "Paramatthadīpanī", which is the commentary to the "Udāna", the "Itivuttaka", the "Petavatthu", the "Theragāthā", the "Therīgāthā", the "Cariyāpiṭaka" and the "Vimānavatthu";[19]

- The "Jātakatthavaṇṇanā", which is the commentary to the "Jātaka";[20]

- The "Saddhammapajjotika", which is the commentary to the "Mahā-Niddesa" and the "Cūḷa-Niddesa";

- The "Saddhammappakāsinī", which is the commentary to the "Paṭisambhidāmagga";

- The "Visuddhajanavilāsinī", which is the commentary to the "Apadāna";

- The "Madhuratthavilāsinī", or "The Clarifier of Sweet Meaning" (P.T.S.), which is the commentary to the "Buddhavaṃsa".

The Abhidhamma Piṭaka consists of the following seven Books:

- "Dhammasaṅgaṇī" (translated by PTS as "Buddhist Psychological Ethics," and also translated by U Kyaw Khine) and this has as commentary the "Aṭṭhasālinī" ("The Expositor");

- "Vibhaṅga" or "The Book of Analysis," which has as commentary the "Sammohavinodanī" or "Dispeller of Delusion";[21]

- "Dhātukathā" or "Discourse on Elements";

- "Puggalapaññatti" or "a Designation of Human Types";

- "Kathāvatthu" or "Points of Controversy";

- "Yamaka";[22]

---

[19]Translated into English are: the "Udāna" commentary (two volumes), the "Itivuttaka" commentary (two volumes), the commentary to the "Vimānavatthu", "Vimāna Stories," the commentary to the "Petavatthu", "Peta Stories," the commentary to the "Therīgāthā", "Commentary on the Verses of the Therīs."

[20]In the English edition of the "Buddha's Birth Stories", parts of the commentary have been added.

[21]In two volumes.

[22]Yamaka means pair. This has not been translated into English.

- "Paṭṭhāna" or "Conditional Relations".[23]

As to the commentary to the last five Books of the Abhidhamma, this is the "Pañcappakaraṇatthakathā".[24]

The greater part of the commentaries to the Tipiṭaka is from the hand of the great commentator Buddhaghosa.[25] He translated into Pāli, compiled and arranged material from the ancient commentaries, which were in Sinhalese. These commentaries, the "Mahā-Atthakathā", the "Mahā-Paccarī" and the "Kuruṇḍi", stemmed from the time of the Thera Mahinda, the son of the great King Asoka who came to Sri Lanka in order to propagate Buddhism.

Furthermore, there are sub-commentaries, called ṭīkā in Pāli, which explain the commentaries. These are the "Sāratthadīpanī", a sub-commentary to the "Samantapāsādikā", which is the commentary to the Vinaya; the "Sārattha Mañjūsā", a sub-commentary to the Suttanta Piṭaka, the "Paramatthapakāsinī", a sub-commentary to the Abhidhamma Piṭaka; and the anuṭīkā (anu meaning: along, alongside), which explains words and expressions in the sub-commentaries. Apart from the aforementioned works, there are several other texts in Buddhism needed for the study of the Dhamma that were composed by the "Elders"[26] who were qualified to pass on the tradition of the Dhamma. These are the following texts:

- "Milindapañha" or "Milinda's Questions,"[27] composed about 500 Buddhist Era (43 B.C.);

- "Visuddhimagga" or "Path of Purification,"[28] an Encyclopedia on Buddhism, composed by Buddhaghosa about 1000 B.E. (457

[23]There is a translation of part of the "Paṭṭhāna". There is also a "Guide to Conditional Relations", explaining part of the "Paṭṭhāna", by U Narada, Myanmar.

[24]Only the commentary to the "Kathāvatthu" has been translated into English, with the title of "Debates Commentary".

[25]He lived in the fifth century of the Christian era and stayed in the "Great Monastery" of Anurādhapura, in Sri Lanka.

[26]Thera can be translated as Elder or senior monk, a monk who has been ordained for at least ten years.

[27]In two volumes. One translation by the P.T.S. and another one by T.W. Rhys Davids.

[28]One edition as translated by Ven. Nyāṇamoli, Colombo, and one edition as translated by Pe Maung Tin, P.T.S.

A.D.);

- "Abhidhammattha Saṅgaha" or "A Manual of Abhidhamma,"[29] composed by Ven. Anuruddha about 1000 B.E. (457 A.D.);[30]

- "Sārattha Saṅgaha", composed by Nanda about 1000 B.E. (457 A.D.);

- "Paramattha Mañjūsā", a sub-commentary to the "Visuddhimagga", composed by Ven. Dhammapāla;

- "Saccasaṇkhepa" (meaning Exposition of the Truth), composed by Ven. Dhammapala;

- "Abhidhammattha-vibhāvinī-ṭīkā", a sub-commentary to the "Abhidhammattha Saṅgaha"[31] composed by Sumangala, of Sri Lanka;

- "Moha Vicchedanī", an explanation of the "Dhammasangaṇi" and the "Vibhaṅga" (the first and second Books of the Abhidhamma), composed by Ven. Kassapa of Sri Lanka, about 1703 B.E. (1160 A.D.);

- "Mangalattha Dīpanī", an explanation of the Mangala sutta (Good Omen Discourse, Khuddakapāṭha, "Minor Readings", no 5) composed by Ven. Sirimangala in Chiangmai.[32]

---

[29]It has been translated into English and published by the P.T.S. under the title of "Compendium of Philosophy", and by Ven. Nārada, Colombo, under the title of "A Manual of Abhidhamma". It has also been translated by the Venerable Bhikkhu Bodhi as "A Comprehensive Manual of Abhidhamma". Moreover, it has been translated together with its commentary as "Summary of the Topics of Abhidhamma" and "Exposition of the Topics of Abhidhamma", by R.P. Wijeratne and Rupert Gethin.

[30]The P.T.S. edition suggests that the date is between the 8th and the 12th century A.D.

[31]Translated into English by by R.P. Wijeratne and Rupert Gethin, see footnote 29.

[32]I could add to this enumeration the "Nettippakaraṇa", translated as "The Guide," P.T.S. and the "Peṭakopadesa" which has been translated as "Piṭaka Disclosure" by Ven. Ñāṇamoli. They are compilations of a school, which, according to tradition, traced its descent to Mahā-Kaccana, one of the great disciples of the Buddha. Dhammapāla has written a commentary on the "Nettippakaraṇa", probably late fifth century A.D.

3
The Buddha

The Omniscient Buddha, the Exalted One, attained parinibbāna, his final passing away, between the twin Sāla trees in the Salwood, a place of recreation for the Mallas of the city of Kusināra. From then on, the living beings in this world no longer had an opportunity to hear the teaching of the Dhamma directly from the Buddha himself. However, the Buddha left us the Dhamma and the Vinaya he had taught and laid down as our teacher, representing him after he had finally passed away.[1]

The measure of regard and respect Buddhists have for the Buddha's excellent Dhamma is in accordance with the degree of their knowledge and understanding of the Dhamma and Vinaya. Even if a man were to see the outward appearance of the Buddha, emanating his excellence, listen to the teaching of the Dhamma directly from him, or seize the hem of his garment and walk behind him step by step, but did not understand the Dhamma, he would not really see the Buddha. But if one sees and understands the Dhamma, one is called a person who sees

[1]Dialogues of the Buddha II, no 16, Mahā Parinibbāna Sutta.

the Tathāgata.[2]

There are three levels of understanding of the Buddhist teachings, the Dhamma as taught by the omniscient Buddha, namely:

- the level of pariyatti, or study of the Dhamma and Vinaya;
- the level of paṭipatti, or practice, the development of understanding of the Dhamma with the purpose to realize the Dhamma by which defilements are eradicated and the ceasing of dukkha is reached;
- the level of paṭivedha, or penetration, the direct realization of the Dhamma by which the defilements are eradicated and the ceasing of dukkha is reached.

The saying of the Buddha that whoever sees the Dhamma sees the Tathāgata, refers to the seeing and realization of the Dhamma the Buddha attained at the moment of his enlightenment. This is the Dhamma consisting of the nine supramundane, or lokuttara, dhammas.[3] The direct realization of the Dhamma, which is the level of paṭivedha, is the result of the practice, paṭipatti, the development of the understanding of the Dhamma. The level of paṭipatti must depend on pariyatti, the study of the Dhamma and the Vinaya. The study is the refuge on which we depend, it is the way leading step by step to the Dhamma of the level of paṭipatti, the practice, and then to the Dhamma of the level of paṭivedha, the realization.

The Dhamma, the teaching of the Buddha, has been preserved by memorizing and was passed on by oral tradition. It was recited from memory as heard from the disciples who were arahats and who had established the three parts of the teachings, called the Tipiṭaka at the first Council, held shortly after the Buddha's parinibbāna in Rājagaha. The Dhamma was recited from memory and passed on until it was committed to writing in the first century B.C. The Dhamma and Vinaya

[2]"Khuddaka Nikāya", "Minor Readings", "As it was said" ("Itivuttaka"), The Threes, Ch V, no. 3. Tathāgata is an epithet of the Buddha.

[3]There are eight types of lokuttara cittas (supramundane consciousness), which realize the lokuttara dhamma that is nibbāna. There are four stages of enlightenment and for each of those there are two types of lokuttara citta, path-consciousness and fruition-consciousness. This will be explained later on.

as established at the Council by the disciples who were arahats consists of three parts, namely:

- the Vinaya Piṭaka,
- the Suttanta Piṭaka,
- the Abhidhamma Piṭaka.

The Vinaya Piṭaka concerns mostly the rules of conduct for the monks so that they can lead the "holy life" (brahma cariya)[4] perfectly, to the highest degree. The Suttanta Piṭaka mostly concerns the principles of the Dhamma as preached to different people at different places. The Abhidhamma Piṭaka deals with the nature of dhammas, realities, and their interrelation by way of cause and result.

The Buddha had realized the true nature of all realities and also their interrelation, by way of cause and effect, through his enlightenment. The Buddha explained the Dhamma, which he had realized through his enlightenment, in order to help other beings living in this world. In his incomparable wisdom, purity and compassion, he explained the Dhamma from the time of his enlightenment until the time of his parinibbāna, his final passing away. The Buddha fulfilled the perfections in order to become the Perfectly Enlightened One, the Arahat, the Sammāsambuddha.[5] He was endowed with extraordinary accomplishments (in Pāli, sampadā),[6] and these were the "accomplishment of cause" (hetu), the "accomplishment of fruition" (phala) and the "accomplishment of assistance to other beings" (sattupakāra)[7].

As regards the "accomplishment of cause," this is the fulfilment of the right cause, namely the perfections necessary to attain enlightenment and become the Sammāsambuddha.

As regards the "accomplishment of fruition," this is the attainment of four fruits or results that are the following accomplishments:

---

[4]Brahmacariya, the life of those who develop satipaṭṭhāna, right understanding of realities, in order to become an arahat.

[5]Universal Buddha, who found the Path all by himself and could teach the truth to others.

[6]"Abhidhammattha-vibhāvinī-ṭīkā".

[7]Satta is being and upakāra is assistance.

1. The accomplishment of wisdom (ñāṇa sampadā), the wisdom arising with the path-consciousness, at the moment of his enlightenment.[8] This wisdom is the basis and root-cause of his omniscience and his ten powers[9] (dasa bala).

2. The accomplishment of abandoning (pahāna sampadā). This is the complete eradication of all defilements, together with all accumulated tendencies for conduct which may not be agreeable, called in Pāli: vāsanā. Vāsanā is conduct through body or speech, which may not be agreeable and has been accumulated in the past. This disposition can only be eradicated by a Sammāsambuddha.[10]

3. The accomplishment of power (ānubhāva sampadā), which is the power to achieve what one aspires to.

4. The accomplishment of physical excellence (rūpa-kāya sampadā). This consists of the special bodily characteristics manifesting his excellent qualities accumulated in the past[11] and also, apart from these, other physical qualities, which were pleasing to the eye, impressive to all people, and which gave them joy.

When the cause, the perfections, has been fulfilled, it is the condition for the accomplishment of fruition, the attainment of enlightenment and becoming the Sammāsambuddha. Not just for his own sake did he become the Sammāsambuddha, gaining freedom from dukkha (suffering, inherent in the cycle of birth and death). He fulfilled the perfections in

[8]The magga-citta is the lokuttara citta, supramundane citta, experiencing nibbāna and eradicating defilements. It is accompanied by wisdom, paññā, which is called magga-ñāṇa.

[9]These powers are his perfect comprehension in the field of wisdom, such as comprehension of deeds (kamma) which bring their appropriate results, comprehension of the elements, the khandhas (mental and physical phenomena), the āyatanas (sense-fields), comprehension of the inclinations of other beings, remembrance of his former lives, knowledge of the passing away and rebirth of other beings, the destruction of defilements. ("Middle Length Sayings" I, no. 12, The Greater Discourse on the Lion's Roar).

[10]Even arahats, those who have no defilements, can have behaviour which is not pleasing, such as speaking fast or running, accumulated in the past. Such conduct is not motivated by akusala citta, unwholesome consciousness, since they have eradicated all defilements.

[11]See "Dialogues of the Buddha" III, no. 30, The Marks of the Superman.

order to attain enlightenment and acquire omniscience of the Dhamma so that he could teach the Dhamma to the living beings in this world who could also thereby become liberated from dukkha. If the Buddha had fulfilled the perfections in order to eradicate defilements and to become freed from dukkha only for his own sake, he could not be called the Sammāsambuddha.

There are two kinds of Buddha: the Sammāsambuddha and the Pacceka Buddha, or "Silent Buddha."[12]

As regards the Sammāsambuddha, he is someone who has realized by his profound wisdom, all by himself, the truths concerning all dhammas, which he had never heard before, and has attained omniscience of those dhammas as well as mastery of special powers in the field of knowledge.

As regards the Pacceka Buddha, he is someone who, by himself, has thoroughly realized the truths concerning all dhammas, which he had never heard before, but has not attained omniscience of them, nor mastery of special powers in the field of knowledge.

Thus, the cause, the fulfilment of the perfections, brings its result, which is the attainment of Buddhahood accordingly. Cause and result are different for the Sammāsambuddha and for the Pacceka Buddha.

The third accomplishment of the Buddha regards the assistance to living beings (sattupakāra). This is the accomplishment of constant assistance to the living beings of this world because of his disposition and his efforts to do so. He wanted to help even people of evil character such as Devadatta.[13] In the case of people whose faculty of understanding was not yet strong enough, the Buddha waited with the teaching of Dhamma until the time was ripe for them. He taught Dhamma with the sole purpose to help people to gain freedom from all dukkha, without any consideration of gaining possessions, honour, and so on, for himself.

When the Sammāsambuddha had fulfilled the accomplishment of cause and the accomplishment of fruition, he was ready to help those who were receptive to his teaching, to be freed from dukkha, and this was the accomplishment of assistance to other beings. Thus, he was

[12] "Puggala Paññatti", "Designation of Human Types," Ch I, Division of Human Types by One, 28, 29. Pacceka is derived from the Pāli paṭi eka, by himself. Eka means alone.

[13] He tried to kill the Buddha on various occasions.

the Sammāsambuddha because he fulfilled the three accomplishments of cause, of fruition and of assistance to other beings.

Therefore, the Dhamma that the Sammāsambuddha taught is the Dhamma he completely penetrated when he attained enlightenment. Through the realization of the Dhamma at the time of his enlightenment, his defilements were completely eradicated. The Buddha taught the Dhamma he had realized himself so that those who practised the Dhamma accordingly would also become free from defilements.

The followers of the Buddha should investigate and study the truth of the Dhamma that the Buddha realized through his enlightenment, in order to find out what this truth exactly is. In which way is the truth the Buddha realized different from the truth of the conventional world?

The Buddha realized the truth through his enlightenment and taught it to his followers so that they too would have understanding and practise the Dhamma accordingly until they would realize the truth themselves. The truth the Buddha taught is that everything which appears is a type of dhamma,[14] a reality that is not self, not a being, not a person. All dhammas that arise do so because there are conditions for their arising, such as attachment, anger, regret, unhappy feeling, happy feeling, jealousy, avarice, loving-kindness, compassion, seeing, hearing; all of these are different types of dhammas. There are different kinds of dhammas because they arise on account of different conditions.

One erroneously takes attachment, anger, and other dhammas that arise, for self, for a being, for a person, and that is wrong view, wrong understanding. It is wrong understanding because those dhammas, after they have arisen, fall away, disappear, are subject to change all the time, from birth to death. The reason for erroneously taking dhammas for self, a being or a person, is ignorance of the truth about dhammas.

Whenever one sees, one takes the seeing, which is a kind of dhamma, for self; one clings to the idea of "I am seeing." When one hears, one takes the dhamma that hears for self; one clings to the idea of "I am hearing." When one smells, one takes the dhamma that smells for self; one clings to the idea of "I am smelling." When one tastes, one takes the dhamma that tastes for self; one clings to the idea of "I am tasting." When one experiences tangible object through the bodysense, one takes

[14]Dhamma has several meanings, it does not only mean doctrine. In this context dhamma means everything which is real, reality.

the dhamma that experiences this for self, one clings to the idea of "I am experiencing." When one thinks of different subjects, one takes the dhamma that thinks for self; one clings to the idea of "I am thinking."

After the Buddha had realized through his enlightenment the truth of all dhammas, he taught this truth to his followers so that they too would understand that dhammas are not self, not a being, not a person. He taught about paramattha dhammas, ultimate realities, each with its own characteristic that is unalterable. The characteristics of paramattha dhammas cannot be changed by anybody, whether he knows them or does not know them, whether he calls them by a name in whatever language, or does not call them by a name. Their characteristics are always the same. The dhammas that arise do so because there are the appropriate conditions for their arising and then they fall away. Just as the Buddha said to the venerable Ānanda,[15] "Whatever has arisen, has come into being because of conditions, is by nature subject to dissolution."

Because of ignorance, one has wrong understanding and takes the dhammas that arise and fall away for self, a being or a person. This is the cause of desire and ever growing infatuation with one's rank, title or status, with one's birth, one's family, the colour of one's skin and so on. In reality, what one sees are only different colours appearing through the eyes, not self, not a being, not a person. The sound one hears is not self, not a being, not a person. What appears through the senses are only different kinds of dhammas that arise because of their appropriate conditions.

The wrong view that takes dhammas for self, a being or a person, has been compared to the perception of a mirage. People who are travelling in the desert may perceive a mirage of water ahead of them, but when they come close the mirage disappears because in reality there is no water. The mirage they perceived was a deception, an optical illusion. Even so is the wrong understanding that takes dhammas for self, a being or a person, a deception caused by ignorance, by wrong perception or remembrance, and by wrong belief.

Words such as being, person, woman or man are only concepts used to designate what we see or hear. Moreover, it is evident that the dif-

[15] "Dialogues of the Buddha" II, no. 16, Mahā Parinibbāna Sutta, Ch V, 144.

ferent colours, sounds, odours, cold, heat, softness, hardness, motion or pressure could not appear if there were no dhammas that can experience them, namely, seeing, hearing, smelling, tasting, experiencing cold, heat, softness, hardness, motion or pressure, knowing the meaning of the different things and thinking.

The dhammas that can experience different things, such as the dhamma which experiences colour, the dhamma which experiences sound, the dhammas which experience odour, flavour, cold, heat, softness, hardness, motion, pressure, the dhamma which knows the meaning of the different things and the dhamma which thinks about different subjects, all these dhammas, experiencing different things, have been classified by the Sammāsambuddha as citta, consciousness.

4

Exposition of Paramattha Dhammas I

4.0.1 Citta and Cetasika

Citta, or consciousness, is the dhamma that is the leader in knowing what appears, such as seeing or hearing. Cittas have been classified as 89 types in all, or, in special cases, as 121 types.[1]

Cetasika, or mental factor, is another type of dhamma, which arises together with citta, experiences the same object as citta, falls away together with citta and arises at the same base as citta. Cetasikas each have their own characteristic and perform their own function. There are 52 types of cetasikas in all.

Rūpa, or physical phenomena, is the dhamma that does not know or experience anything, such as colour, sound, odour or flavour. There are 28 types of rūpas in all.

Nibbāna is the dhamma that is the end of defilements and the ceasing of dukkha. Nibbāna does not have conditions that can cause its arising; it does not arise and fall away.

[1] This will be explained later on.

4.0.2 Citta paramattha dhamma

When we see different colours, the eyes themselves do not see. The eyes are only a condition for the arising of seeing, which is a citta. When sound impinges on the ear, the sound and the ear do not experience anything, the ear is not citta. The dhamma that hears the sound, that experiences the sound, is citta. Thus, citta paramattha[2] is the dhamma which experiences colour, sound or other objects. These paramattha dhammas, which are real, are "abhidhamma,"[3] non-self, beyond control, dependent on the appropriate conditions. Even if a Buddha had not been born and discovered the truth, dhammas arise and fall away because of their own conditions and their own true nature. We read in the "Gradual Sayings," Book of the Threes, Ch XIV, §134, Appearance, that the Buddha said:

> "Monks, whether there be an appearance or non-appearance of a Tathāgata, this causal law of nature, this orderly fixing of dhammas prevails, namely, all phenomena are impermanent. About this a Tathāgata is fully enlightened, he fully understands it. So enlightened and understanding he declares, teaches and makes it plain. He shows it, he opens it up, explains and makes it clear: this fact that all phenomena are impermanent."

The same is said about the truth that all conditioned dhammas are dukkha and that all dhammas are non-self.

The Sammāsambuddha was the pre-eminent preceptor, because he realized all by himself, through his enlightenment, the nature of all dhammas. He realized the truth that dhammas are non-self, not a being, not a person, and that they cannot be controlled by anybody.

The term "abhi" can mean great, mighty. Abhidhamma is the dhamma that is mighty; it is anattā, non-self, it is beyond anybody's control. When the Buddha had attained enlightenment, he taught all

---

[2]The Pāli term paramattha is derived from parama, superior, highest, and attha, which is "meaning." Paramattha dhammas are realities in the highest or ultimate sense.

[3]Abhidhamma, the third part of the Tipiṭaka, means "higher Dhamma," Dhamma in detail. It deals with ultimate or absolute realities, different from conventional truth. Ultimate reality or paramattha dhamma can also be called "abhidhamma".

the dhammas he had realized himself. He taught their true nature and also their different conditions. The Buddha respected the Dhamma he had penetrated. We read in the "Kindred Sayings" (I, Sagāthā-vagga, Ch VI, §2, Holding in Reverence) that the Buddha, shortly after his enlightenment, while staying at Uruvelā, was considering to whom he could pay respect. But he could find nobody in the world who was more accomplished than himself in morality, concentration, insight, emancipation, or knowledge of emancipation. We then read that he said:

> "This Dhamma then, wherein I am supremely enlightened – what if I were to live under It, paying It honour and respect!"

The Buddha did not teach that he could control the dhammas he had realized. He proclaimed that even he could not cause anybody to attain the path-consciousness and fruition-consciousness that experience nibbāna at the moment of enlightenment and to become liberated from dukkha. He taught that only the practice of the Dhamma is the condition for the person who practises to attain path-consciousness and fruition-consciousness that experience nibbāna at the moment of enlightenment, and to become liberated from dukkha.

Paramattha dhamma, or abhidhamma, is not a dhamma that is beyond one's ability to understand because paramattha dhamma is reality. Right view, right understanding, is actually knowing the characteristics of paramattha dhammas as they really are.

Citta is the paramattha dhamma that arises and cognizes different objects, such as colour, sound, odour, flavour, tangible object or other things, depending on what type of citta arises. For example, the citta that arises and sees colour through the eyes is one type of citta. The citta that arises and hears sound through the ears, is another type of citta. The citta that arises and experiences cold, heat, softness, hardness, motion or pressure through the bodysense is again another type of citta. The citta that arises and thinks, which knows through the mind-door different subjects, is again another type of citta. All this occurs in accordance with the type of citta that arises and with the conditioning factors that cause the arising of different types of citta.

At the moment when citta sees something, there is not just the citta that sees, or only the object which is seen. There must be citta that sees, as well as the object that is seen by the citta. Whenever there is an object that is seen, colour, it is evident that there must also be a reality that sees, the citta that sees. However, if one is only interested in the object which is seen, it prevents one from knowing the truth, from knowing that the object which is seen can only appear because citta arises and performs the function of seeing that object. When one thinks of a special subject or story, it is citta that thinks of concepts or words at those moments. When citta arises, it experiences something, and that which is known by citta is called in Pāli ārammaṇa, object.

The Pāli term ārammaṇa (or ālambana), in the teaching of the Sammāsambuddha, refers to that which citta knows. When citta arises and sees what appears through the eyes, that is the object of citta at that moment. When citta arises and hears sound, sound is the object of citta at that moment. When citta arises and experiences odour, odour is the object of citta at that moment. It is the same in the case of the citta which tastes flavour, the citta which experiences cold, heat, softness, hardness, motion or pressure through the bodysense or the citta which thinks of different subjects; whatever is known or experienced by citta is the object of citta at that moment. Whenever there is citta, there must be an object together with the citta each time. When citta arises, it must experience an object; there cannot be a citta that does not know anything. There cannot be just citta alone, the dhamma that knows something, without an object, that which is known by citta.

Citta, the reality that knows an object, does not only exist in Buddhism or in the human world. The citta that sees or hears etc. is a paramattha dhamma, it is universal and does not belong to anyone. If someone conceives the idea of "this person sees" or "that being hears," it is due to the outward appearance and to his memory. If there were no outward appearance and no memory, one would not conceive the citta that sees as "this person sees," or the citta that hears as "that being hears." Citta is paramattha dhamma. No matter which being or which person sees, the citta that arises and sees can only see what appears through the eyes. The citta that hears can only hear sound. The citta that sees cannot experience sound, and the citta that hears cannot experience what appears through the eyes. It is not in anyone's power to alter the characteristic and the nature of a paramattha dhamma.

Citta, a paramattha dhamma that arises and cognizes an object, can arise because the appropriate conditions are there for its arising. If there are no conditions, citta cannot arise. If, for example, sound does not arise and impinge on the earsense, the citta that hears cannot arise. If odour does not arise and impinge on the smelling-sense, the citta that experiences odour cannot arise. The different types of citta can only arise because there are conditions that are appropriate for the arising of those types of citta. There are 89 different types of citta, or, in special cases, 121 types, and for the arising of each of these types there are not just one condition, but several conditions. For example, the citta which sees needs for its arising the condition which is the eye, the rūpa which is eyesense (cakkhuppasāda),[4] and the rūpa which is visible object or colour, that which appears through the eyes.

Citta is a paramattha dhamma that is not rūpa. The paramattha dhammas that are not rūpa are nāma-dhammas. Citta, cetasika and nibbāna are nāma-dhammas and rūpa is rūpa-dhamma.[5]

4.0.3 Cetasika paramattha dhamma

When citta arises and cognizes an object, another kind of nāma-paramattha dhamma arises together with the citta and experiences the same object as the citta. That nāma-paramattha dhamma is cetasika (mental factor). Cetasikas are, for example, anger, love, happy feeling, unhappy feeling, avarice, jealousy, loving-kindness or compassion. These dhammas are cetasika paramattha dhamma, not citta paramattha dhamma.

Phenomena such as anger, affection, happy or unhappy feeling are dhammas which are real, they are not self, not a being, not a person. They are dhammas that must arise together with citta. If there were no citta, cetasikas such as anger, love or unhappy feeling could not arise. There are 52 kinds of cetasika paramattha dhammas in all. Anger (dosa) is one type of cetasika with the characteristic of coarseness or ferociousness. Love or attachment is another type of cetasika, lobha cetasika, with the characteristic of clinging, not letting go, desiring the object that is experienced. Thus, we see that cetasikas are not all of the same type, that each of them is a different dhamma with its own

[4] Cakkhu means eye, and pasāda means clearness or sense-faculty. The cakkhu pasāda rūpa is able to receive the impingement of colour.

[5] "Dhammasangaṇi", "Buddhist Psychological Ethics", Book III, Nikkhepakaṇḍaṃ, The Deposition, Part II, 1309, 1310.

characteristic. They do not only have different characteristics, but the manifestations and the conditions that make them arise are different for each of them.

Citta paramattha dhamma and cetasika paramattha dhamma are nāma-dhammas which experience an object and which arise together. Cetasika arises and falls away together with citta, experiences the same object as citta and arises at the same physical base as citta. Thus, wherever citta arises and falls away, cetasika also arises and falls away. Citta paramattha dhamma and cetasika paramattha dhamma cannot be separated, they do not arise and fall away without one another.

However, they are different types of paramattha dhamma. Citta is the leader in knowing an object and the different cetasikas that arise together with the citta experience the same object as the citta, but they each have a different characteristic and a different function with regard to the experience of the object. It is because of the fact that each citta that arises is accompanied by a different number of cetasikas and by different types of them that there are 89 or, in special cases, 121 different types of citta. Each type of citta is different, because cittas know different objects, they have different functions and they are accompanied by different types of cetasikas. Some cittas, for example, have that which appears through the eyes as their object; some have sound as object. Some cittas perform the function of seeing, some the function of hearing. Some cittas are accompanied by lobha cetasika (attachment); some cittas are accompanied by dosa cetasika (aversion or anger).

When people who can receive the teachings listen to the Abhidhamma and investigate the paramattha dhammas that appear, by paññā (understanding) accumulated in the past, they can, at that moment, penetrate the true nature of paramattha dhammas. Therefore, in the time of the Buddha, when the Buddha, who was pre-eminent in teaching, had finished his exposition of the Dhamma, there were many people who could attain enlightenment and experience nibbāna. Those people listened to the Dhamma, they understood and investigated the truth and came to know the paramattha dhammas that appeared at that moment as they really are. When the Buddha, for example, taught that seeing-consciousness, the citta which performs the function of seeing, is impermanent, they had sati-sampajañña (sati and paññā)[6] and when they were seeing they knew the true nature of that citta; they realized it as a nāma-dhamma, not self, not a being, not a person. When they were hearing they had sati-sampajañña and they knew the characteristic of the dhamma that was hearing. When paññā penetrates the characteristic of impermanence, of the arising and falling away, of the paramattha dhamma which appears at that moment, and realizes it as dukkha, there can be elimination of attachment and of wrong view that paramattha dhammas are self, permanent and happiness.

Therefore, we should correctly understand that the Dhamma the Buddha realized through his enlightenment and taught, and which has been compiled and recorded as the Tipiṭaka, deals with the true nature of all dhammas. When we have studied paramattha dhammas and understood what they are, we should investigate the paramattha dhammas that are appearing so that we can realize the true nature of their characteristics. In this way, doubt and ignorance of the characteristics of paramattha dhammas can truly be abandoned.

When one studies paramattha dhammas with the purpose of having more understanding of them, one should also investigate, in relation to them, the different causes which bring different effects. This is the way to thoroughly understand their nature. We should, for example, know whether the dhamma that sees is the same as the dhamma that hears, or whether this is not the case. We should know in which respect they are the same and in which respect they are different. It is true that the dhamma which sees and the dhamma which hears are citta paramattha dhamma. However, they are different cittas because the conditions for their arising are different. The citta that sees is dependent on visible object, which impinges on the rūpa that is eyesense (cakkhuppasāda); this conditions its arising. Whereas, the citta which hears is dependent on sound which impinges on the rūpa which is earsense (sotapasāda); this conditions its arising. Thus, the citta that sees and the citta that hears have different functions and are dependent on different conditions.

[6] Sati is the cetasika that is mindfulness. Its function will be explained later on.

5

Exposition of Paramattha Dhammas II

5.0.1 Rūpa paramattha dhamma

Rūpa paramattha dhamma is the reality that does not know anything.[1] It arises and falls away because of conditions, just as in the case of citta and cetasika.

Rūpa paramattha dhamma includes 28 different kinds of rūpa. The meaning of rūpa, material phenomena, or matter, is different from matter in the conventional sense, such as table, chair, or book. Among the 28 kinds of rūpa, there is one kind of rūpa, visible object or colour, citta can experience through the eyes. That which appears through the eyes is the only kind of rūpa that can be seen by citta. As to the other 27 rūpas, these cannot be seen by citta, but they can be experienced through the appropriate doorways by the cittas concerned. Sound, for example, can be experienced by citta through the ears.

---

[1] "Dhammasanganị", "Buddhist Psychological Ethics", Book II, Material Form, Ch I, §595.

Just as twenty-seven rūpas are invisible realities, citta and cetasika are invisible realities, but there is a great difference between rūpa dhamma and nāma dhamma. Citta and cetasika are paramattha dhammas that can experience an object, whereas rūpa is a paramattha dhamma that does not know any object. Rūpa paramattha dhamma is saṅkhāra (conditioned) dhamma; it has conditions for its arising. Rūpa is dependent on other rūpas for its arising, it cannot arise alone, without other rūpas. There must be several rūpas together in a small unit or group that arise together and are dependent on one another. The rūpas in such a group, called in Pāli kalāpa, cannot be separated from each other.

Rūpa is a dhamma that is infinitesimal and intricate. It arises and falls away very rapidly, all the time. When comparing the duration of rūpa with the duration of citta, one unit of rūpa arises and falls away in the time seventeen cittas arise and fall away, succeeding one another. This is extremely fast. For example, it seems that at this moment the citta which sees and the citta which hears appear at the same time, but in reality they arise and fall away separately from each other, with more than seventeen moments of citta in between them. Therefore, the rūpa which has arisen and is the object of the citta which sees, must have fallen away before the citta which hears arises.

Each rūpa is infinitesimal. If a mass of rūpas that arise and fall away together could be split up into the minutest particles, which cannot be divided again, such particles are extremely small units or groups (kalāpas) of rūpas, each consisting of at least eight different rūpas, which cannot be separated from each other. These eight rūpas are called the indivisible or inseparable rūpas, avinibbhoga rūpas. Among these are the four principle rūpas, mahā-bhūta rūpas, which are the following:

- the Element of Earth or solidity (paṭhavi dhātu), the rūpa which is softness or hardness;
- the Element of Water (āpo dhātu), the rūpa which is fluidity or cohesion;
- the Element of Fire or heat (tejo dhātu), the rūpa which is heat or cold;
- the Element of Wind (vāyo dhātu), the rūpa which is motion or pressure.

These four principle rūpas, mahā-bhūta rūpas, arise interdependently and they cannot be separated. Moreover, they are the condition for the arising of four other rūpas. These rūpas, which are dependent on the four principle rūpas, arise together with them in the same group. They are the following rūpas:

- colour or visible object (vaṇṇo), the rūpa which appears through the eyes;
- odour (gandho), the rūpa which appears through the nose;
- flavour (raso), the rūpa which appears through the tongue;
- nutritive essence (ojā), the rūpa which is one of the conditions for the arising of other rūpas.[2]

These four rūpas, together with the four principle rūpas, are included in the eight rūpas that cannot be separated from each other. These eight rūpas constitute the minutest unit, kalāpa, of rūpas that arise and fall away together very rapidly. The four principle rūpas cannot arise without these four derived rūpas (upādāya rūpas)[3], which arise dependent on the four principal rūpas.

The four principle rūpas are the condition, the foundation, for the derived rūpas that arise together with them in the same group. However, although the derived rūpas arise simultaneously with the principle rūpas in the same group and are dependent on them, they are not in their turn the condition for the arising of the four principal rūpas.

There are altogether 28 kinds of rūpas, namely the four principle rūpas and 24 derived rūpas. If the four principle rūpas did not arise, the twenty-four derived rūpas would not arise either.

The twenty-eight rūpas can be classified in different ways, but here they will be explained from the perspective of their interrelation, to facilitate comprehension and memorization.

The different groups, or kalāpas of rūpas, that arise do not fall away immediately. A sabhāva rūpa, a rūpa with its own distinct nature or

[2]Rūpas can be produced by one of the four factors that are kamma, citta, temperature or nutrition.

[3]All rūpas other than the four principle rūpas are derived rūpas, upādāya rūpas, because the latter cannot arise without the four principle rūpas.

characteristic[4] lasts as long as the duration of seventeen cittas arising and falling away, succeeding one another. With regard to the arising and falling away of rūpa, four different aspects can be discerned which have been classified as four lakkhaṇa[5] rūpas:

- upacaya rūpa, the arising or origination of rūpa;[6]
- santati[7] rūpa, the development or continuation of rūpa;
- jaratā rūpa, the decay of rūpa;
- aniccatā rūpa, the falling away of rūpa.

These four lakkhaṇa rūpas are rūpas without their own distinct nature, asabhāva rūpas,[8] but they are themselves characteristics inherent in all rūpas. All rūpas, which have their own distinct nature, sabhāva rūpas, must have these four characteristics. These four characteristics are different: the arising of rūpa, its development, its decay and its falling away are all different characteristics. In other words, upacaya rūpa and santati rūpa are characteristics indicating the moments rūpa has arisen but not yet fallen away, whereas jaratā rūpa indicates the moment close to its falling away and aniccatā rūpa its falling away.

The rūpa that is space, ākāsa rūpa, has the function of limiting or separating all the different groups or kalāpas of rūpas. Space in this context is not outer space, but the infinitesimal space surrounding each kalāpa. After its function, it is also called pariccheda rūpa (pariccheda meaning limit or boundary). What we call matter consists of kalāpas, units of rūpas arising and falling away. The rūpas within a kalāpa hold tightly together and cannot be divided. Matter, be it large or small, can only be broken up because the rūpa space is in between the different kalāpas, allowing them to be distinct from each other. Without space, or pariccheda rūpa, all rūpas would be tightly connected and could not be separated. Pariccheda rūpa is another kind of asabhāva rūpa, which

---

[4] Sabhāva rūpa is a rūpa with its own distinct nature. Sa in Pāli means with, and bhāva means nature. There are also asabhāva rūpas, which, though classified among the 28 kinds of rūpa, are not separate rūpas with their own nature, but special qualities connected with other rūpas. They will be explained later on.

[5] Lakkhaṇa means characteristic.

[6] Upacaya means heaping up.

[7] Santati means continuity.

[8] "A" in Pāli means "not". Asabhāva, without a distinct nature.

does not have its own distinct nature and does not arise separately; it arises simultaneously with the different kalāpas, and in between them.

No matter where rūpa arises, in whichever plane of existence, be it rūpa in living beings or in dead matter, the eight inseparable rūpas (avinibbhoga rūpas), the four lakkhaṇa rūpas and the pariccheda rūpa must be together. These thirteen rūpas are never absent. With regard to the rūpas of the body in people or other living beings, in the planes of existence where there are five khandhas (nāma and rūpa), there are pasāda rūpas, sense organs, produced by kamma as condition. The following five rūpas are sense organs:

- eyesense, cakkhuppasāda rūpa, which can be impinged on by visible object;
- earsense, sotappasāda rūpa, which can be impinged on by sound;
- smelling-sense, ghānappasāda rūpa, which can be impinged on by odour;
- tasting-sense, jivhāppasāda rūpa, which can be impinged on by flavour;
- bodysense, kāyappassāda rūpa, which can be impinged on by tangible object: cold and heat (Element of Fire), softness and hardness (Element of Earth) and motion and pressure (Element of Wind).

Rūpas of the body cannot arise without citta, and, in the planes of existence where there are nāma and rūpa, citta is dependent on rūpas of the body. Each citta must have a particular rūpa of the body as the appropriate base for its arising. Seeing-consciousness (cakkhu-viññāṇa), which performs the function of seeing, arises at the cakkhuppasāda rūpa. Hearing-consciousness (sota-viññāṇa), which performs the function of hearing, arises at the sotappasāda rūpa. It is the same for smelling-consciousness, tasting-consciousness and body-consciousness, they each arise at the rūpa that is the relevant base.

All other cittas, besides these sense-cognitions, arise at the physical base, which is called the heart-base, hadaya rūpa.

Some kinds of rūpa are produced solely by kamma and in each kalāpa the rūpa that is life-faculty, jīvitindriya rūpa, is produced by kamma. This rūpa sustains and maintains the life of the rūpas that it accompanies in one kalāpa; it is not found in dead matter. Therefore, the rūpas in the bodies of people and other living beings are different from the rūpas found in dead matter.

The differences in sex that occur in humans and other living beings is due to two different kinds of rūpa, bhāva rūpas (bhāva meaning nature), which are the following:

- Itthibhāva rūpa, femininity, a rūpa which permeates the whole body, so that it is manifested in the outward appearance, manners, behaviour and deportment which are feminine.

- Purisabhāva rūpa, masculinity, a rūpa which permeates the whole body, so that it is manifested in the outward appearance, manners, behaviour and deportment which are masculine.

Each individual with bhāva rūpa, the rūpa that is sex, has either the rūpa that is femininity or the rūpa that is masculinity. In some cases the bhāva rūpa is lacking. Moreover, those who live in the "Brahma world" (higher planes of existence where one is born as result of jhāna, absorption concentration) do not have conditions for bhāva rūpa.

There can be motion of the body, or by parts of the body, in people and other living beings, owing to citta, but there must also be specific rūpas that originate from citta. If there were rūpas only produced by kamma one could not move or perform different functions. For the movement of the body and the performance of its functions, there are three kinds of vikāra[9] rūpas, rūpas that are changeability, and these are:

- lahūta rūpa, buoyancy or lightness, as occurring in the body of those who are healthy;

- mudutā rūpa, plasticity, the absence of stiffness, as occurs in well-pounded leather;

- kammaññatā rūpa, wieldiness, as occurs in well-melted gold.

[9] Vikāra means change or alteration.

These three vikāra rūpas are asabhāva rūpas, rūpas without their own distinct nature. They constitute the adaptability of the four principle rūpas, the mahā-bhūta rūpas, they cause them to be light, soft and wieldy. The three vikāra rūpas arise only in the bodies of living beings, not in dead matter. The three vikāra rūpas cannot be separated. If there is lahutā rūpa, lightness, in one kalāpa, there must also be mudutā rūpa, plasticity and kammaññatā rūpa, wieldiness. The vikāra rūpas are produced by citta, by temperature and by nutrition. Since citta causes motion in any part of the body, there must also be vikāra rūpas produced by temperature (the right temperature, not too hot, not too cold) and vikāra rūpas produced by nutrition (ojā rūpa, nutritive essence), otherwise the rūpas of the body could not move, even if citta wanted them to do so. For example, when people are paralyzed or incapacitated by a sprain or by other ailments, these vikāra rūpas are not present.

When citta wants to display a sign expressing its intention by means of rūpas of the body, citta produces the rūpa that is bodily intimation, kāyaviññatti rūpa. This is a specific mode of expression by rūpas of the body that arise and display the intention of citta, in the expression of facial features, comportment of the body or gestures. Citta may convey its intention, for example, by staring in a stern way, or by making grimaces displaying contempt or disapproval. If citta does not wish to display its intention, kāyaviññatti rūpa does not arise.

When citta is the condition for sound, such as speech sound or the uttering of other sounds that convey a specific meaning, citta produces the rūpa that is speech intimation, vaciviññatti rūpa. When this arises, it is the condition for the rūpas that are the means of articulation, such as in the lips, to produce speech sound. Without the arising of speech intimation it would not be possible to speak or emit other sounds which convey a specific meaning.

Bodily intimation and speech intimation are asabhāva rūpas, rūpas without their own distinct nature, which arise and fall away together with the citta that produces them.

Some sources classify the three vikāra rūpas (the rūpas which are changeability of rūpa) and the two viññatti rūpas together as five vikāra rūpas.

Another rūpa is sound, sadda rūpa. Sound is different from speech intimation, vaciviññatti rūpa. Sound is the rūpa that contacts the earsense, sotappasāda rūpa, and which is the condition for the arising of hearing-consciousness, sota-viññāṇa. Some sounds arise conditioned by citta, and some do not, such as the sound of thunder, of storm, of engines, of drums, of the radio or of the television.

Summarizing the twenty-eight kinds of rūpa, they are:

the 8 inseparable rūpas, avinibbhoga rūpas, including the 4 principle rūpas, mahā-bhūta rūpas, namely:

- solidity (Earth),
- cohesion (Water),
- temperature (Fire),
- motion or pressure (Wind),

and the 4 derived rūpas which are:

- colour,
- odour,
- flavour,
- nutrition.

Furthermore, there are the following rūpas:

- 1 pariccheda rūpa or space (akāsa), delimiting groups of rūpa;
- 5 pasāda rūpas, sense organs;
- 1 rūpa which is heart-base, hadaya vatthu (base for cittas other than the sense-cognitions);
- 1 rūpa which is life faculty, jīvitindriya rūpa;
- 2 rūpas which are sex, bhāva-rūpas;
- 3 vikāra rūpas, rūpas of changeability (lightness, plasticity and wieldiness);

- 2 rūpas which are body intimation, kāya-viññatti, and speech intimation, vaciviññatti;
- 1 rūpa which is sound;
- 4 lakkhaṇa rūpas (origination, continuity, decay and falling away), characteristics common to all sabhāva rūpas, but which are themselves asabhāva rūpas.

Altogether, there are 28 kinds of rūpa.

In some sources, the number of rūpas that are classified varies. For example, in the "Atthasālinī" ("Expositor" II, Book II, Material Qualities, Ch 3, 339, 340) we find rūpas classified as twenty-six in number, because the elements of earth (solidity), fire (heat) and wind (motion or pressure) are classified together as one kind of rūpa, as tangible object (photthabbāyatana) that impinges on the bodysense, the kāyappasāda rūpa.

There are always several rūpas arising within one kalāpa. The number of rūpas that arise together is different depending on the types of rūpa concerned. There are several ways of classifying the twenty-eight rūpas and this will be dealt with later on in the Appendix.

6

Exposition of Paramattha Dhammas III

6.0.1 Nibbāna paramattha dhamma

Nibbāna paramattha dhamma is another kind of paramattha dhamma. The Buddha called it "nibbāna," because it is the end of "vāna," which means craving.[1] The paramattha dhamma that is nibbāna is the cessation of dukkha. Citta, cetasika and rūpa are dukkha, because they are impermanent, they arise and then fall away. Desire should be eradicated so that there can be an end to dukkha. Desire is the origin, the cause of the arising of dukkha. It is the cause of the arising of the five khandhas, which are citta, cetasika and rūpa.[2] Desire can be eradicated by developing paññā, wisdom, so that the characteristics of the arising and falling away of citta, cetasika and rūpa are penetrated. When paññā has

[1] "Minor Anthologies", "As it was said," the Twos, Ch 2, VII. Vāna means weaving or craving. Ni is a particle meaning negation. Another etymology: vā is blowing. Nibbāna is blowing out, extinction.

[2] The five khandhas are rūpakkhandha (rūpa), vedanākkhandha (feeling), saññākkhandha (remembrance or perception), saṅkhārakkhandha, including all cetasikas except feeling and saññā, and viññāṇakkhandha, including all cittas.

been developed to the degree that nibbāna can be realized and clearly known, clinging and wrong view with regard to citta, cetasika and rūpa can be eradicated. Nibbāna is the dhamma that is the cessation of dukkha and the cessation of the khandhas.[3] Nibbāna is reality, it is a paramattha dhamma, an ultimate reality and it is a dhamma that can be clearly known.

Nibbāna paramattha dhamma[4] has been classified as twofold:

- sa-upādisesa nibbāna dhātu, nibbāna with the khandhas remaining;
- an-upādisesa nibbāna dhātu, nibbāna without the khandhas.[5]

"Upādi" in "upādisesa" is another designation of the five khandhas, which include citta, cetasika and rūpa. As to "nibbāna with the khandhas remaining," this means that all defilements have been eradicated, but that the khandhas remain, arising and falling away in succession. As to "nibbāna without the khandhas remaining," this means the final falling away of the five khandhas, not to arise again, that is, the parinibbāna, the final passing away, of an arahat.

Thus, two kinds of nibbāna have been proclaimed.[6]

When the Buddha attained enlightenment under the Bodhi-tree, he attained nibbāna with the khandhas remaining, sa-upādisesa nibbāna dhātu. He completely eradicated defilements and all the dhammas (citta and cetasikas) accompanying defilements, so that they could never arise again. However, the khandhas were still remaining, namely, citta, cetasika (which were without defilements) and rūpa, arising and falling away in succession.

We read in "As it was said" ("Minor Anthologies", As it was said, the Twos, Ch. II, VII) that the Buddha said to the monks:

> "Of what sort, monks, is nibbāna with the basis still remaining? Herein, monks, a monk is arahat, one who has

[3] So long as there are defilements there are conditions for rebirth. When all defilements have been eradicated, there is the end of the cycle of birth and death, and then the khandhas do not arise again.

[4] "Minor Anthologies", "As it was said," the Twos, Ch 2, VII, and its commentary.

[5] Sa means with, upādi means substratum of life, the khandhas, and sesa means remaining. "A" (becoming "an" before a vocal) indicates a negation.

[6] "As it was said" and commentary.

> destroyed the cankers (defilements), who has lived the life, done what was to be done, laid down the burden, won the goal, worn out the fetter of becoming, one released by perfect knowledge. In him the five sense faculties still remain, through which, as they have not yet departed, he experiences pleasant and unpleasant objects, undergoes pleasure and pain. The end of attachment, aversion and ignorance of that monk, is called, monks, the element of nibbāna with the basis still remaining."

An-upādisesa nibbāna is nibbāna without the khandhas remaining. When the Buddha, between the twin Sal trees, attained parinibbāna, his final passing away,[7] this was an-upādisesa nibbāna, the final falling away of the khandhas. Citta, cetasika and rūpa fell away for good, never to arise again. This was the cessation of rebirth, the end of the cycle of birth and death.

There are four stages of attaining enlightenment and at each of these stages defilements are eradicated. The sotāpanna (stream-winner, who has attained the first stage of enlightenment), the sakadāgāmī (once-returner, who has attained the second stage of enlightenment), and the anāgāmī (non-returner, who has attained the third stage of enlightenment) are "learners" (sekha), because they have to continue to develop higher degrees of paññā in order to eradicate the defilements which are still remaining. The arahat is a "non-learner" (asekha), because he has eradicated all defilements completely, he has reached perfection and does not need to develop higher degrees of paññā any longer.

Nibbāna paramattha dhamma can be classified according to three characteristics:

- voidness, suññatta,
- signlessness, animitta,
- desirelessness, appaṇihita.

Nibbāna is called voidness, suññatta, because it is devoid of all conditioned realities (saṅkhāra dhammas). It is called signlessness, animitta,

[7] "Dialogues of the Buddha" II, no. 16, Mahā Parinibbāna Sutta.

because it is void of "signs" of conditioned realities. It is called desirelessness, appaṇihita, because it is without any basis of desire, namely, conditioned realities.

When someone has developed paññā to the degree that he is about to attain enlightenment, he may penetrate the dhammas that appear at those moments as impermanent, as dukkha, or as anattā. Only one of these three general characteristics can be realized at a time. When he attains nibbāna, his way of emancipation is different depending on which of the three general characteristics of conditioned dhammas he has realized in the process during which enlightenment is attained. When he realizes dhammas that appear as impermanent, he becomes liberated (realizes the four noble Truths) by the emancipation of signlessness (animitta vimokkha).[8] When he realizes dhammas as dukkha, he becomes liberated by the emancipation of desirelessness (appaṇihita vimokkha).[9] When he realizes dhammas as anattā, non-self, he becomes liberated by the emancipation of voidness (suññatta vimokkha).[10]

With regard to these three ways of emancipation, vimokkha, four different aspects can be discerned:[11]

- By predominance – when someone realizes dhammas as impermanent, signlessness emancipation, animitta vimokkha, is predominant. When he realizes dhammas as dukkha, desirelessness emancipation, appaṇihita vimokkha, is predominant. When he realizes dhammas as anattā, voidness emancipation, suññatta vimokkha, is predominant.

- By steadfastness – when someone realizes dhammas as impermanent, the citta is steadfast by signlessness emancipation. When he realizes dhammas as dukkha, the citta is steadfast by desirelessness emancipation. When he realizes dhammas as anattā, the citta is steadfast by voidness emancipation.

[8]Vimokkha means liberation, emancipation.

[9]Dhammas that arise and fall away are not happiness, they are not worth clinging to, they are dukkha. The person who has realized dukkha when he is about to attain nibbāna becomes emancipated by desirelessness.

[10]Dhammas are void of the self.

[11]See "The Path of Discrimination", First Division, V, Treatise on Liberation, third recitation section, 65-66.

- By inclination – when someone realizes dhammas as impermanent, the citta is guided by the inclination to signlessness emancipation. When he realizes dhammas as dukkha, the citta is guided by the inclination to desirelessness emancipation. When he realizes dhammas as anattā, the citta is guided by the inclination to voidness emancipation.

- By the way of being led unto nibbāna – when someone realizes the aspect of impermanence, the citta is being led unto nibbāna, cessation, by the influence of signless emancipation. When he realizes the aspect of dukkha, the citta is being led unto nibbāna by the influence of desirelessness emancipation. When he realizes the aspect of anattā, the citta is being led unto nibbāna by the influence of voidness emancipation.

7

Aspects of the Four Paramattha Dhammas

Citta, cetasika, rūpa and nibbāna are paramattha dhammas; they are reality. Citta, cetasika and rūpa, which arise and fall away in succession, present themselves so that they can be cognized, and thus it can be known that they are reality. For example, when we see colour, hear sound or think, cittas arise and fall away in succession, performing different functions. Some cittas see colour, others hear sound, and others again are thinking, depending on the type of citta and the conditions which cause its arising. The sequences of citta, cetasika and rūpa are extremely rapid and that is why we do not notice the arising and falling away. People may erroneously believe that rūpa gradually changes and that citta arises when a person or other living being is born, that the same citta lasts during life and falls away only when that person or being dies.

If we do not study and investigate the Dhamma, and not develop sati, mindfulness, and paññā, understanding, in order to penetrate the characteristics of citta, cetasika and rūpa, then we shall always be ignorant of the true nature of nāma dhamma and rūpa dhamma, of citta, cetasika and rūpa that arise and fall away in succession, all the time.

The dhammas that arise can do so because there are conditioning factors for their arising. They cannot arise without conditions. The venerable Sāriputta gained confidence in the teachings of the Buddha when he met the venerable Assaji, one of the monks from the group of the first five disciples of the Buddha. The venerable Sāriputta was so impressed by the venerable Assaji's comportment that he followed him, asking him who his preceptor was and what his preceptor was teaching. The venerable Assaji answered:[1]

> "Ye dhammā hetuppabhavā tesaṃ hetuṃ Tathāgato āha, tesañ ca yo nirodho, evaṃvādī Mahāsamaṇo ti."

This means:

> "Those things (dhammas) which proceed from a cause, of these the Truth-finder has told the cause. And that which is their stopping – the great recluse has such a doctrine."

If the Buddha had not taught about the dhammas and the ways they are conditioned, as he had realized through his enlightenment, there would be no one who would know which dhamma arises from what conditions. There would be no one who would know the dhammas that are the conditions for the arising of each type of citta paramattha dhamma, cetasika paramattha dhamma and rūpa paramattha dhamma. The Buddha had, through his enlightenment, penetrated the true nature of all dhammas. He taught that all dhammas that arise do so because of appropriate conditions, and he also taught which conditions bring about the arising of dhammas. Dhammas cannot arise without conditions.

We say of people, of other living beings, or devas, that they are born; but in reality, citta, cetasika and rūpa are born. When a specific type of citta accompanied by cetasikas arises together with rūpa we say in conventional language that a person is born. When citta and cetasikas arise with the rūpa of a deva (a being from a heavenly plane), we say that a deva is born. People, other living beings and devas have different kinds of births because the conditions for their births are different. The conditions that cause different births are numerous and they are

[1] "Book of Discipline" IV, Mahāvagga, the Great Division, 39.

most intricate. However, the Buddha, when he attained enlightenment, penetrated by his omniscience the true nature of all dhammas as well as all the different factors that are the conditions for their arising. He taught the true nature of each dhamma and he explained that whatever dhamma arises has conditions for its arising.

The dhammas that arise are saṅkhāra dhammas, conditioned dhammas. We know that there are citta, cetasika and rūpa, because they arise, and they arise because of the appropriate conditions. Hence, citta, cetasika and rūpa are saṅkhāra dhammas.[2]

The Buddha's teaching is complete as to the letter and meaning. But, he gave further explanations of Dhamma subjects, whose meaning people might misunderstand. He added words that described the meaning, making it even clearer. People might have misunderstandings about saṅkhāra dhamma, dhammas which arise because of conditions: they might mistakenly believe that dhammas that arise could continue to exist. Hence, the Buddha taught that saṅkhāra dhammas are also saṅkhata dhammas,[3] dhammas that have already been conditioned and then fall away.[4] The Buddha used the term saṅkhata dhamma in addition to saṅkhāra dhamma in order to explain that a dhamma that arises has conditions for its arising and that when the conditions fall away, that dhamma, which has arisen because of conditions, also must fall away. Saṅkhata dhamma is the dhamma that has been conditioned and then falls away. Hence, saṅkhāra dhamma, the dhamma that is compounded by conditioning factors, is also saṅkhata dhamma.[5] The paramattha dhammas, which are citta, cetasika and rūpa, are saṅkhāra dhamma as well as saṅkhata dhamma and they have the following characteristics:

- Sabbe saṅkhārā aniccā - All conditioned dhammas are impermanent.

---

[2]Saṅkhāra is derived from saṅkharoti, to combine, put together or compose.

[3]Saṅkhata is the past passive participle of saṅkharoti: what has been put together, has been composed.

[4]"Gradual Sayings" I, Book of the Threes, Ch V, §47.

[5]"Dhammasangaṇi", "Buddhist Psychological Ethics", Book III, Part I, Ch III, the Short Intermediate Set of Pairs, 1085. Saṅkhāra dhamma and saṅkhata dhamma refer to the same realities, but these different terms have been used to explain more clearly the nature of conditioned dhammas. Saṅkhāra dhamma refers to dhamma which depends on other dhammas which condition its arising, whereas saṅkhata dhamma refers to dhamma which has been conditioned to arise and then falls away.

- Sabbe saṅkhāra dukkha - All conditioned dhammas are dukkha.
- Sabbe dhammā anattā - All dhammas are non-self.[6]

7.0.1 All Saṅkhāra Dhammas are Impermanent

All conditioned dhammas are impermanent. The decay and impermanence of rūpa dhamma are apparent but the impermanence of nāma dhamma is hard to notice. We read in the "Kindred Sayings" (II, Nidāna-vagga, XII, the Kindred Sayings on Cause, 7, the Great Chapter §61, The Untaught) that the Buddha, while he was staying near Sāvatthī, at Jeta Grove in Anāthapiṇḍika's Park, said to the monks:

> "The untaught many folk, monks, might well be repelled by this body, where the four great Elements come together, they might cease to fancy it and wish to be free from it. Why so? Seen is the growth and decay of this body, where the four great Elements come together, the taking on (at birth) and laying down of it (at death). Hence well might the many folk be repelled by it, cease to fancy it and wish to be free from it.
>
> Yet this, monks, what we call thought, what we call mind, what we call consciousness (citta), by this the untaught many folk are not able to feel repelled, they are not able to cease fancying it or to be freed from it. Why so? For many a long day, monks, has it been for the uninstructed many folk that to which they cling, that which they call 'mine', that which they wrongly conceive, thinking - that is mine, this I am, this is myself. Hence the untaught many folk are not able to feel repelled by it, are not able to cease fancying it, are not able to be freed from it. . . But as to this, monks, what we call thought, what we call mind, what we call consciousness: one citta arises when another perishes, day and night."

[6] "Khuddaka Nikāya", Mahā-Niddesa, Suddhaṭṭhaka Sutta, The Purified, no. 4. Not translated into English. See also "Dhammapada" ("Minor Anthologies"), vs. 277-280.

Although citta, cetasika and rūpa arise and fall away all the time, it is hard to understand this and to become detached, to eliminate clinging to nāma and rūpa. Nāma and rūpa must be investigated and understood by paññā so that clinging can be eliminated. We read in the "Dhammapada" vs. 277-280 ("Minor Anthologies") that the Buddha said:

> " 'All saṅkhāra dhammas are impermanent', when one discerns this with wisdom, one turns away from dukkha; this is the Path to purity.
>
> 'All saṅkhāra dhammas are dukkha', when one discerns this with wisdom, one turns away from dukkha; this is the Path to purity.
>
> 'All dhammas are non-self (anattā)', when one discerns this with wisdom, one turns away from dukkha; this is the Path to purity."

If one does not realize the arising and falling away of nāma dhammas and rūpa dhammas in order to eliminate clinging to wrong view, one cannot penetrate the four noble Truths and become an ariyan, a "noble person" who has attained enlightenment. The ariyan understands the meaning of "awakening" or Buddhahood, the Buddha's enlightenment. He understands this not merely by theoretical knowledge of the dhammas the Buddha taught, but by direct understanding of the dhammas the Buddha had penetrated by his enlightenment. The ariyan has eradicated all doubt concerning the dhammas the Buddha had penetrated, because the ariyan has realized those dhammas himself.[7] The ariyan has realized the meaning of "Buddhahood" because by attaining enlightenment he has penetrated himself the true nature of the dhammas the Buddha taught. The person who understands and sees the Dhamma, sees the Tathāgata.[8] The person who studies the Dhamma and practises the Dhamma in order to penetrate the true nature of realities can attain enlightenment and eradicate defilements. But this depends on the stage of enlightenment he has attained, be it the stage

[7] "Kindred Sayings" V, Mahā-vagga, Book IV, Kindred Sayings on the Faculties, Ch V, §3, Learner.

[8] "Kindred Sayings" II, Middle Fifty, Ch 4, §87, Vakkali.

of the "stream-winner" (sotāpanna), the "once-returner" (sakadāgāmī), the "non-returner" (anāgāmī) or the arahat.[9]

7.0.2 All Saṅkhāra Dhammas are Dukkha

All saṅkhāra dhammas, conditioned realities, arise and then fall away, be it wholesome citta or unwholesome citta, be it rūpa that is beautiful or rūpa that is ugly, they all arise and fall away alike. The arising and falling away of realities, their impermanence, means dukkha, unsatisfactoriness. The nature of dukkha inherent in all saṅkhāra dhammas is not merely dukkha, suffering, in the sense of bodily pain, illness or tribulations, or suffering caused by separation from what we like and association of what we dislike. The nature of dukkha inherent in all saṅkhāra dhammas is their impermanence; when they have arisen they fall away and thus they should not be taken for happiness. Some people may wonder why all saṅkhāra dhammas are dukkha, why even the citta that experiences happiness and enjoys pleasant objects is dukkha. The citta that experiences happiness does not last and thus it is dukkha. All saṅkhāra dhammas, citta, cetasika and rūpa, are dukkha because they are impermanent, they do not last.

7.0.3 All Dhammas are Anattā

All dhammas are anattā. All four paramattha dhammas, citta, cetasika, rūpa and nibbāna are anattā. They are not self; they are not under anyone's control.

Nibbāna is paramattha dhamma; it is reality. Nibbāna is not saṅkhāra dhamma, it is visaṅkhāra dhamma,[10] unconditioned dhamma. Nibbāna is the dhamma that does not arise,[11] it is the opposite of saṅkhāra dhamma. Saṅkhāra dhamma is the dhamma that arises because of conditions whereas visaṅkhāra dhamma is the dhamma that does not arise, that is unconditioned.

[9] "Minor Anthologies", "Verses of Uplift," Ch V, §5, Uposatha Sutta.

[10] "Vi" is a particle which here denotes negation.

[11] "Minor Anthologies", "The Path of Discrimination", Treatise I, On Knowledge, Ch I, section 1, 18.

Nibbāna is asaṅkhata dhamma, the dhamma that is not saṅkhata.[12] Saṅkhata dhamma is the dhamma that arises and falls away whereas asaṅkhata dhamma is the dhamma that does not arise and fall away. Nibbāna is not conditioned, and, thus, it does not arise and fall away.

Citta, cetasika and rūpa, which are saṅkhāra dhammas, are lokiya, "mundane." They are susceptible to destruction.[13] Nibbāna, which is visaṅkhāra dhamma or asaṅkhata dhamma, is lokuttara. The word lokuttara means beyond the world, supramundane, free from the world.[14]

Summarizing the paramattha dhammas, they are:

- nāma dhamma which knows an object: citta paramattha, 89 or 121 cittas; cetasika paramattha, 52 cetasikas
- rūpa dhamma: rūpa paramattha, 28 rūpas;
- nāma dhamma which does not know an object: nibbāna paramattha.

7.0.4 The Five Khandhas

The five khandhas, groups or aggregates, comprise:

- rūpakkhandha (all rūpas),
- vedanākkhandha (feelings),
- saññākkhandha (remembrance or perception),
- saṅkhārakkandha (all cetasikas, except feeling and remembrance),
- viññāṇakkhandha (all cittas).[15]

[12]The particle "a" denotes negation. See "Gradual Sayings" I, Book of the Threes, Ch 5, §47.

[13]The Pāli term lujjati, to be broken up, has been associated in meaning with "loko," the world. See for example "Kindred Sayings" IV, Second Fifty, Ch 3, §89.

[14]Uttara means higher, beyond. Lokuttara is beyond the world. The cittas that experience nibbāna when enlightenment is attained are lokuttara cittas. This will be explained further on.

[15]"The Book of Analysis," I, Analysis of the Aggregates, 1-32.

7.0.5 Paramattha Dhammas and Khandhas

- Citta is viññāṇakkhandha.
- Cetasika is vedanākkhandha, saññākkhandha, saṅkhārakkhandha.
- Rūpa is rūpakkhandha.
- Nibbāna is not khandha. It is freedom from khandha (khandha vimutti).

The term khandha refers to the dhamma that can be described as past, future or present, internal or external, gross or subtle, inferior or superior, far or near. Hence, khandha is saṅkhata dhamma, the dhamma that is conditioned, which arises and falls away, and thus, it can be described as past, present, future, etc. Whereas asaṅkhata dhamma, nibbāna, is the dhamma that does not arise, that is unconditioned.[16] It cannot be said of nibbāna that it has arisen, that it has not yet arisen, or that it will arise. It cannot be described as past, future or present. Therefore, visaṅkhāra dhamma, nibbāna, is not khandha, it is freedom from khandha (khandha vimutti).

We read in the "Kindred Sayings" (III, Khandhā-vagga, First Fifty, Ch 5, §48, The Factors) that the Buddha, while he was at Sāvatthī, explained to the monks about the five khandhas and the five upādāna khandhas, khandhas of grasping:

> "I will teach you, monks, the five khandhas and the five khandhas that have to do with grasping. Do you listen to it.
>
> And what, monks, are the five khandhas?
>
> Any rūpa, be it past, future or present, inward or outward, gross or subtle, inferior or superior, far or near – that is called rūpakkhandha. Any feeling, any perception, any group of 'activities' (or 'formations', saṅkhārakkhandha), any consciousness, be it past, future or present, inward or outward, gross or subtle, inferior or superior, far or near, that is called viññāṇakkhandha. These five, monks, are called the five khandhas.

[16] "Buddhist Psychological Ethics," Book III, Part II, Appendix II and Book III, Part I, Ch III, §1086.

And what, monks, are the five khandhas that have to do with grasping (upādāna khandhas)? Any rūpa, monks, be it past, future or present... be it far or near, goes together with the āsavas (intoxicants)[17], and is a condition for upādāna, grasping. That is called khandha of grasping, upādāna khandha. Any feeling... any perception... any group of "activities"... any consciousness, monks, be it past, future or present... be it far or near, goes together with the āsavas, and is a condition for upādāna, grasping. These are called the five upadāna khandhas."

7.0.6 The Three Paramattha Dhammas classified as Five Khandhas

- Citta Paramattha Dhamma - all 89 (or 121) types are: Viññāṇakkhandha.

- Cetasika Paramattha Dhamma - 52 types:
  vedanā cetasika is: Vedanākkhandha,
  saññā cetasika is: Saññākkhandha,
  50 cetasikas are: Saṅkhārakkhandha.

- Rūpa Paramattha Dhamma - all 28 types are: Rūpakkhandha.

7.0.7 The Five Khandhas Classified as Three Paramattha Dhammas

- Rūpakkhandha is: Rūpa Paramattha Dhamma (28 rūpas).

- Vedanākkhandha is: Cetasika Paramattha Dhamma (vedanā).

- Saññākkhandha is: Cetasika Paramattha Dhamma (saññā).

- Saṅkhārakkhandha is: Cetasika Paramattha Dhamma (50 cetasikas).

- Viññāṇakkhandha is: Citta Paramattha Dhamma (89 or 121 cittas).

[17] A group of defilements.

Part II

Citta

8

General Introduction

We read in the "Kindred Sayings" (I, Sagāthā vagga, The Devas, Ch 7, §2, Citta sutta) that a deva asked:

```
Now what is that whereby the world is led?
And what is that whereby it is drawn along?
And what is that above all other things
That brings everything under its sway?
```

The Buddha answered:

```
It is citta whereby the world is led,
And by citta it is ever drawn along,
And citta it is above all other things
That brings everything under its sway.
```

This sutta shows us the power of citta.[1] Citta is an element that experiences something, a reality that experiences an object. It is the "chief," the leader in knowing the object that appears.[2] There is not only citta that sees, citta that hears, citta that smells, citta that tastes or citta that experiences tangible object, there is also citta that thinks about many diverse subjects. The world of each person is ruled by his citta. The cittas of some people have accumulated a great deal of wholesomeness (kusala). Even when they meet someone who is full of defilements they can still have loving-kindness, compassion or equanimity because of their accumulations of wholesomeness. Whereas the world of someone else may be a world of hatred, annoyance, anger and displeasure, according to his accumulations. Thus, in reality, each person is all the time his own world.

It seems that we are all living together in the same world. However, in reality all the different rūpas (material phenomena) that appear through the eyes, ears, nose, tongue, bodysense and mind, all those different phenomena, could not appear and be of such importance if there were no citta, the element that experiences them. Since citta experiences the objects that appear through the sense-doors and through the mind-door, the world of each person is ruled by his citta.

Which world is better: the world where a great deal of wholesomeness has been accumulated, so that kindness, compassion, sympathetic joy and equanimity can arise, or the world of hatred, anger and displeasure? Different people may meet the same person and know the same things about him, but the world of each one of them will evolve with loving-kindness or with aversion, depending on the power of the citta that has accumulated different inclinations in the case of each person.

Because of visible object, which appears through the eyes, it seems as if there are many people living together in this world, at a certain time and in a particular location. However, if there is clear comprehension of the characteristic of the element that experiences – the dhamma that arises and sees the object that appears at that moment – one will know that, while there is seeing just for a short moment, there is only the world of seeing. Then there are no people, other living beings or different

[1] Pronounced: "chitta."

[2] Citta is accompanied by cetasikas, mental factors, which also experience the object, but citta is the leader in cognizing the object.

things. At the moment of seeing, thinking about shape and form has not yet occurred; thinking of a story about what is seen has not yet happened.

However, when we think of the world, with its beings, people or different things, we should know that this is only a moment of citta that thinks about what appeared to citta that sees, about visible object. Seeing occurs at a moment different from thinking about what appears. For everyone, citta arises just for a moment, then it is succeeded by the next one; this happens continuously. Thus, it seems that the whole wide world is there, with its many different people and things. But we should have right understanding of what the world is. We should know that realities appear one at a time, and that they appear only for one moment of citta. Since cittas arise and fall away, succeeding one another very rapidly, it seems that the world does not disintegrate, the world lasts, with beings, people and many different things. In reality the world lasts just for one moment, namely, when citta arises and cognizes an object, just for that moment, and then it falls away together with the citta.

In the "Buddhist Psychological Ethics" (the "Dhammasangaṇi", Book I, Part I, Ch I, §6) several synonyms for citta have been given. Citta is called mind (mano or mānasa), heart (hadaya), "that which is pure" (paṇḍara), mind-base (manāyatana), faculty of mind (manindriya), consciousness (viññāṇa), the khandha of consciousness (viññāṇa-kkhandha), and the element of "mind-consciousness" (mano-viññāṇa dhātu).[3]

The Buddha used several synonyms for citta so that the characteristic of citta that is common to everybody could be understood. Citta is reality, it is an element that experiences something, but it is difficult to understand what exactly the characteristic is of the element that experiences. People may more or less understand what citta is; they know that it is the mind, which is common to everybody, but if one only knows this and does not really investigate the nature of citta, one will not know at which moment citta occurs.

The "Atthasālinī", the commentary to the "Dhammasangaṇi", ("Expositor" I, Book I, Part IV, Ch II, 140) states that the reality that is citta is so called because of its variegated nature (the Pāli term vicitta means variegated or various). There is not only one kind of element that

[3]The same synonyms have been given in "Mahā-Niddesa", Pasūra Sutta, No. 319.

experiences, citta, but there are many different kinds of citta. Citta is variegated. Its variegated nature appears when we think of different subjects, when we think, for example, about what we are going to do on a particular day. When we consider this more, we shall find out that thinking occurs according to the variegated nature of all the different cittas that arise.

What shall we do today, this afternoon, tomorrow? If there were no citta we could not perform any action. The fact that we all can perform different actions in a day is due to the variegated nature of the cittas of each one of us. We can see that all our actions in daily life, through body and speech, are different because of the variegated nature of the cittas of each one of us. When we are thinking, citta is the reality that thinks, and each person thinks in a different way. Different people, who are interested in the Dhamma and study it, consider it and ponder over it in different ways. They also have different points of view as far as the practice is concerned. The world evolves in accordance with the variegated nature of the cittas of different people. The world is constituted by different people living in different countries and participating in different groups and these different individuals condition the events in the world. This occurs because of the variety of the thinking of each individual. The world of today evolves in this particular way according to the variegated nature of the cittas of people at this time. How will the world be in the future? It will be again just according to the variegated nature of the cittas that think of many different subjects.

Hence, we see that citta is of a variegated nature. The citta that sees through the eye-door is one type of citta. It is different from the citta that hears through the ears, which is another type of citta. The citta that thinks is again another type of citta.

The "Atthasālinī" states that citta is called "mind" (mano), because it determines and knows an object (ārammaṇa or ālambana). The word object, ārammaṇa, means that which is known by citta. When citta, the dhamma that experiences, arises, it cognizes what is called an "object."

Sound is a reality. When hard things contact each other, it is a condition for the arising of sound. However, when the citta that arises does not experience sound at that moment, sound is not an object. Anything may arise because of conditions, but if citta does not experience it, it is not an object, ārammaṇa.

Citta is named "heart," hadaya, because it is an inward reality. Citta is internal because it is a reality that experiences the object that appears. The object is outside, it is that which citta experiences.

The study of citta is actually investigation of the realities that are appearing at this moment, the realities that are internal as well as those that are external, and in this way we shall come to understand the characteristic of citta. Citta is a reality, but where is it? Citta is an internal reality. When there is seeing, colour appears outside and citta is the reality that is within; it experiences what appears through the eyes.

When we develop understanding, we should investigate the characteristics of realities as they are, according to the truth the Buddha realized through his attainment of Buddhahood, and that he taught to others. He taught the four "Applications of Mindfulness."[4] Mindfulness of citta (cittanupassanā satipaṭṭhāna) means that when there is, for instance seeing, sati is mindful, non-forgetful, of its characteristic. We should investigate, study and apply our attention to the reality of seeing so that we shall gradually have more understanding of it. We can come to know it as the element that experiences what is appearing through the eyes.

When there is hearing of sound, sati can arise and be aware of it, so that hearing can be known as a reality that experiences, and this is an internal reality. It is not easy to investigate this reality and to know it as it is. The reality that hears sound arises, experiences the sound that appears, and then falls away immediately. This is true for each citta: it arises, experiences an object just for an extremely short moment, and then it falls away very rapidly.

When one has right understanding of the citta that sees, the citta that hears or the citta that thinks, satipaṭṭhāna can arise and be aware of the characteristic of citta at that moment, and it can be known as the reality, the element, that experiences something. Paññā can be developed in conformity with the Dhamma the Buddha taught. Then paññā can penetrate the characteristics of realities, so that the four noble Truths can be realized and defilements can be eradicated at the different stages of enlightenment. These stages are: the stage of the

[4]Mindfulness of Body, of Feeling, of Citta and of Dhammas.

"stream-winner" (sotāpanna), of the "once-returner" (sakadāgāmī), of the "non-returner" (anāgāmī) and the stage of the arahat.

Citta is called "pure" or "clear" (paṇḍaraṃ, "Dhammasangaṇi", §6), because citta has only the characteristic of knowing clearly its object. Thus, its nature is pure. The "Atthasālinī" ("Expositor" I, Book I, Part IV, Ch II, 140) states, "Mind also is said to be 'clear' in the sense of 'exceedingly pure' (parisuddhaṭṭhena paṇḍaraṃ), with reference to the life-continuum (bhavanga). So the Buddha has said: 'Bhikkhus, the mind is luminous (pabhassaraṃ), but is corrupted by adventitious corruptions.'," The "Atthasālinī" then explains that when the citta is akusala, it is still called 'pure' (paṇḍaraṃ).[5]

The characteristic of citta is clearly knowing an object, and hence citta is by nature (sabhāva) pure. Even when it is accompanied by upakilesas (accompanying akusala cetasikas) which defile it, it is still called paṇḍaram, pure.

Citta is a reality that arises and then falls away immediately. The falling away of the preceding citta is a condition for the arising of the succeeding citta. The citta that sees arises and falls away; a citta that sees does not arise continuously. There are no cittas that hear, experience tangible object or think continuously. When we are fast asleep and not dreaming, there are cittas arising and falling away, succeeding one another. However, at such moments citta does not experience an object through the eyes, the ears, the nose, the tongue, the bodysense

[5] We find the same text in the commentary to the "Path of Discrimination", the "Saddhammappakāsinī", regarding the 'Treatise on Breathing', section 4, "What are the thirty-two kinds of knowledge in mindful workers," stating that each citta, even akusala citta, can be called paṇḍaram. As to the bhavanga-citta that is called "luminous", phabassaraṃ, the "Atthasālinī" refers to the "Gradual Sayings" I,10: "Bhikkhus, the mind is luminous (pabhassara), but it is corrupted by adventitious corruptions." The bhavanga-citta which is vipākacitta is not involved in outward objects and hence akusala cetasikas do not accompany it. Here it is obvious that the citta is luminous and pure. But also when it is accompanied by defilements, the citta itself is different from the defilements, its nature is pure, pandaraṃ. The "Atthasālinī", in the same section, states: "Though immoral, it is called 'clear' (pandaraṃ) because it issues [^from subconscious vital functions]: just as a tributary of the Ganges is like the Ganges and a tributary of the Godhāvarī is like the Godhāvarī." Even when citta is accompanied by defilements, it does not lose its natural purity, just as the water of a tributary is like the water of the main river. Citta just clearly knows an object.

or the mind-door.

The citta that does not experience an object through any of the six doors is the bhavanga-citta. This citta keeps one alive; it maintains the continuity in one's life as this particular person. Bhavanga-cittas arise and fall away until another type of citta arises that experiences an object through the eyes, the ears, the nose, the tongue, the bodysense or the mind-door. The bhavanga-cittas arise in between the processes of cittas that experience objects through the six doors[6] and this goes on continuously until the end of one's lifespan as a particular person.

The bhavanga-citta does not experience an object through the eyes, the ears, the nose, the tongue, the bodysense or the mind-door. When someone is fast asleep he does not experience like or dislike, he is not jealous, stingy, conceited. He has no loving-kindness or compassion; thus, unwholesome or wholesome qualities do not arise because he does not see, hear, experience tangible object or think.

However, it should be known that whenever the citta that arises experiences an object through one of the six doors, akusala citta is bound to arise because many different defilements have been accumulated and these condition the arising of pleasure and attachment when one sees something pleasant, and the arising of displeasure and annoyance when one sees something unpleasant.

When citta arises and cognizes an object through one of the six doors, what kind of feeling is there? Pleasant feeling, unpleasant feeling and indifferent feeling are not the reality that is citta. They are types of cetasikas, mental factors, the Buddha has called vedanā cetasika, the cetasika that is feeling. Citta as well as cetasika are nāma, but citta is the "chief," the "leader" in knowing an object. Citta is different from vedanā cetasika, which feels pleasant, unpleasant or indifferent about the object that is appearing. Dhammas that arise cannot arise singly, they are dependent on other dhammas that arise simultaneously with them and that condition them. Citta must arise simultaneously with cetasikas, and cetasikas must arise simultaneously with the citta. Citta and cetasikas that arise together fall away together. They experience the same object and they arise and fall away at the same physical base. Each citta that arises is conditioned by different cetasikas that accompany

[6]Cittas that experience objects through the six doors arise in processes, and each citta in that process performs its own function. This will be explained later on.

it. Each citta performs a different function and thus, there is a great diversity of types of cittas.

We do not like it when the citta is annoyed, disturbed, restless, sad or anxious. We like it when the citta is happy, when it is full of joy and when it is infatuated with pleasant objects. However, when the citta is joyful, when it is happy and absorbed in pleasure, the citta is akusala, because it is accompanied by the cetasika that is attachment, lobha cetasika. Lobha is the dhamma that takes pleasure in an object, which clings to it, and is absorbed in it. The Buddha taught people to study and investigate realities so that sati of satipaṭṭhāna could be aware of the characteristics of the realities that are appearing[7] and right understanding of them could be developed. This means that one should investigate realities, notice their characteristics and be aware of them in order to know them precisely, just as they are. In this way, we can come to know which dhammas are kusala, which are akusala and which are neither kusala nor akusala. We can come to know akusala as akusala, no matter of what degree, be it coarse or more subtle. It should be known that not only aversion, dosa, is akusala dhamma, but that there are also many other types of akusala cetasikas.

People ask what they should do to prevent anger. All dhammas are non-self, anattā, and thus, also dosa is anattā. Dosa arises because of its appropriate conditions. There are people who can eradicate dosa for good, so that it does not arise again. Those people have developed paññā and realized the four noble Truths to the degree of the third stage of enlightenment, the stage of the non-returner, anāgāmī.

At each stage of enlightenment, the four noble Truths are realized. The first Truth is the noble Truth of Dukkha. All conditioned dhammas (saṅkhāra dhammas) are impermanent. They arise and fall away immediately and therefore they are dukkha, unsatisfactory, not worth clinging to. They cannot be a refuge. The second noble Truth is the Origin of Dukkha (dukkha samudaya). This is craving (tanhā), which is lobha cetasika. Clinging or craving is the origin, the cause, of the arising of dukkha. The third noble Truth is the Cessation of Dukkha (dukkha nirodha) and this is nibbāna. Nibbāna is the reality that makes an end

[7]Sati, mindfulness, is a cetasika that is non-forgetful of what is wholesome. There are different levels of sati. Sati of satipaṭṭhāna is non-forgetful, mindful of the characteristics of nāma and rūpa.

to dukkha because when nibbāna is attained, defilements that cause the arising of dukkha are eradicated. The fourth noble Truth is the Way leading to the Cessation of Dukkha (dukkha nirodha gāmini paṭipadā). This is the Eightfold Path, which is the development of satipaṭṭhāna, the development of paññā, which can realize the four noble Truths. This is the practice leading to the cessation of dukkha.

The four noble Truths are realized when enlightenment is attained, but there are different degrees of realization at the four stages of enlightenment. The person who has realized the Noble Truths and experiences nibbāna for the first time when he attains enlightenment, is a stream-winner, sotāpanna. The sotāpanna has eradicated wrong view (diṭṭhi) and doubt about the characteristics of realities.

When the sotāpanna has developed paññā further, he can reach the second stage of enlightenment, the stage of the once-returner, sakadāgāmī. Then he realizes the noble Truths to the degree of that stage and experiences nibbāna again. The more coarse attachment to visible object, sound, odour, flavour and tangible object is eradicated at that stage.

When the sakadāgāmi has developed paññā further, he can reach the third stage of enlightenment, the stage of the non-returner, anāgāmī. Then he realizes the noble Truths to the degree of that stage and experiences nibbāna again. Attachment to visible object, sound, odour, flavour, tangible object, and aversion, dosa, are completely eradicated at that stage.

When the anāgāmī has developed paññā further, he can reach the fourth and last stage of enlightenment, the stage of the perfected one, the arahat. He realizes the noble Truths to the degree of that stage and experiences nibbāna again. All remaining akusala dhammas are completely eradicated at that stage. When the arahat passes away, there is the full extinction of the khandhas (khandha parinibbāna); he does not have to be reborn anymore.

Thus, we see that the lokuttara (supramundane) paññā of the ariyan, the person who has attained enlightenment, eradicates defilements stage by stage, that is, according to the stage of enlightenment that has been attained. When we understand this, we should carefully consider what the right way of practice is for the development of paññā, which clearly discerns the dhammas that appear and that can eradicate defilements. The practice should be in conformity with the Dhamma the Buddha taught.

The Buddha explained citta not only as "that which is pure" (paṇḍara), he also used the term "manāyatana," mind-base, for citta, so that the characteristic of citta would be understood even more clearly. "Āyatana" is explained in the "Atthasālinī" (Book I, Part IV, Ch II, §§ 140, 141) as "dwelling place", "place of birth", "place of association" and "cause". It is explained that the place of birth, the meeting-place and cause are suitable terms for citta. Citta is place of birth, because contact, phassa cetasika, and the other cetasikas, arise "in the citta." Citta is a place of association because objects from outside, such as visible object, sound, odour, flavour and tangible object, "meet" in the citta by being its object. As to the meaning of cause, hetu, citta is the cause or condition for contact, phassa, and for the other cetasikas arising together with it; it is conascent-condition (sahajāta-paccaya) for them.

Each citta is a reality, an element, that experiences an object. We shall understand more clearly that citta has the characteristic of anattā if we know that citta is manāyatana, the base on which other realities depend, place of birth, meeting-place and cause.

There may be conditions for the arising of visible object, sound, odour, flavour, tangible objects such as cold, heat, softness or hardness. However, if citta does not arise and experience these objects, if citta is not the "meeting-place" for them, none of these objects can appear. Then, what can be experienced through the eyes cannot appear, neither can sound, odour, flavour, cold, heat, softness or hardness appear. This is because citta is the reality that experiences an object; it is the base, the place of birth, the meeting-place, the cause for realities to appear. The colour behind us cannot appear, because it does not "meet" the citta, it cannot impinge on the eyesense and does not contact the citta. Hence citta cannot arise and see an object behind us.

Although kamma conditions the eyesense that is arising and falling away continuously throughout life, provided we have not become blind, the citta that sees cannot arise continuously. Whenever colour appears, the citta is manāyatana, the meeting-place for the rūpa that is visible object impinging on the eyesense (cakkhuppasāda rūpa) at that moment. The rūpa that impinges on the eyesense is rūpāyatana, the āyatana of visible object, and the eyesense that is impinged on by visible object is cakkhāyatana, the āyatana of eyesense. All the dhammas that "meet" or associate at that moment are āyatanas. The same is true when sound impinges on the earsense and can "meet" the citta that arises and experiences it. Thus, citta is manāyatana, the meeting-place of the dhammas that are appearing.

As we have seen, the "Atthasālinī" states that citta is a cause or condition for phassa, contact, and for the other cetasikas that accompany citta. Phassa, one among the fifty-two types of cetasikas, is a kind of nāma that contacts the object. The contact that is phassa cetasika is mental, it is different from physical contact, which occurs, for example, when a tree falls down and hits the earth. The rūpa that is sound may impinge on the rūpa that is earsense, but if phassa does not arise and contact the sound impinging on the earsense, the citta that hears cannot arise at all.

Phassa is a type of nāma that arises together with the citta and falls away together with it. Phassa experiences the same object as the citta and it arises at the same place of origin as the citta. Therefore, citta is a condition for phassa. In the planes of existence where there are five khandhas (nāma and rūpa), citta and cetasika must always arise at a particular rūpa that is the place of origin for citta and cetasikas. That rūpa is called "vatthu rūpa," physical base. The eyesense is vatthu rūpa, the eye-base, since it is the place of origin for seeing-consciousness and the cetasikas that arise together with it.[8] Realities cannot arise singly, on their own. When a reality arises, there must be other realities that arise together with it at that moment and that condition it. Whatever reality conditions another reality to arise simultaneously with it, conditions that reality by way of conascence-condition, sahajāta-paccaya.[9]

A conditioning dhamma, a paccaya, is a dhamma that assists or supports another dhamma to arise or to subsist. Thus, it is evident that each dhamma that arises is saṅkhāra dhamma, conditioned dhamma, since it is dependent on other dhammas that are the condition for its arising. If there were no conditions, no dhamma could arise.

Different dhammas are different types of conditions. Some dhammas condition other dhammas to arise together with them; they are

[8]There are six rūpas that are vatthu. The five senses are vatthus for the sense-cognitions and the heart-base is vatthu for all the other cittas. Vatthu is not identical with āyatana, which comprises both nāma and rūpa.

[9]Saha means together and jāta means arisen.

conascence-condition, sahajāta-paccaya. Other dhammas arise before the dhammas they condition, they are prenascence-condition, purejāta-paccaya. Other dhammas again arise after the dhammas they condition, they are postnascence-condition, pacchājāta-paccaya.

Citta is conascence-condition for the cetasikas that arise simultaneously and the cetasikas are conascence-condition for the citta they accompany. When contact, phassa, arises and contacts an object, the citta that arises together with phassa cetasika experiences that object, not a different one. When phassa cetasika arises and contacts sound, the hearing-consciousness that arises simultaneously with phassa cetasika, has that sound as its object.

There are four paramattha dhammas: citta, cetasika, rūpa and nibbāna. Each of the paramattha dhammas can be a condition for the arising of other paramattha dhammas that are saṅkhata dhammas, conditioned dhammas. Citta can condition the arising of cetasikas and of rūpas, although not all cittas condition the arising of rūpa. Cetasika conditions the arising of citta and of rūpa, except in some cases. Rūpa is a condition for the arising of other rūpas. Rūpa conditions the arising of citta when it is vatthu, physical base of citta, and when it is the object of citta. All this evolves according to the nature of the paramattha dhammas that are conditioned by way of conascence-condition and by other conditions.

Citta and cetasika are conascence-condition for the rūpa that arises simultaneously with them immediately at the arising moment of citta. Each moment of citta can be subdivided into three extremely short moments:

- the arising moment (uppāda khaṇa);
- the moment of presence (tiṭṭhi khaṇa), when it has not fallen away yet;
- the moment of dissolution (bhaṅga khaṇa).

Citta cannot direct the arising of rūpa. Rūpa that is conditioned by citta (cittaja rūpa) arises simultaneously with the citta, immediately at the arising moment of citta. However, it is different at the moment the rebirth-consciousness (paṭisandhi-citta) arises. At that moment there is no rūpa conditioned by citta, but only rūpa conditioned by kamma (kammaja rūpa) that arises together with the rebirth-consciousness, which is also conditioned by kamma. When the rebirth-consciousness has fallen away, the succeeding citta, the first bhavanga-citta in that life, conditions rūpa to arise simultaneously with it. From that moment on, throughout life, citta conditions rūpa.

However, the sense-cognitions are an exception, they do not produce any rūpa. There are five pairs of sense-cognitions, one citta of each pair is kusala vipāka (result of wholesome kamma) and one citta is akusala vipāka (result of unwholesome kamma). They are the following pairs of citta: seeing-consciousness, hearing-consciousness, smelling-consciousness, tasting-consciousness and body-consciousness. Also, the dying-consciousness of the arahat does not produce any rūpa. Apart from these types of cittas, each type of citta arising in the planes where there are five khandhas conditions rūpa to arise simultaneously with it at its arising moment.[10]

Each person accumulates inclinations that are variegated (vicitta). Some people accumulate a great deal of akusala (unwholesomeness), others a great deal of kusala (wholesomeness). If one has right understanding of the way of developing satipaṭṭhāna, it can be developed. All kinds of kusala that are accumulated are beneficial, they can be "perfections" (pāramīs), supporting conditions for sati to be mindful of the characteristics of realities, which are non-self, not a living being, not a person, so that the four noble Truths can be realized. Defilements can be eradicated in different stages, but for those who only begin with the development of satipaṭṭhāna, satipaṭṭhāna is still weak. The clinging to the concept of self is deeply rooted. Whether one is seeing or hearing, dislikes one's akusala or performs kusala, one takes all these realities for self. One believes that one's kusala belongs to a self.

The study of citta paramattha dhamma can be a supporting condition for the direct understanding of the characteristic of citta appearing right now, at the present moment. Thus, there can be direct understanding of the characteristic of the citta that sees, hears or thinks now. The aim of the study of Dhamma should be the direct understanding

[10]Citta is one of the four factors that produce rūpas of the body. The other factors are kamma, temperature and nutrition. Citta produces groups of rūpas, consisting of the eight inseparable rūpas, and groups which have in addition other types of rūpa.

of realities through satipaṭṭhāna. Satipaṭṭhāna can arise and be aware of the characteristic of the element that experiences whatever object is appearing.

When we study citta, we should not believe that we can immediately have clear understanding of the characteristic of citta. Moreover, the study of citta should not be motivated by the desire to be a person with a great deal of knowledge about citta. The understanding acquired from study can be accumulated together with the other sobhana cetasikas contained in "saṅkhārakkhandha" (the khandha of "formations") and, thus, there are conditions for the arising of sati of satipaṭṭhāna. Sati can be aware of the characteristic of citta that is nāma, the element that experiences an object at this very moment. In this way, paññā can develop and eliminate the wrong view that takes all realities for self. This should be the aim of our study of the Dhamma.

Questions

1. What is life-continuum, bhavanga-citta?
2. When is there citta that is called "that which is pure" (paṇḍara)? And why is it so called?
3. For the arising of which realities can citta and cetasika be a condition?
4. For the arising of which realities can rūpa be a condition?
5. How many stages of enlightenment, that is, of realizing the noble Truths, are there?
6. What is the rūpa that is base, vatthu-rūpa?
7. What is āyatana, and what specifically, are the āyatanas?
8. What is conascence-condition, sahajāta-paccaya?
9. What is the meaning of cittaja rūpa? When does it arise? Which cittas in the five-khandha planes of existence are not conditions for cittaja rūpa?
10. What is the right motivation for the study of the Dhamma?

9

Citta Knows an Object

As we read in the "Atthasālinī", in the section about the aspects of citta (I, Book I, Part II, § 63), citta is so called because it thinks of its object, it clearly cognizes its object. We then read:

> "Or, inasmuch as this word citta is common to all states or classes of citta, that which is known as mundane (lokiya)[1]: kusala (wholesome), akusala (unwholesome), or mahā-kiriya,[2] is termed 'citta', because it arranges itself (cināti) in its own series or continuity by way of javana (impulsion), in a process of citta. And the vipāka is also termed 'citta' because it is conditioned by accumulated (cita)[3] kamma and the defilements.

[1]Mundane, lokiya, is not lokuttara, supramundane. Lokuttara cittas experience nibbāna. Cittas other than lokuttara cittas are mundane. This will be explained in Ch 23.

[2]The arahat has mahā-kiriyacittas instead of mahā-kusala cittas.

[3]In this context the Pāli term cita derived from cinati is used, which means heaped up, accumulated.

> Moreover, all (four classes)[4] are termed citta because they are variegated (citra or vicitta) according to circumstance. The meaning of citta may also be understood from its capacity of producing a variety or diversity of effects."

When we study the texts that have been composed later on we shall find that they deal with six characteristics of citta. These aspects are actually taken from the "Atthasālinī", which is the commentary to the "Dhammasangaṇi" ("Buddhist Psychological Ethics"), the first Book of the "Abhidhamma". The aspects of citta can be classified as five or six categories:

1. Citta is so called because it thinks (cinteti)[5] of an object, it clearly knows an object.
2. Citta is so called because it arranges itself in its own series or continuity, by way of javana in a process.[6]
3. Citta is so called because it is result (vipāka), conditioned by accumulated (cita) kamma and defilements.
4. Citta is so called because it is variegated (vicitta), according to circumstances. In the commentaries composed later on this aspect has been given as twofold:
   - Citta is variegated because it experiences different objects.
   - Citta is variegated because of the accompanying cetasikas, sampayutta dhammas.
5. Citta is so called because of its capacity of producing a diversity of effects.

All these aspects will be dealt with systematically, so that the characteristic of citta will be understood in conformity with the explanation of the "Atthasālinī".

[4] Kusala, akusala, vipāka, result, and kiriya, neither cause nor result. This will be explained further on.

[5] The different Pāli terms used here are word associations with the word citta and they represent the different aspects of citta.

[6] In a process of cittas there are seven javana cittas which are, in the case of non-arahats, kusala cittas or akusala cittas. This will be explained later on.

Citta is so called because it thinks (cinteti) of its object, it clearly cognizes its object. All of us think time and again. If we notice that we are thinking and carefully investigate this, we shall see that we are really quite occupied with thinking, that we think for a long time of a variety of things. We cannot prevent thinking – it goes on and on. Therefore, some people do not want to think; they want to be calm. They believe that it is beneficial to prevent thinking because they see that when they are thinking, they have worry and anxiety; they are restless and disturbed because of attachment or aversion.

We should know that citta is actually the reality that thinks. Rūpa cannot think. When we consider what the subjects are that citta thinks about, we shall know why citta thinks about them, even though we sometimes do not like to think about them at all. It is quite natural that citta arises and thinks time and again about what appears through the eyes, the ears, the nose, the tongue, the bodysense and the mind-door. We believe that all the subjects citta thinks about are very serious and important, but thinking only occurs because citta arises and thinks of an object, and then it falls away. If citta would not think about all those things we take very seriously, they would not exist at all. As we read in the "Atthasālinī", citta is so called because it thinks, it clearly cognizes an object.

As to the dhammas that experience an object, there are different types of realities, each with its own characteristic, which experience an object. Cetasika is a reality that experiences an object, but it is not the "leader" in cognizing an object. Cetasikas arise together with the citta and they experience the same object as the citta, but they each perform their own function. Phassa cetasika (contact), for example, arises together with the citta, but it performs its own function, it experiences the object by contacting it. If phassa cetasika did not arise and perform its function while experiencing an object, there would be no contact with the object. Phassa cetasika experiences the object only in contacting it, but it does not know the object in the same way as citta that clearly cognizes the object.

Paññā is another cetasika that knows, for example, the characteristics of realities that appear as non-self, not a living being, not a person. It penetrates the true characteristics of realities that appear through the six doors. As regards citta, this is the reality that clearly knows its object, as has already been explained. However, citta knows the object differently from phassa, which just contacts the object, or saññā (perception, or remembrance) which recognizes the characteristic of the object, or paññā, which penetrates the true nature of realities.

Citta is the reality that cognizes, that clearly knows the different characteristics of the objects that appear. Is what is appearing through the eyes at this moment one and the same colour, or are there different colours appearing? Reality is true dhamma (sacca dhamma); it can be verified. We should find out whether at this moment we see only one thing, only one colour, or whether we see that which is appearing as different colours, in a detailed way, so that we can distinguish between different things that are perceived. Can we, for example, distinguish between a real diamond and a synthetic diamond?

Citta is the reality that sees and knows clearly; it clearly knows the different characteristics of the different objects, and that even into the smallest details. At this moment, the rūpa that is the eyesense has as its characteristic a special clarity – it can be compared to a mirror in which the image of whatever passes is clearly reflected. The eyesense can come into contact with visible object. The earsense can come into contact just with sound, smelling-sense just with odour, tasting-sense just with flavour, and bodysense just with those rūpas that are tangible object.

Whatever colour appears, the colour of a real diamond, of a synthetic diamond, of jade, of a stone, even the colour of the look in someone's eyes that expresses envy, all that can appear to the citta which sees.

What appears at this moment through the eyes appears to citta, which clearly knows it. It sees all the colours of the different objects that appear, and thus the meaning of things can be known, the shape and form perceived, and there can be thinking about what has appeared through the eyes.

Are sounds that appear through the earsense entirely the same or are there different sounds? Each sound is different depending on the conditions that caused the arising of that sound. No matter how many people there are, the sound of each individual is different. Citta clearly knows each of the different sounds that appear. Citta knows the sound of ridicule, of sarcasm, of contempt, of a fan, of a waterfall, the cry of an animal, the different calls of various kinds of animals, or even the sound of a man who imitates the sound of an animal. Citta clearly knows the characteristics of the different sounds; it hears each different sound.

All kinds of realities can appear when citta arises and clearly knows the object that presents itself. The citta that smells through the nose can arise and clearly know the different odours that appear. It can clearly know the smell of different kinds of animals, plants or flowers, the smell of food, of curry and of sweets. Even if we only smell without seeing anything, we can know what kind of smell it is.

The citta that experiences flavour through the tongue can arise and clearly know different flavours. There are many flavours of food, such as flavour of meat, vegetable or fruit, there is the flavour of tea, coffee, salt, sugar, orange juice, lemon or tamarind. All these flavours are completely different, but the citta that tastes clearly knows each of the different flavours that appear. Citta is able to distinguish clearly the subtlest differences in flavour, it knows them in a detailed way. For example, when we sample food, the citta that tastes the flavour knows exactly whether there is still something lacking. It knows which ingredient should be added, how the food should be seasoned so that it is more tasty.

The citta that experiences tangible object impinging on the bodysense clearly knows the different characteristic of tangible object. It knows, for example, the characteristic of cold of the air, cold of the water, or of the cold weather. It knows the characteristic of silk or of wool that touches the bodysense.

Someone said that while he was standing on the road there was mindfulness of the characteristic of hardness that appeared. He thought that this was hardness of the road, that hardness of his shoes and that hardness of his stockings. All this is thinking about the characteristic of hardness that appears. The citta that thinks arises because of conditions. When hardness impinges on the bodysense and one thinks about what this hardness is, the road, the shoes or the stockings, it can be known that nobody can avoid thinking of different things. However, paññā should understand that citta arises, knows clearly one object at a time and then falls away very rapidly. In this way, the characteristics of realities can be known as they are. Thinking about the road, the shoes or the stockings does not occur at the same time as realizing the characteristic of hardness.

If we clearly understand that it is not a self who thinks, that it is citta that knows the subject about which it thinks, it can be a condition for paññā to develop, so that it comes to know precisely the characteristics of realities as they are. The citta that thinks is different from the citta that sees. The citta that sees knows an object through the eyesense, whereas the citta that thinks knows an object through the mind-door. When a reality appears through the bodysense, be it the characteristic of softness or hardness, it is natural that at that moment we do not yet know what it is that is impinging on the bodysense. Later on we will know what the object is that is hard or soft. If we touch something in the dark, we may turn on the light in order to see what we are touching. Thus, we can understand that at the moment citta experiences hardness, it does not think; that kind of thinking is another type of citta.

When citta experiences just hardness, there is no world of the road, the shoes or the stockings. There is no world of conventional truth, of concepts. There is only the reality that experiences the characteristic of hardness. The reality that experiences hardness is not a living being or a person, it is just a type of nāma that arises and then falls away. The citta that arises later on can think about what has appeared through the eyes, the ears, the nose, the tongue, the bodysense or the mind-door. It thinks about a story, about concepts of what has appeared. Since we are so occupied with our thinking, we forget that the citta that arose and experienced hardness, and the rūpa that is hardness, have fallen away already.

Also, the cittas that are thinking about the hard substance, fall away immediately as well. Nāma and rūpa arise and fall away. Cittas arise and fall away, one after another, continuously, as do rūpas. This happens so rapidly that we do not realize their arising and falling away. We do not realize that the nāma dhammas and rūpa dhammas that arise and fall away are non-self.

Citta is the reality that clearly knows the object that appears, be it through the eyes, the ears, the nose, the tongue, the bodysense or the mind-door. Whatever object phassa cetasika contacts, the citta that arises together with it clearly knows the characteristic of that object; it knows each different object. When it is said of citta, the reality that experiences something, that it has the characteristic of clearly knowing an object, we should understand what that means. It means that citta knows the different characteristics of the different objects appearing through the senses or through the mind-door. Citta is the reality that clearly knows an object, and the object is a condition for citta to arise and to experience that object. The object is object-condition (ārammaṇa-paccaya), it is a condition for the arising of citta by being its object.

Citta cannot arise without knowing an object, but besides object-condition there are also several other conditions for each type of citta that arises.

Questions

1. What are the different ways of knowing an object in the case of phassa cetasika, saññā cetasika, paññā cetasika and citta?
2. What is object-condition?
3. Which objects can be object-condition?

10
A Process of Citta

As we read in the "Atthasālinī" (I, Book I, Part II, § 63) about citta:

> "...Or, inasmuch as this word citta is common to all states or classes of citta, that which is known as mundane: kusala, akusala or mahā-kiriya, is termed 'citta', because it arranges itself (cināti) in its own series or continuity by way of javana (impulsion), in a process of citta."

In order to understand the aspect of citta as that which arranges itself in its own series or continuity by way of javana, we should remember that cittas arise and fall away, succeeding one another very rapidly, and that wholesome and unwholesome qualities, cetasikas, which accompany a citta and fall away with the citta, are accumulated from one moment of citta to the next moment of citta.

When citta arises and sees what appears through the eyes, hears sound through the ears or experiences another sense object, it is usually not known that such experiences are a characteristic of citta. We are more likely to notice citta when it is unhappy, sad or annoyed, when it is happy or pleased, when there is citta with anger or loving-kindness, when there is the inclination to help someone else or to treat him with affection. Each citta that arises and falls away very rapidly is succeeded by the next citta and therefore the accumulations of the preceding citta are going on to the following citta. Whether the citta is kusala citta or akusala citta, each citta that arises and falls away conditions the next citta, which immediately succeeds it. That is why inclinations accumulated in the preceding citta can go on to the next citta, and so it continues all the time.

We can notice that everybody has different inclinations, a different character, and this is so because all the different inclinations have been accumulated in the citta, and these are going on from one citta to the next. Some people are inclined to perform wholesome deeds. They are able to do so because kusala citta that in the past arose and fell away, was succeeded by the next citta that accumulated the inclination toward wholesomeness. Thus, conditions have been created for the arising of kusala citta later on. It is the same in the case of akusala citta, be it akusala citta rooted in attachment, in aversion or in ignorance. When the akusala citta falls away, it conditions the arising of the succeeding citta and thus the inclination to akusala accumulated in the preceding citta goes on to the next citta, and in this way, there are conditions for the arising of akusala citta in the future.

The fact that cittas succeed one another is due to contiguity-condition, anantara-paccaya: each citta is anantara-paccaya for the next citta. This means that the preceding citta conditions the arising of the next citta, which immediately succeeds it, as soon as the preceding citta has fallen away. Each citta is anantara-paccaya for the succeeding one, except the dying-consciousness (cuti-citta) of the arahat. This citta cannot be anantara-paccaya, because when it has fallen away parinibbāna, the final passing away of the khandhas, occurs. Therefore, the dying-consciousness of the arahat is not succeeded by rebirth-consciousness nor by any other citta.

Summarizing the conditions that were already dealt with, they are three:

- conascence-condition – sahajāta-paccaya,
- object-condition – ārammaṇa-paccaya,

- contiguity-condition – anantara-paccaya.

To repeat the "Atthasālinī" about the second aspect of citta:

> "... Or, inasmuch as this word 'citta' is common to all states or classes of citta, that which is known as mundane: kusala, akusala or mahā-kiriya, is termed citta, because it arranges itself (cināti) in its own series or continuity, by way of javana, in a process of citta."

This seems rather complicated, but it refers to realities in daily life. People may have heard time and again the words kusala citta and akusala citta, but they may not be familiar with the terms "mundane," "mahā-kiriyacitta" and with the term "javana in a process."

All the different types of citta can be classified by way of four jātis or categories (jāti meaning birth or nature):

- kusala citta,
- akusala citta,
- vipākacitta,
- kiriyacitta.

Kusala citta is the citta that is wholesome, it is the cause that will produce pleasant result, kusala vipāka, in the future. When kusala citta and the accompanying cetasikas, which are the cause of a future result, have fallen away, the accumulated wholesome qualities of that citta go on to the next citta and again to the following ones. Thus, they are a condition for the arising of kusala vipākacitta and the accompanying cetasikas in the future; they are the result of the kusala citta which formerly arose. It has been explained in the commentary that the cetasikas that accompany the vipākacitta are vipāka cetasikas, but since citta is the "leader" the word vipākacitta is used; the accompanying cetasikas are also vipāka.

Another example where the word citta also refers to the accompanying cetasikas is the term "cittaja rūpa," the rūpa that originates from citta. In fact, cittaja rūpa arises because citta and the accompanying cetasikas are the condition for its arising. Thus, the word cittaja rūpa also refers to the accompanying cetasikas that condition the arising of that rūpa. In the same way, the word vipākacitta also refers to the accompanying vipāka cetasikas.

Akusala citta is a reality that is harmful and dangerous. It causes the arising of unhappy, unpleasant result in the form of different kinds of akusala vipākacittas.

Apart from kusala citta, akusala citta and vipākacitta, there is another class of citta, and this is kiriyacitta, inoperative citta. Kiriyacitta is neither kusala citta nor akusala citta, and, therefore, it is not a cause for the arising of vipākacitta. Nor is it vipākacitta, the result of kusala citta or akusala citta. As we have seen, all cittas can be classified by the four jātis of kusala, akusala, vipāka and kiriya.

If we do not study realities in detail, we shall not know when citta is kusala, when akusala, when vipāka and when kiriya. The rebirth-consciousness, paṭisandhi-citta, is the first citta that has arisen in this lifespan. We all are alive at this moment because the rebirth-consciousness has arisen in this lifespan and it conditions us to be a particular individual. The rebirth-consciousness is neither kusala nor akusala; when it arises it cannot commit any kamma (action) through body, speech or mind. The rebirth-consciousness is vipākacitta; it arises because it is conditioned by a particular kamma. No matter how numerous the kammas may have been which were performed in each of our lifespans, whichever of these kammas conditions the arising of the rebirth-consciousness or any other type of vipākacitta, that kamma is kamma-condition, kamma-paccaya, for the rebirth-consciousness or the other types of vipākacitta. If someone is born in the human plane of existence, which is a happy plane, that birth must be the result of kusala kamma. In such a case, the rebirth-consciousness is kusala vipāka. If one is born in an unhappy plane, a hell plane, as a ghost (peta), as an asura (demon) or as an animal, it is the result of akusala kamma. The rebirth-consciousness that arises in an unhappy plane is akusala vipāka.

A kamma that was formerly committed conditions the arising of the rebirth-consciousness, the first citta of this life, which immediately succeeds the dying-consciousness of the previous life. After the rebirth-consciousness has fallen away, the same kamma is the condition for the arising of the next vipākacittas, which perform the function of life-continuum, bhavanga. The bhavanga-citta maintains the continuation in the life of someone as a particular person. It performs its function throughout life, in between the processes of cittas, until the dying-consciousness arises and one passes away from life in this plane of existence. Then there is no longer this particular person in this lifespan. In the course of life, other kammas can be the condition for the arising of different vipākacittas, which experience objects through the eyes, the ears, the nose, the tongue and the bodysense.

Kusala is the reality that is good, wholesome, blameless, not harmful. Some people think that they can only perform kusala if they are rich and are able to spend money, but they forget that one can be generous and give assistance in other ways. Even if someone does not have much money, he may still have some things he can share with others in order to help them. Can one give assistance to others? If one cannot do this, is that kusala or akusala? If someone with few means does not know that kusala citta is the citta that is good, wholesome and faultless, he will perhaps be unhappy and believe that he cannot perform deeds of merit. But there are actually many other kinds of kusala, apart from donations of money, one can perform. One can have loving-kindness towards someone else. Then one treats him as a fellow human being and the citta is tender and gentle; one can utter affectionate, amiable speech that comes from one's heart. There are always ways and means to give assistance to others and share things with them. At such moments the citta is kusala citta, it is a dhamma that is faultless, which cannot cause any harm or danger.

When there is conceit and someone thinks himself more important, superior or more clever than someone else, when he compares himself with someone else and thinks in terms of "he" and "I," there cannot be kusala citta arising. At such moments one cannot help others, there cannot be any giving or sharing; instead there is akusala citta, the dhamma that is unwholesome and harmful.

If we really understand the characteristic of kusala we shall find ways and means to develop many different kinds of kusala. However, if a person wants to keep things for himself he is unable to be generous. He may have desire for calm, or he may be attached to the idea of eradicating defilements and becoming a sotāpanna, but he is unable to give something away to someone else.

Each person has accumulated inclinations for different kinds of kusala and akusala. We should consider and investigate our own citta and find out whether there is still a great deal of stinginess, or whether we can gradually begin to give away useful things to others. In that way, generosity can become our nature, it can even become a powerful condition, a support for paññā, which eliminates the wrong view that takes nāma and rūpa for self. When paññā has been developed, it can become so keen that nibbāna can be realized.

We may believe that we want to be without defilements, but when defilements actually arise, it seems that we wish to have them. We may have conceit, we may find ourselves important or we may be jealous. Someone else may say that such defilements should be eradicated, that one should rejoice in someone else's happiness or that one should have loving-kindness towards a disagreeable person, but are we able to follow such advice? People who want to be angry, who want to have contempt for others, who want to be arrogant or jealous, cannot follow the advice to cultivate wholesomeness. This shows that the eradication of defilements cannot occur immediately, that it can only be accomplished very gradually. Paññā can gradually be developed so that it can arise from time to time. If we really want to eradicate defilements, we should know that all kinds of kusala should be developed. It is not right to just perform dāna, generosity, and pay no attention to the defilements which still arise. It is essential to know one's defilements.

A person may just want to be calm because he often feels restless and disturbed. Because of his thoughts, he is angry or confused, and there seem to be circumstances that make him feel worried or annoyed all the time. The reason is that at such moments he does not examine his own citta, but instead pays attention only to those he is angry with. If one pays attention to other people in an unwholesome way, so that akusala citta arises, the citta will be disturbed, restless and worried. A person may notice when he is upset and then he just wants to be calm. But he fails to see that when there is no anger he will not be disturbed, whereas when there is anger, he is unhappy and disturbed. When one is angry and disturbed, there is akusala citta, the dhamma that is harmful.

If we can be mindful after we have been angry, and we can then think of others in such a way that loving-kindness, compassion, sympathetic joy or equanimity arises, there will immediately be calmness. When loving-kindness, compassion, sympathetic joy or equanimity accompanies the citta, it is kusala citta, without attachment, aversion and ignorance; and then it is calm. There is true calmness with each kusala citta. Thus, if we want to eradicate defilements we should develop all kinds of kusala, not merely generosity, dāna.

Repeating again the "Atthasālinī" with regard to the second aspect of citta:

> "...that which is known as mundane: kusala, akusala and mahā-kiriya, is termed citta, because it arranges itself in its own series or continuity, by way of javana, in a process of citta."

The word "series" or "continuity", in Pāli "santāna," refers to the arising and falling away of cittas in succession, in their own series. The citta that sees, hears, smells, tastes or experiences tangible object is vipākacitta, not kusala citta or akusala citta. Therefore, these cittas are not javana-cittas which arise and fall away in their own series in the process of cittas.[1] Vipākacittas are results of past kammas. When a deed or kamma has ripened and it is ready to produce result, and there are also other conditioning factors that play their part, vipākacitta can arise. There are different kinds of vipākacitta that perform different functions, such as seeing or hearing. Vipākacitta does not arise in the succession of javana, it is result produced by kusala kamma or akusala kamma that has been accumulated and is therefore the condition for the arising of vipāka. Vipākacitta that arises and then falls away cannot cause the arising of any other vipākacitta.

We should have right understanding of the second aspect of citta, that kusala cittas, akusala cittas and mahā-kiriyacittas arrange themselves in their own series or continuity by way of javana, in the process of cittas. First of all, we have to know what cittas arising in a process, vīthi-cittas, are, which types of cittas they are and when they arise. Javana cittas in a process are a succession or series of kusala cittas or

---

[1]As will be explained, in a process of cittas there are, in the case of non-arahats, usually seven javana cittas which are kusala cittas or akusala cittas, arising and falling away in succession.

akusala cittas. For the arahat there is, instead of kusala citta or akusala citta, mahā-kiriyacitta performing the function of javana.[2] Also, the arahat has different types of cittas that condition the movement of the body, which condition speech and which think, arising in the series of javana-cittas.

We should first of all know that vīthi-cittas, cittas arising in a process, are not rebirth-consciousness, bhavanga-citta or dying-consciousness. All types of cittas other than these are vīthi-cittas. The rebirth-consciousness arises only once in a life span. It succeeds the dying-consciousness of the previous life and it only performs the function of rebirth. At that moment, there is no seeing, hearing, smelling, tasting or the experience of tangible object. Rebirth-consciousness is vipākacitta, the result of kamma. The rebirth-consciousness that arises in the human plane of existence is kusala vipākacitta, the result of kusala kamma.

Kamma not only produces the rebirth-consciousness as result. When the rebirth-consciousness has fallen away, kamma also conditions the arising of the succeeding citta which is the same type of vipākacitta and performs the function of bhavanga, life-continuum. As we have seen, this type of citta maintains the continuation in the life span of someone as a particular person until death. So long as the dying-consciousness has not arisen yet, the bhavanga-cittas that arise and fall away perform the function of preserving the continuity in one's life. They perform their function at the moments when there is no seeing, hearing, smelling, tasting, the experiencing of tangible object or thinking. Thus, the rebirth-consciousness, the bhavanga-citta and the dying-consciousness are cittas that do not arise in processes; they are not vīthi-cittas.

When we are fast asleep, we do not see or experience other sense objects, we do not think. The bhavanga-cittas arise and fall away in succession all the time, until we dream or wake up, and there is again seeing, hearing, the experience of other sense objects or thinking of different subjects of this world. This world does not appear to the rebirth-consciousness, the bhavanga-citta and the dying-consciousness. At the moment the vipākacitta arises and performs the function of rebirth or the function of bhavanga, the different objects of this world, in our case the human world, do not appear. If we would be fast asleep

[2]The arahat does not perform kamma that can produce result. He has reached the end of rebirth. He has no kusala cittas or akusala cittas.

at this moment, we would not know anything, we would not see anyone who is here. We would not experience sound, odour, cold or heat. The bhavanga-citta is not involved with anything in this world. It does not even know who we are, where we are, who are our relatives and friends. It does not know anything about possessions, rank, an honourable position, happiness or misery. Whereas when we are not asleep we remember the things of this world, the different people and the different stories connected with this world.

When we see, there is no bhavanga-citta, but vīthi-citta instead, which arises and sees what appears through the eyes. The citta which sees, the citta which knows what the object is that is seen, the citta which likes what appears through the eyes, the cittas which experience objects through the ears, the nose, the tongue, the bodysense or the mind-door, are all vīthi-cittas. When we hear a sound and then like it or dislike it, there are no bhavanga-cittas, but vīthi-cittas instead.

All the cittas that arise and experience visible object which appears through the eyes, are eye-door process cittas, cakkhu-dvāra vīthi-cittas. There are vīthi-cittas that are ear-door process cittas, nose-door process cittas, tongue-door process cittas, body-door process cittas and mind-door process cittas, all of which experience an object through the corresponding doorway.

The nāma dhammas that naturally occur in our daily life are bhavanga-cittas arising and falling away as well as vīthi-cittas that arise and experience an object through one of the six doors. Successions of bhavanga-cittas and vīthi-cittas arise alternately.

When one is born in a five-khandha plane (where there are nāma and rūpa), kamma conditions the arising of kammaja rūpa (rūpa produced by kamma). These are, among others, the rūpas that are eyesense, earsense, smelling-sense, tasting-sense and bodysense. These rūpas arise and fall away in succession. They provide one with the ability to experience sense objects, thus, they prevent one from being blind, deaf or disabled. However, when kamma at a particular moment no longer conditions the arising of, for example, the rūpa which is eyesense, one will be blind, one will not be able to see anything at all. Thus, the citta which sees and the other sense-cognitions are each dependent on the appropriate conditions which cause their arising.

So long as vīthi-cittas do not arise yet, bhavanga-cittas are arising and falling away in succession. When a rūpa that can be sense object arises and impinges on the corresponding sense-base (pasāda rūpa), vīthi-cittas cannot arise immediately. First, bhavanga-cittas arise and fall away before sense-door process cittas arise, which can experience that rūpa.

Rūpa arises and falls away very rapidly, but citta arises and falls away faster than rūpa. The time one rūpa arises and falls away is equal to the time seventeen cittas arise and fall away. When a rūpa impinges on a sense-base there are, as we have seen, some bhavanga-cittas arising and falling away first. The first bhavanga-citta, which arises when that rūpa impinges on the sense-base, is called atīta-bhavanga, past bhavanga. This bhavanga-citta is of the same type as the bhavanga-cittas that arose before. The name atīta bhavanga is used to point out how long the rūpa that impinges on the sense-base will last so that it can be experienced by vīthi-cittas. Counting from the atīta bhavanga, it cannot last longer than seventeen moments of citta.

When the atīta bhavanga has fallen away, it conditions the succeeding bhavanga-citta, which "vibrates," and which is stirred by the object, so it is called bhavanga calana, vibrating bhavanga.[3] This citta is still bhavanga-citta, since vīthi-citta cannot arise yet and the stream of bhavanga-cittas still continues. When the bhavanga calana has fallen away, the succeeding bhavanga-citta arises, and this is the bhavangupaccheda, arrest bhavanga, which interrupts the stream of bhavanga-cittas, because it is the last bhavanga-citta before vīthi-cittas arise. When the bhavangupaccheda has fallen away, vīthi-cittas arise and experience the object that appears through the eyes, the ears, the nose, the tongue, the bodysense or the mind-door.

All vīthi-cittas that experience visible object through the eyes are eye-door process cittas, cakkhu-dvāra vīthi-cittas, because they experience a visible object that impinges on the eyesense, but has not yet fallen away.

All vīthi-cittas that experience sound through the ears are ear-door process cittas, sota-dvāra vīthi-cittas, because they experience sound, which impinges on the ear-sense and has not yet fallen away. It is the

[3] That bhavanga-citta does not experience the rūpa which impinges on the sense-base, but it is affected or stirred by it, since within an infinitesimally short time vīthi-cittas will arise.

same in the case of the vīthi-cittas that experience objects through the other doorways; they are named after the relevant doorway.

Vīthi-cittas of the mind-door process, mano-dvāra vīthi-cittas, can experience all kinds of objects. When the mind-door process follows upon a sense-door process, the vīthi-cittas of the mind-door process experience visible object, sound, odour, flavour or tangible object that were experienced by the vīthi-cittas of the five sense-door processes. The vīthi-cittas of the mind-door process can also experience dhammārammaṇa, mind-object, which is an object that can be experienced only through the mind-door.

11
Functions of Citta

Citta can experience objects through the six doors. All objects that can be experienced by citta can be classified as sixfold:

1. Visible object, rūpārammaṇa, can be known by citta through the eye-door and through the mind-door.
2. Sound, saddārammaṇa, can be known by citta through the ear-door and through the mind-door.
3. Odour, gandhārammaṇa, can be known by citta through the nose-door and through the mind-door.
4. Flavour, rasārammaṇa, can be known by citta through the tongue-door and through the mind-door.
5. Tangible object, phoṭṭhabbārammaṇa, can be known by citta through the body-door and through the mind-door.
6. Mental object, dhammārammaṇa, can be known by citta only through the mind-door.

The cittas arising in the mind-door process, mano-dvāra vīthi-cittas, can experience all six classes of objects. As regards mental object, dhammārammaṇa, this can be known only by mind-door process cittas.

Each citta that arises performs a function and then it falls away. The rebirth-consciousness, which succeeds the dying-consciousness of the previous life, performs the function of rebirth only once. After that citta has fallen away, bhavanga-cittas arise and all bhavanga-cittas, including the past bhavanga, atīta bhavanga, the vibrating bhavanga, bhavanga calana, and the arrest bhavanga, bhavangupaccheda, perform the function of bhavanga; they preserve the continuity in a lifespan. The bhavangupaccheda is the last bhavanga-citta arising before the stream of bhavanga-cittas is arrested and a series of cittas arising in a process occurs. The bhavangupaccheda is succeeded by the first citta of a process, a vīthi-citta. This citta performs the function of adverting, āvajjana; it pays attention to or adverts to the object that appears through one of the doorways. It does not take part in the succession of bhavanga-cittas, but it turns towards the object that impinges on one of the senses. If the object impinges on the eyesense, the five-sense-door adverting-consciousness, the pañca-dvārāvajjana-citta, arises and performs the function of adverting through the eye-door. If the object impinges on one of the other senses, the five-sense-door adverting-consciousness performs the function of adverting to the object through the relevant doorway. It experiences the object which contacts one of the five sense-doors, but it does not see, hear, smell, taste yet, and there is no body-consciousness yet. If the object contacts the mind-door, not one of the five senses, the mind-door adverting-consciousness, the manodvārāvajjana-citta, arises. This is another type of citta that is different from the five-sense-door adverting-consciousness. It performs the function of adverting to the object only through the mind-door.

During the arising and falling away of bhavanga-cittas, flavour, for example, may arise and impinge on the rūpa which is tasting-sense (jivhāppasāda rūpa). The atīta bhavanga, past bhavanga, arises and falls away and is succeeded by the bhavanga calana, vibrating bhavanga, and this again is succeeded by the bhavangupaccheda, the arrest bhavanga. The bhavangupaccheda is succeeded by the five-sense-door adverting-consciousness. This citta attends to the object, it knows that the object impinges on the tongue-door but it cannot taste yet. It is as if one knows that a visitor has arrived at the door but one does not see him yet and does not know who he is.

We all have guests who come to see us. When we think of guests, we are likely to think of people, but in reality our guests are the different objects that appear through the eyes, the ears, the nose, the tongue, the bodysense and the mind-door. When we see visible object that appears through the eyes, visible object is our visitor. When we hear sound, sound is our visitor. When we do not hear, sound does not appear, and thus, a visitor has not come yet through the ear-door. When flavour appears, flavour is like a visitor, it appears through the door of the tongue just for a moment and then it disappears. Whenever an object appears through one of the doorways, that object can be seen as a visitor who comes through that doorway. It is there just for an extremely short moment and then it disappears completely, it does not come back again in the cycle of birth and death.

Elderly people tend to feel lonely when they lack company. When they were younger they met many people, they enjoyed the company of relatives and friends. When they have become older, the number of visitors, whom they see as people, has dwindled. When one asks elderly people what they like most of all, they will usually answer that they like most of all the company of people. They are happy when other people come to see them, they like to be engaged in conversation. However, in reality everybody has visitors, at each moment one sees, hears, smells, tastes or experiences tangible object. Usually when such visitors come, citta rooted in attachment arises and enjoys what appears through the eyes, the ears, the nose, the tongue or the bodysense.

There are different kinds of visitors. Nobody would like a wicked person as visitor, but a dear relative or friend is most welcome. In reality, the different objects that appear through the senses are only rūpas. Rūpa does not know anything and therefore it cannot have any evil intention towards anybody. When would a visitor be an enemy and when a dear relative or friend? Actually, when an object appears and one enjoys it and clings to it, there is an enemy, because enjoyment with clinging is akusala dhamma. Akusala dhamma is not a friend to anybody. Whereas kusala dhamma is like a close relative who is ready to help one, eager to give assistance at all times. Therefore, we should know the difference between the characteristics of kusala citta and of akusala citta.

Akusala citta is evil, harmful, it is like an enemy, not a friend. When we think of an enemy we may be afraid, and we do not like his company. However, it is akusala citta that is wicked, it is a condition for creating an enemy in the future. Whereas, kusala citta, which is like a dear relative or friend, is a condition for a dear relative or friend to come in the future.[1]

Rūpa is not a condition for foe or friend, because rūpa does not know anything, it has no evil or good intentions. The sound that appears is a reality that does not experience anything, it has no wish for anybody to hear or not hear it. Sound is rūpa that arises because there are conditions for its arising. The kind of sound that will impinge on someone's earsense is dependent on conditions. When we are fast sleep, we do not even hear the deafening, frightening sound of thunder. Then the sound of thunder is not our visitor. However, it can be someone else's visitor when the accumulated conditions, which cause the earsense to be impinged upon by that sound, are there. It is dependent on conditions whether an object will be someone's visitor through the doorway of eyes, ears, nose, tongue or bodysense. Kamma that has been accumulated causes the arising of vipākacitta, which experiences an object through one of the sense-doors.

Thus, the visitors that present themselves through the eyes, the ears, the nose, the tongue and the bodysense are visible object, sound, odour, flavour and tangible object. They appear just for a moment and then they fall away, they disappear, not to return again. There is no living being, person, self or anything there. Nobody knows in a day which visitor will come through which doorway and at which moment.

Whenever citta experiences an object through the eyes, the other senses or the mind-door, it is vīthi-citta, citta arising in a process. The five-sense-door adverting-consciousness, which succeeds the bhavangupaccheda, is the first vīthi-citta in a sense-door process. This citta performs the function of adverting to the object. It merely knows that an object is impinging on one of the five sense-doors. Thus, it is differ-

[1] Akusala citta and kusala citta arise and fall away, but the inclinations to akusala and kusala are accumulated; the accumulated inclinations are the condition for the arising again, later on, of akusala citta and kusala citta.

ent from the citta that performs the function of seeing or from the other sense-cognitions. If the five-sense-door adverting-consciousness had not arisen and fallen away first, the other vīthi-cittas of that sense-door process could not arise, be it a process of the doorway of the eye, the ear, the nose, the tongue or the bodysense.

Thus, the five-sense-door adverting-consciousness is the first vīthi-citta in a sense-door process and it adverts to the object through one of the five sense-doors. Therefore, it is called five-sense-door adverting-consciousness, pañca-dvārāvajjana-citta,[2] and is named after the corresponding doorway, as the case may be. When it adverts to visible object through the eye-door, it is called eye-door adverting-consciousness, cakkhu-dvārāvajjana-citta. In the same way, the adverting-consciousness that adverts to the object through each of the other sense-doors is called ear-door adverting-consciousness, nose-door adverting-consciousness, tongue-door adverting-consciousness and body-door adverting-consciousness. However, the collective name five-sense-door adverting-consciousness can also be used for this type of citta, since it performs the function of adverting through all five sense-doors.

There is also a type of citta that is the first vīthi-citta of the mind-door process that experiences different objects through the mind-door. Before kusala cittas or akusala cittas in a mind-door process arise that may think of different subjects, there must be a citta that performs the function of adverting to the object that contacts the mind-door. This citta, which is the mind-door adverting-consciousness, mano-dvārāvajjana-citta, is the first vīthi-citta of the mind-door process. If this citta does not arise, the next vīthi-cittas that experience an object through the mind-door cannot arise. The mind-door adverting-consciousness is different from the five-sense-door adverting-consciousness. The five-sense-door adverting-consciousness can arise only in the five-sense-door processes, not in a mind-door process. The mind-door adverting-consciousness can perform the function of adverting only through the mind-door.

Thus, there are two types of vīthi-cittas that perform the function of adverting: the five-sense-door adverting-consciousness, which performs the function of adverting through the five sense-doors, and the mind-door adverting-consciousness, which performs the function of adverting

[2] In Pāli, pañca means five, dvāra means door and āvajjana means adverting.

only through the mind-door.

One may wonder whether a five-sense-door adverting-consciousness is arising at this very moment. There must be, otherwise there could not be seeing, hearing, smelling, tasting or the experiencing of tangible object. There is also at this moment mind-door adverting-consciousness. Different vīthi-cittas arise which experience an object through one of the five sense-doors and then they fall away. When the sense-door process is over, there are many bhavanga-cittas arising in succession, and then vīthi-cittas of a mind-door process arise which again experience the same object as the vīthi-cittas of the preceding sense-door process. They experience this object through the mind-door, which is the citta preceding the mind-door adverting-consciousness, the bhavangupaccheda, arrest bhavanga.[3]

When we are fast sleep, we do not experience any object through one of the six doors. The five-sense-door adverting-consciousness or the mind-door adverting-consciousness cannot arise at that time. Also, when we are not asleep there are moments that we do not experience any object through one of the six doors. At such moments, the five-sense-door adverting-consciousness or the mind-door adverting-consciousness do not arise, but there are bhavanga-cittas arising in between the different processes of cittas.

In the five-sense-door process there are seven different types of vīthi-cittas arising in a fixed order. When the first vīthi-citta, the five-sense-door adverting-consciousness, has arisen, has performed the function of adverting to the object and has fallen away, it conditions the arising of the second vīthi-citta. In the case of the eye-door process, seeing-consciousness (cakkhu-viññāṇa) arises and performs the function of seeing (dassana kicca) just once and then it falls away. It is the same in the case of the other sense-door processes: hearing-consciousness, smelling-consciousness, tasting-consciousness and body-consciousness, which arise, perform their function just once and then fall away. Types of citta other than the five sense-cognitions cannot succeed the five-sense-door adverting-consciousness.

The five-sense-door adverting-consciousness is the first vīthi-citta. Seeing-consciousness, or one of the other sense-cognitions, is the sec-

[3]The five sense-doors are rūpas, whereas the mind-door is nāma.

ond vīthi-citta in the process. When the second vīthi-citta has fallen away, it is succeeded by the third vīthi-citta, which is the receiving-consciousness, the sampaṭicchana-citta. This citta performs the function of sampaṭicchana; it receives the object from one of the sense-cognitions. When the sampaṭicchana-citta has fallen away, the fourth vīthi-citta arises, the investigating-consciousness, santīraṇa-citta. This citta performs the function of investigating, it investigates the object just once and then it falls away. The fifth vīthi-citta is the determining-consciousness, votthapana-citta. This is actually the same type of citta that is the mind-door adverting-consciousness, mano-dvārāvajjana-citta. But, in the five-sense-door process, it performs the function of determining the object and it is then called after its function, determining-consciousness, votthapana-citta. It determines whether kusala citta, akusala citta or mahā-kiriyacitta will succeed it. It prepares the way for these types of cittas.

When the determining-consciousness, the votthapana-citta, has fallen away, the sixth type of vīthi-citta arises, and this can be kusala citta, akusala citta or mahā-kiriyacitta. There are different types of kusala cittas, of akusala cittas and of mahā-kiriyacittas, and when the series of javana cittas occurs, these cittas are all of the same type of kusala citta, of akusala citta or of mahā-kiriyacitta. They perform the function of javana, impulsion,[4] "running through" the object. As has been stated, this type of citta "arranges itself in its own series or continuity by way of javana."

All the types of vīthi-cittas that experience an object through the eyes, the ears, the nose, the tongue, the body-sense or the mind-door arise in a fixed sequence. This fixed order of cittas (citta niyāma) takes its course according to conditions and no one has any power or control over this fixed order.

It is because of the appropriate conditions that first the vīthi-citta, which is the five-sense-door adverting-consciousness, arises, performs its function only once and falls away. The second type of vīthi-citta of the sense-door process, which is in the case of the eye-door process seeing-consciousness, arises and performs the function of seeing only once and then it falls away. The third type of vīthi-citta, the receiving-

[4]Javana, which means "impulse," is also translated in some texts as "apperception."

consciousness, sampaṭicchana-citta, arises once and then falls away. The fourth type of vīthi-citta, the investigating-consciousness, santīraṇa-citta, arises only once. The fifth type of vīthi-citta, the determining-consciousness, votthapana-citta, arises only once. The sixth type of vīthi-citta, which may be kusala citta, akusala citta or mahā-kiriyacitta, performs the function of impulsion, javana, and this function is performed seven times by seven javana-cittas arising in succession. It is according to conditions that the javana vīthi-citta arranges itself in its own series or sequence. Conditions also determine that this type of vīthi-citta arises and falls away seven times in succession.

For those who are not arahats, the citta that performs the function of javana is kusala citta or akusala citta. For the arahat there are no kusala cittas or akusala cittas, but there are mahā-kiriyacittas that can perform the function of javana. For the arahat there are only cittas of the jātis (classes) of vipāka and kiriya. There are several types of kiriyacittas. After seeing, hearing, smelling, tasting, the experiencing of tangible object and also while thinking, the javana-cittas of the arahat are "mundane" kiriyacittas. At such moments, the citta experiences visible object, sound, odour, flavour and tangible object, objects which are "the world."

After a single moment of seeing, we enjoy what we have seen and then akusala citta rooted in attachment arises seven times. Thus, akusala citta arises seven times more often than seeing-consciousness, which sees only once. In this way, akusala is actually accumulated in daily life, and this concerns all of us. Because of the persistent accumulation of akusala, the eradication of defilements is extremely difficult, it cannot be achieved without right understanding of realities. If someone believes that it is easy to eradicate defilements, he should learn the truth about the process of accumulation, the accumulation of ignorance, attachment, aversion and of all the other faults and vices. One should know that defilements arise seven times more often than seeing, hearing, smelling, tasting and body-consciousness, the types of citta that arise only once. If someone has expectations and if he is wondering when he will penetrate the four noble Truths, he does not take into account cause and effect, as they really are, he does not consider the conditioning factors that have been accumulated in the cycle of birth and death. We should develop right understanding of the characteristics of all kinds of realities in order to know them as they are. Then we shall penetrate the four noble Truths and defilements can be eradicated stage by stage.

When we are listening to the Dhamma or studying the subject of citta, and sati of satipaṭṭhāna can be aware of the realities as they are, we are following the right practice. This means that we are developing the way eventually leading to the realization of nibbāna, the reality that is the cessation of defilements. Whenever sati is not aware of the characteristics of realities as they appear, one does not develop the way leading to the eradication of defilements, even if kusala dhamma arises.

The "Atthasālinī" states (I, Book I, Part I, Ch I, Triplets in the Mātikā, 44) that akusala dhamma as well as kusala dhamma that are not of the Eightfold Path,[5] are leading to accumulation, to the continuation of the cycle of birth and death. We read about akusala and kusala that are not of the Path:

> "Leading to accumulation (ācayagāmin)' are 'those states which go about severally, arranging (births and deaths in) a round of destiny like a bricklayer who arranges bricks, layer by layer, in a wall."

Whenever we are not aware of the characteristics of realities when they appear, and we do not understand them as they are, no matter whether akusala dhamma or kusala dhamma presents itself, we accumulate and build up life after life, just like the bricklayer who piles up bricks one by one until they become a wall. However, when sati is aware of the characteristics of realities that appear as they really are, this is the Path, it is dispersion (apācayagāmin)[6], because then one does not build up dhammas that lead to accumulation, just as a man tears down the bricks that the bricklayer has piled up. Are we at this moment like the man who knocks down the bricks, or are we like the man who piles them up?

The first vīthi-citta is the five-sense-door adverting-consciousness; the second vīthi-citta, one of the sense-cognitions (pañca-viññāṇas); the

[5] One may perform wholesome deeds without the development of the Eightfold Path, without right understanding of nāma and rūpa. Then there will be no eradication of defilements, no end to the cycle of birth and death.

[6] This is the opposite of ācayagāmin, accumulation.

third vīthi-citta, receiving-consciousness; the fourth vīthi-citta, investigating-consciousness; the fifth vīthi-citta, determining-consciousness. These do not arise in their own series, because there is only one citta of each type that arises and then falls away. Even though the determining-consciousness, votthapana-citta, can arise two or three times when the rūpa that is the object falls away before the javana-citta arises,[7] it cannot be said that the votthapana-citta arises in its own series, like the javana-cittas.

It is only the sixth type of vīthi-citta, the javana-citta, which arranges itself in its own series or continuity, because there are usually seven cittas of this type arising and falling away in succession. When one loses consciousness, the javana-cittas arise and fall away six times in succession, and just before dying they arise and fall away five times in succession. Since the javana-cittas arise and fall away up to seven times in succession, they arise more frequently than the other types of vīthi-cittas. Therefore, it is said that the javana vīthi-citta arranges itself in its own series or sequence.

Questions

1. What is contiguity-condition, anantara-paccaya?
2. How many jātis of citta and cetasika are there, and what are these jātis?
3. What is vīthi-citta? Which citta is not vīthi-citta?
4. What is past bhavanga, atīta bhavanga?
5. Can there be bhavanga-citta when one is not asleep?
6. What objects are known by the five-sense-door adverting-consciousness and through which doorways?
7. Through which doorways does the mind-door adverting-consciousness know an object?

[7] This is the case when the process does not run its full course, as will be explained later on.

8. Through how many doorways does citta know dhammārammaṇa, mental object?
9. What function is performed by the five-sense-door adverting-consciousness, and through which doorways?
10. What functions are performed by the mind-door adverting-consciousness, and through how many doorways?

12

The Duration of Different Processes

When we see and we are then attached to visible object and enjoy it, it seems that it is just "normal" attachment, which is not harmful. However, we should realize that even "normal" attachment is a dhamma that is harmful. Its result is suffering, dukkha, and little by little the conditions are being accumulated for more dukkha later on. It is true that dukkha does not occur immediately when there is just a slight amount of attachment. However, when attachment is accumulated more and more, it becomes powerful and it can reach the degree of a "hindrance" (nīvaraṇa), a defilement that obstructs kusala, which causes worry and is oppressive. Then the characteristic of heaviness is evident, the heaviness of akusala, the dhamma that is restless, not calm.

We can find out for ourselves whether, throughout the whole day, from the time we wake up until we go to sleep, the javana-cittas arise more often in a series of akusala cittas or in a series of kusala cittas. What can be done to cure us of akusala? In fact, we are all taking poison, the poison of akusala, and when we realize this we should look for the right medicine for a cure. If we do not realize that we are taking poison, we will accumulate the inclination to take it. Its harmful effects will gradually increase, evermore. There is only one medicine that can cure us, the development of right understanding of realities, of satipaṭṭhāna. If sati of satipaṭṭhāna does not arise, there is no way to become free from the accumulation of akusala. Akusala will be accumulated evermore and there will not be much opportunity for the arising of different types of wholesomeness. Whereas, when one develops satipaṭṭhāna, it can arise instead of akusala, and votthapana-citta (determining-consciousness arising just before the javana-cittas) can then be contiguity-condition (anantara-paccaya)[1] for the arising of kusala cittas according to one's accumulations. Kusala citta can be accompanied by the degree of sati that is mindful of the reality that is appearing.

The javana vīthi-cittas that are kusala, and those that are akusala, arise and fall away in succession and they accumulate kusala or akusala all the time. This conditions each person to have different inclinations, a different character and different behaviour. The accumulations in the citta of each person are most intricate. Also the arahats, those who have reached perfection, have different inclinations; they excel in different qualities. Venerable Sāriputta was pre-eminent in wisdom, venerable Mahā Moggallāna in superpowers, venerable Mahā Kassapa in the observance of ascetical practices, which he also encouraged others to observe, and venerable Anuruddha was pre-eminent in clairvoyance. The javana vīthi-cittas of each one of us arrange themselves in their own series or sequence and accumulate different kinds of kusala and akusala time and again. This is the reason that, at the present time, we all think, speak and act in completely different ways.

Cittas that are kusala, akusala and mahā-kiriya, which arrange themselves in a series of javana, cause people to have a different behaviour through body and speech. It could happen that people who saw an arahat had contempt for him because they judged him by his outward behaviour, which he had accumulated for an endlessly long time. The Brahman Vassakāra, the Prime Minister of Magadha, for example, made a serious mistake by misjudging an arahat from his outward behaviour. When he saw Mahā Kacchana coming down from a mountain, he said

[1]Each citta is anantara-paccaya, the condition for the arising of the next citta.

that Mahā Kacchana behaved like a monkey. Vassakāra's haughtiness was conditioned by the accumulation of his javana vīthi-cittas. The Buddha told him to ask for Mahā Kacchana's forgiveness, but his accumulated conceit was the condition that made him unable to do so. The Buddha predicted that Vassakāra, after he had died, would be reborn as a monkey in a bamboo wood. Vassakāra had thereupon banana trees planted as well as other things monkeys could eat. Then his food would be all ready for him when he was to be reborn as a monkey in that bamboo wood.

We should see the danger of the accumulation of akusala in the javana vīthi-cittas that arise and fall away in a succession of seven cittas. Akusala is accumulated time and again so that it becomes one's nature and appears in one's behaviour and speech and this accumulated behaviour is called "vāsanā"[2] in Pāli. Even when one has become an arahat, there are inclinations accumulated in the citta that condition different kinds of behaviour. The Buddha is the only person who could eradicate "vāsanā." All arahats have eradicated defilements completely so that not even a germ is left of them, but nevertheless, they are unable to eradicate "vāsanā." This is because they have accumulated "vāsanā" for an endlessly long time in the cycle of birth and death through the power of the javana vīthi-cittas.

Summarising the different types of vīthi-cittas in the five-sense-door process, they are the following seven types:

1. The first vīthi-citta is the five-sense-door adverting-consciousness, pañca-dvārāvajjana-citta.

2. The second vīthi-citta is one of the five pairs[3] of sense-cognitions, dvi-pañca-viññāṇas, which are seeing-consciousness, hearing-consciousness, smelling-consciousness, tasting-consciousness and body-consciousness.

3. The third vīthi-citta is the receiving-consciousness, sampaṭicchana-citta, that receives the object from the preceding citta, one of the sense-cognitions, after this has fallen away.

[2]See Chapter 2.

[3]Of each pair, one citta is kusala vipākacitta and one citta is akusala vipākacitta.

4. The fourth vīthi-citta is the investigating-consciousness, santīraṇa-citta, which examines and considers the object.

5. The fifth vīthi-citta is the determining-consciousness, votthapana-citta, which performs the function of determining whether it will be succeeded by kusala citta, akusala citta or kiriyacitta (in the case of the arahat).

6. The sixth type of vīthi-citta is the javana vīthi-citta of which there are usually seven types in succession. Javana can be translated as impulsion or "running." It goes quickly through the object with kusala citta, akusala citta or kiriyacitta.

7. The seventh type of vīthi-citta is the tadārammaṇa vīthi-citta (tadārammaṇa means: "that object") or tadālambana vīthi-citta (ālambana means delaying, hanging on). This citta is called in English retention or registering-consciousness. It performs the function of receiving the object, hanging on to the object after the javana-cittas, if the object has not yet fallen away, since rūpa lasts no longer than seventeen moments of citta.

The following summary shows the duration of an object that is rūpa, lasting as long as seventeen moments of citta:

- When a rūpa arises and impinges on a sense-base, the first moment of citta that arises and falls away is the bhavanga-citta that is called past bhavanga, atīta-bhavanga.

- The vibrating bhavanga, bhavanga calana, is the second moment of citta.

- The arrest bhavanga, bhavangupaccheda, is the third moment of citta.

- The five-sense-door adverting-consciousness is the fourth moment of citta.

- One of the sense-cognitions is the fifth moment of citta.

- The receiving-consciousness is the sixth moment of citta.

- The investigating-consciousness is the seventh moment of citta.
- The determining-consciousness is the eighth moment of citta.
- The first javana-citta is the ninth moment of citta.
- The second javana-citta is the tenth moment of citta.
- The third javana-citta is the eleventh moment of citta.
- The fourth javana-citta is the twelfth moment of citta.
- The fifth javana-citta is the thirteenth moment of citta.
- The sixth javana-citta is the fourteenth moment of citta.
- The seventh javana-citta is the fifteenth moment of citta.

From the moment of atīta bhavanga when the rūpa that is the object arose, fifteen moments have passed when the seventh javana-citta has fallen away. Thus, there are still two more moments left before the rūpa will fall away, since in comparison with the duration of nāma, rūpa lasts seventeen times longer. People who are born in the sensuous planes of existence have accumulated kamma in the past that is connected with visible object, sound, odour, flavour and tangible object, the sense objects. When the javana-cittas "run through" a sense object and it has not fallen away yet, kamma conditions the arising of vipākacitta after the javana-cittas in the form of tadālambana-citta, retention, which "hangs on" to the object. This is in accordance with the nature of those born in sensuous planes. The tadālambana-citta receives the object after the javana-cittas and there are two types of this citta in succession.

The tadālambana-citta is the last vīthi-citta that performs its function in a process and experiences the object through the corresponding doorway. Then bhavanga-cittas arise again, succeeding one another, until vīthi-cittas of a new process arise and experience an object through one of the doorways.

At the moment of bhavanga-citta, this world does not appear. There is no remembrance connected with the different people and the events of this world. The situation is the same as when one is fast asleep and one is not aware of anything that has to do with this world. At the moments one is fast asleep, and also in between processes, there are just bhavanga-cittas arising and falling away. The rebirth-consciousness, paṭisandhi-citta, the bhavanga-citta and the dying-consciousness, cuti-citta, are not vīthi-cittas, they do not experience an object through one of the six doors.[4] The dying-consciousness is the last citta of this lifespan; it performs the function of passing away from one's life as a particular individual. It is succeeded by the rebirth-consciousness of the next life, and then again there are vīthi-cittas experiencing objects connected with the world of the next life, which is different. So long as the dying-consciousness has not arisen, we are still leading this life. Besides the bhavanga-cittas that do not know anything connected with this world, there have to be again vīthi-cittas which know objects of this world, namely, visible object, sound, odour, flavour, tangible object, objects experienced through the mind-door and different ideas connected with this world.

Summary of a sense-door process that runs its full course, with seven types of vīthi-cittas:

- atīta bhavanga, one moment, not vīthi-citta
- bhavanga calana, one moment, not vīthi-citta
- bhavangupaccheda, one moment, not vīthi-citta
- five-sense-door adverting-consciousness, one moment of vīthi-citta
- one of the sense-cognitions, one moment of vīthi-citta
- receiving-consciousness, one moment of vīthi-citta
- investigating-consciousness, one moment of vīthi-citta
- determining-consciousness, one moment of vīthi-citta
- seven javana vīthi-cittas, kusala citta, akusala citta or kiriyacitta
- two moments of vīthi-citta, tadālambana-citta

[4]As will be explained later on, they experience the object, which was experienced by the last javana-cittas of the previous life.

The duration of one rūpa is equal to the arising and falling away of seventeen moments of citta.

After the vīthi-cittas of a sense-door process have arisen, experienced an object through one of the five sense-doors (which is the pasāda-rūpa) and have fallen away, there will be bhavanga-cittas arising and falling away in succession, in between processes. After that, the mind-door adverting-consciousness arises and experiences through the mind-door (the bhavangupaccheda) the same object as the vīthi-cittas of the preceding sense-door process, which just before experienced that object and then fell away. The process of cittas that experience an object through the mind-door does not last as long as a sense-door process. There is no atīta bhavanga before the mind-door process begins. The object that has just been experienced by cittas of a sense-door process no longer impinges on the eyesense or one of the other senses when the mind-door process begins. There have to be bhavanga-cittas before the mind-door process and the last bhavanga-cittas that arise and fall away are the bhavanga calana that vibrates, that is stirred by the object, and the bhavangupaccheda, the arrest bhavanga.

After this citta has fallen away, the mind-door adverting-consciousness arises and this is the first vīthi-citta of the mind-door process, which experiences the same object as the cittas of the sense-door process. The mind-door adverting-consciousness, which performs the function of adverting to the object through the mind-door, is different from the five-sense-door adverting-consciousness, which performs its function only through five sense-doors. The mind-door adverting-consciousness "ponders over" the object and experiences it through the mind-door. Whenever we think about different subjects, as we do time and again, the citta at such moments does not experience objects through the eyes, the ears, the nose, the tongue and the bodysense.

After the bhavanga calana, the bhavangupaccheda and the mind-door adverting-consciousness have arisen and fallen away, kusala cittas or akusala cittas arise in the case of non-arahats. These types of vīthi-cittas perform the function of javana and they arise and fall away in a succession of seven cittas. After these have fallen away there are, if the object is very clear,[5] tadālambana-cittas arising in a succession of two

[5]This is the case when the sense-door process has run its full course with two

cittas.

Thus, there are only three types of vīthi-cittas arising that experience an object through the mind-door. They are the adverting vīthi-citta, the javana vīthi-citta, of which there are seven cittas in succession, and the tadālambana or tadārammaṇa vīthi-citta, of which there are two types in succession.

Summary of the mind-door process with three types of vīthi-cittas:

- bhavanga calana, one moment (not vīthi-cittas)
- bhavangupaccheda, one moment
- mind-door adverting-consciousness (one moment of vīthi-citta)
- kusala citta, akusala citta or kriyacitta. Seven moments of javana (vīthi-citta)
- kusala citta, akusala citta or kiriyacitta
- kusala citta, akusala citta or kiriyacitta
- kusala citta, akusala citta or kiriyacitta
- kusala citta, akusala citta or kiriyacitta
- kusala citta, akusala citta or kiriyacitta
- kusala citta, akusala citta or kiriyacitta
- tadālambana-citta, two moments of vīthi-citta
- tadālambana-citta

When we see what appears through the eyes, all vīthi-cittas that arise in the eye-door process and experience visible object through the eye-door are eye-door process cittas. Of these vīthi-cittas, there are seven different types in all. They depend on the eye-door and they experience the object that appears through the eye-door, that has not yet fallen away. It is the same in the case of the other sense-door processes. There are in each of these processes seven different types of vīthi-cittas

---

tadālambana-cittas.

experiencing the object that appears through the corresponding doorway and has not yet fallen away.

The number of vīthi-cittas that experience objects in sense-door processes can be different. Four different courses or rounds (vāras) can be distinguished in sense-door processes:

1. the full course ending with the tadālambana-citta (tadālambana vāra);
2. the course ending with the javana-citta (javana vāra);
3. the course ending with the votthapana-citta (votthapana vāra);
4. the futile course (mogha vāra).

A course, or vāra, is a series of vīthi-cittas that arise and fall away in succession and experience the same object through the same doorway. In some courses, seven types of vīthi-citta arise, in others six types, in others again five types, and in some there are no vīthi-cittas arising, there are only the atīta bhavanga and the bhavanga calana.

In the case of the futile course, when a rūpa impinges on one of the senses, the bhavanga-citta that arises at that moment, the atīta bhavanga, is not succeeded immediately by the bhavanga calana, the vibrating bhavanga. There are several moments of atīta bhavanga arising and falling away before the bhavanga calana, which is stirred by the object, arises and this citta is then succeeded by several more moments of bhavanga calana, arising and falling away. Since the object, which is rūpa impinging on one of the senses, is about to fall away (lasting no longer than seventeen moments of citta), there are no conditions for vīthi-cittas to arise and to experience the object that impinged on one of the senses. In that case, it is a futile course.

The futile course of a process can be compared to the situation when someone who is fast asleep and stirred in order to be woken up, does not wake up, and who, when stirred again with force, still does not wake up. In the case of the futile course, the adverting-consciousness does not arise, there are only the atīta bhavanga and the bhavanga calana. The object that impinges when there is a futile course is called "very slight" (atiparitta), because it impinges on one of the senses and only affects bhavanga-cittas, it does not condition the arising of vīthi-cittas; it falls away before there is an opportunity for their arising.

It may also happen that there are several types of atīta bhavanga arising and falling away, followed by several types of bhavanga calana arising and falling away and that after that the bhavangupaccheda arises and the stream of bhavanga-cittas is arrested. Then, the sense-door adverting-consciousness, one of the sense-cognitions, the receiving-consciousness and the investigating-consciousness, can arise and fall away in succession. After that, the determining-consciousness arises, but since the rūpa cannot last longer than seventeen moments of citta, there is no opportunity for the arising of the javana-cittas that experience that rūpa. In that case, two or three moments of votthapana-citta arise and fall away and then, when the rūpa falls away, the process is ended. This course is called the course ending with votthapana (votthapana vāra), since the votthapana-citta is the last vīthi-citta.

All this is according to reality as it occurs in daily life. When an object impinges on one of the senses, the full course of seven types of vīthi-cittas arising and falling away does not always occur. It may happen that there are no vīthi-cittas, thus, there is a futile course, or that the course ends with votthapana-citta (votthapana vāra). In the last case, the object is called "slight" (paritta), because it is the object of only five kinds of vīthi-cittas and then it falls away.

It may also happen, when the votthapana-citta has arisen and fallen away, and is succeeded by the javana-cittas, which arise and fall away in a succession of seven cittas, that then the object falls away. In such a case, the tadālambana vīthi-citta cannot arise and there is a course ending with the javana-citta (javana vāra), with six kinds of vīthi-cittas, where the last type is javana-citta experiencing the object. The object of such a course is called "great" (mahanta), because it is clear and it conditions the arising of kusala citta, akusala citta, or, in the case of the arahat, mahā-kiriyacitta.

Lastly, it may happen that when the javana-cittas have arisen and fallen away in a succession of seven cittas, that the object has not yet fallen away. Then there is a condition for two types of tadārammaṇa-citta (or tadālambana-citta) to arise and to experience the object, which has not yet fallen away. The last vīthi-citta that experiences the object is then tadālambana-citta. This is the course ending with tadālambana-citta (tadālambana vāra). The object of such a course is called "very great" (atimahanta). This object is very clear, the process runs its full course with the tadālambana vīthi-cittas succeeding the javana vīthi-cittas and experiencing the object, which has not yet fallen away.

In the case of the mind-door process, two different courses are possible: the course ending with javana and the course ending with tadālamabana. The object of the course ending with javana is called "obscure" (avibhūta), because it is less clear than the object of the course ending with tadālambana. The object of the course ending with tadālambana is called "clear" (vibhūta), because it is clearer than the object of the course ending with javana.

There are six doorways. A doorway is the means through which vīthi-citta knows an object other than the object of the bhavanga-citta. Of these six doorways, through which vīthi-cittas experience objects, five doorways are rūpa and one is nāma. Summarizing the six doorways, they are:

- the eye-door, cakkhu-dvāra, which is the cakkhuppasāda rūpa,[6]
- the ear-door, sota-dvāra, which is the sotappasāda rūpa,
- the nose-door, ghāṇa-dvāra, which is the ghāṇappassāda rūpa,
- the tongue-door, jivhā-dvāra, which is the jivhāppasāda rūpa,
- the body-door, kāya-dvāra, which is the kāyappassāda rūpa,
- the mind-door, mano-dvāra, which is the bhavangupaccheda citta,[7] preceding the mind-door adverting-consciousness.

Six rūpas are bases, vatthus, where cittas arise, in the planes of existence where there are five khandhas, nāma and rūpa. These rūpas are called vatthu rūpa. Summarizing them, they are:

[6]There are five rūpas, which are pasāda rūpas, the sense organs that can receive the impingement of the relevant sense objects.

[7]The bhavangupaccheda is bhavanga-citta, not vīthi-citta. It does not experience the object, which is experienced by the cittas of the mind-door process. Since it precedes the mind-door adverting-consciousness, it is merely the doorway, the means through which the vīthi-cittas of the mind-door process can experience the object.

- the cakkhuppasāda rūpa, which is the eye-base, cakkhu-vatthu, the place of origin for the two types of seeing-consciousness, cakkhu-viññāṇa;
- the sotappasāda rūpa, which is the ear-base, sota-vatthu, for the two types of hearing-consciousness, sota-viññāṇa;
- the ghāṇappassāda rūpa, which is the nose-base, ghāṇa-vatthu, for the two types of smelling-consciousness, ghāṇa-viññāṇa;
- the jivhāppasāda rūpa, which is the tongue-base, jivhā-vatthu, for the two types of tasting-consciousness, jivhā-viññāṇa;
- the kāyappassāda rūpa, which is the body-base, kāya-vatthu, for the two types of kāya-viññāṇa;
- the hadaya-rūpa, the heart-base, which is the place of origin in the planes where there are five khandhas for all cittas other than the five pairs of sense-cognitions.

The five pasāda rūpas can be doors as well as bases, places of origin. The cakkhuppassāda rūpa (eyesense) is the eye-door for all the cittas of the eye-door process, namely: eye-door adverting-consciousness, seeing-consciousness, receiving-consciousness, investigating-consciousness, determining-consciousness, javana-citta and tadālambana-citta, experiencing visible object which impinges on the eyesense and which has not yet fallen away. However, the cakkhuppasāda rūpa is also the eye-base, cakkhu-vatthu, that is the place of origin, only for the two types of seeing-consciousness (kusala vipākacitta and akusala vipākacitta). With regard to the other cittas of the eye-door process, the eye-door adverting-consciousness, the receiving-consciousness, the investigating-consciousness, the determining-consciousness, the javana-citta and the tadālambana-citta, they arise at the heart-base, hadaya-vatthu. It is the same in the case of the other pasāda rūpas that are the doors of the relevant vīthi-cittas, but which are the base, vatthu, only for the corresponding sense-cognitions.

The hadaya rūpa is the base, the place of origin, for the cittas concerned, but it is not a doorway.

Questions

1. Why are the vīthi-cittas of the mind-door process less in number than those of the five-sense-door processes?
2. Through how many doorways can lobha-mūla-citta, citta rooted in attachment, experience an object?
3. Through how many doorways can the five-sense-door adverting-consciousness experience an object?
4. Through how many doorways can the mind-door adverting-consciousness experience an object?
5. What are the futile course, mogha vāra, the votthapana vāra, the javana vāra and the tadālambana vāra?
6. What object is "obscure" (avibhūta) and what object is "clear" (vibhūta)?
7. Which rūpa is the base for the rebirth-consciousness arising in a plane where there are five khandhas?
8. Which rūpa is the base for the akusala citta arising in a plane where there are five khandhas?
9. Which rūpa is the base for the kiriyacitta arising in a plane where there are five khandhas?
10. .Which rūpas are the bases for the different ear-door process cittas?
11. Which rūpas are the bases for the different cetasikas arising in a plane where there are five khandhas?

13

The Nature of Javana-Citta

The arising and falling away of bhavanga-cittas and of vīthi-cittas, cittas arising in processes, is our ordinary daily life. When one hears about the Dhamma terms that explain the characteristics and functions of the different cittas, but does not understand the meaning of these terms, one may have doubts. All these terms explain the characteristics of realities, and these exist not merely in textbooks, they occur in daily life. They occur each time cittas arise that are seeing, hearing, smelling, tasting, experiencing tangible object or thinking. At this moment, we are seeing, and thus we can know that there are cittas arising in a process. There is the arising of eye-door adverting-consciousness, seeing-consciousness, receiving-consciousness, investigating-consciousness, determining-consciousness and javana-cittas. All these cittas arise and fall away in succession. Right understanding of the Dhamma will remind us to consider whether the javana-cittas that arise after seeing, hearing or the other sense-cognitions are kusala cittas or akusala cittas. The javana-cittas arise in their own series.

When we have learned about the four "jātis" of kusala, akusala, vipāka and kiriya, we shall come to know which citta is cause, producing result in the form of vipākacitta that arises later on. We shall come to know which citta is vipāka, the result produced by a cause, by kamma performed in the past. We should know the jāti, the nature, of the cittas that arise in processes and of those that do not arise in processes. We should, for example, know that rebirth-consciousness is vipākacitta, the result of kamma. One kamma among all the kammas performed in the past is the condition for the rebirth-consciousness to succeed the dying-consciousness of the previous life. The rebirth-consciousness is vipākacitta that performs the function of rebirth only once. It performs this function once and for all in a lifespan, at the first moment of life, when it succeeds the dying-consciousness of the previous life. Thus, it cannot perform this function again in one lifespan. The rebirth-consciousness arises and then falls away immediately; it does not last.

The rebirth-consciousness, which is of the jāti of vipāka, is contiguity-condition, anantara-paccaya, for the immediate arising of the succeeding citta. This citta, which is not vīthi-citta, but performs the function of bhavanga, is also vipāka. Kamma does not only condition the arising of rebirth-consciousness, it also conditions the arising of the succeeding bhavanga-cittas which perform the function of bhavanga, life-continuum. The bhavanga-citta that immediately succeeds the rebirth-consciousness is called "first bhavanga" (paṭhama bhavanga). The next bhavanga-cittas, arising throughout life until the dying-consciousness, are not called by any particular name. They are countless.

Bhavanga-cittas arise and fall away in succession, all the time, until vīthi-citta arises. The vīthi-citta that arises first in a process, before the other vīthi-cittas, is the citta that performs the function of adverting to the object. There are two types of adverting-consciousness: the five-sense-door adverting-consciousness, which performs the function of adverting through the five sense-doors, and the mind-door adverting-consciousness, which performs the function of adverting through the mind-door. Both types of citta are kiriyacitta, thus, not kusala citta, akusala citta or vipākacitta. These types of kiriyacitta can experience an object that is pleasant and agreeable (iṭṭhārammaṇa) as well as an object that is unpleasant (aniṭṭhārammaṇa). In the case of vipākacitta the situation is different, because akusala vipākacitta can experience only an unpleasant object and kusala vipākacitta can experience only a pleasant object.

The "Atthasālinī" (II, Book I, Part X, Ch VI, 293) explains that the characteristic of kiriyacitta is the "mere acting or doing of a function."[1] There are different types of kiriyacitta: those of the arahat, which perform the function of javana, and those which do not perform the function of javana, but carry out other functions and are common to the arahat and the non-arahat. As to the kiriyacittas that do not perform the function of javana, the "Atthasālinī" states that they are "fruitless like a plant with a wind-snapped flower." When a flower drops, there will be no fruit and so the kiriyacitta is like that flower, it cannot produce any result. There are two types of kiriyacitta that do not perform the function of javana: the five-sense-door adverting-consciousness and the mind-door adverting-consciousness. The five-sense-door adverting-conscious-ness performs only one function, the function of adverting through the five sense-doors. Whereas the mind-door adverting-consciousness performs two functions: the function of adverting through the mind-door and the function of determining the object, votthapana, through the five sense-doors.

Apart from these two types of kiriyacitta, which are common to the arahat and the non-arahat alike, there are other types of kiriyacitta which perform the function of javana, but only in the case of the arahat. The "Atthasālinī" refers to these in the same section and explains:

"That which has reached the state of javana (the kiriyacitta of the arahat) is fruitless like the flower of an uprooted tree."

Only the arahat has kiriyacittas that perform the function of javana, and these are neither akusala nor kusala; they cannot produce any result. They are fruitless like the flower of an uprooted tree because the arahat has eradicated all defilements. These types of kiriyacitta merely accomplish the function of javana.

During the eye-door process, when the five-sense-door adverting-consciousness has already fallen away, it is succeeded by seeing-consciousness, which is vipākacitta, the result of kamma that has been performed.

[1] Kiriya or kriyā is derived from karoti, to do. It means action or occupation. Kiriyacitta performs a function. It is translated as "functional," or it is translated as "inoperative," because it does not produce any result. It is neither kusala nor akusala and it is not vipāka.

Kusala kamma conditions seeing-consciousness that is kusala vipāka, which sees a visible object that is beautiful, enjoyable, and, thus, a pleasant object. Akusala kamma conditions seeing-consciousness that is akusala vipāka, which sees a visible object that is not beautiful, not enjoyable, and, thus, an unpleasant object. The vīthi-citta that hears through the ears, hearing-consciousness, is vipākacitta. Nobody knows what kind of sound hearing-consciousness will hear at a particular moment. It is all according to conditions; it depends on kamma that was already performed in the past. When odour is smelled through the nose, it is vipākacitta that is smelling-consciousness. When flavour is tasted through the tongue, it is vipākacitta that is tasting-consciousness. When tangible object is experienced through the bodysense, such as cold, heat, softness or hardness, it is vipākacitta that is body-consciousness. Kamma is the condition for all these vipākacittas to arise and to experience an object, after the five-sense-door adverting-consciousness has performed its function of adverting to that object.

The five pairs of sense-cognitions, such as seeing or hearing, are contiguity-condition, anantara-paccaya, for the arising of the succeeding citta, the receiving-consciousness that receives the object. Receiving-consciousness is vipākacitta, it is the result of the same kamma that produced the preceding sense-cognition. When the receiving-consciousness has fallen away, the same kamma produces the investigating-consciousness, which is also vipākacitta and which performs the function of investigating, after the function of receiving has been performed.

The vīthi-cittas which are vipāka and which arise in the five-sense-door processes are: seeing-consciousness, hearing-consciousness, smelling-consciousness, tasting-consciousness, body-consciousness, receiving-consciousness and investigating-consciousness. These cittas do not arise in their own continuing series like the javana-cittas; they are merely results of kamma. They arise, they perform their own function and then they fall away. After the investigating-consciousness has fallen away, the determining-consciousness, votthapana-citta, arises, and this citta is actually the mind-door adverting-consciousness, mano-dvārāvajjana-citta, performing the function of determining, votthapana, in the five-sense-door processes. The determining-consciousness is kiriyacitta that merely performs its function and then falls away; it does not arise in its own continuing series. When it has fallen away, it is succeeded by javana vīthi-cittas, which perform their function of "running through the object," and these may be kusala cittas or akusala cittas in the case of the non-arahat. As we have seen, for the arahat the javana-cittas are kiriyacittas. There are usually seven javana-cittas and these are of the same type, arising and falling away in succession; thus, these cittas arise in their own continuing series. This is also happening at this very moment.

The "Atthasālinī" (II, Book I, Part X, Ch II, 279, 280) uses a simile in order to explain the arising of vīthi-cittas that experience an object in the five-sense-door process. We read:

A certain king went to bed and fell asleep. His attendant sat shampooing his feet; a deaf doorkeeper stood at the door. Three guards stood in a row. Then a certain man, resident at a border village, bringing a present, came and knocked at the door. The deaf doorkeeper did not hear the sound. He who shampooed the king's feet gave a sign, by which the doorkeeper opened the door and looked. The first guard took the present and handed it to the second guard, who gave it to the third, who in turn offered it to the king. The king partook of it...

When we consider this parable we shall understand the functions performed by each of the vīthi-cittas that arise and experience the object. The impinging of the object on the eyesense is like the knocking on the door by the resident of the border village who brought the present. The resident of the border village cannot enter to visit the king, but his present is handed to the first, second and third guard who then offers it to the king. The function of the five-sense-door adverting-consciousness is compared to the giving of a sign by the attendant, who is shampooing the king's feet. He knows that a guest has come and knocks at the door. The five-sense-door adverting-consciousness adverts to the object that impinges on one of the sense-doors and then it falls away. After that, in the case of the eye-door process, seeing-consciousness arises and performs the function of seeing through the eyesense, which is the eye-door, and this is compared to the doorkeeper who opens the door and looks. The receiving-consciousness is compared to the first guard who receives the present and hands it to the second guard. The investigating-consciousness is like the second guard who examines the present and hands it to the third guard. The determining-consciousness is like the third guard who decides about the present and then offers it to the king. The king who enjoys the present and partakes of it represents the javana-cittas which succeed the determining-consciousness and which enjoy the essential property of the object.

The object has as its only function to impinge on the rūpa that is eyesense (the pasada rūpa). The resident of the border village cannot enter to visit the king, but his present is handed to the first, second and third guard who then offers it to the king. Only seeing-consciousness performs the function of seeing the object impinging on the eye-door. Visible object can only impinge on the rūpa that is eyesense and the cittas of the eye-door process have to know that object; the object cannot escape or intrude on one of the other senses. Seeing-consciousness cannot perform the function of receiving the object, it can only perform the function of seeing while it arises at the eye-base. As we have seen, the receiving-consciousnessis compared to the first guard who receives the present and hands it to the second guard; the investigating-consciousness is compared to the second guard who examines the present and hands it to the third guard; the determining-consciousness is like the third guard who decides about the present and then offers it to the king; the javana-cittas are like he king who partakes of the present and "consumes" it.

The words consuming, partaking of the present, help us to understand the characteristics of the kusala cittas or akusala cittas which perform the function of javana, "running through the object," through the eyes, the ears, the nose, the tongue, the bodysense or the mind-door. The javana-cittas partake of the object with attachment, aversion and ignorance; or they can be kusala citta or, in the case of the arahat, kiriyacitta. The javana-cittas perform their own function; they do not see, receive the object, investigate it or determine it, because the preceding cittas have already performed all these functions. Therefore, there are conditions for the arising of kusala cittas, akusala cittas or kiriyacittas, which run through the object in a succession of seven cittas of the same type. The javana vīthi-cittas can partake of the object, they "consume" it. In the case of a "futile course"[2], sound, for example, may impinge on the ear-sense, but there will not be hearing, and javana-cittas will not arise either. Even so, in the case of a course

[2]See Chapter 11.

ending with determining-consciousness, votthapana-citta, javana-cittas that are kusala cittas, akusala cittas or kiriyacittas do not arise. Then there is no "consuming" of the object. Whereas javana-cittas, which arise and fall away in a succession of seven cittas of the same type, kusala, akusala or kiriya, do partake of the object, they consume it.

It is according to conditions that there are seven javana-cittas arising and falling away in succession that partake of the object. The first javana-citta is repetition-condition (asevana-paccaya) for the second one, which arises and partakes of the object again and so on until the seventh javana-citta, which is not repetition-condition for the succeeding citta. Akusala javana vīthi-citta, kusala javana vīthi-citta and kiriya javana vīthi-citta can be repetition-condition for the arising of the succeeding citta. Through this condition, there is a repetition of cittas of the same jāti (nature), which arise and perform the function of javana, and, thus, kusala citta and akusala citta can acquire strength, they can become kamma-condition for the arising of vipāka in the future. Moreover, they can be natural strong dependence-condition (pakatupanissaya-paccaya) for the arising again in the future of kusala javana vīthi-citta and akusala javana vīthi-citta. The frequent arising in a continuing series of different kinds of akusala javana-cittas conditions an ever-increasing accumulation of akusala. Because of this, we are infatuated with what we see as soon as we wake up and open our eyes. When we are fast asleep and not dreaming, there are bhavanga-cittas, but when we are dreaming or thinking, there are no bhavanga-cittas but cittas arising in mind-door processes, which are thinking. When there are bhavanga-cittas we do not know any object through one of the six doors, any object of this world, but this does not mean that we are without defilements. Also with the bhavanga-cittas there are latent tendencies of defilements, anusaya kilesa.

There are three levels of defilements:

- subtle defilement, anusaya kilesa, accumulated defilements which lie dormant in the citta as latent tendencies;
- medium defilement, pariyuṭṭhāna[3] kilesa, arising together with the javana-citta;

[3]This means prepossession or obsession.

- coarse defilement, vītikkama[4] kilesa, arising together with the javana-citta.

Thus, even with the cittas other than the javana-cittas there are defilements, present in the form of latent tendencies. The arahat has completely eradicated all defilements and thus he has no more latent tendencies.

The vīthi-citta which sees what appears through the eyes, hears sound through the ears or experiences any other sense object, is in that process followed by javana-cittas which arrange themselves in their own series of several kāmāvacara cittas of the same type: akusala citta, kusala citta or kiriyacitta.

In the case of the eye-door process, there are seven different types of vīthi-cittas.[5] It is the same in the case of the ear-door process or the other sense-door processes, there are seven different types of vīthi-cittas. In the case of the mind-door process, there are three different types of vīthi-cittas.

Questions

1. Which vīthi-cittas in a five-sense-door process and in the mind-door process are vipākacittas?

2. How many kiriyacittas does the non-arahat have?

3. How many kiriyacittas that are not javana vīthi-cittas does the arahat have?

4. What is repetition-condition, asevana-paccaya?

5. Which cittas can be repetition-condition?

[4]This means transgression.

[5]See Chapter 10.

14

The Ephemeral Experience of Objects

There are eighty-nine types of citta in all and these can be classified by way of four jātis (jāti being nature of citta):

- Kusala: 21 types of citta
- Akusala: 12 types of citta
- Vipāka: 36 types of citta
- Kiriya: 20 types of citta

When we study the classification of citta by way of jāti, we should know which types of citta arise for the ordinary person (putthujana) and which types for the ariyan (a person who has attained enlightenment):

- The ordinary person has cittas of four jātis: kusala, akusala, vipāka and kiriya.
- The sotāpanna (stream-winner, who has attained the first stage of enlightenment) has cittas of the four jātis.

- The sakadāgāmī (once-returner, who has attained the second stage of enlightenment) has cittas of the four jātis.
- The anāgāmī (non-returner, who has attained the third stage of enlightenment) has cittas of the four jātis.
- The arahat (the perfected one, who has attained the fourth stage of enlightenment) has cittas of two jātis: vipāka and kiriya.

We should not only know the jāti of a particular citta, we should also know the function of that citta. The rebirth-consciousness is vipākacitta, the result of kamma. The citta that performs the function of rebirth in a happy plane is kusala vipāka, the result of kusala kamma. The citta that performs the function of rebirth in an unhappy plane, such as a hell plane, is akusala vipāka, the result of akusala kamma. Not every kusala vipākacitta and akusala vipākacitta perform the function of rebirth. Only the kusala vipākacitta and the akusala vipākacitta that perform the function of rebirth are called rebirth-consciousness.

The kusala vipākacitta or akusala vipākacitta that performs the function of bhavanga (life-continuum) is called bhavanga-citta.

Seeing-consciousness is a vipākacitta that cannot perform the function of rebirth or the function of bhavanga. It can only perform the function of seeing. It is called seeing-consciousness, because it is the citta that clearly knows visible object, it sees the object appearing through the eyes. Thus, we can understand that cittas that clearly know an object through one of the different doorways are named after the function they perform.

Questioner: Why are there not five jātis of citta instead of four, namely, kusala, akusala, kusala vipāka, akusala vipāka and kiriya?

Sujin: You are wondering why there are not five jātis. There are two jātis of cittas that are cause: kusala and akusala, and therefore, you think that there should also be two jātis of cittas that are result: kusala vipāka and akusala vipāka. In that case, there would be five jātis. However, there are only four jātis, because vipāka is mere result, it cannot be called inferior, medium or superior, as is the case with kamma.[1] Kusala citta and akusala citta, the cittas that are cause, have

[1] In the "Dhammasaṇgani" (Book III, Ch I, Group of Triplets, 1025-1027) dham-

many varieties. They are of different shades and degrees, examples of which I shall give below.

Kusala citta and akusala citta are different because of the accompanying kusala dhammas or akusala dhammas when experiencing an object through the eyes, the ears, the nose, the tongue, the bodysense and the mind-door. They are diverse since they can motivate different types of kamma, good deeds and bad deeds. There is kamma of the level of dāna, generosity, sīla, morality and mental development, bhāvana, which includes the development of calm, samatha, through which defilements are subdued, and the development of paññā. The development of paññā has many degrees, such as listening to the Dhamma, explaining the Dhamma or the development of satipaṭṭhāna, which is the development of insight, vipassanā.

Kammas are different since they are performed through body, speech or mind. They are accompanied by different cetasikas and they have different predominant factors.[2] Thus, we see that the realities that are cause, kusala and akusala, are of great diversity, that they have many shades and degrees, whereas vipākacittas do not have such variety. Vipāka is only result of kamma that has been performed already. When kamma has ripened and the right opportunity is there, which conditions it to produce its result, vipākacitta arises. Vipākacitta can perform the functions of rebirth, bhavanga or other functions: it can experience different objects through the eyes, the ears, the nose, the tongue, the bodysense or the mind-door.

Seeing at this moment is vipākacitta; it has arisen because it is conditioned by kamma performed in the past. But the vipākacitta that sees cannot be a cause producing again vipāka.

When hearing-consciousness experiences sound, there is vipākacitta, but hearing-consciousness cannot be a cause producing vipāka. Thus,

---

mas are classified as low, medium and exalted. The "Atthasālinī" (I, Book I, Part I, 45,) explains that "mean" is applied to akusala dhammas, that medium, existing midway between low and exalted, is applied to the remaining dhammas of the three planes of citta (of the sense sphere, rūpa-jhānacittas, arūpa-jhānacittas), and "exalted" to the lokuttara dhammas.

[2] The cetasikas chanda, wish-to-do, viriya, effort, or vīmaṃsā, investigation of the Dhamma, can be accompanying predominant factors and these can be of a lesser degree, medium or superior (see "Visuddhimagga", I, 33). Moreover, citta accompanied by at least two roots can be a predominant factor.

vipākacitta is not cause; it does not produce result. It is incapable of performing deeds through body or speech. It cannot be accompanied by cetasikas that are the wholesome qualities of compassion, sympathetic joy or the three abstinences (virati cetasikas) of right speech, right action and right livelihood.[3]

Vipākacitta itself is not a dhamma that is inferior, medium or superior, but kamma that is inferior, medium or superior produces its result accordingly and therefore, there are different degrees of vipāka. Since vipāka is not a cause, producing result, but only the result of a cause, of kusala kamma or of akusala kamma, there is only one jāti that is vipāka. As we have seen, vipāka does not have such diversity as the dhamma that is cause, namely, kusala and akusala, which are classified as two different jātis. This is the answer to your question.

All vipākacittas are result of kamma that has been performed in the past. There are four types of vipākacittas arising in the eye-door process:

- Seeing-consciousness,
- Receiving-consciousness,
- Investigating-consciousness,
- Registering-consciousness (retention, tadārammaṇa).

We should know when there is vipākacitta, kusala citta, akusala citta or kiriya citta. When we see a pleasant visible object, seeing-consciousness is kusala vipāka. The receiving-consciousness, the investigating-consciousness and the registering-consciousness that follow are also kusala vipāka. After the visible object and the vīthi-cittas of the eye-door process have fallen away, bhavanga-cittas arise and fall away in succession, until vīthi-cittas arise again and know another object that presents itself. We should remember that when seeing-consciousness sees visible object through the eyes, that seeing-consciousness, as well as the other vipākacittas in that process, are the result of kamma that has been performed in the past.

[3]The three abstinences are abstention from wrong speech, wrong action and wrong livelihood. Abstention from wrong livelihood is abstention from wrong speech and wrong action pertaining to one's livelihood.

When we hear a sound, which may be pleasant or unpleasant, it is only one moment of vipāka vīthi-citta that hears the sound and then falls away completely. However, there are conditions for a great number of akusala cittas that like or dislike the rūpas that are appearing through the eyes, the ears, the nose, the tongue or the bodysense. Like and dislike are never lacking in daily life, they arise time and again on account of what appears through the six doors.

Through theoretical understanding, acquired from listening to the Dhamma the Buddha taught, akusala cannot be eradicated. We may know that seeing is only vipāka, the result of kamma performed in the past, but just knowing this in theory is not sufficient. Through theoretical knowledge alone we cannot prevent the arising of attachment, lobha, as soon as we see something pleasant.

We should study realities so that right understanding can develop to the degree that it can see the true nature of realities, that it can see them as not a living being, not a person, not self. When we study the Dhamma and carefully consider it in all details, we shall more and more see the danger of akusala and we shall be inclined to develop all levels of kusala. We should know that if we do not develop kusala, we shall become ever more entangled by defilements.

We may believe that everything belongs to us, but such a belief occurs only at the moments when vīthi-cittas, cittas in processes, arise. When vīthi-cittas do not arise, we do not see, hear, smell, taste or experience tangible object; we do not experience any object through the six doors. At the moments when we are fast asleep, there is no attachment, no longing or yearning, no infatuation with anything; there is no clinging to the khandhas we are used to taking for self. The reason is that at such moments vīthi-cittas do not arise that know objects through the six doors. Thus, only at the moments of our life when we are fast asleep is there no attachment or involvement with the sense objects or with the matters we think about. Why then do we not develop paññā so that attachment and clinging to the objects that appear through the six doors will be eradicated and there will be less akusala?

Realities appear only at the moments vīthi-cittas, cittas in processes, arise. When a citta arises and then falls away, it has disappeared completely. When a rūpa arises and then falls away it has disappeared completely. The visible object that just a moment ago appeared through the eyes has completely fallen away, as have each of the cittas that arose just a few moments ago in the eye-door process. All cittas and all rūpas arise and then fall away and are gone forever.

However, so long as the arising and falling away of nāma and rūpa has not been realized through direct understanding, through insight, we cannot grasp what falling away means. We have not yet realized the falling away of any reality through the development of vipassanā. We may say that at this moment seeing-consciousness falls away, that receiving-consciousness, investigating-consciousness, determining-consciousness, javana-cittas and registering-consciousness fall away, but the falling away of dhammas has not yet been penetrated by insight. Paññā should be developed so that it can penetrate the arising and falling away of nāma and rūpa. Even if paññā has not reached that degree yet, it is most beneficial to listen to the Dhamma and to consider it, so that right understanding can develop and become keener, more refined. Right understanding can be accumulated and then it can be a condition for satipaṭṭhāna to arise and be mindful of the characteristics of the dhammas that arise and fall away. In that way, paññā can gradually develop and penetrate the characteristics of dhammas so that they will be realized as not a living being, not a person, not self.

The "Atthasālinī" (II, Book II, Part II, Discourse on the Chapter of the Summary, Ch I, The Triplets, 361) explains the meaning of past dhammas: "...past means having got beyond the three moments."

These three moments are the moment of arising (uppāda khaṇa), the moment of presence (tiṭṭhi khaṇa) and the moment of falling away (bhanga khaṇa)[4].

Citta has only an extremely short duration: it arises, it is present and then it falls away immediately. Its arising moment is not the moment of its presence nor of its falling away. The moment of its presence is not its arising moment nor the moment of its falling away. The moment of its falling away is not its arising moment nor the moment of its presence. When citta has arisen, it is present and the moment of its presence cannot be called past, but its arising moment belongs already to the past.

When we study rūpa, we learn that rūpa that is originated by kamma

[4]See Chapter 7.

(kammaja rūpa) arises at each of the three moments of citta. Thus, it arises at the arising moment of citta, at the moment of presence of citta and at the moment of the falling away of citta. Rūpa produced by kamma arises at the three moments of citta throughout our life. However, it does not arise anymore during the sixteen moments of citta before the dying-consciousness; rūpa produced by kamma comes to an end when the dying-consciousness falls away.[5] That is the end of the five khandhas that constitute the life of a particular person.

The rūpa that originates from citta (cittaja rūpa) arises at the arising moment of citta. The rebirth-consciousness, the five pairs of sense-cognitions, the four arūpāvacara vipākacittas[6] and the dying-consciousness of the arahat do not produce any rūpa.

The rūpa that originates from temperature (utuja rūpa, the Element of Heat that is of the right temperature) arises at the moment of presence of the temperature that originates it.[7]

The rūpa that originates from nutrition (ahāraja rūpa) arises at the moment of presence of nutritive essence, oja rūpa, present in food that was taken. When the nutritive essence that is in food has been absorbed, it can produce other rūpas.

Citta arises and falls away very rapidly, and thus all three moments of citta disappear immediately. As the "Atthasālinī" explains, any dhamma that is past has got beyond the three moments: the arising moment, the moment of presence and the moment of falling away; it has gone forever, there is nothing left of it.

The "Atthasālinī", in the same section (361), explains synonyms of the word "past." We read:

> "Ceased, that is, has reached cessation." Past dhamma has ceased completely, just as fire that has been extinguished.
>
> "Dissolved, that is, gone to destruction, departed." There is nothing left, just as someone who has died, who is no more. That is the characteristic of falling away.

---

[5]Rūpa does not last longer than seventeen moments of citta. Rūpa originated by kamma cannot survive after death.

[6]The results of kusala cittas of the four stages of arūpa-jhāna, immaterial jhāna. These arise in planes where there is no rūpa.

[7]Rūpa, in this case temperature, is too weak at its arising moment; it can only produce another rūpa at the moment of its presence.

> "Changed, that is, transformed by abandoning the original nature." Thus, so long as a dhamma has its original, usual nature, it exists, but when it abandons its original nature, it does not exist anymore.
>
> "Terminated, this means gone to the term (end) called cessation." It cannot exist any longer, that is the meaning of cessation.
>
> "Exterminated..." This word is stronger then the preceding term "terminated" and the meaning is: it has disappeared completely, there is nothing left of it.
>
> "Dissolved after having arisen, that is, departed after having come to be." This does not mean that the dhamma did not exist. It was, because it had arisen, but after its arising it departed, it disappeared completely, and there is nothing left of it.

We then read: "Which are past dhammas? Rūpa, feeling, perception, formations, consciousness." These are the five khandhas, which are conditioned dhammas, saṅkhata dhammas. The five khandhas comprise the following realities:

- Rūpakkhandha: all rūpas that arise and fall away.
- Vedanākkhandha: all feelings (vedanā cetasika), which arise and fall away.
- Saññākkhandha: remembrance or perception (saññā cetasika), which arises and falls away.
- Saṅkhārakkhandha: fifty cetasikas (formations) such as attachment, aversion, jealousy, avarice, confidence, energy and wisdom; they arise and then fall away.
- Viññāṇakkhandha: each type of citta that arises and falls away.

Everything that arises is conditioned dhamma; it is one of the five khandhas and thus it falls away again. For which of the khandhas are we then still longing, to which of them do we still cling? Each khandha arises and then falls away; it dissolves, disappears completely, there is nothing left of it, there is nothing worth clinging to.

Through knowledge acquired from reading and listening defilements cannot be eradicated, they are still bound to be present in full force. When we consider dhammas and have right understanding of them, conditions are being accumulated for the arising of right awareness. Then sati can be directly aware and attend to the characteristics of the dhammas of which we formerly had theoretical understanding acquired through listening. In this way paññā can penetrate the characteristics of realities that appear and then fall away, and wrong view, which takes realities for a living being, a person or self, can be eliminated.

We are so used to being attached to what appears through the eyes, the ears, the nose, the tongue, the bodysense and the mind-door. We take it for self, for mine, for my property. In reality everything that appears does so only at the moment when citta in a process, vīthi-citta, arises. The dhammas that are vipāka are the results of kamma. We may have a house, many possessions, clothes and ornaments that are all very beautiful and attractive, but in reality there are only vipākacittas, results of past kammas, that arise and experience objects through the eyes, the ears and the other sense-doors. Citta arises and experiences an object just for one moment and then it falls away; it is gone forever, it cannot last at all. Nobody knows which kamma will produce which result in the future. The reason is that we all have performed both kusala kamma and akusala kamma in the past. When there are the right conditions for kamma to produce result, vipākacitta arises and experiences an object through one of the six doors.

When we learn about the truth of impermanence and ponder over it, we can be urged to persevere with awareness of the characteristics of dhammas that appear. If sati can be aware of the characteristics of dhammas and paññā investigates them, over and over again, they can be realized as they are: as not self, as only nāma and rūpa appearing one at a time through the six doors.

Through right understanding of the characteristics of dhammas there will be conditions for kusala javana vīthi-cittas. If we do not listen to the Dhamma and do not investigate realities, we shall not know when there is vipāka, the result of past kamma, and when there are kusala javana vīthi-cittas or akusala javana vīthi-cittas that arise in their own series. If we do not know this, we shall not see the danger and disadvantage of akusala and we shall not be inclined to develop kusala. Then the cycle of birth and death will go on endlessly. Are there more kusala cittas or more akusala cittas during the day? In the future the appropriate result of kamma will arise, be it kusala vipāka or akusala vipāka. It is beneficial to consider and to be aware of the realities that naturally appear in our daily life.

Specifications of Cittas and their Functions

There are fourteen different functions of citta in all:

1. The function of rebirth, paṭisandhi, which follows upon the function of dying, cuti, of the previous life. The cittas that perform the function of rebirth are nineteen types[8] of vipākacittas:

    - kāmāvacara vipākacittas (results of the sense sphere) 10 cittas
    - rūpāvacara vipākacittas (results of rūpa jhāna) 5 cittas
    - arūpāvacara vipākacittas (results of arūpa jhāna)[9] 4 cittas

2. The function of life-continuum, bhavanga, the preservation of continuity in a lifespan. The cittas that perform the function of bhavanga are also nineteen types of vipākacittas. Whatever type of citta performs the function of rebirth in a lifespan also performs the function of bhavanga, after the rebirth-consciousness has fallen away. The bhavanga-cittas that arise during one lifespan are all of the same type as the rebirth-consciousness. They arise and fall away in succession until vīthi-citta arises and experiences an object through one of the six doors, and when the vīthi-cittas of that process have fallen away, bhavanga-cittas of the same type as the rebirth-consciousness follow again. This happens all the time until the dying-consciousness arises at the end of our lifespan.

3. The function of adverting, āvajjana, the adverting to an object that impinges on one of the six doorways. Adverting-consciousness

[8]These will be specified further on in this chapter.

[9]There are five stages of rūpa jhāna, fine material jhāna, and thus, there are five types of vipākacittas that are results. There are four stages of arūpa jhāna and thus, there are four types of vipākacittas that are results.

is the first vīthi-citta that arises in a process and experiences an object through one of the six doorways. There are two types of kiriyacitta that perform the function of adverting:

- the five-sense-door adverting-consciousness, pañca-dvārāvajjana-citta;
- the mind-door adverting-consciousness, mano-dvārāvajjana-citta.

4. The function of seeing, dassana kicca. There are two types of vipākacitta that perform the function of seeing:

   - seeing-consciousness that is akusala vipākacitta;
   - seeing-consciousness that is kusala vipākacitta.

5. The function of hearing, savana kicca. There are two types of vipākacitta that perform the function of hearing:

   - hearing-consciousness that is akusala vipākacitta;
   - hearing-consciousness that is kusala vipākacitta.

6. The function of smelling, ghāyana kicca. There are twotypes of vipākacitta that perform the function of smelling:

   - smelling-consciousness that is akusala vipākacitta;
   - smelling-consciousness that is kusala vipākacitta.

7. The function of tasting, sāyana kicca. There are two types of vipākacitta that perform the function of tasting:

   - tasting-consciousness that is akusala vipākacitta;
   - tasting-consciousness that is kusala vipākacitta.

8. The function of experiencing tangible object through the bodysense, phusana kicca. There are two types of vipākacitta that perform this function:

   - body-consciousness that is akusala vipākacitta;

- body-consciousness that is kusala vipākacitta.

9. The function of receiving, sampaṭicchana kicca, which is the receiving of the object after one of the sense-cognitions has fallen away. There are two types of citta that perform this function:

    - receiving-consciousness that is akusala vipākacitta;
    - receiving-consciousness that is kusala vipākacitta.

10. The function of investigation, santīraṇa kicca, which is the investigation of the object that appears through one of the five sense-doors. There are three types of citta that perform this function:

    - investigation-consciousness accompanied by indifferent feeling (upekkhā) that is akusala vipākacitta;
    - investigation-consciousness accompanied by indifferent feeling that is kusala vipākacitta;
    - investigation-consciousness accompanied by pleasant feeling (somanassa) that is kusala vipākacitta.

11. The function of determination, votthapana kicca, which is the determination of the object so that such or such types of javana-cittas follow in one of the five sense-door processes. There is one type of kiriyacitta that performs this function: the mind-door adverting-consciousness, mano-dvārāvajjana-citta.

12. The function of javana, javana kicca, which is "running through the object" or partaking of the object. There are fifty-five types of citta that can perform the function of javana:

    - akusala cittas 12 cittas[10]
    - ahetuka kiriyacitta (hasituppada citta of the arahat)[11] 1 citta

[10] There are eight types of citta rooted in lobha, attachment, two types rooted in dosa, aversion, and two types rooted in ignorance.

[11] Smile-producing consciousness.

- kāmāvacara kusala cittas (of the sense sphere[12])
  8 cittas
- kāmāvacara kiriyacittas (of the arahat)
  8 cittas
- rūpāvacara kusala cittas (of rūpa-jhāna)
  5 cittas
- rūpāvacara kiriyacittas (of the arahat)
  5 cittas
- arūpāvacara kusala cittas (of arūpa-jhāna)
  4 cittas
- arūpāvacara kiriyacittas (of the arahat)
  4 cittas
- lokuttara cittas (experiencing nibbāna)
  8 cittas

13. The function of registering or retention, tadālambana kicca, which is the function of knowing the object after the javana-cittas have fallen away. There are eleven types of vipākacittas that can perform this function:

- investigation-consciousness, santīraṇa-citta
  3 cittas
- kāmāvacara sahetuka kusala vipākacitta (accompanied by roots)
  8 cittas

14. The function of dying, cuti kicca, the function of departure from this lifespan. After the cuti-citta has arisen, performed this function and fallen away, it is the end of this lifespan and one is no longer this particular individual. There are nineteen types of vipākacittas that can perform the function of dying, and they are of the same types as those that perform the function of rebirth and the function of bhavanga. Whatever type performs the function

[12]Four are accompanied by pleasant feeling, four by indifferent feeling; four are associated with wisdom, four are without wisdom; four are not induced and four are induced. The kāmāvacara kiriyacittas are classified in the same way. See Appendix I to Citta.

of rebirth in a lifespan also performs the function of bhavanga and the function of dying, in the same lifespan.

It is because of conditions that the rebirth-consciousness arises in a particular lifespan with different accompanying cetasikas and together with rūpas of different quality, depending on the strength and the nature of that type of rebirth-consciousness.

There are ten types of kāmāvacara vipākacittas that can perform the function of rebirth in eleven planes of existence of the sense sphere (kāma bhūmi):

- investigating-consciousness (accompanied by indifferent feeling that is akusala vipāka 1 citta)
- investigating-consciousness (accompanied by indifferent feeling that is kusala vipāka 1 citta)
- kāmāvacara sahetuka kusala vipākacittas (mahā-vipāka) 8 cittas

Investigating-consciousness accompanied by indifferent feeling, that is akusala vipāka, is the result of akusala kamma and it can perform the function of rebirth in four classes of unhappy planes of existence: the hell planes, the ghost-realm (of petas), the demon-world (asura-kāya) and the animal world.[13]

Investigating-consciousness accompanied by indifferent feeling that is kusala vipāka, is the result of kusala kamma that is weak, and it can perform the function of rebirth in the human plane. In that case, akusala kamma has the opportunity to make that person suffer, and cause him to be handicapped from the time of his conception. He will be born mentally handicapped, mute, blind, cripple or with other kinds of weaknesses. It can also perform the function of rebirth in the lowest heavenly plane, the plane of the "Four Guardian Deities" (Cātummahārājika).

The eight types of mahā-vipākacittas can perform the function of rebirth in the human plane and in six classes of heavenly planes, and their

[13]Investigating-consciousness, santīraṇa-citta, performs the function of investigating in a sense-door process, but this type of citta can also perform the function of rebirth-consciousness. In the latter case, it is still called investigating-consciousness since it is the same type of citta as that arising in a sense-door process.

different qualities depend on the strength and the degree of excellence of the kusala kammas that condition them.[14]

The five types of rūpāvacara vipākacittas perform the function of rebirth in fifteen rūpa-brahma planes, and the different degrees of these kinds of rebirth depend on the rūpāvacara kusala citta that is the cause of them.

The four types of arūpāvacara vipākacittas perform the function of rebirth in four arūpa-brahma planes, and the different degrees of these kinds of rebirth depend on the arūpāvacara kusala citta that is the cause of them.

The eleven kinds of tadālambana-cittas, which perform the function of retention or registering and which follow upon the javana-cittas, do not arise in the rūpa-brahma planes and the arūpa-brahma planes.[15]

There are two types of cittas performing five functions, which are the function of rebirth, bhavanga, santīraṇa, tadālambana and dying, namely: investigating-consciousness accompanied by indifferent feeling that is akusala vipāka and investigating-consciousness accompanied by indifferent feeling that is kusala vipāka.

The eight types of mahā-vipākacittas perform four functions, which are the function of rebirth, bhavanga, tadālambana and dying.

The five types of rūpāvacara vipākacittas perform three functions and the four types of arūpāvacara vipākacittas also perform three functions, which are the function of rebirth, of bhavanga and of dying.

There are two types of citta that can perform two functions, namely the mind-door adverting-consciousness[16] and the investigating-consciousness accompanied by pleasant feeling.[17]

---

[14]There are 8 types of mahā-vipākacitta, which are results of the eight types of mahā-kusala citta; they are accompanied by pleasant feeling or indifferent feeling, accompanied by wisdom or unaccompanied by wisdom, arising without being induced, or being induced. These details will be explained further on.

[15]Only in the planes where there are sense impressions there are, after the javana-cittas, conditions for kamma to produce vipākacittas which "hang on" to the object experienced during that process.

[16]It performs the function of adverting in the mind-door process and it performs the function of determining, votthapana, in the sense-door process.

[17]This type of citta can only perform the function of investigation in a sense-door process when the object is very pleasant. It can also perform the function of retention or registering.

All the other types of cittas perform only one function, their own proper function.

Questions

1. Of which jāti is registering-consciousness, tadārammaṇa-citta? By which kamma is it produced?
2. When does rūpa originating from kamma arise? And when does it not arise?
3. When does rūpa originating from citta arise? When does it not arise?
4. Which function is performed by akusala citta?
5. Of which jātis are the cittas performing the function of javana?
6. Can kusala citta and kiriyacitta perform the function of retention (tadārammaṇa)?
7. Which functions can be performed by investigating-consciousness accompanied by indifferent feeling?
8. Which functions can be performed by investigating-consciousness accompanied by pleasant feeling?
9. Of which jātis are the cittas of the arahat?
10. Of which jātis are the cittas of the non-arahat?

15

The Cycle of Birth and Death

As we have seen, the first aspect of citta given by the "Atthasālinī" is clear knowledge of an object. Remembrance of this aspect can be a supporting condition for sati to arise and to be aware of the characteristic of citta when there is seeing, hearing, smelling, tasting or the experience of tangible object. Such experiences can then be realized as citta, not self, who experiences. Citta is the reality, the dhamma, which clearly knows the object that is appearing.

The second aspect of citta is the aspect of javana-citta, which arranges itself in its own series of cittas of the same type. People have diverse inclinations because of different accumulations of kusala and akusala. Some people have accumulated a great deal of attachment, aversion and ignorance, whereas others have accumulated many wholesome qualities. Because of different accumulated inclinations people have different characters.

The third aspect of citta is the aspect of vipāka, of citta as result, conditioned by accumulated kamma and defilements.[1] If one has right

[1]In this connection, there is a word association between citta and cito, which

understanding of vīthi-citta, citta arising in a process, it will be clearer what the cycle of birth and death is. We are born and we revolve in a threefold cycle: the cycle of defilement, the cycle of kamma and the cycle of vipāka. This threefold cycle is summarized in the third aspect of citta, citta as vipāka, conditioned by accumulated kamma and defilements.

Kusala dhammas and akusala dhammas that arise at the moment of javana-citta fall away again, but they are not lost, they are accumulated and go on from one moment of citta to the next moment of citta. Citta that arises falls away again, but its falling away is a condition for the arising of the succeeding citta and all accumulations present in the preceding citta go on to the succeeding citta. That is the reason why akusala javana vīthi-citta and kusala javana vīthi-citta, which arrange themselves in their own continuing series, can condition the arising of vipāka later on.

As we have seen, the cycle of birth and death is threefold: the cycle of defilement, the cycle of kamma and the cycle of vipāka. The cycle of defilement revolves when objects are experienced through the sense-doors and through the mind-door. Defilements that arise in the series, or succession of javana, are the condition for the cycle of kamma. Akusala kamma and kusala kamma, performed through body, speech and mind are the condition for the cycle of vipāka.

When vipākacitta arises and experiences an object through the eyes, the ears, the nose, the tongue or the bodysense, defilements are bound to arise on account of the object that is experienced, and then the cycle of defilement revolves again. Time and again the defilements of like or dislike arise because of what appears through the sense-doors or the mind-door. Defilements again condition the performing of kamma, kusala kamma and akusala kamma, and these produce kusala vipāka and akusala vipāka. Thus, there is no end to the threefold cycle. So long as paññā has not been developed and is not powerful enough to reach the stage of being able to realize the four noble Truths, the threefold cycle of defilement, kamma and vipāka is bound to revolve all the time.

The "Dependent Origination," Paticca Samuppāda, which is the teaching of the arising of phenomena in dependence upon each other, can be considered under the aspect of the threefold cycle. Ignorance,

---

means accumulated.

avijjā, is the condition for the arising of kamma-formation, saṅkhāra. This means that the cycle of defilement conditions the cycle of kamma. Kamma-formation, saṅkhāra, is the condition for the arising of consciousness, viññāṇa (in this case vipākacitta); this means that the cycle of kamma conditions the cycle of vipāka.[2]

Ignorance, avijjā, is actually moha cetasika, the akusala dhamma that does not know realities as they are. It represents the cycle of defilement that conditions the arising of kamma-formations.

Kamma-formation, saṅkhāra, which is the fruit of ignorance, is threefold:

- meritorious kamma-formation (puññābhisaṅkhāra)[3];
- demeritorious kamma-formation (apuññābhisaṅkhāra)[4];
- imperturbable kamma-formation (āneñjābhisaṅkhāra).

Meritorious kamma-formation is volition, cetanā, performing kusala kamma that is dependent on rūpa, materiality, and this includes kāmāvacara kusala kamma (of the sense sphere) and rūpāvacara kusala kamma (rūpa-jhāna, of the fine-material sphere).

Demeritorious kamma-formation is the volition that performs akusala kamma.

Imperturbable kamma-formation is arūpāvacara kusala kamma, volition arising with the four types of arūpa-jhāna kusala citta (immaterial jhāna).

Meritorious kamma-formation, demeritorious kamma-formation and imperturbable kamma-formation are conditions for the arising of viññāṇa.

---

[2]Kusala kamma and akusala kamma condition the revolving in the cycle of birth and death. They condition birth in a new existence; they condition seeing, hearing, smelling, tasting and the experience of tangible object. These experiences (vipāka) are the condition again for the cycle of defilements.

[3]Puññā is merit, kusala. Abhisaṅkhāra stands for cetanā, volition or intention. Although at the moment of kusala citta there is no ignorance with the citta, ignorance can still condition kusala kamma. So long as ignorance has not been eradicated, one has to continue in the cycle of birth and death, performing both good deeds and evil deeds that bring results. Only the arahat who has eradicated ignorance is freed from the cycle. He does not perform kusala kamma nor akusala kamma, deeds that bring results.

[4]Apuññā is demerit, akusala.

Viññāṇa is a synonym of citta, consciousness, but in the context of the "Dependent Origination" it is vipākacitta. The vipākacitta that is rebirth-consciousness arises in different planes of existence, in accordance with the cause, kamma, that produces it.

The Buddha explained the Dhamma by different methods, for example, by way of the four paramattha dhammas, by way of the four noble Truths or by way of the "Dependent Origination." These different methods concern the dhammas that occur at each moment, even now, at this very moment.

The third aspect of citta is citta as vipāka. Vipāka is conditioned by accumulated kamma and defilements. This shows us that in daily life there are defilements, kamma or vipāka at different moments. Right understanding of vīthi-citta is a condition for mindfulness and investigation of different cittas arising in processes that experience visible object, sound, the other sense objects or mental object. Then paññā can come to know when there is defilement, when kamma and when vipāka.

For example, with regard to cittas arising in the eye-door process, some cittas are vipāka and some are not:

- the five sense-door adverting-consciousness is not vipākacitta;
- seeing-consciousness is vipākacitta;
- receiving-consciousness is vipākacitta;
- investigating-consciousness is vipākacitta;
- determining-consciousness is not vipākacitta;
- javana-cittas that are kusala, akusala or kiriya are not vipākacitta;
- registering-consciousness is vipākacitta.

We may wonder of what use it is to know in detail at which moment there is vipāka and at which moment there is not vipāka in the eye-door process. It is useful to know that the dhammas that are cause are different from the dhammas that are result. Akusala dhammas and kusala dhammas are cause, not vipāka. When there is vipākacitta, there is result originating from a cause; vipāka itself is not a cause. If we understand at which moment there is vipāka, result produced by past kamma, such as seeing now, can we still believe that there is a self who can cause the arising of particular vipākas? If we have right understanding of the citta that is cause and of the citta that is result, we shall know the meaning of anattā, non-self. We shall understand anattā when seeing, hearing, smelling, tasting, experiencing tangible object or thinking. This understanding can be a supporting condition for sati to be aware of the realities that appear at such moments and, thus, there will be more understanding of the different characteristics of these realities that arise, each because of its own conditions.

Some people fear that vipāka will not arise anymore, they are afraid that vipāka will come to an end at death. There is no reason to be afraid of this, we do not have to worry that vipāka will not arise anymore today, tomorrow, the next days, the coming months, years or lives. When someone is not yet an arahat, there are still conditions present for the continuation of vipāka; it will arise time and again. We should consider what kind of kamma is going to produce vipāka in the future. We can verify in this life, in the case of different individuals, to what extent there is vipāka produced by kusala kamma and to what extent vipāka produced by akusala kamma.

In the commentary to the "Gradual Sayings," the "Manoratha Pūraṇi", in the commentary to the Nidāna Sutta (Book of the Threes, Ch IV, §33, Causes), there is an explanation of this sutta according to the Abhidhamma method.[5] Kamma is classified as sixteen kinds: eight kinds of akusala kamma and eight kinds of kusala kamma. Akusala kamma as well as kusala kamma need other conditions to be able to produce their results. Four of these conditioning factors are favourable or advantageous (sampatti) and four are unfavourable or disadvantageous (vipatti). Some akusala kammas that have been performed can be prevented from producing result through four favourable factors: favourable place of birth (gati), favourable bodily condition (upadhi), favourable time (kāla) and success in means or occupation (payoga).[6] Thus, when

[5]The teachings can be explained according to the Suttanta method or the Abhidhamma method. The Buddha preached the Suttas to people with different accumulations and he used conventional terms so that they could understand his teaching more easily. The explanation according to the Abhidhamma method is by way of paramattha dhammas, ultimate realities.

[6]These factors will be explained further on.

someone has a favourable place of birth, has a favourable bodily condition, lives in a favourable time and has success in his means or occupation, some akusala kammas do not have an opportunity to produce results.

Some akusala kammas have the opportunity to produce result because of four unfavourable factors: unfavourable place of birth, unfavourable bodily condition, unfavourable time and failure in one's means or occupation.

It is the same in the case of kusala kamma. If someone has the factors of unfavourable place of birth, unfavourable bodily condition, unfavourable time and failure in occupation, some kusala kammas do not have an opportunity to produce result.

Some kusala kammas have the opportunity to produce result because of four favourable factors: favourable place of birth, favourable bodily condition, favourable time and success in occupation. Thus, when we take into account the four favourable factors and the four unfavourable factors in the case of kusala kamma and of akusala kamma, kamma can be classified as sixteen-fold.

Favourable place of birth (gati sampatti) is a happy plane of existence where one is born. Unfavourable place of birth (gati vipatti) is an unhappy plane of existence where one is born, such as a hell plane.

We all have to be reborn as soon as the dying-consciousness falls away, but nobody knows whether the place one will go to will be happy or unhappy. Some people wish to be reborn into a family where there is no addiction to alcohol or intoxicating drugs, but so long as the moment of dying has not come yet, one does not know what types of javana vīthicittas that condition rebirth will arise before the dying-consciousness. One does not know which kamma will produce vipāka after the dying-consciousness, in the form of rebirth and in which plane there will be rebirth.

When kusala kamma produces result in the form of rebirth in a happy plane, there is a favourable place of rebirth. There is not only the kusala kamma that produces rebirth in a happy plane, but there are also other kusala kammas performed in the cycle of birth and death. On account of a happy rebirth these kammas can have an opportunity to produce, in the course of life, kusala vipākacittas that experience pleasant objects. However, one also committed akusala kamma in the past and thus one cannot experience only pleasant objects. When akusala kamma produces result, there is the experience of unpleasant objects through the eyes, the ears, the nose, the tongue or the bodysense. We all have performed both kusala kamma and akusala kamma but the opportunity for them to produce result depends on the factors of favourable or unfavourable place of birth and on other conditions.

Bodily condition (upadhi)[7] is another factor that can be favourable or unfavourable. Dukkha, suffering, is inherent in bodily condition. Even when someone is born as a human being, thus, in a happy plane, akusala kamma that was committed in the past can be the condition for having a body with defects or handicaps. A defective body is an unfavourable bodily condition that contributes to akusala kamma producing results more often than kusala kamma.

Apart from this factor there is the time factor, which can be favourable (kāla sampatti) or unfavourable (kāla vipatti). The factor of time that is favourable conditions kusala kamma that has been performed in the past to produce result. When one lives in a favourable time, there is an abundance of food, enough fish in the water and plenty of rice in the fields. Then it is not difficult to obtain food and food is not expensive. When the country where one lives is prosperous and there is peace, when one can live in comfort, with an abundance of all the things one needs, kusala kamma has the opportunity to condition the arising of kusala vipākacitta. Then vipākacitta experiences pleasant objects through the eyes, the ears, the nose, the tongue and the bodysense.

It may happen that one lives in an unfavourable time, when the country is in a state of unrest, when food is hard to obtain and expensive. Then kusala kamma does not have an opportunity, to the same extent as when the time is favourable, to condition the arising of kusala vipākacitta that experiences pleasant objects through the senses. Even upright people who do not cause trouble to anybody may still have unpleasant experiences, they may suffer from pain or sickness or they may lose their lives, because they live in an unfavourable time. One may have accumulated kusala kamma, but if one lives in an unfavourable time, when one's country is in disorder and confusion, akusala kamma committed in the past has the opportunity to produce result in the form

[7] Upadhi means foundation or substratum.

of akusala vipākacitta, and this can happen also at this time.

Success or failure in one's means or occupation (payoga sampatti and vipatti) are also factors that condition kamma to produce result or that can prevent kamma from producing result. Someone is successful in his occupation when he is skilful, diligent and clever in the performing of his tasks. Each kind of occupation, even that of a thief, needs expertise and skill for the accomplishment of one's tasks. The ability to accomplish one's work is success in occupation, be it in a wholesome way or in an unwholesome way. No matter which profession or task one performs, one needs success in occupation, skilfulness and competence in the accomplishment of one's work. Then akusala kamma that has been committed in the past has no opportunity to condition vipākacitta. Someone may be upright, but he may lack expertise, knowledge and competence in his profession or task, and thus there is failure in occupation. This may prevent the arising of kusala vipāka.

The Buddha taught in detail about the causes that bring their appropriate results and he also explained about the different conditioning factors necessary for the arising of results. His teaching about this subject illustrates the truth of anattā. There is no self who can cause anything to arise at will. Each citta that arises is dependent on different conditions. As we have seen, the producing of result by kusala kamma or akusala kamma is also dependent on other conditioning factors, which are: favourable or unfavourable place of birth, favourable or unfavourable bodily condition, favourable or unfavourable time and success or failure in one's occupation.

Right understanding of cause and result, that is, of defilements, of kamma and of vipāka, can be a condition for a decrease in the suffering, dukkha, which is inherent in the cycle of birth and death. We should know with regard to the vīthi-cittas, for example, those of the eye-door process, what is vipāka and what is kamma, and we should know that vipākacittas cannot perform kamma. The vipākacittas in that process are, as explained before, seeing-consciousness, receiving-consciousness that receives the object after the seeing-consciousness, and investigating-consciousness that investigates the object after the receiving-consciousness. When one performs kusala kamma there are no vipākacittas but kusala javana-cittas.

When one hears a pleasant sound, the vipākacitta that is hearing-consciousness arises and just hears, the receiving-consciousness receives that sound, the investigating-consciousness investigates it, examines it. These vipākacittas cannot perform any akusala kamma or kusala kamma.

When one smells a fragrant odour that impinges on the nose, the vipākacitta that is smelling-consciousness arises and experiences that odour. The receiving-consciousness receives that smell and the investigating-consciousness examines it. These vipākacittas cannot perform kamma; they cannot cause the movement of any rūpa of the body to perform kamma.

When we speak, walk, lift our hands, or when the body moves for the performing of different functions, the citta at such moments is different from the vipākacitta that sees, hears, tastes, smells or experiences tangible object. The javana vīthi-cittas, be they kusala or akusala, can cause the movement of rūpas of the body. Thus, we can understand that the cittas that perform kamma are altogether different from vipākacittas.

While we are eating different types of citta arise. The citta that sees is vipākacitta, the citta that likes the food that is seen is akusala citta rooted in attachment, the citta that dislikes the food that is seen is akusala citta rooted in aversion. The citta that tastes a sour or sweet flavour is vipākacitta. The citta that, with desire, conditions the movement of the body when taking the food, when chewing and swallowing it, is akusala citta rooted in attachment. Sati can arise and be aware of the characteristics of the different kinds of cittas as they naturally appear, so that they can be known as they are. One should not try to flee from lobha, but one should know it as it is; and only thus can it be eventually eradicated.

Since the time of our birth there were conditions for the arising of attachment, time and again, in daily life, and therefore attachment has become our nature. While we are doing our work there is, most of the time, attachment; thus, the moments of attachment that arise in a day are countless. However, if we see the benefit of kusala, there can also be conditions for the arising of kusala citta. While we are eating, javana vīthi-cittas with attachment are likely to arise and fall away, but the javana-cittas in the next process may be different. If sati can be mindful of the citta that enjoys the food, there are kusala javana-cittas. Or sati can be mindful of the characteristics of rūpas, such as softness, hardness, cold, heat, motion, pressure, or of the flavour that appears, which may be sour, sweet or salty.

When one develops satipaṭṭhāna, right understanding can come to know the nature of citta. Akusala can be known as it is, before there is any action through body or speech. Sati can be aware of the citta that sees and then there can be right understanding of its characteristic, as being different from the citta with attachment to the object that appears.

As we have seen, the third aspect of citta is the aspect of citta as vipāka, conditioned by accumulated kamma and defilements. Defilement is the dhamma that is impure. When one desires something or wishes to obtain something for oneself, there is no contentment, no peace. Whereas, if one does not want anything for oneself and attachment does not arise, there is contentment. When one longs for something, when one is attached, there is ignorance which is unable to see that at such moments there are impure dhammas, that there is no inward peace but confusion caused by clinging. Whenever one is disturbed by selfish desire, by clinging, there are impure, akusala dhammas. People sometimes mistake attachment for confidence in kusala (saddhā).[8] If sati does not arise and paññā does not investigate realities, it will not be known when there is attachment that is akusala and when there is confidence in wholesomeness that is kusala.

Monks and laypeople, who still have defilements, are not free from attachment; it arises in daily life. So long as defilements have not been eradicated, be it in the case of layman or monk, attachment to what appears through the eyes, the ears, the nose, the tongue, the bodysense or the mind-door will arise. The different defilements that arise time and again can be very strong, and then they are of the degree of akusala kamma committed through the body or through speech. If defilements would be eradicated, akusala kamma could not arise. When one has performed kamma, the citta and cetasikas that arose together at that moment have fallen away, but kamma is never lost. It is accumulated and goes on from one citta to the next citta, since each citta that falls

[8] One may, with confidence in kusala, perform good deeds. At another moment one may, with attachment, take delight in one's own good deed and take one's attachment for confidence. Or, one may take attachment to a teacher for confidence that is wholesome.

away is succeeded by the next citta, all the time. Because of this, there can be kamma-condition (kamma-paccaya), that is, kamma that conditions the arising of result, vipākacitta and its accompanying cetasikas.

We should know when there are defilements, when kamma and when vipāka. The cittas that see, hear, smell, taste or experience tangible object are vipākacittas, results of kamma. We all like to see only pleasant things and we never have enough of seeing them. We have eyesense, a rūpa that is conditioned by kamma, thus we have the ability to see, but we cannot be sure whether we shall see a pleasant object or an unpleasant object. It depends on kamma-condition whether a pleasant object or an unpleasant object will impinge on the eyesense and appear to seeing-consciousness. When kusala kamma is kamma-condition, it causes seeing-consciousness that is kusala vipākacitta to arise and to experience a pleasant object. When akusala kamma is kamma-condition, it causes seeing-consciousness that is akusala vipākacitta to arise and to experience an unpleasant object. When hearing-consciousness hears a pleasant sound, it is the result of kusala kamma. When hearing-consciousness hears an unpleasant sound, it is the result of akusala kamma. The arising of kusala vipāka or akusala vipāka at this moment or the next moments depends on kusala kamma or akusala kamma that is the condition for the vipākacitta that experiences an object through one of the senses.

There are twenty-four principal conditions for all realities that arise.[9] Kamma-condition, kamma-paccaya, is one condition among them, being the condition for the arising of vipāka. Seeing, hearing, smelling, tasting, or the experience of tangible object, are vipākacittas accompanied by vipākacetasikas that arise because of kamma-condition. Nobody can cause the arising of vipāka according to his wish. At this moment, we have seen already, we have heard already. Who can prevent seeing or hearing when they have already arisen because of kamma-condition?

Citta and cetasikas that experience an object appearing through the senses are vipākacitta and vipākacetasikas that arise together. Vipākacitta is a condition for vipākacetasika and vipākacetasika is a condition for vipākacitta, and, thus, since they are both vipāka they condition one another by way of vipaka-condition, vipaka-paccaya. The citta and

[9] The seventh Book of the Abhidhamma, the "Paṭṭhāna," deals with all the conditions for the phenomena that arise.

cetasikas that arise together and are vipāka, condition one another; each of them, citta and each of the accompanying cetasikas, is vipāka-condition for the other conascent dhammas.

The rūpa that is conditioned by kamma is not vipāka, although it is the result of kamma. Rūpa is altogether different from nāma, it does not know anything and thus it is not vipāka that is the mental result of kamma. Vipāka is nāma, the reality that experiences an object.

Questions

1. What is kamma-condition?
2. What is vipāka-condition?
3. Is the rūpa that originates from kamma, vipāka? Explain your answer.

16

The Nature of Vipāka

Vipāka is produced by kamma performed in the past. It is not easy to understand that kamma, which already belongs to the past, can still be a condition for the arising of vipākacitta and vipākacetasikas in the present time. The nature of vipāka should be examined in detail, so that there can be right understanding of kamma and vipāka. The reality of vipāka is nāma, citta and cetasikas that arise because they are conditioned by kamma that has been performed already.

When a person is confronted with an unpleasant or a pleasant event in his life, people usually say, "This is his kamma." We should say that it is the result of kamma performed in the past, so that people can have right understanding of kamma and vipāka. If one does not express oneself precisely and, for example, says that an accident is the kamma of that person, the truth of cause and result will not be clear to other people who are not familiar with this subject. They will confuse kamma and vipāka and take vipāka for kamma.

When we consider the aspect of citta as vipāka, conditioned by accumulated kamma and defilements, we shall see more clearly the true nature of different dhammas. We should remember that without the doorways of the senses and the mind-door, by means of which objects are received and experienced, vipākacittas could not arise in our daily life; the result of kamma could not be received. When seeing arises, there is vipāka, the result of kamma. The result of kamma is received not only when we have an accident, when we suffer from sickness or pain, when we experience gain and loss, honour and dishonour. Also at each moment of seeing, hearing or the other sense-cognitions, when we experience the ordinary objects in daily life, there is result of kamma performed in the past. Sati can be aware of the reality that is vipāka when there is seeing, hearing, smelling, tasting or the experience of tangible object in daily life.

Vipākacitta is bound to arise; it is the result of kamma that has been performed. We cannot know by which kamma in the past the vipākacittas arising in the different processes are conditioned. For example, we do not know which kamma produces the vipākacitta that hears the sound of a child playing football. It is difficult to understand the subject of kamma in detail. It is one of the subjects that are "unthinkable," subjects one cannot fathom, and therefore one should not speculate about them.[1]

Kamma that has been performed already is a cause stemming from the past. Even if kamma has been performed at a time that lies far back in the cycle of birth and death, it can still condition the arising of vipākacitta. If someone speculates about which kind of kamma conditions as its result the seeing of this object or the hearing of that sound, he will not be freed from ignorance and confusion. He will be speculating about something he cannot fathom, because he does not have paññā to the degree of penetrating the truth of kamma and vipāka. Vipāka, however, the result of kamma, which experiences objects through the senses, is appearing at this moment, and thus it can be known.

Among the four "Applications of Mindfulness" the third one is "Mindfulness of Citta."[2] The first type of citta mentioned in this section is citta with attachment (sarāgacitta). Sati can arise and be aware of the characteristic of the citta with attachment and clinging that appears

[1]The Sutta about the "Unthinkables" is quoted further on in this chapter.

[2]The other three are "Mindfulness of the Body", "Mindfulness of Feeling," "Mindfulness of Dhammas."

time and again in daily life. If sati does not arise, it will not be known that, when there is seeing of an object, cittas with attachment and clinging to what is seen arise, succeeding one another very rapidly. If paññā knows the characteristics of dhammas that naturally appear, defilements can eventually be eradicated. Paññā can know the difference between the characteristic of vipākacitta, the result of past kamma, and the characteristic of kusala citta and of akusala citta. Kusala citta and akusala citta of the degree of kamma performed at the present time can condition the arising of vipākacitta in the future. We should not only know the characteristic of vipāka which is more obvious, such as in the case of a pleasant or an unpleasant event, but also the characteristic of vipāka which is the experience through the senses of the manifold objects in daily life.

If we understand that vipākacitta that arises is the result of kamma we performed ourselves, can we still be angry with other people or blame them for the vipāka we receive? In the Scriptures we read about events in the lives of people of old who received different vipākas. Also, in the present time different events occur which clearly show that each person has to receive vipāka, the result of past kamma, but we cannot predict in which way it will appear. For example, a building may collapse and crush the owner so that he dies. A bomb is not the cause that the building collapses and crushes that man. His death is not caused by being shot or assaulted. Kamma performed in the past is the cause for receiving results through the eyes, the ears, the nose, the tongue or the bodysense. Therefore, one should not be angry with someone else or blame him for the vipāka one receives. Sati can be aware of the characteristic of the dhamma that is vipākacitta, not a being, person or self.

Thus, one can come to understand that the moment of vipāka is the result of past kamma, different from the moments of attachment, aversion and ignorance, or the moments of kusala dhammas. The kusala dhammas and akusala dhammas that arise are causes in the present that will condition the arising of results in the future.

The things outside as well as the rūpas of the body that appear to seeing and are perceived as being tall, short, dark or light, appear actually only at the moment they impinge on the eyesense. If there is no eyesense and we do not see, we cannot think of shape and form, of tall, short, dark and light we take for our body.

Therefore, in reality, one's own body and all the things outside do not belong to anyone. They appear just at the moment seeing-consciousness arises and then they fall away very rapidly.

It is the same with sound that only appears when it impinges on the earsense, and then falls away completely. It does not belong to anybody. By being aware of the characteristics of realities, just as they naturally appear in daily life, the wrong view can be eradicated which takes realities for a being, a person or self.

In daily life there arises, time and again, just a moment of seeing, of hearing, of smelling, of tasting, of body-consciousness or of thinking, and all these passing moments are real. They can be objects of satipaṭṭhāna so that paññā can investigate their characteristics, and in this way realities can be known as they are: not a being, person or self.

We should carefully consider what our possessions we believe we own really are. The moments we do not see them we can merely think about them, but we believe that we own many things. However, of what use can these things be to us during the moments we do not see or touch them? When the characteristics of paramattha dhammas have been understood as they are: not a being, person or self, it will be realized that paramattha dhammas are the same for all people, and that in that respect all people are equal. When seeing-consciousness arises, it sees what appears and then it falls away. The seeing-consciousness and what appears to seeing, visible object, do not belong to anybody. Therefore, we should not take anything for "I" or "mine." All people are equal, they are the same as far as paramattha dhammas are concerned. The defilement, however, which takes realities for "I" or "mine" is of a different degree for each person.

We are used to enjoying our possessions, but we may begin to realize that we have no possessions at all, that there is just seeing-consciousness that arises and sees and then falls away very rapidly. Where are our possessions at the moments seeing-consciousness does not arise? Our possessions are only that which seeing-consciousness sees when it arises just for a short moment, and therefore, is it right to take what is seen for our possessions? What appears just for an extremely short moment cannot become one's property, it cannot be owned; it can only appear through the eyes when it is impinging on the eyesense.

It is the same with sound, odour, flavour and tangible object. They impinge just for a moment on the relevant sense-door and, thus, we should not take these realities for "I" or "mine."

We all want to possess many things, we want to have as much as other people, but it all depends on kamma; the vipāka which appears in the present time is produced by a past cause. Therefore, result or vipāka is not in anyone's power. Nobody can predict which kamma will produce which vipākacittas as result, arising in the different processes when there is seeing, hearing, smelling, tasting or the experience of tangible object.

In the "Gradual Sayings" (II, Book of the Fours, Ch VIII, §7, Unthinkable) we read that the Buddha said:

> Monks, there are these four unthinkables, not to be thought of, thinking of which one would be distraught and come to grief. What are the four?
>
> Of Buddhas, monks, the range (field of knowledge) is unthinkable, not to be thought of... Of one who has attained jhāna, monks, the range of jhāna is unthinkable, not to be thought of... The fruit of kamma, monks, is unthinkable, not to be thought of... Speculation about the world, monks, is unthinkable, not to be thought of, thinking of which one would be distraught and would come to grief. These, monks, are the four unthinkables..."

While we are seeing now, there is vipākacitta that experiences an object through the eyes. Sati can be aware of the characteristics of realities: of nāma, the reality which experiences an object, and of rūpa, that which appears. Sati can only be aware of these characteristics and more than that cannot be known. It cannot be known which kamma of which past life has conditioned the seeing arising at this moment as its result. It is impossible to find this out. When there is seeing, sati can be mindful and paññā can clearly know the difference between seeing, which is vipāka, and akusala citta with like or dislike or kusala citta, which can arise after seeing.

The fourth aspect of citta as stated by the "Atthasālinī" is its variegated nature (vicitta). Citta is variegated because of the different accompanying dhammas, sampayutta dhammas, namely, the cetasikas that arise together with the citta. The accompanying cetasikas are different; each person has accumulated different inclinations. It is impossible that each person thinks in the same way or adheres to the same belief. People have a different outer appearance and also their ways of thinking, their points of view and their beliefs are not the same. Even the Buddha, during the time he was still alive, before his parinibbāna, could not cause all people to have right view. For those who have accumulated the right conditions, kusala vipākacitta and kusala citta can arise, so that they are able to hear the Dhamma, study it and investigate the truth the Buddha taught. When one has listened to the Dhamma, one should test its meaning, carefully consider it in all details and develop paññā so that the characteristics of realities can be known as they really are, in conformity with the truth the Buddha taught.

Wrong view does not only occur in other beliefs. Also, those who are Buddhists engage in different practices depending on the ideas and points of view they have accumulated.

After the second Council (of Vesāli), the monks of the Vajjiyan Clan, on account of whom the second Council had been convened, propagated different doctrines in conformity with their own opinion. One of their statements was that, in order to attain enlightenment, one should merely recite:

> "Dukkha, dukkha" ("Kathāvatthu", "Points of Controversy", Nidānakathā).

Thus, we see that wrong understanding and wrong practice have occurred since the past. We all should, in the present time, study the Dhamma and investigate it in detail.

We read in the "Puggala Paññatti" ("Human Types", Ch IV, §5)[3] that with regard to the grasping of the Dhamma there are four types of people: people who quickly grasp the Dhamma, can realize the four noble Truths and attain enlightenment even during a discourse (ugghaṭitaññū), people who attain enlightenment after a more detailed explanation of a discourse that was uttered in brief (vipacitaññū), people who require guidance and have to study and develop paññā a great deal (neyya puggala), and people who, although they listen to the Dhamma, read a

[3]See also "Gradual Sayings," II, Book of the Fours, Third Fifty, Ch XIV, §3.

great deal, often discuss and explain the Dhamma to others, cannot attain enlightenment yet (pada parama)[4]. In the present time, there are no people of the first and second category, there are only those of the third and fourth category.

We all should study in order to know what the realization of the four noble Truths means, and in what way paññā can be developed that realizes the arising and falling away of the dhammas appearing through the eyes, the ears, the nose, the tongue, the bodysense and the mind-door. Thus we shall know that the study of the Dhamma is of great benefit, that it is a supporting condition for sati to be aware of the characteristics of realities which the Buddha penetrated by his enlightenment and which he, out of compassion, taught to others in all details. The characteristic of citta, such as the citta that sees, can be object of satipaṭṭhāna, since it is reality. Right understanding can be developed of realities, so that the characteristic of anattā, non-self, can be clearly known. Realities arise and fall away in daily life, they are not a being, a person or self, not a thing that exists.

[4]Pada means "word" of the text and parama means highest.

17
Citta and Cetasika

The "Atthasālinī" mentions several aspects of citta:

- Citta is so called because it clearly knows an object.
- Citta is so called because it arises in its own series by way of javana.
- Citta is so called because it is result conditioned by accumulated kamma and defilements.
- Each citta is so called because it is variegated (vicitta) according to circumstances, because of the accompanying dhammas (sampayutta dhammas).

The fact that cittas are variegated (vicitta) means that all of them are different. They are variegated because of the accompanying dhammas. Citta is saṅkhāra dhamma; it arises because of conditions and different combinations of cetasikas condition it. Cetasika is another kind of paramattha dhamma that arises and falls away together with the citta, experiences the same object as the citta and arises at the same physical base as the citta. Therefore, the cetasikas that are the accompanying dhammas arising together with the citta are the condition for cittas to be variegated.

The cittas of one person are completely different from the cittas of any other person. Different accumulated kamma of the past conditions the result, the vipāka in the present, to be varied for different people. Animals and human beings in this world are different because of the diversity of the cause, of kamma. The outward appearance and bodily features of living beings are different, and they also experience different worldly conditions of gain, loss, honour, dishonour, well-being, misery, praise and blame. All these factors are just results that arise from various causes from the past. Past causes condition the results in the present to be varied for different people, from birth to death. It is unknown on which day and at which moment we shall depart from this world. Nobody can tell in which situation he will die, outside his home or inside, on land, in the water or in the air, due to sickness or due to an accident. It all depends on kamma that has been performed in the past. Not only the vipākacittas in the present are variegated for different people, but also the cittas that are causes in the present, kusala cittas and akusala cittas, are variegated. These are the condition for the results arising in the future to also be varied.

The diversity of cittas is endless. They are variegated because of the cetasikas that arise together with the citta, the sampayutta dhammas. We should know the meaning of sampayutta dhamma, associated dhamma. There are four kinds of paramattha dhammas: citta, cetasika, rūpa and nibbāna. Citta and cetasika are realities that have to arise together, they cannot be without one another; they cannot be separated from each other. When they arise together, they also fall away together. They share the same object and they have the same base, place of origin, in the planes where there are five khandhas, that is, nāma and rūpa. These are the characteristic features of their being associated dhammas, sampayutta dhammas.

The characteristics of sampayutta dhammas, citta and cetasikas, have been explained in detail so that it can be clearly known that nāma is completely different from rūpa. When we listen to the teachings and study them, conditions are gradually being built up (as saṅkhārakkhandha)[1] for the arising of sati and paññā. Thus, satipaṭṭhāna will arise and the characteristics of nāma and rūpa will be investigated and known, one at a time. They will appear as clearly distinct from each other, as being not associated (not sampayutta), although they can arise at the same time.

The "Atthasālinī" (I, Book I, Part II, Analysis of Terms, Ch I, 70) explains that when rūpa-dhammas and arūpa-dhammas (nāma-dhammas) are produced together, rūpa arises together with arūpa (nāma), but it is not associated or conjoined with it. The same is true for rūpa arising with rūpa. But arūpa is always accompanied by, coexistent, associated and conjoined with arūpa.

Thus, being associated is a characteristic that only pertains to nāmas, to citta and cetasika that arise and fall away together and experience the same object. Rūpa is completely different from nāma. Rūpa is not a dhamma that experiences an object. Rūpas that arise and fall away together cannot be associated dhammas. The realities that are associated dhammas can only be nāma-dhammas, elements that experience something. They are closely conjoined, since they arise at the same base, share the same object and fall away together.

In the "Atthasālinī" it has been stated as to the fourth aspect of citta, that each citta is variegated (vicitta), according to circumstances, because of the accompanying dhammas, sampayutta dhammas.

There are fifty-two kinds of cetasikas in all, but not all of them accompany each citta. Cittas are different because of the amount of cetasikas and the different types of cetasikas that accompany them. It depends on the type of citta and on its jāti (nature) by which cetasikas it is accompanied. The eighty-nine types of citta that arise are different as to their jāti, which may be kusala, akusala, vipāka or kiriya, one of these four jātis. The classification of citta by way of jāti is a classification as to the nature of citta. Citta that is kusala by nature cannot be anything else but kusala, no matter for whom, where or when it arises. The citta that is akusala cannot be anything else but akusala; no matter for whom it arises. Akusala is akusala, whether one is a monk or lay follower, no matter what rank one has, of what race one is, which colour

[1] In combination with other wholesome qualities comprised in saṅkhārakkhandha, the khandha of formations or activities.

of skin one has. The nature of citta cannot be changed, because citta is a paramattha dhamma, an absolute or ultimate reality. When the associated dhammas, the cetasikas, are akusala, the citta is akusala. When the associated dhammas are sobhana (beautiful), citta can be kusala, kusala vipāka or sobhana kiriyacitta (of the arahat), in accordance with the jāti of the citta.[2]

The "Atthasālini" (I, Book I, Part IV, Ch II, Section of Exposition, 142) states that the Buddha has accomplished a difficult matter, namely, that he classified cittas and cetasikas, designated them and gave them a name. The "Atthasālinī" uses a simile to illustrate this:

> "...True, it would be possible to find out by sight, or by smell, or by taste the difference in colour, smell and taste of a variety of waters or a variety of oils which have been placed in a jar and churned the whole day, yet it would be called a difficult thing to do. But something of greater difficulty has been accomplished by the supreme Buddha, who brought out the designation of nāma dhammas, after making an individual classification of them, namely of citta and the cetasikas which have arisen on account of one object..."

Nāma is more complex and intricate than rūpa, but the Buddha had, for each kind of nāma, designated four characteristic features:

- the specific characteristic which appears,
- the function,
- the mode of manifestation,
- the proximate cause or immediate occasion for its arising.

Citta is the "leader," the "chief," in knowing an object. The "Atthasālinī" (II, Book I, Part VIII, Ch I, the first Path, 214) states that citta is a base (bhūmi). It is the ground or soil for the accompanying cetasikas that are dependent on it. If there were no citta, there could not be, for example, the cetasika that is pleasant feeling, because then there would

[2]Sobhana cetasikas are wholesome qualities, which can accompany cittas of three jātis. Further on, the term sobhana will be explained more in detail.

be no foundation for it. Whenever pleasant feeling arises, the citta is the base on which the accompanying feeling depends. Thus, citta is the base on which the associated dhammas (sampayutta dhammas), happy feeling and the other accompanying cetasikas, are dependent.

As we have seen, citta can be classified by way of the four jātis of akusala, kusala, vipāka and kiriya. No matter which citta one refers to, one should know of which jāti it is. Vipāka is the result of kamma, and since there are both kusala kamma and akusala kamma, there also have to be both kusala vipāka and akusala vipāka.

When one refers to the result of akusala kamma, one should call it "akusala vipāka," and one should not abbreviate it as just "akusala." Akusala vipākacitta is the result of akusala kamma, it is not of the jāti that is akusala, and kusala vipākacitta is the result of kusala kamma, it is not of the jāti that is kusala.

Kiriyacitta, which is again another kind of citta, is not kusala, akusala or vipāka. It is a citta that arises because of conditions other than kamma-condition (kamma-paccaya). It is not result. Neither is it a cause that can condition the arising of vipāka. The arahat has kiriyacittas instead of akusala cittas or kusala cittas, because he no longer has conditions for akusala and kusala. For him there is only vipākacitta, the result of past kamma, and kiriyacitta.

The Buddha did not only classify cittas and cetasikas by way of the four jātis of kusala, akusala, vipāka and kiriya, he also used other methods of classification. He classified all dhammas as threefold ("Atthasālinī", Book I, Part I, Mātikā, Ch I, The Triplets, 39):

- kusala dhammas,
- akusala dhammas,
- indeterminate (avyākata) dhammas.

All paramattha dhammas that are not kusala dhammas or akusala dhammas are indeterminate dhammas, avyākata dhammas.[3] Thus, when citta and cetasika are classified according to this threefold method, the cittas and cetasikas which are avyākata dhammas are: cittas and cetasikas which are vipāka, and cittas and cetasikas which are kiriya.

[3] Avyākata means undeclared. They are not "declared" as kusala or akusala.

The four paramattha dhammas of citta, cetasika, rūpa and nibbāna can be classified according to the threefold classification of kusala dhamma, akusala dhamma and avyākata dhamma. Then the four paramattha dhammas are classified as follows:

- kusala citta and cetasikas: kusala dhamma;
- akusala citta and cetasikas: akusala dhamma;
- vipākacitta and cetasikas: avyākata dhamma;
- kiriyacitta and cetasikas: avyākata dhamma;
- all rūpas: avyākata dhamma;
- nibbāna: avyākata dhamma.

Questions

1. Can rūpa be associated dhamma, sampayutta dhamma, with nāma?
2. Can rūpa be sampayutta dhamma with rūpa?
3. Is colour that appears through the eyes, kusala dhamma or avyākata dhamma? Explain the reason.
4. Is seeing-consciousness kusala dhamma, akusala dhamma or avyākata dhamma? Explain the reason.
5. Can nibbāna be kusala dhamma?
6. Which citta has no jāti?
7. With which dhamma can citta be associated dhamma, and when?
8. Can one type of citta be associated dhamma with another type of citta?
9. Can akusala dhamma be associated dhamma with kusala dhamma?
10. With which dhamma can nibbāna be associated dhamma?

18

Cittas of the Sense-Sphere

There are eighty-nine different types of citta and these can be classified according to different grades, namely as four planes (bhūmi) of citta:

- sensuous plane, kāmāvacara bhūmi,
- fine-material plane, rūpāvacara bhūmi (rūpa-jhāna),
- immaterial plane, arūpāvacara bhūmi (arūpa-jhāna),
- supramundane plane, lokuttara bhūmi.

The "Atthasālinī" (I, Book I, Part II, Analysis of terms, 62) gives an explanation of the meaning of kāmāvacara, sensuous, according to different methods. According to one method of explanation, kāmāvacara is used for the citta that is involved in kāmāvacara dhammas, thus, it is the citta which is of the grade of the sensuous plane of consciousness. "Kāmāvacara" is the complete term,[1] but the abridged form of "kāma"

[1] Avacara means moving in or frequenting.

is also used. Citta of the grade or plane of kāma, kāmāvacara citta, frequents objects of sense, namely: visible object, sound, odour, flavour and tangible object.

At each moment in daily life there is kāmāvacara citta, except when there is citta of another grade or plane that is more refined than that of the kāmāvacara citta. When one develops kusala citta with calm by means of a meditation subject that is dependent on rūpa, materiality, and calm becomes firmly established so that it reaches the level of attainment concentration (appanā samādhi), there is rūpa-jhānacitta, which has an object that is still dependent on rūpa. Then there is a higher plane of citta, the fine material plane of citta, rūpāvacara bhūmi, and the citta of this plane, the rūpāvacara citta, is free from kāma, sensuousness. A plane of citta that is still higher is the arūpa bhūmi, immaterial plane. The citta of this plane, the arūpāvacara citta, is of a higher degree of calm and more refined, firmly established in calm with an object that is not dependent on rūpa. The citta that is even more refined than arūpāvacara citta is lokuttara citta which realizes the characteristic of nibbāna. That is the citta of the supramundane plane, lokuttara bhūmi. Thus, cittas are varied as they are of different planes of citta. The eighty-nine cittas can be classified according to the planes of citta in the following way:

- 54 kāmāvacara cittas,[2]
- 15 rūpāvacara cittas,[3]
- 12 arūpāvacara cittas,[4]
- 8 lokuttara cittas.[5]

[2]Included are 12 akusala cittas, 8 kusala cittas, 8 mahā-vipākacittas, 8 mahā-kiriyacittas (of the arahat). Also included are the ahetuka vipākacittas that are the ten sense-cognitions (two pairs), 2 receiving-consciousnesses and 3 investigating-consciousnesses, the ahetuka kiriyacittas that are the sense-door adverting-consciousness, the mind-door adverting-consciousness and the smile-producing-consciousness of the arahat.

[3]For each of the five stages of rūpa-jhāna there are rūpāvacara kusala citta, vipākacitta and kiriyacitta.

[4]For each of the four stages of arūpa-jhāna there are arūpāvacara kusala citta, vipākacitta and kiriyacitta.

[5]For each of the four stages of enlightenment there are the path-consciousness, magga-citta, and its result, the fruition-consciousness, phala-citta.

There is kāmāvacara citta at the moments when there is not rūpāvacara citta, arūpāvacara citta or lokuttara citta.

The "Atthasālinī" (in the same section) states that the term kāma, sensuousness, has two meanings:

- sensuousness of defilements, kilesa kāma,
- the base or foundation of sensuousness, vatthu kāma.

The "Atthasālinī" states:

> "The sensuousness of the defilements is so termed because it desires, and the other, the sensuousness of base, is so termed because it is desired by the sensuousness of defilements."

Kilesa kāma is sense desire (chanda rāga) that is lobha cetasika, the dhamma that enjoys objects, is pleased with them and clings to them. Vatthu kāma are the objects that are the basis on which desire or clinging depends, that which is desired. Vatthu kāma also comprises the three classes of planes of existence where a person can be reborn: the sensuous planes of existence (kāma bhūmi), the fine material planes (rūpa bhūmi)[6] and the immaterial planes.[7] So long as lobha has not been eradicated, one is not free from the cycle of birth and death and, thus, one can be reborn in those planes. They are vatthu kāma, the objects for kilesa kāma, the sensuousness of defilements.

Kāmāvacara citta that is attached to visible object, sound, odour, flavour and tangible object clings firmly to them, even though they appear just for a moment. Visible object appears for an extremely short moment, when it impinges on the eyesense. Sound appears just for an extremely short moment, when it impinges on the earsense. It is the same with odour, flavour and tangible object. All of them are insignificant dhammas (paritta dhammas), they appear just for a moment and then they fall away. Nevertheless, citta is attached and clings all the time to these insignificant dhammas. Since these dhammas that arise and fall away are succeeding one another, it seems that they can last, that they do not fall away.

---

[6]Birth in these planes is the result of rūpa-jhāna.

[7]Birth in these planes is the result of arūpa-jhāna.

There is no end to clinging to all the sense objects, to visible object, sound, odour, flavour and tangible object. We are infatuated with them and keep on clinging to them. These objects fall away, but they are replaced; the rūpas that fall away are succeeded by new ones. We are deluded and cling again to visible object, sound and the other sense objects that replace those which have fallen away and thus clinging continues all the time. When we see visible object and we like it, we want to see it again and again. When we hear a sound that we like we want to hear it again, and it is the same with odour, flavour and tangible object that we like. When we are eating and we like a particular flavour, we wish to eat the same food again and taste that flavour again. Clinging to the sense objects arises each day, time and again. It is our nature to cling through the eyes, the ears, the nose, the tongue, the bodysense and the mind-door.

When we like something we see, we wish to see it all the time, but that is impossible. All conditioned dhammas, saṅkhāra dhammas, arise and then fall away; that is their nature. When a delicious flavour appears, attachment depending on the tongue arises. At that moment attachment through the eyes, the ears, the nose or the bodysense cannot arise. When odour appears and attachment to it arises, there cannot be attachment through the eyes, the ears, the tongue or the bodysense, since only one citta arises at a time. There cannot be the arising of two cittas at the same time. We all are attached to the objects that appear alternately through the eyes, the ears, the nose, the tongue, the bodysense and the mind-door. We are not attached just to colour, just to sound or just to one of the other sense objects; we are attached to all of them. The reason is that attachment to all the sense objects has been accumulated continuously, from the past to the present time, and it will be accumulated on to the future.

Thus, kāmāvacara citta, citta of the sense sphere "travels" to, frequents visible object, sound, odour, flavour and tangible object; it clings to these objects, it is not free from them. Some people who want to be free from sense objects say that, as a result of having performed meritorious deeds, they want to be reborn in heaven. Even heavenly planes are not free from sense objects, but they are more refined than the objects in the human world.

From birth to death, when citta has not attained calm to the degree of attainment concentration (appanā samādhi), that is, when citta is not jhānacitta, and when citta is not lokuttara citta, citta is kāmāvacara citta. Whether we are asleep or awake, whether we see, hear, smell, taste, experience tangible object or think of different subjects, at all such moments there is no living being who experiences objects, there is no person, no self. There are only cittas of the grade of kāma, sensuousness, kāmāvacara cittas that experience objects.

The person who is not an anāgāmī (non-returner who has attained the third stage of enlightenment) or an arahat still clings to visible object, sound, odour, flavour and tangible object. This shows how difficult it is to eradicate clinging to the sense objects that appear through the six doors. Even if someone has cultivated calm to the degree of jhāna and he is reborn in a brahma plane,[8] clinging to the sense objects cannot be completely eradicated. If he is not yet an anāgāmī, he will again and again return to a life of clinging to visible object and the other sense objects that appear through six doors. Therefore, we should not be negligent with regard to the defilements. We should understand realities as they are; we should understand which cause brings which effect. Then we shall be able to develop right understanding of the eightfold Path, which can eradicate defilements completely.

Kāmāvacara is a name for the citta that is involved in dhammas of the sense sphere, kāmāvacara dhammas. The "Atthasālinī" explains that the planes of existence of the kāmāvacara dhammas, that is, the sensuous planes of existence, extend from the lowest plane, which is the "Avīci hell," up to the highest sensuous plane which is a heavenly plane, called the "paranimmita vasavatti deva plane" (the plane of heavenly beings with power over the creations of others). In all these planes there are sense objects.

As regards the term basis of sensuousness or clinging, vatthu kama, this has, according to the "Atthasālinī, a wider meaning than visible object, sound, odour, flavour or tangible object. Any kind of dhamma that is a basis or foundation for attachment is actually vatthu kāma. Lobha cetasika is the reality that is attached, which clings to everything, except lokuttara dhammas.[9] Lobha clings to the rūpa-brahma planes

---

[8]Rebirth in a rūpa-brahma plane is the result of rūpa-jhāna and rebirth in an arūpa-brahma plane is the result of arūpa-jhāna.

[9]Nibbāna and the lokuttara cittas that experience it cannot be objects of clinging.

and the arūpa -brahma planes, thus, these are vatthu kāma, the basis on which clinging depends. All dhammas other than lokuttara dhammas are vatthu kāma, they are the basis of clinging.

The "Atthasālinī" (§ 61-63) uses several methods to explain the meaning of kāmāvacara citta. According to the first explanation, kāmāvacara citta is the citta of the grade or plane of sensuousness, kāma; it is not free from kāma, sensuousness. According to the second method, kāmāvacara citta is the citta which frequents, "travels" to the sensuous planes of existence: the four unhappy planes,[10] the human plane and the six classes of heavenly planes (of the devas). According to the third explanation, kāmāvacara citta is so called because it attends to, frequents, the sense objects: visible object, sound, odour, flavour and tangible object. Since the citta takes these sense objects as its objects of experience, citta is called kāmāvacara citta.

It is easy to understand that any citta that is involved in sense objects, thus, visible object and the other sense objects, is kāmāvacara citta.

Questioner: Does the arahat have kāmāvacara citta?

Sujin: Yes. When the arahat sees visible object that appears through the eyes, the citta that sees is kāmāvacara citta, because visible object is a sense object. Whenever citta experiences visible object and the other sense objects, it is kāmāvacara citta, no matter whether it is the citta of the Buddha, an arahat disciple or anybody else.

According to the fourth method of explanation, citta is kāmāvacara citta because it causes rebirths in sensuous planes of existence, namely the four unhappy planes, the human plane and the six classes of heavenly planes.

All of us here are in the human plane, because kāmāvacara kusala citta has conditioned kāmāvacara vipākacitta to perform the function of rebirth in the human plane, which is a sensuous plane of existence.

Someone may develop samatha to the degree of attainment concentration (appanā samādhi) and attain rūpa-jhāna or arūpa-jhāna. If he does not lose his skill in jhāna and jhānacitta arises just before the dying-consciousness, the jhānacitta does not condition rebirth in this

[10]The hell planes, the animal world, the plane of petas (ghosts) and the plane of asuras (demons).

world but in a rūpa-brahma plane or an arūpa-brahma plane, depending on the degree of jhāna. Rebirth as a human being is the result of kāmāvacara kusala citta that performs dāna, generosity, observes sīla, morality, develops samatha or vipassanā. These ways of kusala, performed by kusala citta of the sense-sphere, citta that is not free from kāma, have rebirth in sensuous planes of existence as a result.

The term bhūmi, base or plane, has two different meanings: plane or grade of citta and plane of existence. As to the first meaning, bhūmi designates the citta that is the base or foundation for the accompanying dhammas (sampayutta dhammas), all cetasikas that arise together with the citta. As we have seen, we can classify cittas by way of four bhūmis or planes of citta: the cittas of the sense-sphere, kāmāvacara cittas, rūpa-jhānacittas, arūpa-jhānacittas and lokuttara cittas. As to the second meaning of bhūmi, this designates the plane of existence, the situation or place where a living being is born. The human world is one bhūmi, a plane where one is born. It is one plane among thirty-one planes of existence.

Citta is variegated. There are different types of citta and even cittas of the same type are varied. Kāmāvacara kusala cittas that arise are varied because the accompanying cetasikas are different and have different intensities, such as saddhā, confidence in kusala, which can be of different intensities, and paññā which can be of different levels. There is a great variety of the accompanying cetasikas. Thus, their result is rebirth in different happy planes, not only in the human plane.

When one commits akusala kamma, it can be noticed that akusala kammas are of different degrees, they can be more serious or they can be of a lesser degree. Sometimes there may be a great deal of hate or vengefulness, sometimes there may not be so much aversion. Sometimes one does not make a great effort to hurt or kill other beings; the intention to kill may not be very strong, and moreover, only tiny beings may die as a consequence of one's effort to kill. Since the different akusala kammas are performed by cittas that are accompanied by various cetasikas of different intensities, their results are varied, in the form of vipākacittas performing the function of rebirth in four different classes of unhappy planes. Since both kusala kamma and akusala kamma are variegated, causing variegated results, there must be many different planes where there can be rebirth. Besides the human plane, there are other planes of existence.

Questions

1. What is the difference between sensuousness of defilements, kilesa kāma, and sensuousness of base, vatthu kāma?
2. What is the meaning of "insignificant dhammas," paritta dhammas?
3. Did the Buddha have citta of the sense sphere, kāmāvacara citta?
4. What are the meanings of bhūmi, plane?

19
Planes of Existence

The term "bhūmi" can mean plane or grade of citta as well as plane of existence. Bhūmi as plane of existence is the world or place where living beings are born. There are thirty-one planes of existence, and these are in conformity with the different grades of citta which condition birth in these planes. The planes of existence are the following:

- 11 sensuous planes, kāmabhūmi,
- 16 rūpa-brahma-bhūmi,
- 4 arūpa-brahma-bhūmi.

This is a classification as thirty-one planes by way of different levels. Actually, there are many more places of birth included in each of these planes. Even this human plane is not the only human world, besides this human world there are others.

The eleven classes of kāmabhūmi include:

- four unhappy planes,

- the human plane,
- six heavenly planes or deva planes.

The four unhappy planes can be summarized as follows:

- hell planes,
- the animal world,
- the world of ghosts or petas (pettivisaya),
- the world of demons (asuras or asurakāyas).

There is not only one abyss of hell. There is a great abyss of hell and this has several abysses, such as the Sañjīva Hell, the Kalasuta Hell, the Sanghāta Hell, the Roruva Hell, the Mahāroruva Hell, the Tāpana Hell, the Mahātāpana Hell and the Avīci Hell. Apart from the great hells there are minor hells, but in the scriptures there is not much reference to these in detail. The Buddha explained about the different planes in order to point out cause and result. Kusala kamma and akusala kamma are causes that bring their corresponding results. What one cannot see clearly through direct experience should not be explained in a very detailed way and to the same extent as the realities one can verify oneself through the development of insight.

There are four classes of unhappy planes where living beings can be reborn. If rebirth is the result of very heavy akusala kamma there is rebirth in the "Great Hell," the "Avīci Hell," where one suffers extreme torments. When one is freed from that great abyss of hell and the working of kamma is not yet exhausted, one is reborn in a small abyss, a minor hell. When someone commits very heavy akusala kamma, he does not realize that rebirth in a hell plane lies ahead, since he has not gone there yet. So long as one is still a human being, living in this world, one does not go to another plane, even though the cause of rebirth in an unhappy plane, akusala kamma, may already be there. When someone has committed akusala kamma, it is a condition for rebirth in an unhappy plane after he has passed away.

The result of akusala kamma of a lesser degree conditions rebirth in other unhappy planes, such as the animal world. We can notice that there is an extraordinary variety in the bodily features of animals. Some kinds have many legs, some only a few, some are without legs. Some have wings, some are without wings. They live in the water or on land. It is due to the variegated nature of citta that their bodily features are so varied. The variety of bodily features of human beings is not as manifold as those of animals. All humans have a body and they generally have eyes, ears, nose and tongue. It is true that there are differences in skin colour and the length of the body, and that there is variety in outward appearance. However, even if one would take into account the differences in bodily features of all humans in the world, including people in the past, the present and the future, their diversity is not as great as the diversity of animals. The amount of variety in animals, including those in the water, on land and those that can fly, is far greater. All this is due to kamma, which causes such variety.

The result of akusala kamma of a lesser degree than that which conditions rebirth in the animal world, conditions rebirth in the planes of ghosts or petas. A ghost is tortured all the time by hunger and weariness. There are many different ghost planes. Every human being has a daily recurring disease, namely hunger, and that is the reason why one can say that it is impossible to be without disease. Hunger is a grave disease; one can notice this when one suffers from hunger. If there is but a slight feeling of hunger and one then eats delicious food, one forgets that hunger is a kind of suffering, something that has to be completely cured. It may happen that someone is very hungry but unable to eat because of circumstances, and then he will know the nature of suffering from hunger.

One day, a person who had many friends received their telephone calls from morning until evening, and, thus, he had no time to eat. Late at night he realized that hunger is a great torment and he understood the expression "pangs of hunger," referring to the stings in the stomach or the intestines, caused by hunger. He experienced what they were like. When he could finally eat, it was not possible to take a lot of food, all at once, to cure his hunger. This is harmful for the body and can cause fainting. He had to eat little by little, but he still fainted. This example shows that hunger is a grave disease, a daily recurring disease. Ghosts suffer tremendous hunger, for in the ghost plane there is no means of curing hunger. Agriculture is not possible on that plane, one cannot plant rice or obtain other crops. One cannot prepare any food, there is no trade by means of which one can obtain food. Thus, birth in a ghost plane is the result of akusala kamma. Ghosts can rejoice in the kusala of humans when humans extend merit to them in order to let them share in their kusala. When ghosts rejoice with kusala citta in the good deeds of others it can be a condition for them to receive food that is suitable in that plane. Or they may become released from life in the ghost plane; they may pass away from that life and be reborn in another plane. This can happen if the kamma that conditioned their birth as a ghost has been exhausted.

Another unhappy plane is the plane of the asuras, demons. Rebirth as an asura is the result of akusala kamma that is less grave than the akusala kamma that produces rebirth in one of the other unhappy planes. If someone is reborn as an asura he has no entertainment; no way to amuse himself with pleasant objects, such as there are in the human plane and in the heavenly planes. In the human plane one can read books, one can watch plays and attend concerts. In the asura plane there are no such ways of amusement with pleasant objects. Since akusala kammas are various and of different degrees, the planes where one can be reborn are also various, in conformity with the kammas that cause rebirths.

There are seven happy planes of rebirth that are the results of kāmāvacara kusala kamma, namely, one human plane and six heavenly planes or deva planes. In the Tipiṭaka it is explained that there are four human planes where one can be reborn:

- The Pubbavideha continent, situated to the East of Mount Sineru;
- The Aparagoyāna continent, situated to the West of Mount Sineru;
- The Jambudīpa continent, situated to the South of Mount Sineru, and this is the human world where we live;
- The Uttarakurū continent, situated to the North of Mount Sineru.[1]

[1]See "Visuddhimagga", VII, 42-44 and footnote 15. A circle of world-sphere mountains encloses the ocean. In the centre of the ocean is Mount Sineru or Mount Meru. The Southern continent of Jambudīpa, Rose-Apple Land, is the known inhabited world. Sometimes Jambudīpa refers to India.

Human beings who live in this world, the Jambudīpa continent (Rose-Apple Land), can only perceive this world. Wherever they travel, they see only the objects of the Jambudīpa continent. They are not able to go to the other three human worlds.

There are six heavenly planes and these have different degrees of excellence. As to the first plane, this is the heaven of the four deva rulers or guardians of the world, the "cātu-mahārājika plane."[2] These four deva rulers are:

- Dhaṭarattha, sometimes called Inda, ruling over the East, over the Gandhabba devas;
- Virūḷha, sometimes called Yama, ruling over the South, over the Khumbhaṇḍa devas;
- Virūpaka, sometimes called Varuṇa, ruling over the West, over the Nagas;
- Kuvera, sometimes called Vessavaṇa or Vesuvanna, ruling over the North, over the Yakkas.

The heavenly plane of the four deva rulers is the lowest class of heaven and this is not as far away from the human world as the higher heavenly planes.

There are higher deva planes and these have different degrees of excellence corresponding with the levels of these planes.

The second heavenly plane is the Heaven of the Thirty-three, Tāvatimsa, and this plane is higher than the plane of the four deva rulers. Inda is the chief of this plane. In the heaven of the Thirty-three there are four heavenly groves:

- Nandana Grove in the East,[3]
- Cittalatā Grove in the West,
- Missaka Grove in the North,
- Phārusaka Grove in the South.

[2]See "Visuddhimagga" VII, 40, footnote 14.
[3]See Jātakas VI, no. 545.

The third heavenly plane is the Yāma heaven, which is higher than the heaven of the Thirty-three.

The fourth heavenly plane is Tusita, which is higher than Yama.

The fifth heavenly plane is the "heaven of the devas who delight in creating," Nimmānarati, which is higher than Tusita.

The sixth heavenly plane is the "heaven of devas who rule over others' creations," Paranimittavasavatti, which is higher than Nimmānarati. This plane is the highest of the sense sphere planes.

To which heavenly plane would we like to go? Someone who is not an arahat still has to be reborn, but where will he be reborn? It will probably not be in a brahma plane, because birth as a brahma in a brahma plane is the result of kusala jhānacitta if this arises just before dying, as has been explained. Thus, rebirth in a sensuous plane is more likely. Whether there will be rebirth in an unhappy plane or a happy plane depends on the cause that produces rebirth, namely kamma, a deed that has been performed during the cycle of lives.

The rūpāvacara bhūmis, fine material planes of existence, are the planes where rūpa brahmas are born. Birth in these planes is the result of fine-material jhāna, rūpa-jhāna. There are sixteen rūpa brahma planes.[4]

The result of the first jhāna can be birth in three planes:

- birth in the Pārisajja plane, the result of kusala jhānacitta of a weak degree;
- birth in the Purohita plane, the result of kusala jhānacitta of medium degree;
- birth in the Mahābrahmā plane, the result of kusala jhānacitta of superior degree.

The result of the second jhāna of the fourfold system (and the third jhāna of the fivefold system)[5] can be birth in three planes. This depends

[4]See the Second Book of the Abhidhamma, the "Book of Analysis," Ch 18, 6, Age limit.

[5]For some individuals rūpa-jhāna is of four stages, and for some it is of five stages. Jhāna factors are successively abandoned as higher stages of jhāna are reached. For those who have abandoned the two factors of applied thinking and sustained thinking

on the degree of jhāna, which can be weak, medium or superior. These planes are:

- Parittābha bhūmi,
- Appamāṇabha bhūmi,
- Ābhassara bhūmi.

The result of the third jhāna of the fourfold system (and the fourth jhāna of the fivefold system) can be birth in the following three planes, depending on the degree of jhāna:

- Parittasubha bhūmi,
- Appamāṇasubha bhūmi,
- Subhakiṇha bhūmi.

The result of the fourth jhāna of the fourfold system (and the fifth jhāna of the fivefold system) can be birth in the Vehapphala bhūmi.

Moreover, there can be birth in the Asaññāsatta bhūmi as result of the fifth jhāna. Beings who are born in this plane are born only with rūpa, not with citta and cetasika.[6]

There are five Suddhāvāsā planes (Pure Abodes) for anāgāmīs and these births are the results of the fourth jhāna of the fourfold system (and the fifth jhāna of the fivefold system). They are:

- Aviha bhūmi,
- Atappa bhūmi,
- Sudassa bhūmi,
- Sudassi bhūmi,
- Akaṇiṭṭha bhūmi.

at the second stage there are only four stages of jhāna. For those who have abandoned only the factor of applied thinking and not the factor of sustained thinking at the second stage, there are five stages of jhāna.

[6]They have seen the disadvantages of nāma and this is the condition for them to be reborn without nāma.

There are four arūpa-brahma planes. Birth in these planes is the result of immaterial jhāna, arūpa-jhāna. The meditation subject of arūpa -jhāna is no longer dependent on rūpa. Corresponding with the four stages of arūpa-jhāna, these planes are the following:

- the plane of infinite space, ākāsānañcāyatana bhūmi;
- the plane of infinite consciousness, viññāṇañcāyatana bhūmi;
- the plane of nothingness, ākiñcaññāyatana bhūmi;
- the plane of neither perception nor non-perception, n'evasaññā-n'āsaññāyatana bhūmi.

In these four arūpa-brahma planes there are only nāma-khandhas, cittas and cetasikas, there is no arising of any rūpa at all.

In the "Gradual Sayings" (I, Book of the Threes, Ch VIII, § 80, Abhibhu, 3) we read that the Buddha explained to Ānanda about the manifold world systems. In the "thousand lesser worlds" are included a thousandfold of the four human planes, of the deva planes and of the brahma worlds. We read that the Buddha said:

> "As far as moon and sun move in their course and light up all quarters with their radiance, so far extends the thousandfold world-system. Therein are a thousand moons, a thousand suns, a thousand Sinerus, lords of mountains; a thousand Rose-Apple Lands, a thousand Western Oxwains (Aparagoyāna), a thousand northern Kurus, a thousand Eastern Videhās; four thousand mighty oceans, four thousand Mighty Rulers, a thousand "Four Great Rulers" (the four world guardians), a thousand heavens of the Thirty-three, a thousand Yama worlds, a thousand heavens of the Devas of Delight, a thousand heavens of the Devas that delight in creation, a thousand heavens of the Devas that delight in others' creations, and a thousand Brahma worlds. This, Ānanda, is called 'The system of the thousand lesser worlds.' A system a thousandfold the size of this is called 'The Twice-a-thousand Middling Thousandfold World-system.' A system a thousandfold the size of this is called 'The Thrice-a-thousand

> Mighty Thousandfold World-system.' Now, Ānanda, if he wished it, the Tathāgata could make his voice heard throughout this last-named world-system, or even further, if he chose."

The explanation of the world-systems may not be as detailed as some people who have doubts would wish, but it shows the perfection of wisdom (paññā pāramī) of the Buddha, who is the "Knower of the Worlds" (lokavidū), the person who clearly knows all worlds.

As we have seen, the fourth aspect of citta, mentioned by the "Atthasālinī" is that citta is variegated according to circumstance, because of the sampayutta dhammas, the accompanying cetasikas. Therefore, cittas can be classified as different kinds in various ways. Cittas can be classified by way of the four jātis of kusala, akusala, vipāka and kiriya. Cittas can also be classified by way of the four planes of consciousness: kāmāvacara citta, rūpāvacara citta, arūpā-vacara citta and lokuttara citta.

Kāmāvacara cittas can be of the four jātis of kusala, akusala, vipāka and kiriya. The cittas of the higher planes, namely rūpāvacara cittas, arūpāvacara cittas and lokuttara cittas, cannot be of the jāti of akusala. Lokuttara cittas cannot be of the jāti of kiriya either.

Thus, rūpāvacara cittas can be of three jātis: kusala, vipāka and kiriya. Rūpāvacara kusala citta can cause the arising of rūpāvacara vipākacitta that performs the function of rebirth in one of the rūpabrahma planes of existence. The rūpāvacara kusala citta of the fifth stage of jhāna can condition rebirth as asaññāsatta, a being with only rūpa, in the asaññāsatta plane. As we have seen, there are sixteen rūpabrahma planes in all. The arahat who attains the stages of rūpa-jhāna has rūpāvacara kiriyacitta.

The arūpāvacara kusala citta can cause the arising of arūpāvacara vipākacitta that performs the function of rebirth in one of the four arūpa-brahma planes. The arahat who attains the stages of arūpa-jhāna has arūpāvacara kiriyacitta.

Rūpāvacara citta and arūpāvacara citta are sublime consciousness, mahaggatā citta. The "Atthasālinī" (I, Book I, Part I, Ch I, Mātikā, Triplets, 44) states:

> " 'Sublime' (mahaggatā) means, 'having reached greatness'[7],

[7] Mahā means great and gata means gone or reached.

from ability to discard corruptions, from the abundance of fruition, from the length of duration..."

It is most difficult to discard defilements. As soon as we have seen an object, like or dislike arises. However, when there is attainment concentration (appanā samādhi), thus, when jhānacitta arises, the citta is calm and one-pointed on the meditation subject that is experienced through the mind-door. At such moments, there is no seeing, hearing, smelling, tasting or the experience of tangible object. When there are jhānacittas, no matter for how long, there cannot be bhavanga-cittas in between, such as in the case of kāmāvacara cittas.[8] Kāmāvacara cittas experience an object for an extremely short moment, they are insignificant dhammas (paritta dhammas). The kāmāvacara cittas of seeing, hearing or thinking occur in processes that are of extremely short duration, they experience an object just for a moment. When cittas of the eye-door process arise and experience visible object which appears through the eye-door, and then fall away, there have to be bhavanga-cittas immediately afterwards. Bhavanga-cittas arise before there are cittas in the mind-door process that cognize the visible object that was experienced in the preceding eye-door process. Kāmāvacara dhammas, which are visible object, sound, odour, flavour, tangible object as well as the cittas that experience these sense objects, are all insignificant dhammas (paritta dhammas).

The mahaggatā cittas, "sublime cittas," namely the rūpāvacara cittas and the arūpāvacara cittas, are cittas that have reached excellence because they can subdue defilements. When there is attainment concentration, when jhānacittas arise and fall away in succession, there is no seeing, no hearing, no experience of an object through one of the sense-doors, neither is there thinking about these objects. That is the reason why it is said that mahaggatā citta discards defilements. However, when the jhānacittas have fallen away completely, kāmāvacara cittas arise again. When there are cittas arising in processes that experience objects through the different doorways, akusala javana-citta

[8] Those who are skilled in jhāna can have jhānacittas in succession for a long period of time. That is why jhānacitta is called sublime because of its duration. During the attainment of jhāna there is no bodily suffering. The jhānacitta is sublime because of its fruition; it can cause rebirth in rūpa-brahma planes and arūpa-brahma planes.

has the opportunity to arise if one does not perform kusala. So long as defilements have not been eradicated completely, akusala citta is likely to arise after seeing, hearing, smelling, tasting and the experience of tangible object. Do we realize that akusala citta arises time and again? If one does not realize this, one cannot subdue defilements nor can one develop the way leading to the eradication of defilements.

Before the Buddha's enlightenment, there were people who saw the disadvantages and the danger of akusala cittas which arise very soon after seeing, hearing and the other sense-cognitions. Therefore, they tried to find a way to temporarily subdue defilements. They found out that the only way leading to that goal was not to see, to hear or to experience the other sense objects. When one experiences sense objects, one cannot prevent the arising of defilements. People who understood this could cultivate the way of kusala which leads to true calm, temporary freedom from attachment (lobha), aversion (dosa) and ignorance (moha), and this is realized at the moment of attainment concentration, appanā samādhi.

At the moment of jhānacitta there are no sense impressions. There is only the experience of the meditation subject through the mind-door and this is a condition for the citta to be firmly established in calmness and one-pointedness on that object. Attainment concentration that is reached when jhānacitta arises does not lead to the complete eradication of defilements. When the jhānacittas have fallen away, defilements have the opportunity to arise again. Only at the moments of rūpāvacara citta and arūpāvacara citta, citta has reached excellence; it is mahaggatā citta, because it can subdue defilements by not seeing, hearing, smelling, tasting or experiencing tangible object.

This is different in the case of the anāgāmī (non-returner), the person who has reached the third stage of enlightenment. He sees, but there is no attachment to visible object, since he has eradicated attachment to sense objects. He hears, smells, tastes and experiences through the bodysense the tangible objects of heat, cold, hardness, softness, motion and pressure, but he has no attachment, he has eradicated attachment to these objects. The lokuttara kusala citta, which is the magga-citta, path-consciousness, can eradicate defilements completely. Thus, we see that citta is variegated as there are four planes of citta that are the four grades or levels of kāmāvacara, rūpāvacara, arūpāvacara and lokuttara.

Rūpāvacara citta and arūpāvacara citta can be of three jātis: kusala, vipāka and kiriya.

Lokuttara citta is of two jātis: kusala and vipāka. There is no lokuttara kiriyacitta.

There are eight types of lokuttara citta, corresponding with the four stages of enlightenment. For each stage there is the magga-citta, path-consciousness, which is lokuttara kusala citta, and the fruition-consciousness, phala-citta, which is lokuttara vipākacitta. The eight types of lokuttara cittas are the following:

- path-consciousness of the sotāpanna (sotāpatti magga-citta), which is lokuttara kusala citta;
- fruition-consciousness of the sotāpanna (sotāpatti phala-citta) which is lokuttara vipākacitta;
- path-consciousness of the sakadāgāmī (sakadāgāmī magga-citta), which is lokuttara kusala citta;
- fruition-consciousness of the sakadāgāmī (sakadāgāmī phala-citta), which is lokuttara vipākacitta;
- path-consciousness of the anāgāmī (anāgāmī magga-citta), which is lokuttara kusala citta;
- fruition-consciousness of the anāgāmī (anāgāmī phala-citta), which is lokuttara vipākacitta;
- path-consciousness of the arahat (arahatta magga-citta), which is lokuttara kusala citta;
- fruition-consciousness of the arahat (arahatta phala-citta), which is lokuttara vipākacitta.

The lokuttara kusala citta is the condition for the lokuttara vipākacitta to succeed it immediately; there is no other type of citta arising in between the lokuttara kusala citta, which is cause, and the lokuttara vipākacitta, which is result. Apart from the lokuttara kusala citta, no other type of kusala citta can produce vipākacitta immediately succeeding it.

As soon as the magga-citta of the sotāpanna, which is lokuttara kusala citta, has fallen away, it is succeeded by the phala-citta that is lokuttara vipākacitta. It is the same in the case of the magga-citta and the phala-citta of the sakadāgāmī, the anāgāmī and the arahat.

The four types of lokuttara vipākacitta, the phala-cittas, cannot perform the functions of rebirth, bhavanga and dying. They are different from mundane vipākacittas.[9] The lokuttara vipākacitta that immediately succeeds the lokuttara kusala citta also has nibbāna as object. The lokuttara vipākacitta, the phala-citta, performs the function of javana in the same process as the lokuttara kusala citta that precedes it. The phala-citta is the only type of vipākacitta that can perform the function of javana in a process. It performs the function of javana and it has nibbāna as object. Each type of lokuttara kusala citta arises only once in the cycle of birth and death and it eradicates defilements completely, in conformity with the stage of enlightenment that has been attained. However, there are two or three lokuttara vipākacittas arising after the lokuttara kusala citta; these succeed one another and have nibbāna as object. It depends on the type of person who attains enlightenment whether phala-citta arises two or three times.

The sotāpanna cannot be reborn more than seven times. As we have seen, the phala-citta of the sotāpanna cannot perform the function of rebirth. The type of vipākacitta which performs for the sotāpanna the function of rebirth is in accordance with the plane of existence where he will be reborn. If the sotāpanna is reborn in a heavenly plane, kāmāvacara vipākacitta performs the function of rebirth. If the sotāpanna is reborn in a brahma plane, rūpāvacara vipākacitta or arūpāvacara vipākacitta performs the function of rebirth in accordance with that plane.

As we have seen, the word bhūmi, plane, can refer to the grade of citta as well as to the plane of existence for living beings. Summarizing, when bhūmi is used in the sense of grade of citta, there are four bhūmis: kāmāvacara citta, rūpāvacara citta, arūpāvacara citta and lokuttara citta. When bhūmi is used in the sense of the place where living beings are born, the world where they live, there are thirty-one planes and

[9]The magga-citta does not lead to rebirth; it eradicates defilements, the conditions for rebirth.

these correspond with the different grades of citta: eleven kāma bhūmis, sixteen rūpa-brahma planes and four arūpa-brahma planes.

Questions

1. What is the Suddhāvāsā plane (Pure Abodes) and who can be born there?
2. Of how many jātis can rūpāvacara citta and arūpāvacara citta be?
3. Of how many jātis can lokuttara cittas be?
4. Which types of citta are mahaggatā, sublime?
5. Which type of vīthi-citta, citta arising in a process, is the lokuttara citta?

20
Feelings

Cittas are variegated because of different sampayutta dhammas, the accompanying cetasikas. Cittas can be classified by way of the different accompanying feelings:

- cittas accompanied by pleasant feeling, somanassa sahagata;[1]
- cittas accompanied by unpleasant feeling, domanassa sahagata;
- cittas accompanied by indifferent feeling (neither pleasant nor unpleasant), upekkhā sahagata;
- citta accompanied by bodily pleasant feeling, sukha sahagata;
- citta accompanied by (bodily) painful feeling, dukkha sahagata.

Every citta that arises is accompanied by the cetasika that is feeling, vedanā. The different cittas are accompanied by specific feelings,

[1] Sahagata means accompanied.

depending on the type of citta. Citta is the "leader" in knowing the different characteristics of objects and cetasika is the dhamma which feels on account of the object that is experienced; it can be happy feeling, unhappy feeling, pleasant bodily feeling, painful feeling or indifferent feeling.

Citta is different according to its jāti, that is kusala, akusala, vipāka or kiriya, and the accompanying cetasikas, are of the same jāti as the citta. Akusala cetasikas cannot accompany kusala citta, vipākacitta or kiriyacitta. Kusala cetasikas cannot accompany akusala citta, vipākacitta or kiriyacitta. Vipāka cetasikas cannot accompany akusala citta, kusala citta or kiriyacitta. Just as in the case of the other cetasikas, feeling is varied as it accompanies cittas of the different jātis of kusala, akusala, vipāka or kiriya.

If the Buddha had not explained in detail the characteristics of all kinds of dhammas, people would continue to have wrong understanding about vedanā cetasika, feeling. For example, painful feeling that is experienced when one has discomfort, sickness or pain, arises together with body-consciousness, the vipākacitta, which experiences tangible object through the bodysense just for one short moment. This feeling is not the same as (mental) unpleasant feeling, domanassa, arising when one is annoyed about an unpleasant object that impinges on the bodysense. Cittas are varied as they are accompanied by different feelings. The Buddha taught in detail which kind of feeling accompanies each kind of akusala citta, kusala citta, vipākacitta and kiriyacitta, and this is a most intricate subject.

Whenever we feel pain there is bodily painful feeling and this is akusala vipāka. However, when we are unhappy, disturbed and anxious because of that painful feeling, it is not vipāka. At that moment akusala feeling accompanies akusala citta that is displeased.

When we study the Abhidhamma in detail, we can have right understanding of vedanā cetasika that accompanies citta. If one does not study realities, one does not know whether feeling at a particular moment is kusala, akusala, vipāka or kiriya, and therefore, one is bound to be infatuated with pleasant mental feeling, pleasant bodily feeling or indifferent feeling.

We read in the "Gradual Sayings" (I, Book of the Twos, Ch VIII, On Characteristics, §7) that the Buddha said:

> "Along with feeling, monks, arise evil, unprofitable dhammas, not without them. By abandoning just those feelings, those evil, unprofitable dhammas do not exist."

Then the same is said about the other nāma-khandhas, apart from vedanākkhandha, namely: saññākkhandha, saṅkhārakkhandha and viññāṇakkhandha.

Vedanā cetasika, feeling, is the basis of clinging and clinging is very persistent. If one does not know the truth about vedanā cetasika, one cannot abandon the view that feeling is self.

The understanding of the nature of vedanā cetasika is a supporting condition for sati to begin to be aware of the characteristic of feeling. If one does not understand what feeling is, one will not notice that feeling is reality; that it arises time and again in our daily life, just like the other dhammas that appear through the sense-doors and the mind-door. These dhammas can only appear because citta arises and experiences them, and each citta is accompanied by feeling.

We should remember that if there were no feeling on account of what is seen, heard, smelt, tasted and experienced through the bodysense, there would not be anxiety and akusala dhamma would not arise. However, since feeling arises, there is clinging to feeling, holding on to it. One wants to obtain for oneself things that can condition pleasant feeling. Thus, akusala dhammas continue to arise, but one does not notice this.

All dhammas are anattā; nobody can prevent feeling cetasika from arising. No matter what type of citta arises, it must be accompanied by feeling cetasika, which feels on account of the object that is experienced at that moment. Now, at this very moment, there must be some kind of feeling, be it indifferent feeling, bodily pleasant feeling, painful feeling, (mental) pleasant feeling or unpleasant feeling. The study of the Dhamma is not merely knowledge of names and numbers. The aim of the study is knowing the characteristics of realities, thus also of feeling which is arising now. There may not yet be awareness of the characteristic of the feeling of this moment, but we should remember that the feeling of this moment is a reality that has arisen and fallen away already. If one does not know the true characteristic of feeling, one is bound to take pleasant and painful bodily feeling, mental pleasant and unpleasant feeling and indifferent feeling for self.

If sati is not aware of the characteristic of feeling, it will not be possible to abandon the wrong view that dhammas are living beings, persons or self. We all consider feeling as something very important in life. We all want pleasant feeling, nobody wants to have unpleasant feeling. Therefore, we strive with all means to have bodily pleasant feeling or mental pleasant feeling. However, one may not know that there is at such moments clinging, that one tries to hold on to feeling which arises because of its own conditions and then falls away again.

The Buddha classified feeling cetasika as a separate khandha, vedanākkhandha, because people attach great importance to feeling and cling to it. It is a reality people take for self, as a living being or a person, as being of the greatest value. It is necessary to listen to the Dhamma and study it evermore in detail, to consider what one has learnt and to investigate the truth of dhammas in daily life, so that sati can arise and be aware of the characteristics of the dhammas that appear.

Vedanā cetasika can be of the four jātis of kusala, akusala, vipāka and kiriya. Feeling is a conditioned dhamma, saṅkhāra dhamma. It arises because of its appropriate conditions. Feeling which is vipāka arises because of kamma-condition, kamma-paccaya. Feeling which is kusala, akusala or kiriya is not vipāka, it cannot arise because of kamma-condition, but it arises because of other conditions. There are different ways of classifying feeling, but when it is classified as fivefold,[2] pleasant bodily feeling and painful feeling are of the jāti that is vipāka, they are the results of kamma. Kamma that has been performed in the past conditions accordingly the arising of the feelings that are vipāka, which feel on account of the objects impinging on the sense-doors and the mind-door.

Seeing-consciousness, which is vipākacitta, is accompanied by indifferent feeling, which is vipāka cetasika, and also by other cetasikas. It is the same in the case of hearing-consciousness, smelling-consciousness and tasting-consciousness. However, it is different in the case of body-consciousness. Body-consciousness which is akusala vipāka and which experiences a characteristic of tangible object impinging on the bodysense,

[2] Feeling can also be classified as threefold: pleasant feeling, unpleasant feeling and indifferent feeling. It can be classified by way of contact through the six doorways, and by other ways.

is accompanied by painful feeling. Body-consciousness that is kusala vipāka is accompanied by pleasant bodily feeling.

Nobody can change the conditions for the arising of the feelings that accompany these different types of citta. Body-consciousness arises because of kamma-condition. When the Great Elements (hardness, softness, heat, cold, motion or pressure) that are pleasant objects (iṭṭhārammaṇa) impinge on the rūpa that is bodysense (kāyappasāda rūpa), pleasant bodily feeling arises. When the Great Elements that are unpleasant objects, (aniṭṭhārammaṇa) impinge on the bodysense, painful bodily feeling arises. The feeling that arises at the bodysense can only be painful feeling or pleasant bodily feeling, not indifferent feeling, pleasant (mental) feeling or unpleasant feeling. The bodily feelings and the mental feelings should be distinguished from each other. When body-consciousness arises, the accompanying feelings, pleasant bodily feeling and painful feeling, are of the jāti that is vipāka, they are results of past kamma. However, when one is disturbed or anxious, there is unhappy feeling and this is not the result of past kamma. It arises because it is conditioned by accumulated akusala dhamma.

Apart from painful and pleasant bodily feeling, which can only be of the jāti which is vipāka, and unpleasant (mental) feeling, which can only be of the jāti which is akusala, there are other kinds of feelings, namely pleasant (mental) feeling and indifferent feeling. These can be kusala, akusala, vipāka or kiriya. The fact that there is such a variety of feelings makes it clear to us that realities can only arise because of their appropriate conditions.

Have we ever been aware of the characteristics of different feelings? At this moment, feeling arises and falls away. Some people may have begun to be aware of the characteristics of rūpas appearing through the eyes, the ears, the nose, the tongue or the bodysense. Others may be inclined to consider and be aware of characteristics of nāmas, elements that experience objects, when there is seeing, hearing, smelling, tasting, body-consciousness or thinking. However, this is not enough. Sati should be aware of the characteristics of dhammas which are classified as the five khandhas: rūpakkhandha, vedanākkhandha, saññākkhandha, saṅkhārakkhandha (formations or activities, the cetasikas other than vedanā and saññā, remembrance) and viññāṇakkhandha. If sati is not yet aware of these dhammas, defilements cannot be eradicated. Defilements cannot be eradicated if there is ignorance of realities, thus, if sati is not aware of the characteristics of all realities that are appearing.

Is there feeling while we are asleep? Dhamma is a subject that we should reflect on time and again. The more we investigate the Dhamma the more shall we gain clear understanding of it. Therefore, we should consider whether there is feeling cetasika, also while we are asleep. When we are fast asleep we do not experience any object of this world. There are no objects appearing through the six doors. At such moments, we do not think, nor do we dream. What we saw or heard before, what we liked or thought about does not appear. However, also when we are fast asleep, there must be cittas arising and falling away, so long as our life term has not come to an end. These are bhavanga-cittas, life-continuum, which preserve the continuity in one's life as this particular individual. As soon as we wake up the objects of this world appear, until it is time to go to sleep again.

While we are fast asleep, the bhavanga-cittas that are arising and falling away in succession are vipākacittas, the result of past kamma; kamma is the condition for the bhavanga-cittas to arise in succession and to preserve the continuity in the life of a person. Therefore, the person who sleeps does not die yet. The four nāma-khandhas, citta and cetasikas, have to arise together, they cannot be separated from each other. Each time citta arises there must be cetasikas that accompany the citta. Feeling arises with every citta. The feeling cetasika that accompanies bhavanga-citta is vipāka cetasika and it feels on account of the object that is experienced by the bhavanga-citta. All the accompanying cetasikas share the same object with the citta. The function of feeling cetasika is feeling on account of the object that is experienced by the citta. The object of the bhavanga-citta is not an object of this world; it is the same object as experienced shortly before the dying-consciousness of the preceding life. We do not know this object. Neither do we know the characteristic of the feeling accompanying the bhavanga-citta.

When we compare the situation of being asleep with the situation of being awake, it helps us to see more clearly the conditions for the experience of objects. The objects of this world can only appear because there are processes of cittas that experience them through the six doorways.

We should investigate further what exactly wakes up when we wake up and what exactly is asleep when we are asleep. Rūpa is the dhamma that does not know anything, thus, rūpa does not wake up nor does it sleep. Nāma is the dhamma that experiences an object. When nāma does not know an object appearing in this world, this state is called "being asleep." Also, while we are asleep, there are cittas arising and falling away in succession, preserving the continuity in one's life, so long as one does not pass away.

When we wake up, what is it that wakes up? Citta and cetasikas wake up, because they arise and experience an object through the eyes, the ears, the nose, the tongue, the bodysense or the mind-door. Thus, when we experience an object of this world we are awake. If we reflect on this fact in a more detailed way, it will be a supporting condition for the development of satipaṭṭhāna. The aim of the teaching of Dhamma is awareness of the characteristics of realities in order to know them as they are. The Buddha's words can encourage us to have right effort (viriya) for satipaṭṭhāna, the development of right understanding of the realities of this moment.

As we have seen, when we wake up, citta and cetasikas know the objects of this world. We have to consider more deeply what actually wakes up: citta and cetasikas wake up together. Vipākacitta arises and sees what appears through the eyes or it experiences what appears through the ears, the nose, the tongue or the bodysense. No one can prevent this; it is beyond control. Vipākacitta, which is the result of kamma, arises, experiences an object and then falls away. It would be impossible to sleep continuously; kamma causes one's birth into this life and it does not condition a person to be asleep his whole life until he dies. It is kamma which produces eyes, ears, nose, tongue and bodysense so that there are conditions for the arising of citta which sees a pleasant object, and this is the result of kusala kamma, or citta which sees an unpleasant object, and this is the result of akusala kamma. Citta that hears a pleasant sound is the result of kusala kamma, and citta that hears an unpleasant sound is the result of akusala kamma. It is the same with regard to the other doorways.

Thus, vipākacitta and cetasikas that arise wake up and experience objects through each of the doorways in daily life. Apart from these types of cittas what else is there? When one has woken up there are also akusala dhammas, all kinds of defilements which begin to wake up.

When one is asleep there are no akusala cittas, but there are the latent tendencies of defilements (anusaya kilesas), which lie dormant in the citta. The defilements that have not been eradicated are accumulated from one citta to the next citta, since cittas arise and fall away in succession. Thus, also when one is asleep, the accumulated defilements are carried on from one moment of bhavangacitta to the next moment of bhavangacitta. At these moments, defilements do not arise and there cannot be like or dislike of an object, since one does not see yet, one does not hear, smell, taste or experience tangible object yet, one does not experience any object of this world. When we are asleep, all the defilements are also asleep. However, when we wake up, the defilements wake up. After seeing, hearing and the experience of the other sense objects, all kinds of defilements arise with akusala citta, depending on the conditions that cause the arising of particular akusala dhammas.

As we have seen, cittas can be classified by way of four planes, bhūmis, of citta, namely, kāmāvacara bhūmi, rūpāvacara bhūmi, arūpāvacara bhūmi and lokuttara bhūmi. Cittas are more refined as they are of higher planes.

Cittas are mostly of the kāmāvacara bhūmi, of the sense sphere; thus, one experiences visible object, sound, odour, flavour or tangible object. Kāmāvacara citta is of the plane that is of the lowest grade. As soon as we wake up we see and hear. Citta turns towards the objects appearing through the eyes, the ears, the nose, the tongue, the bodysense and the mind-door. Citta frequents these sense objects. The cittas that arise in a day are of the lowest plane and moreover, they are usually of the most inferior jāti, that is, akusala. Usually it is akusala citta that wakes up, unless there are conditions for kusala. When we see, clinging follows seeing most of the time. We hear and then we are attached to the sound that was heard, and this is natural. Citta rooted in attachment arises more often than citta rooted in aversion, the citta that is annoyed and harsh.

We should face the truth that there are more often akusala cittas than kusala cittas in a day. If we do not realize this, we cannot develop kusala in order to be free from cittas that are inferior and mean. Then there will continue to be innumerable akusala cittas, just as usual. When we do not see the danger and disadvantage of akusala, we may even enjoy our akusala. Thus, we should remember that it is usually defilement, kilesa, which wakes up. Defilements arise in the processes of the eye-door, the ear-door, the nose-door, the tongue-door, the door of the bodysense and the mind-door.

It depends on the individual to what extent defilements will cause suffering of mind and body. When we realize the confusion and suffering caused by defilements, we shall apply ourselves to the development of kusala, be it dāna, sīla, samatha or satipaṭṭhāna. When one develops satipaṭṭhāna, there is awareness of the characteristics of the realities that are appearing.

Some people believe that they should try to eradicate lobha first, so that they are able to develop the paññā that leads to the stage of enlightenment of the sotāpanna. However, this is impossible. Lobha, attachment, arises, it is a type of reality that arises because of the appropriate conditions. It is not a being, person or self. However, paññā should consider the characteristic of lobha so that it can be known as it is: a type of reality that arises and then falls away.

The types of feeling arising with different cittas can be classified as fivefold in the following way:

- pleasant bodily feeling, accompanying body-consciousness that is kusala vipāka;
- painful feeling, accompanying body-consciousness that is akusala vipāka;
- unpleasant feeling, accompanying the two types of dosa-mūla-citta;
- pleasant (mental) feeling, which can accompany cittas that are kusala, akusala, vipāka and kiriya;
- indifferent feeling, which can accompany cittas that are kusala, akusala, vipāka and kiriya.

Unpleasant feeling cannot accompany cittas that are kusala, vipāka and kiriya. It can accompany only akusala citta, namely, the two types of dosa-mūla-citta, citta rooted in aversion.[3] If one does not know this,

[3]One type is not induced and one type is induced. This will be explained later on.

one may take for kusala what is in fact akusala. This may happen, for example, when one feels sorry for people who suffer and who are in trouble. One wants to help them so that they are relieved from their distress. There may be conditions for kusala citta with true compassion, karuṇā cetasika. However, one should know the characteristic of the feeling that accompanies the citta, one should know whether one has unpleasant feeling or not. When one has unpleasant feeling, when one is sad, there is akusala citta. Akusala citta is completely different from kusala citta that is accompanied by compassion, karuṇā cetasika. If one truly understands this, one can abandon the sad, unhappy feeling that is akusala. Then one will be able to help someone else to be free from suffering with feeling that is happy, not unpleasant or sad.

Therefore, one should know precisely when the citta is akusala, so that akusala can be eliminated. People usually believe, when they have compassion for someone who suffers, that they should also take part in his sadness and unhappiness. They do not realize that this is not true compassion.

People are usually ignorant of their feelings. If someone is asked what feeling he has at this moment, he may only know vaguely whether he feels indifferent, happy or unhappy. Feeling arises with each citta, but it is not easy to realize its true nature, even when there is awareness of feeling. Feeling is only a reality that experiences, a kind of nāma. When sound appears, the citta that is hearing-consciousness hears sound. At that moment there is feeling, vedanā cetasika, which accompanies hearing-consciousness. When the cetasika that is contact, phassa, contacts the object, vedanā cetasika must also arise. If sati can begin to be aware of the characteristic of citta or of feeling, supporting conditions are accumulated for being less forgetful of realities when we have indifferent feeling, happy feeling, bodily pleasant feeling, painful feeling or unhappy feeling. We may be sad, but instead of giving in to unhappy feeling, there can be sati that is aware of it and then it can be known as only feeling cetasika arising because of conditions. Thus, we see that satipaṭṭhāna is beneficial, that right understanding can relieve suffering when one is distressed and feels unhappy.

Questions

1. Of which jātis can indifferent feeling and pleasant feeling be?
2. Of which jāti are painful feeling and bodily pleasant feeling?
3. Of which jāti is unpleasant feeling?
4. Of which jāti is the feeling when one is fast asleep?
5. Can rūpa wake up or be asleep? Explain the reason.

21 Associated Dhammas

Cittas can be classified by way of different associated dhammas, sampayutta dhammas, and these are the accompanying cetasikas that cause them to be variegated. Cittas can be classified as sampayutta, associated with particular cetasikas, and as vippayutta, disassociated from them. When cittas are differentiated by this way of classification, five particular cetasikas are referred to, namely wrong view (diṭṭhi), aversion (dosa), doubt (vicikicchā), restlessness (uddhacca) and wisdom, paññā. Four of these cetasikas are akusala and one is sobhana. As regards the akusala cetasikas citta can be associated with, there is the following classification:

- diṭṭhigata-sampayutta: citta associated with diṭṭhi cetasika, wrong view;
- paṭigha-sampayutta: citta associated with dosa cetasika;
- vicikicchā sampayutta: citta associated with vicikicchā cetasika, doubt about realities;

- uddhacca-sampayutta: citta associated with uddhacca cetasika, restlessness.

As regards the sobhana cetasika citta can be associated with, there is the following classification: ñāna-sampayutta, citta associated with paññā cetasika.

The twelve types of akusala cittas which will be dealt with hereafter can be classified as associated, sampayutta, and dissociated, vippayutta, in the following way: of the eight types of lobha-mūla-citta, four types are associated with wrong view, diṭṭhigata-sampayutta; and four types are dissociated from wrong view, diṭṭhigata-vippayutta.

The two types of dosa-mūla-citta are associated with paṭigha, which is dosa cetasika, the reality that is coarse and harsh.

One type of moha-mūla-citta is associated with doubt, vicikicchā-sampayutta, and one type is associated with restlessness, uddhacca-sampayutta.

Thus, of the twelve types of akusala citta, eight types are sampayutta and four types are vippayutta.

The lobha-mūla-cittas that are associated with and dissociated from wrong view can be differentiated because of the accompanying feelings. Two of the four types that are associated with wrong view are accompanied by pleasant feeling and two types by indifferent feeling. Even so, two of the four types that are dissociated from wrong view are accompanied by pleasant feeling and two types by indifferent feeling.

Moreover, there is still another differentiation to be made. Lobha-mūla-cittas can arise without being prompted, asaṅkhārika, and they can arise because they are prompted, sasaṅkhārika.[1] Four types are unprompted and four types are prompted. The eight lobha-mūla-cittas are classified as follows:

1. Accompanied by pleasant feeling, with wrong view, unprompted (somanassa-sahagataṃ, diṭṭhigata-sampayuttaṃ, asaṅkhārikam ekaṃ).

2. Accompanied by pleasant feeling, with wrong view, prompted (somanassa-sahagataṃ, diṭṭhigata-sampayuttaṃ, sasaṅkhārikam ekaṃ).

[1] This will be explained further on.

3. Accompanied by pleasant feeling, without wrong view, unprompted (somanassa-sahagataṃ, diṭṭhigata-vippayuttaṃ, asaṅkhārikam ekaṃ).

4. Accompanied by pleasant feeling, without wrong view, prompted (somanassa-sahagataṃ, diṭṭhigata-vippayuttaṃ, sasaṅkhārikam ekaṃ).

5. Accompanied by indifferent feeling, with wrong view, unprompted (upekkhā-sahagataṃ, diṭṭhigata-sampayuttaṃ, asaṅkhārikam ekaṃ.

6. Accompanied by indifferent feeling, with wrong view, prompted (upekkhā-sahagataṃ, diṭṭhigata-sampayuttaṃ, sasaṅkhārikam ekaṃ).

7. Accompanied by indifferent feeling, without wrong view, unprompted (upekkhā-sahagataṃ, diṭṭhigata-vippayuttaṃ, asaṅkhārikam ekaṃ).

8. Accompanied by indifferent feeling, without wrong view, prompted (upekkhā-sahagataṃ, diṭṭhigata-vippayuttaṃ, sasaṅkhārikam ekaṃ).

The two types of dosa-mūla-citta are associated with paṭigha, repulsion or anger, which is actually dosa cetasika, and, thus, they are both paṭigha-sampayutta. When there is unpleasant feeling, it is each time accompanied by dosa cetasika, the dhamma that is coarse, harsh and vexatious. The characteristic of unpleasant feeling is quite different from pleasant feeling and indifferent feeling. The two types of dosa-mūla-citta, which are both paṭigha-sampayutta, are accompanied by unpleasant feeling. The two types of dosa-mūla-citta are different in as far as one type is asaṅkhārika, unprompted, without instigation, and one type is sasaṅkhārika, prompted. They are classified as follows:

1. Accompanied by unpleasant feeling, with anger, unprompted (domanassa-sahagataṃ, paṭigha-sampayuttaṃ, asaṅkhārikam ekaṃ).

2. Accompanied by unpleasant feeling, with anger, prompted (domanassa-sahagataṃ, paṭigha-sampayuttaṃ, sasaṅkhārikam ekaṃ).

There are two types of moha-mūla-citta. One of them is vicikicchā-sampayutta, accompanied by doubt (vicikicchā cetasika), which doubts about the Buddha, the Dhamma, the Sangha, the khandhas, the dhātus (elements), the past, the present, the future and other matters. The second type of moha-mūla-citta is called uddhacca-sampayutta, accompanied by restlessness.

Moha cetasika (ignorance) does not know realities as they are. Moha experiences an object, it is confronted with an object but it is unable to know the true characteristic of the object that appears. For example, when one is seeing now, one may not know that what appears through the eyes is just a rūpa, a kind of reality. There may also be doubt about realities. One may doubt whether it is true that one does not see people or things, as one always believed, but only a rūpa, appearing through the eyesense. Doubt does not arise all the time, but whenever there is doubt about the Buddha, the Dhamma, the Sangha and about the characteristics of realities that appear, there is moha-mūla-citta vicikicchā-sampayutta.

When we have seen, heard, smelt, tasted or experienced tangible object through the bodysense, the javanacittas that follow, when the cittas are not kusala, are often moha-mūla-cittas which are uddhacca-sampayutta, accompanied by restlessness. These types arise when the akusala citta is not accompanied by lobha cetasika, dosa cetasika or vicikicchā cetasika (doubt). Then we can know the characteristic of moha-mūla-citta that is uddhacca-sampayutta, arising when we are forgetful of realities and do not know the characteristic of the object that appears.[2]

The two types of moha-mūla-citta are classified as follows:

1. Accompanied by indifferent feeling, with doubt (upekkhā-sahagataṃ, vicikicchā-sampayuttaṃ).

2. Accompanied by indifferent feeling, with restlessness (upekkhā-sahagataṃ, uddhacca-sampayuttaṃ).

As we have seen, of the twelve types of akusala cittas, eight types are sampayutta, and four types are vippayutta.

As regards sobhana (beautiful) cittas, associated with paññā cetasika, these are called ñāṇa-sampayutta (ñāṇa is paññā cetasika).

[2]Uddhacca accompanies each akusala citta, but the second type of moha-mūla-citta is called uddhacca-sampayutta and in this way it is differentiated from the first type.

Cittas can be differentiated as unprompted, asaṅkhārika, or prompted, sasaṅkhārika. The term "saṅkhāra" which is used in the Tipiṭaka has several meanings. It is used in the following composite words: saṅkhāra dhammas, saṅkhārakkhandha, abhisaṅkhāra, as well as asaṅkhārika and sasaṅkhārika. In each of these cases, saṅkhāra has a different meaning.

Saṅkhāra dhammas are dhammas that arise because of their appropriate conditions. When they have arisen, they fall away again. All saṅkhāra dhammas are impermanent. There are four paramattha dhammas: citta, cetasika, rūpa and nibbāna. The three paramattha dhammas that are citta, cetasika and rūpa are saṅkhāra dhammas; they arise because of conditions, they are present for an extremely short moment and then they fall away completely. Nibbāna is not dependent on conditions, it is the dhamma that does not arise and fall away. Nibbāna is the unconditioned dhamma (visaṅkhāra dhamma).

The three saṅkhāra dhammas that are citta, cetasika and rūpa can be classified as five khandhas:

- rūpakkhandha, all rūpas;
- vedanākkhandha, feeling, vedanā cetasika;
- saññākkhandha, remembrance or perception, saññā cetasika;
- saṅkhārakkhandha, "formations", the other fifty cetasikas;
- viññāṇakkhandha, all cittas.

As regards saṅkhārakkhandha, this comprises the cetasikas other than vedanā and saññā, that is, fifty cetasikas. As regards saṅkhāra dhammas, these are all cittas, or eighty-nine cittas, all cetasikas, or fifty-two cetasikas, and all rūpas, or twenty-eight rūpas.

Saṅkhāra dhamma includes more realities than saṅkhārakkhandha: all cittas, cetasikas and rūpas are saṅkhāra dhammas, whereas only fifty cetasikas are saṅkhārakkhandha.

Among the fifty cetasikas that are saṅkhārakkhandha, volition or cetanā cetasika, is preponderant; it is foremost as kamma-condition. It is "abhisaṅkhāra"; abhi is sometimes used in the sense of preponderance. In the "Dependent Origination" (Paticcasamuppāda), ignorance, avijjā, conditions saṅkhāra and saṅkhāra conditions viññāṇa. Saṅkhāra as a factor of the Dependent Origination refers to cetanā cetasika, which is abhisaṅkhāra, the dhamma that is foremost in conditioning, as "kamma formation". It is actually kusala kamma or akusala kamma which conditions the arising of result in the form of vipākacitta, referred to as viññāṇa in the Dependent Origination. It is true that the other cetasikas are also conditions for the arising of citta. Phassa cetasika, contact, is for example, an important condition. If there were no phassa cetasika, which contacts an object, there could not be cittas that see, hear, smell, taste, experience tangible object or think about different matters.

However, phassa is not abhisaṅkhāra. It only contacts the object and then it falls away completely.

Thus, among the fifty cetasikas that are saṅkhārakkhandha, only cetanā cetasika is abhisaṅkhāra: cetanā that is kusala kamma or akusala kamma is a foremost condition, it is kamma-condition for the arising of vipākacitta.

Saṅkhāra as a factor of the Dependent Origination is threefold:

- meritorious kamma formation, puññ'ābhisaṅkhāra (puññā is merit, kusala);
- demeritorious kamma formation, apuññ'ābhisaṅkhāra;
- imperturbable kamma formation, aneñj'ābhisaṅkhāra.

Meritorious kamma formation is cetanā cetasika arising with kāmāvacara kusala citta and rūpāvacara kusala citta. Demeritorious kamma formation is cetanā cetasika arising with akusala citta. Imperturbable kamma formation is cetanā cetasika arising with arūpāvacara kusala citta, and this is kusala citta that is firm and unshakable.

Kāmāvacara kusala citta (of the sense sphere) arises only for a very short moment and this kind of kusala is not unshakable. It arises merely seven times in one process.[3] It is only occasionally that there is dāna, abstention from akusala or the development of other kinds of kusala. When there is no such opportunity, akusala citta arises very often, during many processes. Rūpāvacara kusala citta is kusala citta that is ñāṇa-sampayutta, accompanied by paññā cetasika. It is the citta that

[3]There are seven javana-cittas in a process, which are kusala cittas or akusala cittas in the case of the non-arahat.

has reached calm to the stage of appanā samādhi, attainment concentration or jhāna. Rūpāvacara citta is mahaggata kusala, kusala which "has reached greatness", which is sublime. However, it is still close to kāmāvacara kusala, since it has an object connected with rūpa.

Imperturbable kamma formation is cetanā arising with arūpa-jhānacitta. This citta is of the same type as the fifth rūpa-jhānacitta,[4] but it has an object that is immaterial, not connected with rūpa, and therefore it is more refined; it is unshakable. It produces abundant result; it conditions the

arising of arūpa-jhāna vipākacitta in the arūpa -brahma planes. In these planes the duration of a lifespan is extremely long, and this is in conformity with the power of the arūpa-jhāna kusala citta. Birth in a heavenly plane is a happy birth, because there is in such planes no disease, pain, bodily ailments or other discomforts such as occur in the human plane and in the unhappy planes. However, the duration of the lifespan in heavenly planes is not as long as in the rūpa-brahma planes, and the lifespan in the rūpa-brahma planes is not as long as in the arūpa-brahma planes. As we have seen, birth in the latter planes is the result of cetanā arising with arūpa-jhāna kusala citta. This type of cetanā or kamma is abhisaṇkhāra that is imperturbable or unshakable, āneñj'ābhi-saṅkhāra.

Summarizing the meanings of saṅkhāra in different composite words, they are the following:

- saṅkhāra dhammas, which are citta, cetasika and rūpa;
- saṅkhārakkhandha, including fifty cetasikas (vedanā and saññā are each a separate khandha);
- abhisaṅkhāra, which is cetanā cetasika, one among the fifty cetasikas included in saṅkhārakkhandha.

In addition, the terms asaṅkhārika and sasaṅkhārika are used for the differentiation of cittas. Kusala citta, akusala citta, vipākacitta and kiriyacitta can be without instigation, asaṅkhārika, or with instigation, sasaṅkhārika.

[4]The arūpa-jhānacittas are accompanied by the same jhāna factors as the fifth rūpa-jhānacitta. This will be explained further in the section on Samatha.

We read in the "Atthasālinī" (I, Part IV, Ch V, 156) that sasaṅkhārika means "with effort" or "with instigation". The instigation can come from oneself or from someone else. Someone else may urge one or order one to do something. It is the nature of citta as it naturally arises in daily life to be asaṅkhārika or sasaṅkhārika. No matter whether the citta is kusala or akusala, sometimes it arises of its own accord, because of accumulations that have been formed in the past and are thus a strong condition for its arising. Then it has the strength to arise spontaneously, independent of any instigation. The nature of such a citta is asaṅkhārika. Sometimes kusala citta or akusala citta that arises is weak, it can only arise when there is instigation by oneself or by someone else. Then the citta is sasaṅkhārika. Thus we see that kusala citta and akusala citta have different strengths, as they are asaṅkhārika and sasaṅkhārika.

Sometimes akusala citta is strong, it arises immediately because of accumulated like or dislike of the object that is experienced at that moment. Sometimes this is not the case. For example, someone may have no inclination at all to go to the cinema or theatre. However, when members of his family or friends urge him to go, he will go. Does the citta at such a moment really like to go? Someone may be indifferent to go or not to go, but if people urge him, he will go. If he were on his own, he would not go. Sometimes one may think that a particular film is worth seeing and enjoyable, but one still does not go because one does not have the energy, one does not feel the urgency to go immediately. This is reality in daily life. We can find out when there is citta with strength and when there is citta that is weak, no matter whether it concerns akusala, such as lobha and dosa, or kusala. Some people, when they have heard that there is a "Kaṭhina" ceremony, the offering of robes to the monks after the rainy season, want to attend immediately and they also urge others to attend. Some people, when they hear that this or that particular person will not attend a ceremony, may decide not to go, even though they have been urged to go. Thus, kusala citta as well as akusala citta have different degrees of strength and this depends on the conditions for their arising.

The Buddha explained that particular cittas can be asaṅkhārika or sasaṅkhārika in order to show us how intricate citta is. Cittas that arise may be accompanied by the same cetasikas, but the nature of these cittas can be different in as far as they are asaṅkhārika or sasaṅkhārika, depending on the strength of the accompanying cetasikas. The Buddha taught the Dhamma in detail and this shows his great compassion.

We read in the "Atthasālinī" (Book I, Part IV, Ch VIII, 160, 161) about four "Infinites", namely, space, world-systems, groups of sentient beings and the knowledge of a Buddha:

> "There is, indeed, no limit to space reckoned as so many hundreds, thousands, or hundred thousands of yojanas (one yojana being 16 kilometres) to east, west, north or south. If an iron peak of the size of Mount Meru were to be thrown downwards, dividing the earth in two, it would go on falling and would not get a footing. Thus infinite is space.
>
> There is no limit to the world-systems reckoning by hundreds or thousands of yojanas. If the four great Brahmās, born in the Akaniṭṭha mansion (the highest rūpa-brahma plane), endowed with speed, and capable of traversing a hundred thousand world-systems during the time that a light arrow shot by a strong archer would take to travel across the shadow of a palmyra tree, were with such speed to run in order to see the limit of the world-systems, they would pass away without accomplishing their purpose. Thus the world-systems are infinite.
>
> In so many world-systems there is no limit to beings, belonging to land and water. Thus infinite are the groups of beings.
>
> More infinite than these is a Buddha's knowledge."

With regard to infinite space, nobody can measure how many hundreds, thousands or hundreds of thousands yojanas space is. Neither can one count the world-systems. If one were to count the stars and the world-systems, one would never be able to finish, the world-systems are infinite. One cannot determine the number of living beings of all the different groups that live in the world-systems: the human beings, devas, brahmas, animals living on land or in the water, all beings in the unhappy planes. The wisdom of the Buddha is called infinite, there are no limits to it and it is more infinite than the other three infinites.

When we think of all beings that live in the countless world systems, the diversity of the cittas of all those beings must be endless. With regard to one individual there is a great variety of cittas, even of one class of citta, such as kāmāvacara kusala citta. Every citta arises only once, it is unique. The same type arises again but it is then a different citta. When we take into consideration the cittas of innumerable beings, we cannot imagine the variety of even one type of citta arising for living beings in the different planes.

The "Atthasālinī" states as to the type of kāmāvacara kusala citta, accompanied by pleasant feeling, associated with paññā, which is asaṅkhārika, thus, powerful, that it is classified as one type among the eight types of kāmāvacara kusala cittas. This is classified as just one type, although there is an endless variety even of this type of kāmāvacara kusala citta for one being and even more so for countless other beings.

Further on, we read in the "Atthasālinī" with regard to the classification of the kāmāvacara kusala cittas as eight types:

"Now, all these classes of kāmāvacara kusala citta arising in the countless beings in the countless world systems, the Supreme Buddha, as though weighing them in a great balance, or measuring them by putting them in a measure, has classified by means of his omniscience, and has shown them to be eight, making them into eight similar groups."

This classification as eight types of mahā-kusala[5] cittas is in accordance with the truth. They are classified as eight types: they can be accompanied by pleasant feeling, somanassa vedanā, or by indifferent feeling, upekkhā vedanā, accompanied by paññā or without paññā, asaṅkhārika or sasaṅkhārika. Summarizing them, they are:

1. Accompanied by pleasant feeling, with wisdom, unprompted (somanassa-sahagataṃ, ñāṇa-sampayuttaṃ, asaṅkhārikam ekaṃ).

2. Accompanied by pleasant feeling, with wisdom, prompted (soma-0nassa-sahagataṃ, ñāṇa-sampayuttaṃ, sasaṅkhārikam ekaṃ).

3. Accompanied by pleasant feeling, without wisdom, unprompted (somanassa-sahagataṃ, ñāṇa-vippayuttaṃ, asaṅkhārikam ekaṃ).

[5]Mahā means great. Mahā-kusala cittas are kusala cittas of the sense sphere, kāmāvacara kusala cittas. Mahā-kiriyacittas and mahā-vipākacittas are also cittas of the sense sphere, accompanied by beautiful roots, sobhana hetus.

4. Accompanied by pleasant feeling, without wisdom, prompted (somanassa-sahagataṃ, ñāṇa-vippayuttaṃ, sasaṅkhārikam ekaṃ).

5. Accompanied by indifferent feeling, with wisdom, unprompted (upekkhā-sahagataṃ, ñāṇa-sampayuttaṃ, asaṅkhārikam ekaṃ).

6. Accompanied by indifferent feeling, with wisdom, prompted (upekkhā-sahagataṃ, ñāṇa-sampayuttaṃ, sasaṅkhārikam ekaṃ).

7. Accompanied by indifferent feeling, without wisdom, unprompted (upekkhā-sahagataṃ, ñāṇa-vippayuttaṃ, asaṅkhārikam ekaṃ).

8. Accompanied by indifferent feeling, without wisdom, prompted (upekkhā-sahagataṃ, ñāṇa-vippayuttaṃ, sasaṅkhārikam ekaṃ).

Do we at times feel tired and bored, without energy? Sometimes the citta thinks of performing a particular kind of kusala, but then it is too weak, and fatigue and boredom arise. Can sati at such moments be aware of the characteristic of citta that is weak and without energy for kusala? If there is no awareness, there is a concept of self who feels that way. Fatigue, weakness, boredom, a feeling of being downcast, in low spirits and without energy, all such moments are real. If sati is not aware of the characteristics of such realities as they naturally appear, it will not be known that they are not a living being, not a person, not a self. They are only characteristics of citta that arises because of conditions and then falls away again.

The Buddha explained citta under many different aspects. One of these aspects is the classification of citta as asaṅkhārika and sasaṅkhārika. Lobha-mūla-citta can be asaṅkhārika or sasaṅkhārika. Also, dosa-mūla-citta and kusala citta can be asaṅkhārika or sasaṅkhārika. When sati can be aware of the characteristics of these realities, they can be known as nāma, different from rūpa. A feeling of being downcast or disheartened, of being in low spirits, without energy for kusala, is not rūpa. It is the nature of citta that is sasaṅkhārika, there is at such moments a citta that is weak.

Cittas differentiated as asaṅkhārika and sasaṅkhārika can only be kāmāvacara cittas. Kāmāvacara cittas are of the lowest grade of citta. These are cittas that usually arise in daily life, when there is seeing, hearing, smelling, tasting, experiencing tangible object or thinking about the sense objects. The kusala cittas or akusala cittas which arise on account of the sense objects sometimes have strength and, thus, arise spontaneously, and sometimes they are weak and arise with instigation. It all depends on conditions.

The cittas that are of a higher grade, namely, rūpāvacara cittas, arūpāvacara cittas and lokuttara cittas, are not classified by way of asaṅkhārika and sasaṅkhārika. All of them are prompted, sasaṅkhārika. The reason for this is that they are dependent on the appropriate development as a necessary condition for their arising. In this context, being sasaṅkhārika does not mean that they are weak, such as in the case of kāmāvacara cittas that are prompted, sasaṅkharika. Before rūpāvacara citta, arūpāvacara citta and lokuttara kusala citta arise, there must be kāmāvacara kusala citta accompanied by paññā each time. This is a necessary factor that induces or prompts their arising. Therefore, the cittas of the higher planes, rūpāvacara cittas, arūpāvacara cittas and lokuttara cittas are each time sasaṅkhārika and ñāṇa-sampayutta, accompanied by paññā.

We can come to know whether cittas in different circumstances of our daily life are asaṅkhārika or sasaṅkhārika. When we, for example, come to listen to the Dhamma, do we need to be urged by someone else? At first, we may not want to come of our own accord, we need to be urged. However, later on we come of our own accord, without being urged. In each of these cases the nature of citta is different, being sasaṅkhārika or asaṅkhārika. The citta is not all the time sasaṅkhārika or all the time asaṅkhārika. One may, for example, go to the cinema after having been urged, and, thus, the cittas are weak. However, afterwards, when one sits comfortably, one may enjoy oneself, one may be amused and laugh, and then the cittas are not weak, because one does not need any instigation to laugh or to have fun. While one enjoys oneself and laughs, the cittas with pleasant feeling are strong, arising of their own accord; they are asaṅkhārika. This shows us that citta is each time anattā, that it arises because of its own conditions. The citta that arises at this moment may be this way, the next moment it is different again, depending on conditions.

Questions

1. With how many types of citta does wrong view, diṭṭhi, arise?
2. With which types of feeling can diṭṭhi cetasika arise?
3. With which type of feeling does dosa cetasika arise?
4. With which types of akusala citta does pleasant feeling, somanassa vedanā, arise?
5. With which types of akusala citta does indifferent feeling, upekkhā vedanā, arise?
6. What is the meaning of the terms saṅkhāra dhammas, saṅkhārakkhandha, abhisaṅkhāra, asaṅkhārika and sasaṅkhārika?
7. When we take into account the eight lobha-mūla-cittas and the eight mahā-kusala cittas, in which ways are these two classes similar and in which ways are they different?

22
Roots

Cittas are variegated on account of the associated dhammas, sampayutta dhammas, which are roots, hetus.

The realities that are saṅkhāra dhammas, conditioned dhammas, cannot arise just by themselves, without being dependent on conditions for their arising. There are three kinds of paramattha dhammas that are saṅkhāra dhamma: citta, cetasika and rūpa. Citta is dependent on cetasika as condition for its arising and cetasika is dependent on citta for its arising. Some cittas are dependent on both cetasika and rūpa as conditions for their arising. Rūpas are dependent on other rūpas as condition for their arising. Some rūpas are dependent on citta, cetasika and other rūpas as condition for their arising.

Cittas are variegated on account of the different roots, hetus, which accompany them. Some cittas arise together with cetasikas that are hetus, whereas other cittas arise without hetus. Only six cetasikas are hetus:

3 akusala hetus:

- lobha cetasika is the hetu that is lobha

- dosa cetasika is the hetu that is dosa
- moha cetasika is the hetu that is moha

3 sobhana hetus:

- alobha cetasika is the hetu that is alobha
- adosa cetasika is the hetu that is adosa
- paññā cetasika is the hetu that is amohal

Dhammas other than these six cetasikas cannot be root-condition, hetu-paccaya. The cetasikas that are not hetus condition citta while they arise together with it, but they are not a condition by way of hetu-paccaya, by being roots. Hetu-paccaya is only one condition among the twenty-four principal conditions for phenomena.

The six cetasikas which are roots, hetus, can be compared to the roots of a tree, which make it thrive and become fully grown, so that it flowers and bears much fruit. When the six kinds of hetus arise, they also make the dhammas they accompany thrive and develop so that they can produce much fruit, evermore, again and again. Those who are not arahats still have both akusala hetus and kusala hetus. For the arahat there are no akusala hetus nor are there kusala hetus. The cetasikas alobha, adosa and paññā (amoha), that accompany the kiriyacitta which performs the function of javana in the case of the arahat are indeterminate roots, avyākata hetus, roots that are neither kusala nor akusala.[1]

Indeterminate dhammas, avyākata dhammas, are realities that are neither kusala nor akusala, namely: vipākacitta, kiriyacitta, vipāka cetasikas, kiriya cetasikas, rūpa and nibbāna.

As we have seen, the six hetus can be classified as twofold: as the three akusala hetus of lobha, dosa and moha, and as the three sobhana hetus of alobha, adosa and paññā. In this classification the term sobhana, beautiful, is used and not kusala. The hetus that are kusala condition kusala vipāka, result, which arises later on. Whereas sobhana

[1] As we have seen, the arahat does not perform kamma which can produce result, and thus, kiriyacittas perform the function of javana.

hetus arise with kusala citta, with kusala vipākacitta[2] and with sobhana kiriyacitta. Thus, sobhana hetus do not merely arise with kusala citta.

The four paramattha dhammas can be classified as twofold by way of not hetu (in Pāli na-hetu) and hetu:

- citta: not-hetu (na-hetu);
- cetasika: only six of the fifty-two cetasikas are hetu, the other forty-six cetasikas are not-hetu (na-hetu);
- rūpa: not-hetu (na-hetu);
- nibbāna: not-hetu (na-hetu).

Citta and forty-six cetasikas are na-hetu. Some cittas and cetasikas are accompanied by cetasikas that are hetus; they are sahetuka citta and cetasika.[3] Some cittas and cetasikas are not accompanied by hetus, they are ahetuka citta and cetasika.

Seeing-consciousness, which sees visible object that appears, is accompanied by only seven cetasikas: by contact, feeling, remembrance, volition, life faculty, one-pointedness and attention. Contact, phassa cetasika, performs the function of contacting the visible object that impinges on the eye-sense. Feeling, vedanā cetasika, performs the function of feeling; in this case it is upekkhā vedanā, which feels indifferent about visible object. Remembrance or perception, saññā cetasika, performs the function of remembering visible object that appears through the eyesense. Volition, cetanā cetasika, which performs in this case, since it is neither kusala nor akusala, the function of coordinating and urging citta and the accompanying cetasikas to accomplish their own tasks. Life faculty, jīvitindriya cetasika, performs the function of watching over citta and the accompanying cetasikas, maintaining their life, but only so long as they are present. One-pointedness or concentration, ekaggatā cetasika, performs the function of focussing on the object that appears. Attention, manasikāra cetasika, performs the function of being attentive to the visible object.

[2] Kusala vipākacitta can be accompanied by sobhana hetus or it can be ahetuka, without hetus.

[3] "Sa" means with.

These seven cetasikas are not-hetu, and, therefore, seeing-consciousness is ahetuka vipākacitta. Lobha-mūla-citta, which may arise after seeing, is accompanied by two cetasikas which are hetus: lobha, the dhamma which enjoys what appears and clings to it, and moha, the dhamma which is ignorant of realities. Thus, lobha-mūla-citta is sahetuka citta, accompanied by roots.

When we take into consideration hetu and na-hetu, and also sahetuka and ahetuka, saṅkhāra dhammas can be classified as follows:

- rūpa: is na-hetu and ahetuka;
- citta: is na-hetu; some cittas are sahetuka and some are ahetuka;
- cetasika: forty six cetasikas are na-hetu; some cetasikas are sahetuka and some are ahetuka. Six cetasikas are hetu: lobha, dosa, moha, alobha, adosa and paññā; the cetasikas that are themselves hetu are sahetuka when accompanying other hetus. Moha which accompanies moha-mūla-citta is ahetuka.

Lobha cetasika is sahetuka because every time it is accompanied by another hetu, by moha. If moha cetasika does not arise, lobha cetasika cannot arise either. Dosa cetasika is also sahetuka, since it has to be accompanied every time by moha. Moha that accompanies lobha-mūla-citta is sahetuka, because it arises in that case together with the hetu that is lobha. Moha that accompanies dosa-mūla-citta is sahetuka, because it arises in that case together with the hetu that is dosa. Moha that accompanies moha-mūla-citta is ahetuka, because moha is in that case the only root, it does not arise together with lobha or dosa.

Contact, phassa cetasika, which accompanies every citta, is not-hetu, na-hetu. Whenever citta arises together with a cetasika that is hetu, the accompanying phassa is sahetuka. Whenever ahetuka citta arises, the accompanying phassa is also ahetuka. Thus phassa, which is na-hetu, is sometimes sahetuka and sometimes ahetuka.

Our daily life consists of sahetuka cittas as well as ahetuka cittas. If one has not listened to the Dhamma and studied it, one will not know when there are sahetuka cittas and when ahetuka cittas. The Buddha explained in detail which cittas are ahetuka and which are sahetuka. He explained which types of hetus, and which types of other cetasikas are accompanied by sahetuka cittas; he also indicated the number of accompanying dhammas. For example:

- Moha-mūla-citta is accompanied by one hetu, by moha; it is eka-hetuka (eka means one).
- Lobha-mūla-citta is accompanied by two hetus, by moha and lobha; it is dvi-hetuka (dvi is two).
- Dosa-mūla-citta is accompanied by the hetus of moha and dosa; it is also dvi-hetuka.

As regards kusala citta, this must be accompanied by sobhana hetus, otherwise it would not be kusala. Kusala cittas can be differentiated as unaccompanied by paññā cetasika and as accompanied by paññā cetasika. Kusala citta which is unaccompanied by paññā arises with two hetus, with alobha, non-attachment, and adosa, non-aversion, and, thus, it is dvi-hetuka. Kusala citta that is accompanied by paññā arises with three hetus: alobha, adosa and amoha, thus, it is ti-hetuka (ti means three). Kusala citta cannot be accompanied by one hetu, it needs to be accompanied each time by at least the two hetus of alobha and adosa.

Root-condition, hetu-paccaya, is one condition among the twenty-four conditions. A conditioning factor is a dhamma which assists other dhammas and conditions their arising or maintains them, depending on the type of condition. Phassa cetasika, for example, is different from lobha cetasika, but both phassa and lobha are conditioning factors that assist other dhammas, citta, cetasika and rūpa, in conditioning their arising. However, since the characteristic and function of phassa are different from those of lobha, these two cetasikas are each a different kind of condition.

Phassa cetasika is nutrition-condition, āhāra-paccaya. This type of condition brings its own fruit or result, in this case feeling.[4] This type of condition is different from root-condition, hetu-paccaya; a root is a firm foundation for the dhammas it conditions. As we have seen, the hetus have been

[4]Material food, contact, cetanā and viññāṇa can be āhāra-paccaya. In the case of āhāra-paccaya, the conditioning dhamma maintains the existence of and supports the growth of the conditioned dhamma. See Appendix to Cetasika, under phassa.

compared to the roots of a tree, which make the tree thrive and develop. However, a tree does not solely depend on the roots for its growth and development. It also needs earth and water, it needs nutrition so that it is able to bear fruit. If, on the other hand, the roots are lacking, earth and water alone will not be able to make it grow and prosper. Thus, a tree needs different conditions for its growth. Even so, there are six hetus, which are root-condition, but besides these there are also other types of conditions. Phenomena condition other phenomena in different ways.

In the seventh book of the Abhidhamma, the "Conditional Relations," the "Paṭṭhāna", all the different ways of conditionality have been expounded. The first condition that is mentioned is root-condition, hetu-paccaya. Thus, we can see the importance of the dhammas that are hetus. When during a cremation ceremony the monks chant texts from the Abhidhamma, they start with "hetu-paccaya," comprising the six hetus of lobha, dosa, moha, alobha, adosa and amoha. Thus it is emphasized that the dhammas that are these hetus bring results, that they condition rebirth, and that, in this way, the cycle of birth and death goes on.

There are many kinds of conditions and all of them are important. The Buddha did not teach solely root-condition, hetu-paccaya. Nor did he teach solely object-condition, ārammaṇa-paccaya. In the case of object-condition, the object is a condition for citta to arise and to know that object. The Buddha taught all the different conditions in detail. He taught twenty-four principal conditions and also other conditions that are derived from some of the principal conditions.

The rūpa that is eyesense, cakkhuppasāda rūpa, does not arise from hetu-paccaya, but from other conditions. In its turn it is a condition for other dhammas as faculty-condition, indriya-paccaya. It is leader in its own function: it is the faculty that conditions seeing-consciousness to arise and to see the visible object that appears. Thus, it conditions seeing-consciousness by way of faculty-condition, indriya-paccaya. If there were no rūpas of eyesense, earsense, smelling-sense, tasting-sense and bodysense, the body would be like a log of wood. One would not be able to see, to hear or to experience the other sense objects. The five pasāda rūpas, the senses, are faculty-condition, they are leaders in performing their function, each in their own field. Eyesense is the leader as to its own function of receiving visible object, it is the condition for seeing-consciousness to arise and to see visible object. The other rūpas could not perform this function. It depends on the keenness of the eyesense whether what appears through it is clear or vague. This has nothing to do with someone's will or wish; it depends on the eyesense, which is faculty-condition for seeing.

Each kind of dhamma is a condition for the arising of other dhammas and there are different ways of conditionality. Lobha, dosa, moha, alobha, adosa and paññā condition other dhammas by being their roots. Many times a day akusala hetus arise, they arise more often than kusala hetus. At times there are kusala hetus and when these gradually develop and become more powerful, akusala hetus will dwindle. Paññā should be developed so that the characteristics of realities can be known as they are. It is paññā, the hetu of amoha, which understands realities as they are. So long as paññā does not clearly know the characteristics of realities, the akusala hetus of lobha, dosa and moha are bound to thrive and develop. There is no reality other than paññā, amoha, which can eradicate the akusala hetus. When one studies the Dhamma, understands the characteristics of the realities appearing through the six doors and develops satipaṭṭhāna, the kusala cetasika amoha, or paññā, will gradually grow. When one realizes the four noble Truths at the attainment of the first stage of enlightenment, the stage of the sotāpanna, different kinds of defilements are eradicated in conformity with that stage. It is at the attainment of arahatship that all defilements are eradicated.

The noble persons of the stages of the sotāpanna, the sakadāgāmī and the anāgāmī are called "learners," sekha puggala. They have to continue to develop paññā until, at the attainment of arahatship, akusala hetus as well as kusala hetus do not arise anymore. The arahat who has eradicated all defilements and has reached the end of rebirth, does not have kusala hetus, because these would be a condition for the arising of kusala vipāka in the future, endlessly. The arahat has cittas accompanied by alobha, adosa and amoha, but these are indeterminate roots, avyākata hetus, which do not condition vipāka in the future.

One may wonder whether one will ever reach that stage. We shall reach that stage one day if we are patient and persevere with the development of right understanding, day in day out. There were many people in the past who attained arahatship and if it were impossible to attain this result, there would not have been anybody who attained it. However, it cannot be attained as quickly as one would hope, the result is in conformity with the cause. If paññā does not arise yet, if it does not develop, defilements cannot be eradicated. Paññā can be gradually developed, stage by stage, and then it will be able to penetrate the true characteristics of realities. In this way, defilements can be eradicated.

We should never forget the aim of the study of citta, cetasika and rūpa. The aim is the development of satipaṭṭhāna, thus, the understanding of the true characteristics of citta, cetasika and rūpa, just as they naturally appear; one at a time. This is the truth the Buddha realized through his enlightenment and taught to others. It may happen that one has studied the Dhamma but does not practise in conformity with what one has learnt. That is an inconsistency. When one has studied the realities from the texts but one does not learn to directly understand them as they are when they appear, it is impossible to eradicate defilements.

The akusala hetus of lobha, dosa and moha that arise are of the jāti that is akusala, they cannot be of another jāti. The akusala hetus condition the arising of akusala citta and they are accumulated evermore and carried on to the future. The three sobhana hetus of alobha, adosa and paññā can be of the jātis that are kusala, vipāka and kiriya, as they accompany kusala citta, kusala vipākacitta or kiriyacitta. As we have seen, sobhana comprises more dhammas than kusala. Sobhana dhammas comprise realities which are kusala, kusala vipāka and sobhana kiriya.

When all dhammas are classified as three groups, namely as kusala dhammas, akusala dhammas and indeterminate dhammas, avyākata dhammas, the six cetasikas which are hetus are classified as nine in the following way:

- three akusala hetus, namely, lobha, dosa and moha;
- three kusala hetus, namely, alobha, adosa and paññā;
- three avyākata hetus, namely, alobha, adosa and paññā.

Questions

1. What is root-condition, hetu-paccaya, and which paramattha dhammas are root-condition?
2. What is indeterminate root, avyākata hetu, and which are the indeterminate roots?
3. What is avyākata dhamma and which realities are avyākata dhammas?
4. What is the difference between kusala hetus and sobhana hetus?
5. Which realities are na-hetu, not-root?
6. What is sahetuka and which realities are sahetuka?
7. Which of the hetu cetasikas are ahetuka and which are sahetuka?
8. Which akusala cittas are accompanied by one root, eka-hetuka, and which are accompanied by two roots, dvi-hetuka?
9. Can kusala citta be eka-hetuka? Explain this.
10. Is contact, phassa cetasika, hetu or na-hetu? Can it be ahetuka or sahetuka? Can it be eka-hetuka, dvi-hetuka or ti-hetuka, thus, accompanied by one root, two roots or three roots?
11. When hetus are classified as nine, which are they?

23
Sobhana and Asobhana

Cittas can be classified as sobhana and asobhana. Sobhana dhammas are realities that are "beautiful." Sobhana dhammas do not only comprise kusala dhammas, but also dhammas which are kusala vipāka, the result of kusala kamma, and sobhana kiriya dhammas, the cittas of the arahat who has neither kusala nor akusala.

Asobhana dhamma is the opposite of sobhana dhamma. Asobhana dhammas are dhammas that are not sobhana, not beautiful. Asobhana dhammas do not only comprise akusala citta and cetasika, but also all cittas and cetasikas that are not accompanied by sobhana cetasikas. Thus, when cittas are classified by way of associated dhammas, sampayutta dhammas, which condition citta to be varied, cittas can be differentiated as sobhana and asobhana. This means that cittas are classified as accompanied or unaccompanied by the cetasikas that are the sobhana hetus of alobha, adosa and paññā. The sobhana hetus are sobhana cetasikas, which condition citta to be sobhana. Therefore, the classification of citta as sobhana and asobhana should follow upon the classification of citta by way of hetus. All cittas that are accompanied by sobhana hetus are sobhana cittas and all cittas that are not accompanied by sobhana hetus are asobhana cittas.

When we study paramattha dhammas we should carefully investigate cause and result. If we clearly understand cause and result, we shall not have any misunderstanding as to sobhana dhammas and asobhana dhammas.

Akusala citta arises together with the akusala cetasikas of lobha, dosa and moha and thus it is clear that it is not sobhana citta.

Seeing-consciousness cannot arise together with lobha, dosa or moha, or with any of the sobhana cetasikas. Seeing-consciousness is accompanied only by seven cetasikas: contact (phassa), feeling (vedanā), remembrance (saññā), volition (cetanā), one-pointedness or concentration (ekaggatā), life-faculty (jīvitindriya) and attention (manasikāra). These seven cetasikas are the universals (sabbacitta-sādhāraṇā); they have to accompany each and every citta. Citta cannot arise without these seven cetasikas, no matter whether it is akusala citta, kusala citta, vipākacitta, kiriyacitta, lokuttara citta or any other type of citta. The seven "universals" and six other cetasikas, the particulars (pakiṇṇakā), which do not arise with every citta, can be of four jātis according to the type of citta they accompany.[1] The "universals" and the "particulars", taken together, are the aññasamāna cetasikas.[2] When the aññasamāna cetasikas arise with akusala citta, they are akusala, and when they arise with kusala citta, they are kusala. Whereas akusala cetasikas accompany only akusala citta and sobhana cetasikas accompany only sobhana citta.

Seeing-consciousness is vipākacitta, which is accompanied only by the seven universals, not by sobhana cetasikas or by akusala cetasikas. Thus, seeing-consciousness is asobhana citta, but it is not akusala citta.

When one studies the Dhamma, one should understand precisely the difference between akusala dhammas and asobhana dhammas. Akusala dhammas are realities that are mean, inferior, dangerous. They are causes that produce unpleasant and sorrowful results. Asobhana dhammas are citta and cetasika that are not accompanied by sobhana cetasikas. The Buddha taught the Dhamma by various methods and under differ-

[1]This will be explained further in the Appendix.

[2]Añña means other and samāna means common. When kusala citta is taken into account, akusala citta is taken as "other," and vice versa.

ent aspects, according to the true characteristics of realities. When we study the Dhamma we should investigate the characteristics of realities in detail, so that we can understand them as they are. As we have seen, dhammas can be classified as threefold, as kusala dhamma, akusala dhamma and avyākata (indeterminate) dhamma. We should remember that kusala dhammas are realities that are cause, producing kusala vipāka. Akusala dhammas are realities that are cause producing akusala vipāka. Avyākata dhammas are realities that are neither kusala nor akusala. They are vipākacitta and cetasika, kiriyacitta and cetasika, rūpa and nibbāna. Thus, avyākata dhamma comprises not only citta and cetasika that are vipāka and kiriya, but also the paramattha dhammas that are rūpa and nibbāna. Rūpa and nibbāna cannot be kusala or akusala because they are not citta or cetasika. Thus, all four paramattha dhammas can be classified as these three groups of dhammas. When dhammas are classified as four jātis, this classification refers only to citta and cetasika.

The cittas and cetasikas of the four jātis can be classified as sobhana and asobhana in the following way:

- akusala citta and accompanying cetasikas which are asobhana,
- kusala citta and accompanying cetasikas which are sobhana,
- vipākacitta and kiriyacitta (unaccompanied by sobhana cetasikas such as alobha and adosa) which are asobhana,
- vipākacitta and kiriyacitta (accompanied by sobhana cetasikas) which are sobhana.

Seeing-consciousness that is kusala vipāka and seeing-consciousness that is akusala vipāka are accompanied only by the seven universals. It is the same for the other four pairs of sense-cognitions, they are accompanied only by the seven universals. Thus, the five pairs of sense-cognitions, the dvipañcaviññāṇa, are asobhana cittas. Moreover, there are cittas other than these ten that are asobhana, not accompanied by sobhana cetasikas.

Some kusala vipākacittas are asobhana and some are sobhana, accompanied by sobhana cetasikas. Each citta that arises in daily life is different. The rebirth-consciousness arising in the human plane of existence is different from the rebirth-consciousness arising in an unhappy plane, they are results produced by different kammas. A being born in an unhappy plane has a rebirth-consciousness that is akusala vipāka, the result of akusala kamma. Rebirth-consciousness that is akusala vipāka can arise in a hell plane, a ghost plane (pitti visaya), in the plane of demons (asuras) or in the animal world. The rebirth-consciousness arising in the human plane or in one of the deva planes is kusala vipākacitta; birth in these planes is a happy rebirth, the result of kusala kamma.

Rebirth-consciousness arising in the human plane is kusala vipāka, but there are different degrees of kamma producing kusala vipāka. Those who are handicapped from the first moment of life have a rebirth-consciousness that is the result of a very weak kusala kamma, unaccompanied by the sobhana cetasikas of alobha, adosa and paññā. Since the rebirth-consciousness of such a person is the result of weak kusala kamma, akusala kamma has the opportunity to cause him to be troubled by a handicap from the time of his birth.

As regards human beings who are not handicapped from the first moment of their life, they are born in different surroundings: they are born into different families, some of which are poor, some rich; they are of different ranks; there are differences in the number of their attendants or companions. All these varieties are due to a cause, namely, the difference in strength of the kusala kamma that produced as result the vipākacitta performing the function of rebirth. If kusala kamma is accompanied by paññā of a low degree or unaccompanied by paññā, it can produce as result rebirth-consciousness which is kusala vipāka accompanied by sobhana cetasikas and the two hetus of alobha and adosa. That person is then dvi-hetuka, born with a rebirth-consciousness accompanied by two sobhana hetus but without paññā. In that life he cannot attain jhāna nor enlightenment.

When someone is born with a rebirth-consciousness accompanied by paññā, as result of kamma accompanied by paññā, then he is ti-hetuka, born with a rebirth-consciousness accompanied by the three sobhana hetus of alobha, adosa and amoha or paññā. When that person listens to the Dhamma, he is able to consider the Dhamma and to understand it. In that life he can, if he develops paññā of the level of samatha, attain jhāna. Or he can develop insight and, if the right conditions have been accumulated, he can realize the four noble Truths and attain enlightenment. Nevertheless, one should not be neglectful as to the development of paññā. Someone may have been born with three sobhana hetus and he may have accumulated sati and paññā, but if he neglects developing kusala or listening to the Dhamma, he may only be skilful as to worldly knowledge. If one does not develop insight, one will not realize the characteristics of realities as they are.

In former lives, people may have been interested in the Dhamma, they may have studied it and they may even have been ordained as a bhikkhu or a novice. However, for the attainment of enlightenment it is necessary for everybody to develop paññā, no matter whether he is a bhikkhu or a lay follower. Nobody knows in what state of life, as a bhikkhu or a layman, he will attain enlightenment. One must know as they are the characteristics of realities that appear; paññā must be developed life after life, until, during one life, it has become so keen that it can penetrate the four noble Truths.

In the past someone may have been interested in the Dhamma and occupied with the study of the Dhamma and applied it in his life, but one should never forget that so long as enlightenment has not been attained, accumulated defilements can condition one to go astray. Defilements are so persistent, so powerful, they can condition people to be neglectful of kusala and to be engrossed in akusala. Someone may have been born with a rebirth-consciousness that is ti-hetuka, with alobha, adosa and paññā, but if he is neglectful and does not listen to the Dhamma, if he does not consider it carefully and if he is not aware of realities, there cannot be any development of paññā in that life. It is to be regretted that someone born as ti-hetuka wastes his life by not developing paññā.

It is not sure which kamma will produce the rebirth-consciousness of the next life. It may happen that akusala vipākacitta will perform the function of rebirth in an unhappy plane, or that ahetuka kusala vipākacitta will perform the function of rebirth, in which case a person is handicapped from the first moment of life, or that dvi-hetuka vipākacitta performs the function of rebirth in a happy plane. In that case, someone is born without paññā and he is not able to develop paññā to the degree that the four noble Truths can be realized and enlightenment attained. Instead of neglecting the development of paññā one should persevere with its development so that it can grow and become keener.

When the rebirth-consciousness is sobhana citta, the bhavanga-citta is also sobhana citta. A human being who is not born with an ahetuka kusala vipākacitta, thus, who is not handicapped from birth, has, when he is fast asleep, sobhana bhavanga-cittas. If he is born with the two hetus of alobha and adosa, the bhavanga-cittas that are of the same type as the rebirth-consciousness are also dvi-hetuka. If he is born with the three hetus of alobha, adosa and paññā, the bhavanga-cittas are ti-hetuka. When we are fast asleep, defilements do not arise; we have no like or dislike, because we do not yet experience objects through the sense-doors. We do not see, hear, smell, taste, experience objects through the bodysense or think about different objects. When we wake up, happiness or unhappiness arises due to the different types of akusala cittas that arise in a day. When we are awake, there are more asobhana cittas than kusala cittas. Seeing-consciousness arises and sees what appears through the eyes just for one moment and then there are usually akusala javana vīthi-cittas, seven moments of them. Thus, javana citta arises seven times more than seeing-consciousness that performs the function of seeing just for one moment. A great deal of akusala dhammas has been accumulated from one moment of citta to the next moment, day in day out. Therefore, we should not be neglectful in the development of understanding while we study the Dhamma the Buddha explained in detail. The Buddha explained which cittas are sobhana, which cittas are asobhana and which of the asobhana cittas are akusala, vipāka or kiriya.

Questioner: Does the arahat have asobhana cittas?

Sujin: Yes, he has.

Questioner: Does the arahat have akusala cittas?

Sujin: No, he has not. The arahat has asobhana cittas but he does not have akusala cittas. For the arahat the sense-cognitions such as seeing or hearing arise, which are asobhana cittas, but he has neither akusala cittas nor kusala cittas.

There are fifty-two cetasikas in all: thirteen aññasamāna cetasikas, which can be of four jātis and which are of the same jāti as the citta and cetasikas they accompany, fourteen akusala cetasikas and twenty-five sobhana cetasikas.[3]

[3]This will be explained further in the Appendix.

It is important to have right understanding of the realities that are sobhana or asobhana. The Pāli term sobhana is often translated into English as beautiful, but this word may cause misunderstandings. One may believe that everything that is beautiful or pleasant must be sobhana. One may for example think that pleasant bodily feeling is sobhana, but this is not so. We should consider the reality of pleasant bodily feeling. As we have seen, feelings can be classified as fivefold:

- pleasant feeling,
- unpleasant feeling,
- indifferent feeling,
- pleasant bodily feeling,
- painful bodily feeling.

Pleasant bodily feeling, sukha vedanā, accompanies body-consciousness that is kusala vipāka, experiencing a pleasant tangible object. Body-consciousness is not accompanied by the sobhana cetasikas of alobha, adosa or paññā. Thus, the reality of pleasant bodily feeling is asobhana, not sobhana. If we do not correctly understand the Pāli terms that represent the different dhammas, we shall have misunderstandings about them.

We should know precisely which dhammas can be sobhana and which dhammas cannot be sobhana. Rūpa cannot be sobhana dhamma, although it can be a beautiful, pleasant object. Rūpa is the dhamma that does not know anything; it can neither be kusala nor akusala. It cannot be accompanied by kindness, compassion, sympathetic joy or any other sobhana dhamma. Only citta and cetasika can be sobhana or asobhana. Rūpa can be an object that conditions citta to arise and to like or dislike it, but rūpa itself is indeterminate dhamma, avyākata dhamma. Rūpa does not know that citta likes it or dislikes it. Rūpa itself has no intention or wish to be liked or disliked by citta, since rūpa is not a dhamma that can experience something. Citta experiences objects; it wants to see visible object, to hear sound, to smell odour, to experience pleasant tangible object, so that happy feeling can arise again and again. One wants pleasant feeling every day, whenever objects are experienced through the senses, or even whenever there is thinking about all these objects.

The five khandhas are objects of clinging, and this is shown in different similes. In the commentary to the "Visuddhimagga", the "Paramattha Mañjūsa" (See Vis. XIV, 221, footnote 83)[4] it is said that rūpakkhandha is like a dish because it bears the food which will bring happiness. Vedanākkhandha is like the food in that dish. Saññākkhandha is like the curry sauce poured over the food that enhances its flavour; because, owing to the perception of beauty it hides the nature of the food that is feeling. Saṅkhārakkhandha is like the server of the food being a cause of feeling. Viññāṇakkhandha is like the eater, it is helped by feeling.

Citta is the leader in knowing an object. Citta and cetasikas, the four nāmakkhandhas, must arise together, they know the same object and they cannot be separated from each other. All four nāmakkhandhas must arise together; there cannot be less than four nāmakkhandhas. In the planes where there are five khandhas, the nāmakkhandhas are dependent on rūpakkhandha, which conditions their arising.

We study the different types of citta so that we can understand precisely the characteristics of cittas that can be classified in different ways. They can be classified by way of the four jātis, the four classes as to their nature of kusala, akusala, vipāka and kiriya; by way of the three groups of kusala dhamma, akusala dhamma and indeterminate dhamma, avyākata dhamma; by way of hetus; by way of asaṅkhārika and sasaṅkhārika; by way of sobhana and asobhana. These classifications make it clear to us that cittas are accompanied by different cetasikas that cause them to be variegated. If we understand these classifications it can be a condition for sati to arise and to be aware of realities, so that they are known as anattā, not a self or a being. They are just nāma and rūpa, each with their own characteristic, appearing one at a time. Visible object appearing through the eyes is one characteristic of reality, sound is another characteristic of reality.

[4]The Commentary to the "Abhidhammattha Sangaha": "The body, being the support of feeling, represents the vessel; feeling, being the thing enjoyed, represents the food; recognition (saññā), being the means by which one savours the feeling, represents the seasoning; formations, as putting things together, represents the cook; consciousness, being the one who enjoys (it all), represents the one who eats".

Odour, flavour and tangible object are all different realities, each with their own characteristic. Kusala citta and avyākata citta are different realities each with their own characteristic.

If there is more understanding of all these realities which each have their own characteristic, conditions are accumulated for the arising of sati which can be aware and which can investigate the characteristics of realities that appear. In this way, the true nature of each dhamma can be penetrated.

Questions

1. Can rūpa be sobhana dhamma? Explain the reason.
2. What is the difference between a person born with a rebirth-consciousness that is kusala vipākacitta unaccompanied by sobhana cetasikas and a person born with a rebirth-consciousness that is kusala vipākacitta accompanied by sobhana cetasikas?
3. What type of kamma produces as result rebirth-consciousness accompanied by two hetus, thus, which is dvi-hetuka?
4. What is the difference between a person who is dvi-hetuka and a person who is ti-hetuka (born with three hetus)?
5. When a person is fast asleep, is the citta then sobhana or asobhana?

24
The World

Cittas can be classified as mundane, lokiya, and supramundane, lokuttara. First of all, we should understand the meaning of the world, loka, "according to the discipline of the ariyan", as the Buddha explained in the "Kindred Sayings" (IV, Kindred Sayings on Sense, Second Fifty, Ch IV, §84, Transitory). We read:

Then the venerable Ānanda came to see the Exalted One... Seated at one side the venerable Ānanda said to the Exalted One:

> " 'The world! The world!' is the saying, lord. Pray, how far, lord, does this saying go?"
>
> "What is transitory by nature, Ānanda, is called 'the world' in the ariyan discipline. And what, Ānanda, is transitory by nature? The eye, Ānanda, is transitory by nature, visible object is transitory by nature, seeing-consciousness is transitory by nature, eye-contact is transitory by nature, pleasant feeling, unpleasant feeling or indifferent feeling that arises owing to eye-contact, that also is transitory by nature.

(The same is said with regard to the other doorways.)

> What is thus transitory, Ānanda, is called 'the world' in the ariyan discipline."

For the ariyan, the person who has attained enlightenment, the transitoriness of realities is natural, but this is not so for the person who does not yet realize the arising and falling away of realities. Someone cannot become an ariyan if he does not see the arising and falling away of the realities that appear. The Buddha said to Ānanda that whatever is transitory by nature is the world in the ariyan discipline. The world is everything that arises and falls away. The dhamma that does not arise and fall away is not the world; it is distinct from the world, supramundane, lokuttara. This is nibbāna.

We can classify cittas as lokiya and lokuttara. The citta that does not clearly realize the characteristic of nibbāna, thus, which does not have nibbāna as object, is mundane, lokiya citta. The citta that has nibbāna as object and eradicates defilements is the path-consciousness or magga-citta, and the citta that has nibbāna as object after defilements have been eradicated is the fruition-consciousness or phala-citta, immediately succeeding the magga-citta; both types of citta are supramundane, lokuttara cittas.

One should develop lokiya paññā that realizes the characteristics of nāma and rūpa in order to become an ariyan. Lokiya paññā is not technical knowledge or the knowledge one needs to have in science. Lokiya paññā in Buddhism is just the understanding of the characteristics of nāma and rūpa.

Lokiya paññā knows the characteristics of the "world," namely, the realities that appear through the eyes, the ears, the nose, the tongue, the bodysense and the mind-door. It knows the realities other than nibbāna.

There are four magga-cittas and these are the lokuttara kusala cittas of the four stages of enlightenment, which have nibbāna as object while they eradicate defilements in accordance with these stages. There are four phala-cittas and these are the lokuttara vipākacittas which have nibbāna as object when the defilements have been eradicated in accordance with the stages of enlightenment. All other types of citta are lokiya cittas.

There are four pairs of lokuttara cittas, namely the lokuttara kusala citta and the lokuttara vipākacitta of the sotāpanna, the stream winner, of the sakadāgāmī, the once-returner, of the anāgāmī, the non-returner and of the arahat:

- sotāpatti magga-cittasotāpatti phala-citta,
- sakadāgāmī magga-cittasakadāgāmī phala-citta,
- anāgāmī magga-cittaanāgāmī phala-citta,
- arahatta magga-cittaarahatta phala-citta.

When the magga-citta of the sotāpanna arises, it performs the function of eradicating defilements while it has nibbāna as object, and then it falls away. It is succeeded immediately by the phala-citta of the sotāpanna. This citta also has nibbāna as object and when it arises, the defilements have already been eradicated by the magga-citta of that stage. The sotapatti magga-citta is lokuttara kusala citta, and it conditions the lokuttara vipākacitta to succeed it immediately, without any interval. The expression "without delay," "akaliko," is used in the Tipiṭaka, referring to the fact that the lokuttara magga-citta produces its result immediately.[1] One does not have to wait for the arising of result until the next life. In the case of other kusala kamma or akusala kamma, the result does not succeed the kamma immediately.

The person who develops samatha until the jhānacitta arises will not receive its result so long as he is in the human plane. The reason is that jhāna vipākacitta performs the functions of rebirth, bhavanga and dying in a brahma plane.[2] If one's skill in jhāna does not decline and jhānacitta arises shortly before the dying-consciousness, it will, after the dying-consciousness has fallen away, produce vipākacitta. This vipākacitta performs the function of rebirth in one of the brahma-planes. For example, the kusala jhānacitta of the first stage of rūpa-jhāna conditions the jhānacitta that is vipāka to perform the function of rebirth

[1] See also "Visuddhimagga" VII, 80, 81.

[2] The rebirth-consciousness, the bhavanga-cittas and the dying-consciousness are, in one lifespan, the same type of vipākacitta, result of the same kamma.

in the brahma plane of the first stage of rūpa-jhāna. It is the same in the case of the higher stages of rūpa-jhāna; they produce rebirth-consciousness accordingly in the higher rūpa-brahma planes. The kusala arūpa-jhānacitta of the first stage, the arūpa -jhāna of "infinite space", conditions the arūpa-jhāna vipākacitta to perform the function of rebirth in the arūpabrahma plane of infinite space. It is the same in the case of the higher stages of arūpa-jhāna kusala citta; they produce their results accordingly in the higher arūpa-brahma planes.

Thus, in the case of jhānacitta, kamma does not produce result in the same life. In the case of kāmāvacara kusala kamma (of the sense sphere), its result may arise in the same life, but not immediately; numerous cittas arise and fall away in between the time kamma is performed and its result is produced. Or the result may arise in a future life, or even after many lives. Only in the case of lokuttara kusala citta it is different. As soon as lokuttara magga-citta has fallen away, it is succeeded immediately by its result. The lokuttara vipākacitta does not perform the function of rebirth, bhavanga and dying, nor any of the functions other vipākacittas perform.

The "Atthasālinī" (I, Book I, Part II, Ch II, the Couplets, 47, 48) states about lokiya and lokuttara:

> "In the expression 'worldly phenomena,' the cycle of rebirth is called 'the world' (loka), because of its dissolving and crumbling (lujjana). States that are joined to the world by being included therein are termed 'worldly.' To have passed beyond the worldly is to be supramundane, literally 'ulterior' (uttara dhamma). Dhammas which have passed the worldly, being not included therein, are termed 'lokuttara dhamma'."

Citta, cetasika and rūpa are saṅkhāra dhammas, realities that arise and fall away. Also lokuttara citta and cetasikas that have nibbāna as object arise and fall away. However, cittas are classified as mundane, lokiya, and supramundane, lokuttara, because lokiya cittas do not have nibbāna as object, whereas lokuttara cittas have nibbāna as object. Magga-citta has nibbāna as object and it eradicates defilements, and phala-citta has nibbāna as object after the defilements have been eradicated according to the stages of enlightenment.

We read in the "Kindred Sayings" (IV, Kindred sayings on Sense, Second Fifty, Ch IV, § 85, Void):

> Then the venerable Ānanda came to see the Exalted One... Seated at one side the venerable Ānanda said to the Exalted One: " 'Void is the world! Void is the world!' is the saying, lord. Pray, lord, how far does this saying go?"
>
> "Because the world is void of the self, Ānanda, or of what belongs to the self, therefore is it said 'Void is the world.' And what, Ānanda, is void of the self or of what belongs to the self?
>
> The eye is void of the self or of what belongs to the self. Visible object is void of the self or of what belongs to the self. Seeing-consciousness is void of the self or of what belongs to the self. Eye-contact is void of the self or of what belongs to the self. Pleasant feeling, unpleasant feeling or indifferent feeling which arises owing to eye-contact is void of the self or of what belongs to the self." (The same is said with regard to the other doorways.) "That is why, Ānanda, it is said 'Void is the world.',"

Voidness cannot be realized so long as there is ignorance of realities. One should know what voidness is and of what there is voidness. One should know the meaning of voidness of the self and of what belongs to the self, as it really is. The dhammas that can be experienced through the eyes, the ears, the nose, the tongue, the bodysense and the mind-door arise and then fall away; they are void of the self and of what belongs to the self.

Some people believe that at times they experience that there is nothing that belongs to a self. They wonder why they did not have such an experience before. Formerly they used to believe that there was a self and things belonging to a self. However, because they often listened to the Dhamma they came to the conclusion that there is nothing which belongs to a self and that they should not cling to such a wrong view anymore. This is only thinking about the truth. Theoretical understanding is not enough, because it cannot eradicate defilements. If a person does not realize that he has merely theoretical understanding, he may mistakenly believe that he has already a great deal of paññā and that he will soon attain enlightenment. People may think in such a way because they have found out something they did not know before and they take this knowledge for something extraordinary.

One should know that defilements cannot be eradicated through thinking about the truth. Defilements cannot be eradicated if one does not yet know the characteristic of nāma, the element that experiences something, such as seeing, hearing, smelling, tasting, experiencing tangible object or thinking. It is not a self who has these experiences. When someone has not developed paññā through awareness of the characteristics of the realities that are appearing, he does not penetrate the true nature of nāma and rūpa, and he cannot realize their arising and falling away. Nāma and rūpa that are arising and falling away are actually the world that is arising and falling away at this moment.

People may reflect on the characteristics of nāma and rūpa and they may have understanding of them, but they should not erroneously believe that paññā has already been developed to the degree of eradicating defilements. If sati does not arise, if there is no awareness and investigation of the characteristics of realities that are appearing one at a time, the difference between nāma and rūpa cannot be realized. The difference between the characteristic of nāma and the characteristic of rūpa should be realized through the mind-door as they appear one at a time, so that they are clearly known as they are. This is realized at the first stage of insight,[3] but so long as this stage has not been reached, paññā cannot develop further to the degree of knowing that all conditioned dhammas are merely the world which is void, void of what one takes for self, for a being or for a person.

We read in the "Culla Niddesa", in "Mogharāja's Questions" ("Khuddaka Nikāya")[4] that the Buddha spoke to the monks about detachment. He said:

> "Just as if, monks, a man should gather, burn or do what he please with all the grass, all the sticks, branches and stalks in this Jeta Grove, would you say 'this man is gathering, burning us, doing what he please with us'?"

[3]The stages of insight will be explained further on in this book.

[4]Not translated into English, but this text is similar to "Kindred Sayings" III, Khandhāvagga, First Fifty, §33.

"Surely not, lord."

"Why so?"

"Because, lord, this is not our self, nor belonging to ourselves."

"Even so, monks, what does not belong to you, detach from it. If you detach from it, it will be for your profit and welfare. The body is not yours, detach from it. If you detach from it, it will be for your profit and welfare. Feeling... remembrance... formations (saṅkhārakkhandha)... consciousness, detach from them. If you detach from them it will be for your profit and welfare. One should consider the world as void in this way..."

Further on we read that when someone sees with understanding the world as merely grass and sticks, he does not wish for rebirth in other existences, he only has inclination towards nibbāna which is the end of rebirth. Thus, he considers the world as void.

One is used to taking rūpas and feelings for self. When saññā remembers what is experienced in the wrong way, one perceives a self and clings to names that are used in the world. One is used to taking all conditioned realities for self, no matter whether it is kusala dhamma or akusala dhamma.

If one is not convinced of the truth that they are like grass, sticks, branches and leaves, one cannot become detached from the realities that are the five khandhas.

If people do not study and consider the Dhamma the Buddha taught and if they do not develop satipaṭṭhāna, they do not really know the world, even if they have been in this world for an endlessly long time. If one does not know the world as it is, one cannot be liberated from it. Someone may think that life in this world is pleasant when he experiences a great deal of happiness, but there cannot be happiness continuously. Happy feeling arises only for one moment and then it falls away. If people do not study realities and do not know them as they really are, they do not know what the world is and of what it consists.

We all know that there are objects appearing through the eyes and the other senses. Sound, for example, appears when there is hearing. We should remember that if there were not the element which experiences, the element that is hearing, sound could not appear. The different objects which appear through the eyes, the ears, the nose, the tongue, the bodysense and the mind-door, make it evident that there is citta, the reality which experiences, the element which experiences. We can know the characteristic of citta, the element that experiences and which arises and falls away, because different objects appear. Thus, we can know that the world arises and falls away each moment.

So long as we do not penetrate the characteristics of realities which arise and fall away, succeeding one another very rapidly, we take what appears for a "whole," a being, person or thing. Then we do not know the world as it really is. Someone may have studied the world from the point of view of worldly knowledge, geography, history or science, but all technical knowledge and science cannot cause him to be liberated from the world, not even after innumerable periods of time. If a person does not know the world as it really is, he cannot become liberated from it.

Can the world be our refuge in life? We are attached to happy feeling, but it arises and then falls away completely each time, and that feeling cannot return anymore. If someone were to undergo excruciating suffering, he would indeed want to escape from the world, he would not take refuge in it. However, he cannot escape so long as he does not know the world as it really is.

It is important to consider whether one is ready to give up the idea of being, person or self, or not yet. At this moment there is no self, but is one ready to become detached from the world? First of all, one should clearly know that there is no self, being or person, so that one can become detached from the world and be liberated from it.

Some people cannot bear the truth that there is no self who is seeing, hearing or experiencing the other sense objects. They cannot accept it that there are, in the absolute sense, no relatives and friends, no possessions, no things they could enjoy. Usually, people do not believe that they should be liberated from the world. In order to abandon the clinging to the view of self or mine, one should develop the paññā that knows all realities that appear as they really are. Then one will truly know the world that consists of these realities.

It is not easy to know the world as it really is. Those who have learnt the truth about the world the Buddha realized himself by his enlightenment and taught to others, should carefully consider what they have learnt and apply it in their daily life. They should continue to develop paññā so that it can become keener and know the characteristics of realities that constitute the world as they really are. We should know the world at this very moment, not at another time. We should know the world when there is seeing, hearing, smelling, tasting, experiencing tangible object or thinking, at this very moment. We should listen to the Dhamma and study it, so that there can be awareness, investigation and understanding of the characteristics of realities appearing through the six doors. This is the only way that paññā can develop and know the world which arises and falls away now.

We read in the "Kindred Sayings" (IV, Saḷāyatanavagga, Kindred Sayings on Sense, Second Fifty, Ch II, §68, Samiddhi sutta) that when the Buddha was staying near Rājagaha, in Bamboo Grove, Samiddhi came to see him and addressed him:

> " 'The world! The world!' is the saying, lord. Pray, lord, to what extent is there the world or the concept of 'world'?"
>
> "Where there is eye, Samiddhi, visible object, seeing-consciousness, where there are dhammas cognisable by the eye, there is the world and the concept of 'world'."
>
> (The same is said with regard to the other doorways.)

The world is known because there is the eye and through that doorway the colours of the world can be seen. Through the ear the sounds of the world can be heard. Through the nose the odours of the world are smelled. Through the tongue the flavours of the world are tasted. Through the bodysense the heat, cold, hardness, softness, motion and pressure of the world are experienced. If there were not these doorways could the world appear? If there were no seeing, hearing, smelling, tasting, the experience of tangible object or thinking, the world could not appear. We cling to the idea that the world appears because we see the world. What appears through the eyes is the world of colour. It is the same in the case of the other doorways. Thus, the world consists of visible object, sound, odour, flavour and tangible objects, and the world can appear because there are the senses and the mind-door. The eye is a condition for seeing, the ear for hearing and the other doorways for the experience of the relevant sense objects. Through the mind-door there is thinking about the objects that appear through the six doors. We do not have to look for another world. No matter in which world one lives, that world appears through one of the six doorways.

Further on in the same sutta we read that the Buddha said to Samiddhi:

> "But where there is no eye, no visible object, no seeing-consciousness, no dhammas cognisable by seeing-consciousness, there is, Samiddhi, no world, no concept of 'world'."
>
> (The same is said with regard to the other doorways.)

If we do not know the world as it really is, it is impossible to be liberated from it, even if we wanted to. We will be in this world and in other worlds for a long time. In past lives we lived also in other worlds and even so in the future we will live in the world for an endlessly long time. We will be reborn again and again, going around in the cycle of birth and death, experiencing happiness and sorrow.

Some people believe that the Buddha still exists, although he attained parinibbāna. They want to visit him in order to offer food to him. We should consider the Phagguna Sutta ("Kindred Sayings" IV, Saḷāyatana vagga, Kindred Sayings on Sense, Second Fifty, Ch III, §83)[5]:

> "Then the venerable Phagguna approached the Blessed One... and said to him: 'Venerable sir, is there any eye by means of which one describing the Buddhas of the past could describe them - those who have attained final Nibbāna, cut through proliferation, cut through the rut, exhausted the round, and transcended all suffering?..."

He then asked the same about the ear, the nose, the tongue, the bodysense and the mind. Thus, he asked whether after the Buddha's parinibbāna there would still exist eye, ear, nose, tongue, bodysense or mind. We read that the Buddha answered that there is no such eye, ear, nose, tongue, bodysense or mind.

When the Buddha attained parinibbāna, he passed finally away. There were no longer eyes, ears, nose, tongue, bodysense and mind.

[5] I used the translation of Ven. Bodhi, in "the Connected Discourses of the Buddha".

He did not go to a particular place where he could personally receive people's offerings after his parinibbāna. If he would still have senses and mind arising and falling away, he would not be liberated from the world. There would still be dukkha, he would not be free from dukkha.

The world is what appears through the six doors. If citta did not arise and see, hear, smell, taste, experience tangible object or think, the world would not appear. When sati is aware, the objects that appear can be studied and investigated, and these are the characteristics of the world appearing through the six doors. Thinking about the world is not the same as knowing the characteristics of realities as they are, realizing them as not a being, not a person, not self. If someone merely thinks about the world, he thinks actually about beings, people, self or different things, and then he knows the world by way of conventional truth (sammuti sacca), not be way of absolute truth (paramattha sacca).

Do we realize in our daily life whether we are in the world of conventional truth or in the world of absolute truth? Citta is the reality that experiences objects through the six doors. There is citta at each moment, but the world does not appear at each moment. When there is no seeing, hearing, smelling, tasting, the experience of tangible object or thinking, this world does not appear. The rebirth-consciousness, the first citta in this life, does not experience an object of this world. It is vipākacitta, the result of kamma. Kamma conditions the rebirth-consciousness to succeed the dying-consciousness, the last citta of the preceding life. The rebirth-consciousness experiences the same object as the cittas that arose shortly before the dying-consciousness of the preceding life. Since the rebirth-consciousness does not know an object of this world, this world does not appear yet at that moment. When the rebirth-consciousness has fallen away, the kamma which conditioned its arising also conditions the succeeding bhavanga-citta. The bhavanga-citta experiences the same object as the rebirth-consciousness. When bhavanga-cittas are arising and falling away in succession, performing the function of preserving the continuity in a lifespan, the objects of this world are not experienced. Bhavanga-cittas do not see, hear, smell, taste, experience tangible object or think. Thus, so long as these cittas are arising and falling away, this world does not appear.

When there are cittas arising in processes, the world appears. There are six doors through which vīthi-cittas, cittas arising in processes, know the world. Five doors are rūpa and one door is nāma, and they are the following:

- the cakkhuppasāda rūpa, the eye-door,[6]
- the sotappasāda rūpa, the ear-door,
- the ghāṇappasāda rūpa, the nose-door,
- the jivhāppasāda rūpa, the tongue-door,
- the kāyappasāda rūpa, the body-door,
- the bhavangupaccheda-citta, the mind-door.

The five senses, which are the five pasāda rūpas, each have their own specific characteristic, and they can be impinged on just by the relevant rūpas which each of them is able to receive. Thus, each of the pasāda rūpas can be the doorway for the cittas concerned, which can experience the sense object that impinges on that particular pasāda-rūpa. In daily life there is not only seeing, hearing, smelling, tasting or the experience of tangible object, there is also thinking about different objects. When citta receives and experiences an object after it has been experienced through the eye-door or through the other sense-doors, the citta is at such moments not dependent on the pasāda rūpas that are the sense-doors. It is then dependent on the mind-door, the arrest bhavanga, bhavangupaccheda,[7] which arises before the mind-door adverting-consciousness, the manodvārāvajjana-citta. The mind-door is the doorway for the vīthi-cittas of the mind-door process that arise after the sense-door process and which experience the sense object which has just fallen away, or for the cittas which think of different objects. If the bhavangupaccheda-citta would not arise, then the first citta that experiences an object through the mind-door, the manodvārāvajjana-citta, mind-door adverting-consciousness, could not arise either. The mind-door and the mind-door adverting-consciousness are different dhammas. The mind-door that is the bhavangupaccheda-citta, is a vipākacitta not

[6]See for these terms Ch 4, Exposition of Paramattha Dhammas II.

[7]The last bhavanga-citta before vīthi-cittas arise and the stream of bhavanga-cittas is arrested.

arising in a process, thus, it is not vīthi-citta. The manodvārāvajjana-citta is a kiriyacitta, the first vīthi-citta that arises and knows an object through the mind-door.

This is ordinary, daily life. We should understand the characteristics of the doorways, so that we can investigate and know realities as they are: they are arising and falling away and they are not a being, a person or a self.

At this moment, we may not think of the eyesense, the cakkhup-pasāda rūpa, but it is a reality, a rūpa that arises and falls away in the middle of the eye.

In the "Atthasālinī" (II, Book II, Ch III, Derived Rūpas, 307) we read that the āyatana of the eye, cakkhāyatana, is the eyesense, and that it is derived from the four great Elements. We read:

> " 'Included in personality', it is comprised in and depending on just that.
>
> 'Invisible': what cannot be seen by visual cognition.
>
> 'Reacting': reaction, friction is here produced.[8] "

It cannot be seen, but it can be impinged on by visible object. The term cakkhāyatana is composed of cakkhu and āyatana. Cakkhu means eye. Āyatana is meeting-place or birthplace. Thus, cakkhāyatana is the eye as meeting-place and birthplace. When the eyesense is impinged on by visible object, there is a condition for seeing-consciousness to arise at the eye-base and to experience visible object.

The Buddha explained that when the cittas that arise in the eye-door process and experience visible object through the eye-door have fallen away, there are many bhavanga-cittas arising and falling away. Then cittas arise which experience through the mind-door the visible object that was just before experienced by cittas through the eye-door. The cittas of the mind-door process follow extremely rapidly upon the cittas of the eye-door process, even though there are bhavanga-cittas in between the processes. We should appreciate the value of the Buddha's teaching about the doorways in detail. His teaching can help us not to confuse the cittas that experience visible object through the eye-door and the cittas that experience the object through the mind-door, after

[8] By impingement of visible object on the eyesense.

the eye-door process is over. It is the same in the case of the other sense-doors. When the cittas that experience an object through one of the other sense-doors have fallen away, there is each time, after bhavanga-cittas have arisen and fallen away in succession, a mind-door process of cittas that know the same object through the mind-door.

Nāma dhammas, citta and the accompanying cetasikas, arise and fall away, succeeding one another extremely rapidly. Right now it seems that we are seeing and hearing at the same time. However, in reality one citta arises at a time and experiences one object while it is dependent on one doorway. Then it falls away extremely rapidly. A process consists of several cittas that arise and fall away in succession. The cittas in one process are dependent on one and the same doorway. Since cittas succeed one another so rapidly, one may not know the true characteristics of the cittas arising in the eye-door process, one may not realize that they only experience the reality appearing through the eyes. Cittas of the mind-door process arise afterwards, and they receive and experience the visible object that appeared just before through the eyesense. After that there are processes of cittas which notice and remember the shape and form of what appeared and then one tends to forget that what appears through the eyes is in reality only visible object.

The eyesense has been compared to an ocean that is so large that it can never be satiated. We can see the colour of the moon, the sun and the stars. Although they are infinitely far away, their colours can contact the eyesense and then they are experienced by the vīthi-cittas of the eye-door process. It seems that there is the universe, the world full of beings, people and things. However, in reality there is citta that thinks about the shape and form of the Four Great Elements of earth, water, fire and wind. They appear in different combinations, they appear as beings, people, the moon, the sun, the stars, as many different things. When we experience things through touch, only cold, heat, softness, hardness, motion or pressure appears. If we know dhammas as they are, we realize what the world is: the dhammas that arise and fall away very rapidly, which are transitory.

All dhammas that arise have to fall away, without exception. If one does not realize the arising and falling away of dhammas, one only pays attention to conventional truth. The cittas of the mind-door process remember a "whole," the shape and form of what appears through the eyes, they remember the meaning of high and low sounds which appear through the ears. The names of different things are remembered, and then only concepts are known.

Questions

1. What is the world?
2. What is mundane paññā, lokiya paññā?
3. Does the rebirth-consciousness know an object of this world? Explain your answer.
4. What object does the bhavanga-citta know?
5. Is the mind-door adverting-consciousness the same as the mind-door?
6. Of which jāti is the mind-door?
7. Of which jāti is the mind-door adverting-consciousness?

25

The Variegated Nature of Citta

Citta is variegated, vicitta, and it causes a great variety of effects. We read in the Atthasālinī (I, Book I, Part II, Ch I, 64):

> "How is citta capable of producing a variety or great diversity of effects in action? There is no art in the world more variegated than the art of painting. In painting, the painter's masterpiece is more artistic than the rest of his pictures. An artistic design occurs to the painters of masterpieces that such and such pictures should be drawn in such and such a way. Through this artistic design there arise operations of the mind (or artistic operations) accomplishing such things as sketching the outline, putting on the paint, touching up, and embellishing. Then in the picture known as the masterpiece is effected a certain (central) artistic figure. Then the remaining portion of the picture is completed by the work of planning in mind as, 'Above this figure let this be; underneath, this; on both sides, this.' Thus all classes of arts

> in the world, specific or generic, are achieved by citta. And owing to its capacity thus to produce a variety or diversity of effects in action, citta which achieves all these arts, is itself variegated like the arts themselves. Nay, it is even more variegated by nature than the art itself because the latter cannot execute every design perfectly. For that reason the Blessed One has said, 'Bhikkhus, have you seen a masterpiece of painting?' 'Yes lord.' 'Bhikkhus, that masterpiece of art is designed by citta. Indeed, Bhikkhus, citta is even more variegated than that masterpiece.',"

The diversity in pictures that are painted is only a trivial matter, citta is more variegated than that. The great diversity of actions we perform in daily life make the variegated nature of citta evident. There is kamma performed through body, speech and mind. There is kusala kamma, which is dāna, sīla or bhāvanā. There are different kinds of akusala kamma, for example, killing or stealing. The variegated nature of citta appears from all the different kinds of actions that are performed.

We may be impressed by the great diversity of rūpas outside, which are not of living beings, when we reflect on the variety of vegetation, of trees, plants, flowers and leaves, or the variety in nature, such as mountains or rivers. All this variety in nature occurs because the Four Great Elements of earth, water, fire and wind arise in various combinations. Earth has the characteristic of hardness or softness, water has the characteristic of fluidity or cohesion, fire has the characteristic of heat or cold and wind has the characteristic of motion or pressure. There are different degrees of these characteristics of the Great Elements which arise together in different combinations, and that is why the rūpas outside have a great deal of variety. However, more variegated than all these combinations of rūpas outside is the variegated nature of citta that achieves such a variety of things.

Akusala kamma is variegated and, therefore, it is the condition for an immense diversity in the features of animals. There are animals with two legs, with four or more than four legs, or without legs. Some live in the water, some on land. Kusala kamma, which is variegated, causes human beings to be different as to sex, bodily appearance or facial features. Citta is variegated in its accomplishments to such an extent that a great diversity of terms in language is needed for the designation and naming of all these characteristics thatappear. The need of terms to describe the variegated nature of citta in its accomplishments will never end and will go on in the future.

No matter where we are, no matter what we see, no matter what the topic of our conversation is, the variegated nature of citta that accomplishes so many diverse things appears all the time.

The Buddha reminded us to consider the characteristic of citta at this moment, while we notice the diversity of effects due to the variegated nature of citta. The citta at this moment causes a variety of action, so that there are diverse effects in the future. We should not merely consider the different outward effects of citta. The Buddha reminded us to investigate the characteristic of citta arising at this moment, and this is "mindfulness of citta," one of the four "applications of mindfulness."[1] In order to understand the characteristic of citta we should be aware of citta which sees at this moment, which hears, smells, tastes, experiences tangible object or thinks at this moment, thus, of the citta which is dependent on one of the six doors.

We all think of many different topics and stories. When the citta thinks of something, that subject is present only for the moment citta is thinking about it. Citta is the reality that thinks. If one does not consider citta while there is seeing now, or the experience of one of the other sense objects now, or thinking now, when will one ever be able to understand the characteristic of citta?

Citta thinks of many different things, citta is always travelling. Citta is travelling when there is seeing through the eyes, hearing through the ears, smelling through the nose, tasting through the tongue, the experience of tangible object through the bodysense and experiencing an object through the mind-door. We all like travelling, who wants to be always in the same place, being inactive, leading a monotonous life? We want to see, hear, smell, taste and experience tangible object. We wish to experience all the different sense objects, it never is enough. Citta arises and frequents the different objects that appear through the six doors, it never is inactive. If one realizes the characteristics of realities as they are, one can know that citta arises, experiences an object and

[1]The others are: mindfulness of body, of feeling and of dhammas.

then falls away. That is the true characteristic of citta.

We read in the "Kindred Sayings" (III, Khandhavagga, Kindred Sayings on Elements, Middle Fifty, Ch V, §99, The Leash, I) that the Buddha, while he was at Sāvatthī, said to the monks:

> "Incalculable, monks, is this round of rebirth. No beginning is made known of beings wrapt in ignorance, fettered by craving, who run on, who fare on the round of rebirth...
>
> Just as a dog, tied up by a leash to a strong stake or pillar, keeps running round and revolving round and round that stake or pillar, even so, monks, the untaught manyfolk, who discern not those who are ariyans... who are untrained in the worthy doctrine, regard body as the self, regard feeling, perception, the activities, regard consciousness as having a self, as being in the self or the self as being in consciousness... run and revolve round and round from body to body, from feeling to feeling, from perception to perception, from activities to activities, from consciousness to consciousness... they are not released therefrom, they are not released from rebirth, from old age and decay, from sorrow and grief, from woe, lamentation and despair... they are not released from dukkha, I declare."

We then read that for the ariyan the opposite is the case, he is released from dukkha. In the following sutta, "The Leash" II (§100), we read that the Buddha used a simile of a dog which was tied up by a leash to a pillar and which would always stay close to the pillar, whatever posture he would take. Even so people stay close to the five khandhas, they take them for self. Further on we read that the Buddha said:

> "Wherefore, monks, again and again must one regard one's own citta thus: 'For a long, long time this citta has been tainted by lust, by hatred, by illusion.' By a tainted citta, monks, beings are tainted. By purity of citta beings are made pure.

Monks, have you ever seen a picture which they call a show-piece?"[2]

"Yes, lord."

"Well, monks, this so-called showpiece is thought out by citta. Wherefore, monks, citta is even more diverse than that showpiece.

Wherefore, monks, again and again must one regard one's own citta thus: 'For a long, long time this citta has been tainted by lust, by hatred, by illusion.' By a tainted citta, monks, beings are tainted. By purity of citta beings are made pure.

Monks, I see not any single group so diverse as the creatures of the animal world. Those creatures of the animal world, monks, have their origin in citta.[3] Wherefore, monks, citta is even more variegated than those creatures of the animal world.

Wherefore, monks, a monk must again and again thus regard his own citta: 'For a long time this citta has been tainted by lust, by hatred, by ignorance.' By a tainted citta, monks, beings are tainted. By purity of citta beings are made pure.

Just as if, monks, a dyer or a painter, if he has dye or lac or turmeric, indigo or madder, and a well-planed board, or wall or strip of cloth, can fashion the likeness of a woman or of a man complete in all its parts, even so, monks, the untaught many folk creates and recreates its body, feelings, perception, activities, consciousness.

As to that, what do you think, monks? Is body permanent or impermanent?"

"Impermanent, lord."

"And so it is with feelings, perceptions, the activities, consciousness. Wherefore, monks, so seeing... a monk

---

[2] "Show-piece" is a translation of the Pāli: citta-caraṇa, citta which is called caraṇa, travelling. The Commentary to this passage adds that the artists went about, that they were travelling, exhibiting their work of art.

[3] Being born as an animal is the result of kamma. Citta is the source of good and bad actions which are performed and which will bring different results.

knows: 'For life in these conditions there is no hereafter.',"

A painter depends on paints of various colours so that different pictures can be made. At this moment the citta of each one of us is like a painter, it creates the khandhas of rūpa, feeling, perception, activities and consciousness that will arise in the future.

We all are different, we have different appearances and this is due to different kammas that have been performed a long time ago. The citta that performs varied actions is the condition for diverse effects in the future. There will be diverse effects by way of place of birth, sex, outward appearance, possessions, honour, well-being, pain, praise and blame. We should be aware of the characteristic of the citta that is appearing now, which is "painting" or creating all the realities that will arise in the future. If we are not aware of its characteristic we shall not understand the variegated nature of citta, which can cause so many different effects. Cittas arise and fall away now, succeeding one another very rapidly. There is citta that sees visible object through the eyes, citta that hears sound through the ears, and, even though we may be sitting still, there is citta that travels very far while we are thinking. We may think of where we shall go on a journey, or we may think of all the diverse things that we are going to achieve.

The painter takes his picture for something important, and evenso the citta of the ordinary person, who is not an ariyan, takes the sense objects which are only rūpas for beings, people or self; he takes them for a thing which exists, and he will continue to do so in each new life. So long as one does not yet know the characteristics of the five khandhas, realities that arise and fall away, as they are, one will take them for something, for self.

As we have seen in the sutta "The Leash" (II), the Buddha used the simile of a dog tied to a pole. When standing, he has to stand close to the pole, when sitting, he has to sit close to the pole, he cannot get away from it. Even so the ordinary person cannot get away from the five khandhas, he is inclined to take them for self.

We read in the "Kindred Sayings" (I, Sagāthā vagga, Ch IV, 2, Māra, §6, the Bowl):

> "On one occasion, at Sāvatthī, the Exalted One was instructing, enlightening, inciting and inspiring the monks by a ser-

> mon on the five khandhas of grasping. And the monks with their whole mind applied, attentive and intent, listened with rapt hearing to the Dhamma..."

We then read that Māra[4] wanted to distract the monks. He took the appearance of a bullock and went towards their bowls which were drying in the sun, whereupon the Buddha told the monks that it was not a bullock but Māra. The Buddha then said to Māra that the five khandhas are not self, and that the forces of Māra will never find the person who sees thus and has become detached, without defilements.

The commentary to this sutta, the Sāratthappakāsinī, gives an explanation of the words used in this sutta to describe the way the Buddha spoke to the monks while he was instructing them. He was inciting and inspiring them so that they would apply the Dhamma. In this connection, the Pāli term "samādana" is used, which means applying, undertaking what one considers worthwhile. The Buddha preached to the monks so that they would consider the Dhamma and have correct understanding of it. The Buddha explained the Dhamma for people's benefit so that, when they had listened they could understand it and apply it. He explained the Dhamma in detail so that people would correctly understand kusala dhamma as kusala dhamma and akusala dhamma as akusala dhamma and not mistake akusala for kusala. Kusala dhamma and akusala dhamma have each their own characteristic and they should not be confused. The Buddha taught in all details about the five khandhas of grasping, which are citta, cetasika and rūpa. We cannot escape the five khandhas, no matter where we go or what we are doing. People should carefully study and consider the five khandhas so that they will not have wrong view about them, but understand them as they are.

The commentary explains that the Buddha incited the monks so that they would have energy (ussaha) and perseverance for the application of the Dhamma.

Right understanding of the Dhamma is not easy and it cannot be acquired rapidly, within a short time. The Buddha explained the Dhamma so that people would persevere in its application, have courage and take the effort to consider it carefully, in order to have right understanding

[4]The Evil One. The word Māra has several meanings; it can also represent defilements and all that is dukkha.

of it. In this way sati could arise and be mindful of the characteristics of realities as they naturally appear in daily life, and paññā could realize their true nature. The Buddha did not teach what cannot be verified, he did not teach what does not appear right now. The Buddha taught about seeing, about visible object appearing through the eyes, about hearing, the reality which experiences sound, about sound appearing through the ears, he taught about all realities which are appearing at this moment, which can be verified. People who have listened to the Dhamma can be encouraged to persevere with its application, to study the Dhamma, to consider it and to be aware again and again of the characteristics of realities that appear, so that their true nature can be realized, just as the Buddha taught.

The commentary also states in connection with the Buddha's preaching, that the monks were inspired, gladdened and purified because of the benefit they acquired from their understanding of the Dhamma.

Do we apply the Dhamma with perseverance and courage, and are we inspired and gladdened because of it? We can take courage and be inspired when kusala citta arises. Some people may be unhappy, they may worry about it that they are becoming older and that sati arises very seldom. When someone worries the citta is akusala. We should not worry, or have akusala cittas, because of the Dhamma. The Buddha taught the Dhamma so that people would be encouraged to apply it, to develop it with perseverance and gladness, and be inspired by it. All akusala arises because of conditions; there is no self who can prevent its arising. When akusala citta has already arisen, we should not be downhearted, but we can take courage. If there can be awareness of the characteristic of akusala that appears we can be inspired by the Dhamma. If we investigate the characteristic of akusala dhamma that appears at that moment, we shall know that it is not a being, not a person or self. We can clearly see that at the moment of awareness there is no akusala, that we are not downhearted. If one does not take akusala for self one will not be disturbed or discouraged because of it.

Akusala dhamma arises because of conditions, and when it has arisen, we should, instead of worry about it again and again, be aware of its characteristic, investigate it and understand it as not self. This is the only way to have less akusala and to eventually eradicate it.

When satipaṭṭhāna is developed people will come to know what it means to be inspired, gladdened and purified because of the benefit acquired from the realization of the Dhamma. They will experience that the truth of the Dhamma they realize is purifying and that it is to their benefit. We shall know this when the characteristics of realities can be known as they are.

The monks were inspired and gladdened because of the benefit they acquired from the teachings. The commentary adds, "We all can attain this benefit." The development of satipaṭṭhāna should not discourage us. The realities that appear can be penetrated and realized as they are: they arise and fall away, they are not self, not a being or person. One should not worry about it that one cannot know today realities as they are. Sati can arise today and begin to be aware, and then the characteristics of realities will surely one day be wholly penetrated and clearly known as they are.

If people understand the great value of the Dhamma, if they see that the truth of the Dhamma is to their benefit and that they can attain it one day, although not today, they will not be discouraged. They will continue to listen and to study the realities the Buddha taught in detail, and then there will not be forgetfulness of realities, there will be conditions for the arising of sati.

The Buddha taught realities and these are as they are, they cannot be changed into something else. In the "Debates Commentary" (Ch XXI, 188), the "Pañcappakaraṇatthakathā", commentary to the "Kathāvatthu" ("Points of Controversy"), one of the topics discussed is whether one can make the "sāsana," the Buddha's teachings, anew, change into something else; whether one can change satipaṭṭhāna into something else, or change akusala dhamma into kusala dhamma.

Everybody should investigate this point. We should consider whether kusala dhammas and akusala dhammas can be changed, whether akusala dhamma can be kusala dhamma. Can satipaṭṭhāna be changed into something else?

If we consider cause and effect in the right way, we can understand that the dhammas the Buddha taught cannot possibly be altered. He realized the truth of the Dhamma by his enlightenment and he taught the truth to others. Someone may have wrong understanding of realities, but the true characteristics of realities cannot be changed by anybody.

There are many aspects with regard to the variegated nature of citta.

As we have seen, citta is classified in many different ways and this shows its variegated nature. We read in the Atthasālinī (I, Part II, Ch I, 64) that citta is also variegated because of the many different objects it can experience. Citta can experience any kind of object, no matter how varied and intricate it may be. Citta experiences paramattha dhammas as well as concepts and it knows words denoting concepts. It knows words used in different languages, it knows names and it thinks of many different stories. Thus, citta is variegated because of the objects that are variegated.

Citta cognizes, clearly knows its object, that is its specific characteristic (sabhāva lakkhaṇa). There are also general characteristics (samañña lakkhaṇa) of all conditioned realities, namely, the three characteristics of impermanence, dukkha and anattā. Citta has these three general characteristics.

We read in the Atthasālinī (I, Book I, Part IV, Ch I, 112) about the specific characteristic, function, manifestation and proximate cause of citta.

> Its characteristic is cognizing an object.
>
> Its function is being a forerunner, precursor. It is like a town-guard, seated at a crossroads in the middle of town. He notes each townsman or visitor who comes, that is, the object. Thus it is the chief or leader in knowing an object.
>
> It has connection as manifestation. We read, "The citta which arises next does so immediately after the preceding citta, forming a connected series." Cittas arise and fall away, succeeding one another.

The proximate cause of citta is nāma-dhammas and rūpa-dhammas. Citta is a conditioned dhamma, saṅkhāra dhamma. Conditioned dhammas cannot arise singly, and thus, citta does not arise without accompanying cetasikas. In the planes of existence where there are five khandhas, citta is dependent on nāma-dhammas as well as rūpa-dhammas as proximate cause for its arising. In the planes where there is only nāma, in the arūpa brahma planes, citta has as proximate cause for its arising only nāma-dhammas, cetasikas.

Questions

1. What is the cause of the diversity of rūpa-dhammas that we notice in vegetation, plants, flowers, mountains and rivers, in equipment and other things we use?
2. Can citta experience objects other than paramattha dhammas?

Part III

Concepts

26
Concepts (I)

Paramattha dhammas[1] are realities; they are not beings, people, or self. The paramattha dhammas that arise are only citta, cetasika, and rūpa,[2] each of which has its own characteristic, its own nature. They arise because of conditions and then they fall away again very rapidly. If one does not know the characteristics of citta, cetasika and rūpa, namely, the paramattha dhammas that arise, fall away and succeed one another very rapidly, one knows just concepts. One takes rūpa and nāma,[3] which arise and fall away in succession, for things that are lasting. Thus, one lives in the world of conventional truth, sammutti sacca. When realities appear, one clings to shape and form, to a "whole," one takes fleeting

[1]Paramattha dhammas: usually translated as ultimate, absolute, or fundamental realities.

[2]Citta, cetasika, and rūpa: Citta is a moment of consciousness which cognizes an object; seeing, for example cognizes colour. There is one citta at a time and it is accompanied by several cetasikas, mental factors, each performing its own function. Rūpa (physical phenomenon, materiality, matter), does not know anything.

[3]Nāma: mental phenomena, that is, citta and cetasika. Rūpa: physical phenomena.

realities for things that exist.

However, when one has studied paramattha dhammas and knows how to develop paññā (wisdom), there can be awareness of the characteristics that appear and paññā can become keener. Then the stage of insight can be reached which is the clear understanding of realities that arise and fall away at this moment. One will clearly see that there is no being, person or self. One will know that there are only paramattha dhammas appearing one at a time. This is in accordance with the truth the Buddha realized at his enlightenment and taught to others.

Ignorance is deeply rooted and very persistent. It conditions us to cling to conventional truth and to take realities for things, beings, and people. From the moment of rebirth-consciousness there are nāma and rūpa which arise and fall away, succeeding one another all the time. When we leave our mother's womb and enter this world, we experience the sense objects that appear through the six doors. We see, hear, smell, taste, and experience cold and heat through the bodysense. We do not know that what appears through the eyes is only a kind of reality that can be seen, visible object.

Realities arise, fall away and succeed one another all the time, but it seems as if they do not arise and fall away and thus they are taken for "something." We cling to a concept of things as a mass, a conglomeration or whole (gaṇa paññatti). We may do this even when we don't know yet the conventional terms of things. Small children who cannot talk yet and do not know the meaning of things as expressed in language, as well as animals, know concepts of a "whole." When a child grows up it learns the correct meaning of the words used in language, which denote concepts. Thus, the child becomes familiar with conventional truth.

If we only know conventional truth, and do not develop right understanding of nāma (mentality) and rūpa (physical phenomena), realities appear as if they do not arise and fall away. It seems that we see things, beings, and people. We may touch a cup, a plate, a spoon or fork, but in reality it is just the element of earth[4] or hardness that is touched. What do we see or touch in daily life? When we touch something, we are not used to realizing that the reality of hardness is touched. We have the feeling that we touch a spoon, a fork, a plate, or a cup.

[4]The element of earth denotes solidity appearing as hardness or softness. It can be experienced through touch.

Since realities arise and fall away and succeed one another very rapidly, we cling to the shape and form of things, to a conglomeration or mass. It seems that a spoon is hard, a fork is hard, a cup is hard and a plate is hard. In reality, what is touched is only the rūpa (physical phenomenon) which is hardness, the element of hardness. Since we remember different shapes and forms of things, we know that a cup is not a dish, a spoon is not a fork. What is real in the absolute sense is rūpa dhamma, which has the characteristic of hardness, but we remember only what is real in the conventional sense. We remember that a dish is for serving rice, a bowl for curry and a spoon for serving food.

One recognizes conventional things that are in reality different elements. When one sees, for example, a radio or a television, one takes it for granted that they are composed of iron, plastic, and other materials. However, in reality the component parts are only different rūpa elements. One may be forgetful of the characteristics of nāma dhammas and rūpa dhammas that appear one at a time and then fall away. One remembers the conventional terms of things after seeing what appears through the eyes. All the time, more and more conventional terms are needed because there are new inventions every day. When we know the shape and form of different things that appear as a mass or a whole, we know concepts, conventional truth, and not absolute truth.

We know the concept of a whole or a mass (gaṇa paññatti) because of the experience of visible object. Apart from this, we know a concept of sound, (sadda paññatti), that is, we know the meaning of sounds. All this occurs in daily life. We should know precisely what is absolute truth and what is conventional truth when we recognize the shape and form of things and they appear as a cup, a dish, a spoon, a radio, a car, or a television.

Human beings can utter sounds that form up words; they use conventional terms with which they name things that appear. Thus, we can understand what it is that is being referred to. Animals cannot, to the same extent as human beings, refer to things by means of language. Sound is a reality; different sounds constitute words or names. There cannot be words or names without sounds. When someone has eyesight, he can see different things, but he also needs speech sounds that form up words and names in order to refer to what he sees. When someone knows the meaning of the sounds that form up words, he can speak; he can name things and refer to different subjects. We all cling to names which are used in conventional language.

We should also know ultimate realities. We should know the characteristic of sound, a kind of reality that can be heard. The reality of sound is named differently in different languages. In English, the word "sound" is used to denote this reality. In Pāli, it is called "sadda-rūpa." No matter how one names it, it is a reality that has its own characteristic: it is a rūpa (physical phenomenon) which appears through the ears. It is not nāma (mentality), a reality which experiences.

The commentary to the "Abhidhammattha Sangaha",[5] the "Abhidhammattha Vibhāvinī", (Book 8), gives an explanation of paramattha dhammas (fundamental or ultimate realities), sammutti (conventional truth) and paññatti (concepts). This subject pertains to daily life, it is deep in meaning and it should be correctly understood. Names can be given because there is the reality of sound. Sounds form up names, in Pāli, nāma. In this context the word nāma does not refer to nāmadhamma, the reality that experiences. A name "bends towards," conveys the meanings of things. "Namati" in Pāli means: to bend, incline towards. According to the sub-commentary, there are two kinds of names: names that are suitable to convey meaning, and names that are used because of preference.

About what do we speak in daily life? Why do we speak? We speak so that someone else will understand the subject we refer to. Thus, sadda-rūpa (sound) functions then as name, nāma, it "bends towards", conveys the meaning of the different subjects we want to make known. The fact that someone else understands the meaning of what we say and the subjects we speak about depends on the words we use to convey the meaning; it depends on the language we choose to express ourselves.

The "Abhidhammattha Vibhāvinī" deals with several other aspects concerning different kinds of names. It distinguishes between four kinds

[5] "Abhidhammattha Sangaha": an encyclopaedia of Abhidhamma, ascribed to Anuruddha and composed sometime between the 8th and 12th centuries A.D. It has been translated into English and published by the P.T.S. under the title of "Compendium of Philosophy", by Ven. Nārada, Colombo, under the title of "A Manual of Abhidhamma", and by Bhikkhu Bodhi as "A Comprehensive Manual of Abhidhamma". Moreover, it has been translated together with its commentary as "Summary of the Topics of Abhidhamma" and "Exposition of the Topics of Abhidhamma", by R.P. Wijeratne and Rupert Gethin.

of names. There are names which are generally agreed upon (sāmañña nāma), such as sky, rain, wind, or rice. There are names denoting a special quality (guṇa nāma), such as Arahatta Sammāsambuddho.[6] Someone who does not have the special qualities of a Buddha cannot have this name. Then there are names denoting activity (kiriya nāma) and names that are given according to one's liking. The Dhamma is very intricate and detailed. We should study all realities that the Buddha realized at his enlightenment and taught to others. He wanted to help people to understand the true nature of the realities that appear. The "Abhidhammattha Vibhāvinī" states:

"Question: For which reason did the Buddha teach the Dhamma in such an extensive way?

Answer: Because he wished to help three groups of beings. There are beings that are slow in understanding nāma (mentality), beings that are slow in understanding rūpa (materiality, physical phenomena), and beings that are slow in understanding both nāma and rūpa. They have different faculties: some have keen faculties, some have faculties of medium strength, and some have weak faculties. There are people who like short explanations, there are people who like explanations of medium length, and there are people who like detailed explanations.

Those among the different groups who are slow in understanding nāma can understand realities as explained by way of the five khandhas,[7] because nāma is classified by way of four khandhas, thus, in a more extensive way. Those who are slow in understanding rūpa can understand realities as explained by way of āyatanas.[8] The five senses and the five sense objects are ten kinds of rūpa which are āyatanas. As to dhammāyatana, this comprises both nāma and rūpa. Thus, in this classification rūpa is explained more extensively. Those who are slow in understanding as to both nāma and rūpa can understand realities

[6]The Fully Enlightened One, an epithet for the Buddha.

[7]The Five Khandhas (aggregates) are rūpa (materiality), vedanā (feeling), saññā (perception, memory), saṅkhāra (all other mental factors) and viññāna (citta or consciousness).

[8]The twelve āyatanas (bases) are eye-base, visible object-base, ear-base, sound-base, nose-base, odour-base, tongue-base, flavour-base, body-base, tangible-data-base (includes hardness, softness, heat, etc.), mind-base, dhammāyatana. Mind-base, manāyatana, includes all cittas. Dhammāyatana includes cteasikas, subtle rūpas and nibbāna, which are experienced through the mind-door.

as explained by way of elements, dhātus,[9] because in this classification both nāma and rūpa are explained in detail."

We should consider whether we are people who are slow in understanding only nāma (mentality), only rūpa (materiality) or both nāma and rūpa. If we are slow in understanding both nāma and rūpa, we need to listen to the Dhamma very often, and we need to study different aspects of the teachings in detail. This is necessary in order to have right understanding of realities and to be able to cultivate all kinds of kusala. In this way, there will be supporting conditions for satipaṭṭhāna to arise and to be aware of the characteristics of realities, just as they naturally appear in daily life.

The "Abhidhammattha Vibhāvinī" (Book 8) distinguishes between six kinds of concepts that are names, that is, "nāma-paññatti" (see "Visuddhimagga" VIII, note 11).

1. Vijjamāna paññattis, concepts which make known what is real, for example, the words rūpa, nāma, vedanā (feeling), or saññā (perception).[10]

2. Avijjamāna paññattis, concepts that make known what is not real, such as the words Thai or foreigner. These concepts do not represent absolute realities, citta and cetasika that are nāma, and rūpa. Thai or foreigners are not real in the absolute sense; they are conventional realities, sammutti dhammas. Could akusala citta[11] (unwholesome consciousness) be Thai or foreign? Akusala citta is a paramattha dhamma (a reality); it is a dhamma that has its own characteristic. It is not Thai or foreign.

3. Vijjamānena avijjamāna paññattis, concepts of what is not real based on what is real. There is the expression "the person with the six abhiññās."[12] The six abhiññās are real, but person is not. Thus, this is concept of what is not real based on what is real.

[9]The eighteen dhātus (elements) include three for each sense-door. For the eye-door these are: eye element, visible object element, seeing consciousness element. The other five doors are ear, nose tongue, body and mind. (See "Visuddhimagga" XV,17)

[10]Vedanā and saññā are cetasikas that accompany each citta.

[11]Akusala citta can be rooted in greed, delusion, or aversion. Kusala citta, citta that is wholesome or skilful.

[12]Abhiññās are supernatural powers.

4. Avijjamānena vijjamāna paññattis, concepts of what is real based on what is not real. There is the expression "woman's voice." The sound is real, but the woman is not real.

5. Vijjamānena vijjamāna paññattis, concepts of what is real based on what is real. There is the term cakkhu-viññāṇa (eye-consciousness). Cakkhu (eye) is a reality, namely the cakkhuppasāda-rūpa (eyesense, a reality sensitive to colour or visible object), and viññāṇa (consciousness) is also a reality, namely the reality that experiences.

6. Avijjamānena avijjamāna paññattis, concepts of what is not real based on what is not real. There is the expression "the king's son." Both king and son are not real; they are sammutti dhammas, conventional realities.

There are objects that are real and objects that are not real. Objects can be experienced through the six doors and they can be classified as sixfold:

- Visible object (rūpārammaṇa) can be known through the eye-door.
- Sound (saddārammaṇa) can be known through the ear-door.
- Odour can be known through the nose-door.
- Flavour can be known through the tongue-door.
- Tangible object can be known through the body-door.
- Dhammārammaṇa (mental object) can be known only through the mind-door.

As to visible object, this is the reality that appears through the eyes. It is the object of vīthi-cittas[13] that arise depending on the eyesense, the cakkhuppasāda-rūpa. When visible object has fallen away there

[13] Cittas experiencing objects that impinge on the six doors arise in a process of cittas; they are vīthi-cittas. Visible object is not only experienced by seeing-consciousness, but also by other cittas arising within a process. See appendix.

are many bhavanga-cittas[14] arising and falling away, and then vīthi-cittas of the mind-door process experience the visible object which has just fallen away. Thus, visible object can be experienced through two doors: through the eye-door and, after there have been bhavanga-cittas in between, through the mind-door.

As to sound, this is the reality that appears through ears. It is the object of vīthi-cittas that arise depending on the earsense, the sotappasāda-rūpa. It appears through the mind-door after there have been bhavanga-cittas in between. There have to be bhavanga-cittas after each process of cittas. Thus, there must always be bhavanga-cittas in between a sense-door process and a mind-door process. When we hear sound and know the meaning of what is heard, these are different processes. When one knows the meaning of a word there are mind-door processes of cittas that think of that word. These cittas are different from cittas of the ear-door process that experience the sound that has not yet fallen away.

As regards odour, this is the reality that appears through the nose. It is the object of cittas that arise depending on the rūpa that is smelling-sense. After there have been bhavanga-cittas in between, there are cittas of the mind-door process which experience odour.

As to flavour, this is the reality that appears through the tongue. It is the object of cittas that depend on the rūpa that is tasting-sense. After there have been bhavanga-cittas in between, there are cittas of the mind-door process which experience flavour.

Tangible objects are cold, heat, softness, hardness, motion and pressure that appear through the bodysense. They are the objects of cittas that arise depending on the bodysense. After there have been bhavanga-cittas in between, there are cittas of the mind-door process which experience tangible object.

The five classes of sense objects, which have just been mentioned, can appear through the six doors. When the cittas of the eye-door process have arisen and experienced visible object through the eye-door, there are, after there have been bhavanga-cittas in between, cittas of the mind-

[14]Bhavanga-cittas are translated as life continuum. Bhavanga-cittas arise in between the processes of cittas. They do not experience the objects that impinge on the five sense-doors and the mind-door. They experience the same object as the rebirth-consciousness, the first citta in life. See appendix.

door process which experience visible object through the mind-door. It is the same with the experience of the other sense objects. These objects are experienced by the cittas of the corresponding sense-door processes, and then, after there have been bhavanga-cittas, they are experienced through the mind-door. Thus, each of the five classes of sense objects is experienced through its corresponding sense-door and through the mind-door. They are experienced through the six doors: the eye-door, the ear-door, the nose-door, the tongue-door, the body-door and the mind-door.

There is another class of objects, namely dhammārammaṇa (mental objects). This class of objects can only be experienced through the mind-door. There are six kinds of dhammārammaṇa:

- The five pasāda-rūpas (senses),
- Sixteen subtle rūpas (sukhuma rūpas),[15]
- Citta,
- Cetasika,
- Nibbāna,
- Concepts (paññattis).

Five classes of dhammārammaṇa, namely, the pasāda-rūpas, the subtle rūpas, citta, cetasika, and nibbāna are paramattha dhammas. One class, the paññattis, is not paramattha dhamma.

The cittas of the eye-door process, namely, the eye-door adverting-consciousness, seeing-consciousness, receiving-consciousness, investigating-consciousness, determining-consciousness, the javana-cittas[16] and the

[15]There are 28 kinds of rūpas. Twelve are gross and sixteen are subtle. The gross rūpas are the five sense organs and the sense objects that can be experienced through eyes, ears, nose, and tongue, and three rūpas that can be experienced through the bodysense, namely, solidity, temperature, and motion. Subtle rūpas include, for example, cohesion and nutritive essence

[16]Javana literally means "running through," impulsion; the javana-cittas arise in the sense-door processes and in the mind-door process, and they "run through the object." There are usually seven javana-cittas in a process of cittas, and these are kusala or akusala in the case of non-arahats. Arahats do not have kusala cittas or akusala cittas; they have kiriyacittas.

tadālambana-cittas[17] (retention), experience visible object that has not yet fallen away. They do not have a concept as object.

The cittas of the ear-door process experience sound that has not yet fallen away, they do not have a concept as object. It is the same with the cittas of the nose-door process, the tongue-door process and the body-door process.

When the vīthi-cittas of a sense-door process have fallen away, there are many bhavanga-cittas in between, and then there are cittas of the mind-door process. The first series of cittas of the mind-door process that arise after a sense-door process experience a sense object which has only just fallen away; they do not have a concept as object.

In each series of mind-door process cittas there are two or three kinds of vīthi-cittas, namely: one moment of mind-door adverting-consciousness, seven moments of javana-cittas and two moments of tadālambana-cittas. When the first series of mind-door process cittas has fallen away, there are many bhavanga-cittas in between. Then there will be another series of mind-door process cittas that can have as its object a concept (such as shape and form, or the image of something as a "whole") on account of a sense object.

When this series of mind-door process cittas has fallen away, there are bhavanga-cittas in between, and then there will be more rounds of mind-door process cittas that follow. They know the meaning of something; they know words and names. In between the different series there are bhavanga-cittas. When we know that we see people or different things, the citta experiences a concept, not a paramattha dhamma that is rūpa. The object that is paramattha dhamma appearing through the eyes are only different colours. When the vīthi-cittas of the mind-door process know that there are beings, people and different things, then the cittas have paññattis, concepts, as object. They know what a particular thing is.

Paramattha dhammas are not paññatti dhammas. Paramattha dhammas are realities that each have their own characteristic that can be directly experienced, even if one does not use terms to name it. Paññatti dhammas, concepts, are not absolute realities. We may see a painting of fruit, such as grapes, or mangoes, and we may see real grapes and man-

[17] Tadālambana is also called tadārammaṇa. See Appendix.

goes. What is then a concept? When we see a painting of mountains, of the sea, or trees, we know that it is a picture. When we see "real" mountains or trees, do we believe that these are realities, not concepts?

It is evident that names are concepts, paññattis, because they convey the characteristics or the meaning of phenomena. However, even if one does not yet name things, or there is not yet a name, one can already think of a concept of a "whole" or a mass. There can be a concept or idea of "something" that appears even though one does not know any language or words to express its meaning. When we know what it is that appears, even without naming it, we know a paññatti (concept).

When we see what is only a painting of fruit and real fruit, both the painting and the real fruit are paññattis. A paññatti (concept) is not a paramattha dhamma (reality). As we have seen, there are many aspects of paññatti. It can be an idea of a whole or a mass; or it can be a name or term that refers to something, be it real or not real.

What is the difference between real fruit and a painting of fruit? What appears through the eyes while one sees are not beings, people, or different things. No matter whether one sees a painting of grapes or real grapes, only colour appears through the eyes. We may believe that only the picture is a paññatti and that the "real" grapes are not a paññatti (concept). However, in reality, the picture as well as the real grapes that appear are objects that are paññattis experienced by mind-door process cittas. The cittas of the eye-door process experience only colour that appears. The cittas of the mind-door process that experience a concept know the meaning of something; they know what something is. They know that there are grapes. Thus, the cittas (moments of consciousness) that know that there are grapes have a concept, a paññatti, as object, and not a paramattha dhamma.

When we see somebody, we should know that this is in reality the same as seeing a picture, thus, we know in both cases a concept. It is difficult to separate concepts from realities, for example, when we notice that there is a chair. The object that is the paramattha dhamma appearing through the eyes and the object which is the paramattha dhamma appearing through the bodysense are not paññattis.

Questioner: I do not understand conventional realities very well. At this moment, I see a pen. You say that when one sees a pen, it is evident that the sense-door process has passed and that there is a mind-door process. I do not know how I should study or practise so that I won't let the sense-door process pass without knowing it.

Sujin: One should listen to the Dhamma so that one will really understand when the object of citta (consciousness) is a concept and through which door citta knows a concept. When citta has a paramattha dhamma (ultimate reality) as object, there are no beings, people or things, there is no self. At this moment, realities arise and fall away and succeed one another so rapidly that it seems that we see a thing, such as a fan. The fan rotates, and it seems that we can see rūpas (matter) moving. In reality, there are many series of mind-door process cittas that have paññatti (concept) as object and, thus, the characteristics of the paramattha dhammas are hidden. One does not know the characteristics of the paramattha dhammas as they really are.

Questioner: If this is so, how can we do away with concepts?

Sujin: That is not possible. However, one should understand correctly that, when one knows that there are beings, people or things, there are at such moments mind-door process cittas that have a concept as object.

Questioner: Are there then cittas that think of words?

Sujin: Even when we do not think of words we can know a concept. When we know the shape and form of something, when we have a concept of something as a whole or know the meaning of something, that is, we know what something is, then the object is a paññatti (concept), not a paramattha dhamma (reality). The characteristics of realities should be known precisely so that their arising and falling away can be realized. Someone may believe that he does not see that a chair falls away. When we cannot distinguish the different characteristics of paramattha dhammas, as they appear one at a time, we take them all together as a whole. When we see a chair we know a concept. How could a concept fall away?

As to the example of a picture of grapes and real grapes, is there any difference when one touches them and there is the experience of tangible object through the bodysense? Is the element of hardness not the same in both cases? The element of hardness originates from different factors and this is the condition that there are different degrees of hardness and softness. Hardness is a reality that appears through the bodysense, whether it is a picture of grapes or real grapes.

However, the grapes in the picture do not have the flavour of real grapes. Real grapes can be recognized because there are different types of rūpas (physical phenomena) which arise together. Flavour is one type of rūpa; odour is another type. Cold or heat, softness or hardness, motion or pressure, these are all different types of rūpas that arise together and fall away very rapidly and are then succeeded by other rūpas. Thus we think of a concept of a thing that does not seem to fall away. In reality, the rūpas that constitute grapes, such as cold or heat, hardness or softness, or flavour, fall away. Each rūpa lasts only as long as seventeen moments of citta, no matter what colour, sound or other type of rūpa it may be. Paññā (wisdom) should consider realities and know them one at a time; it should resolve the whole that is remembered by saññā (remembrance or perception) into different elements. Thus it can be known that what one takes for particular things are in reality only different paramattha dhammas, each with its own characteristic, which arise and fall away together. When we join them together and have an image of a whole, there are mind-door process cittas, which have a concept of a whole (gaṇa paññatti) as object.

Questioner: If it is known through the mind-door that there is a pen, is that right or wrong?

Sujin: It is not wrong. The object at that moment is a concept which is included in dhammārammaṇa (mind-door object). However, paññā should realize the difference between the mind-door process and the eye-door process. When one does not develop paññā one cannot distinguish the sense-door process and the mind-door process from each other and then one believes that there are beings, people and different things. To what are we attached in daily life? What does lobha (mental factor of craving) like? It likes everything, and what does this mean?

Questioner: All things which are desirable.

Sujin: Lobha likes everything, including concepts. The world is full of concepts. We cannot stop liking paramattha dhammas as well as paññattis. Whenever we like something, we do not merely like a paramattha dhamma, we also like a concept. When we, for example, like a particular belt, we like the colour which appears through the eyes.

Questioner: We also like its trademark.

Sujin: We like everything. When we say that we like colours, what are these colours? They are the colours of eyebrows, eyes, nose, or mouth. If there were no colours appearing how could there by eyebrows, eyes, nose, or mouth? There could not be. However, when we see colours such as red, green, grey, blue, or white we should know that colour is only the reality that appears through the eyes. Nevertheless, we like the colours of eyes, nose, and mouth. Thus, we like concepts. Paramattha dhammas are real. However, when we like something we like both the paramattha dhamma that appears and the concept, which is conceived on account of that paramattha dhamma.

27

Concepts (II)

The "Atthasālinī" (II, Part II, 400) explains about being unguarded as to the "controlling faculties," the indriyas. Here, the indriyas of eyes, ears, nose, tongue, bodysense and mind are referred to. We read:

> "Grasps the general appearance, i.e., grasps by way of lusting, desire a sign such as is of the male, or female, pleasant, etc., and which is the basis of corruption."

When we cling to the general appearance of male or female, it shows that the object is not a paramattha dhamma. When we know that we see a man or woman, we don't just know the reality that appears through the eyes, but we have an image (nimitta), a concept on account of what appears through the eyes. The image of the general appearance of a man or woman is the foundation of defilements.[1] Through the power of desire (chanda raga) we take that image for something attractive. When

[1] There are numerous defilements (unwholesome mental factors), such as lobha, greed, attachment, aversion, ignorance and wrong view.

we like a concept such as a belt, it shows that the belt is an attractive image. One is attached to it, one is ruled by desire. If the belt is not beautiful, if it is not an attractive image (nimitta), one does not like it. On account of colours that appear through the eyes, there can be different "nimittas", attractive or unattractive.

We read further on in the "Atthāsalinī":

> "Grasps the details (anuvyañjana), i.e., takes the various modes of hands and feet, of smiling, laughing, speaking, looking straight ahead, looking askance, which have earned the name of 'details' from the manifesting, the revealing of the lower nature."

The "details" are the condition that causes defilements to appear. When someone likes a belt, he likes the general appearance, the image, and the details. If all belts were the same, if there were no variety of them, the details would not be different. However, there are many kinds of belts and they are different as to the details. The details condition the arising of different kinds of defilements.

Questioner: If we don't cling to concepts, I fear that we will not know that this is a pen.

Sujin: That is not so. We should know realities in accordance with the truth. What appears through the eyes falls away, and then there are mind-door process cittas, which arise afterwards and know a concept. Paññā (wisdom) should know realities as they are. It should know what is visible object, which appears through the eye-door. It should know that the experience of visible object is different from the moment that citta knows a concept. Thus we can become detached from the idea that visible object that appears are beings, people, or things; we can become detached from that which is the foundation of clinging. We should understand that when it is known that there is a man, a woman, beings, or different people, the object is an image or concept known through the mind-door. When we develop satipaṭṭhāna, we should know the characteristics of the realities just as they naturally appear, in order to be able to realize the arising and falling away of nāma and rūpa. It should be known that paramattha dhammas are not concepts. One should continue to develop paññā when realities appear through eyes, ears, nose, tongue, bodysense, and mind-door.

Questioner: Did you say that a concept is a kind of dhammārammaṇa (mind-door object)?

Sujin: A concept is dhammārammaṇa. It is an object that can only be known through the mind-door.

Questioner: Are there also paramattha dhammas (ultimate realities) which are dhammārammaṇa?

Sujin: There are six classes of dhammārammaṇa.[2] Five classes are paramattha dhammas and one class is not paramattha dhamma. We should know when an object is a concept. When an object is not a paramattha dhamma, the object is a concept.

When we think of concepts in daily life, the characteristics of the paramattha dhammas, which are experienced through the six doors, are hidden. Thus, realities are not known as they are. One does not know that what appears through the eyes is not a being, person or self. It is only colour that appears when it impinges on the eyesense. When will paññā become keener so that it will know the truth when there is seeing?

When the truth is known, we will let go of the idea that there is a self, that there are beings or people. One will be able to distinguish between the object which is a paramattha dhamma and the object which is a concept and one will have right understanding of the realities which appear through the six doors.

Questioner: Which object is experienced while we are dreaming?

Sujin: Everyone, except an arahat, is sure to dream. When we wake up, we say that in our dream we saw a relative who passed away. While we were dreaming, did we see a concept or a paramattha dhamma? If we do not consider this, we will not know the truth. It seems as if we can really see in our dreams. However, if we ask someone what he sees in his dreams, he will answer that he sees people, relatives and friends, that he sees different beings. Thus, when we dream, we "see" concepts. At such moments, the eye-door process cittas do not arise because we are asleep. However, cittas arising in the mind-door process are thinking, they "see" beings and people. When we are dreaming we think of concepts that are conceived on account of what we formerly saw, heard or experienced through the other senses.

---

[2]The six classes are the five sense organs, the sixteen subtle rūpas, citta, cetasika, nibbāna, and concept.

Also, when we read about different subjects in the newspaper and see pictures, we only think of concepts; we don't know the characteristics of paramattha dhammas (ultimate realities) that appear. We don't know the difference between concepts and paramattha dhammas. When we read or perform our tasks in daily life, there is seeing of what appears through the eyes, but we pay attention only to concepts and keep on thinking of them.

Concepts are conceived on account of what was heard. A small child often hears sounds but it does not yet know words; it does not understand conventional language. It sees, hears, smells, tastes, experiences tangible object, it experiences pain, it is angry, it has likes and dislikes, and it cries. However, it does not know words with which it can explain its feelings, it cannot speak yet until it has become older. Can anybody remember all that has happened from the moment he was born? Seeing, hearing, and other sense-cognitions arose but we could not use words to express ourselves since we did not yet understand the meaning of the different sounds used in speech. That is why the memory of the events of early childhood fades away. When we grow up we know the meaning of the different sounds which form up words in current speech, which are used to express ourselves. We take in more and more impressions through eyes and ears and combine these experiences, and thus many kinds of events of our lives can be remembered. The world of conventional truth expands and there is no end to its development.

When one reads a story one also wants to see a moving picture of it and hear the corresponding sounds. We should realize to what extent the world of conventional truth hides realities, paramattha dhammas. We should consider what are concepts, not paramattha dhammas, when we, for example, watch television, when we watch a play and look at people talking. It seems that the people who play in a film on television are real people, but the story and the people who play in it are only concepts. The paramattha dhammas that appear fall away very rapidly and then they are succeeded by other realities. When we know that there is a particular person, the object of the citta is a concept.

The characteristics of paramattha dhammas are hidden because of ignorance, avijjā, which does not know the difference between paramattha dhammas and concepts, paññattis. Therefore, one is not able to realize that the realities appearing through the eyes, ears, nose, tongue, bodysense and mind-door are not beings, a person, or self. If we study citta, cetasika (mental factors), and rūpa in more and more detail, the intellectual understanding of the Dhamma will develop. This understanding is accumulated and thus conditions are developed for the arising of sati (mindfulness) which can be directly aware of the characteristics of paramattha dhammas. Thus, there can be more detachment from the outward appearance (nimitta) and the details (anuvyañjana) which are forms of paññatti.

Questioner: Can a concept be an object of satipaṭṭhāna?

Sujin: It cannot.

Questioner: From what I heard just a moment ago, it seems that a concept can be the object of satipaṭṭhāna.

Sujin: Only paramattha dhammas can be the object of satipaṭṭhāna. When flavour impinges on the rūpa that is tasting-sense, there are conditions for the arising of cittas that experience flavour through the tongue-door. First, there is the five-sense-door adverting-consciousness and then there are tasting-consciousness, receiving-consciousness, investigating-consciousness, determi-ning-consciousness, the javana-cittas and the tadālambana-cittas (registering or retention). Then the flavour falls away and, thus, there is no grape in the absolute sense. However, when one joins different realities together into a whole, such as a grape, then the object is a concept.

Satipaṭṭhāna is developed when there is awareness of the characteristics of paramattha dhammas and they are realized as not a being, a person or self. When sati does not arise, the characteristics of paramattha dhammas cannot be discerned, only concepts are known. Then, there will be ideas of beings, people and self all the time.

Questioner: You said that concepts could be known through the mind-door. Therefore, I am inclined to think that if there is awareness through the mind-door, concepts can be the object of satipaṭṭhāna.

Sujin: In order to have more understanding of satipaṭṭhāna, we should begin with this very moment. Is there a concept while you hear sound now? Sound is a paramattha dhamma. When citta knows the meaning of the sound it knows a concept and it knows this through the mind-door. Citta thinks about different words. Sati can follow and be aware of that citta, so that it can be realized as just a type of citta that thinks of words.

Questioner: Thus, satipaṭṭhāna can know the reality that is thinking, but it cannot know concepts. As far as I understand, each of the sense-door processes has to be followed by a mind-door process, it cannot be otherwise. When there is seeing there is an eye-door process, and after there have been bhavanga-cittas in between, there is a mind-door process of cittas which experience visible object. Is that right?

Sujin: The vīthi-cittas of the mind-door process, which follow vīthi-cittas of a sense-door process, have to experience the same rūpa. If the javana-cittas of the sense-door process are lobha-mūla-cittas[3] (cittas rooted in attachment), the javana-cittas of the first mind-door process after that sense-door process have to be the same types of lobha-mūla-citta. The mind-door process follows extremely rapidly upon the sense-door process. With respect to this, there is a simile of a bird perching on a branch. As soon as the bird perches on the branch, its shadow appears on the ground. Even so, when the object has been experienced through the sense-door and there have been many bhavanga-cittas in between, arising and falling away very rapidly, it is immediately afterwards experienced through the mind-door. Since cittas succeed one another so rapidly, one does not know that visible object which is experienced through the eyes is only a paramattha dhamma that can appear because it has impinged on the eye-sense.

Questioner: When there is seeing through the eyes and we know that it is a pen, it shows that we know the word pen through the mind-door. Is that right?

Sujin: Before we can think of the word pen, we already know a concept. A paññatti is not merely sadda paññatti, a concept of sound, a word or name.

Questioner: After seeing I remember what was seen. Is the object then already a concept?

Sujin: The Pāli term paññatti means: it makes something known (derived from paññāpeti).

Questioner: Must each of the sense-door processes be followed by a mind-door process?

---

[3]Unwholesome cittas, akusala cittas, are cittas rooted in unwholesome roots, akusala hetus. They are lobha-mūla-cittas, dosa-mūla-cittas (cittas rooted in aversion or hate) or moha-mūla-cittas, cittas rooted in ignorance.

Sujin: The five sense objects, which are visible object, sound, odour, flavour, and tangible object, appear through two doorways. Thus, visible object appears through the eye-door and then, after there have been bhavanga-cittas in between, it appears through the mind-door. In the same way, sound, odour, flavour, and tangible object appear through the corresponding sense-doors and then through the mind-door.

Questioner: When we taste a sour flavour and we notice that it is sour, do we experience a concept?

Sujin: What is sour?

Questioner: For example, a sour orange we eat.

Sujin: The flavour is a paramattha dhamma, and when we think of a sour orange, the object is a concept. The words sour oranges are "sadda paññatti" ("sadda" meaning sound or word). When we name something, the object is nāma paññatti, a concept that is a name. If there were no sounds, there would be no words, and we would not think of the meaning of things; we would not pay much attention to objects. When sound is the object of cittas of the ear-door process, and then of cittas of the mind-door process, saññā (remembrance), which remembers the meaning of the different sounds, conditions thinking about words and names.

Everything can be called by a name, such as a pen, a pencil, a table or a chair; these are all names. There is no dhamma that cannot be called by a name. Since dhammas have distinctive characteristics, names are needed to make these known. Thus, dhammas are the cause of name giving. The "Atthasālinī" (Book II, Part II, Ch. II, 391) describes the process of name giving. We read:

> "There is no being, no thing that may not be called by a name. Also, the trees in the forest, the mountains are the business of the country folk. For they, on being asked, 'What tree is this?' say the name they know, as 'Cutch,' 'Mango tree.' Even of the tree, the name of which they know not, they say, 'It is the nameless tree.' And that also stands as the established name of that tree..."

If there were no names, it would be most difficult for people to understand one another. Even paramattha dhammas need to be named.

The Buddha used concepts to classify dhammas according to their characteristics, such as the following names:

- The five khandhas,
- The twelve āyatanas,
- The eighteen elements,
- The four noble Truths,[4]
- The twenty two indriyas,[5]
- The different groups of people (puggala).

Thus, the Dhamma the Buddha taught needs different terms and names in order to be understood.

The "Atthasālinī" uses different synonyms for nāma paññatti, concepts that are names.[6] It is an interpretation, an expression that renders the meaning of something in language (nirutti). A name is a distinctive sign that shows the meaning of something (vyañcana). There are sounds which people utter, sounds combined as words which express the meaning of something (abhilāpa, meaning, phrasing or expression). These synonyms explain the meaning of nāma paññatti, a name or term. A term makes the meaning of something known. The idea or notion that is made known can also be called a concept. Thus, there are, generally speaking, two kinds of paññatti:

1. That which is made known (paññāpiyattā or atthapaññatti).
2. That which makes known (paññāpanato), the name or term (sadda paññatti or nāma paññatti) which makes known the meaning of things.

---

[4]The four noble Truths are dukkha (suffering), the origin of dukkha, the cessation of dukkha, and the way leading to the cessation of dukkha.

[5]Indriya (faculties): see "Visuddhimagga" XVI, 1.

[6]See "Dhammasaṅgaṇī" (translated as Buddhist Psychological Ethics by P.T.S.) §1306.

If we remember these two classes of concepts, it will be easier to understand what a concept is. There are many kinds of concepts and they can be classified in different ways. One way of classifying them is the following (see also "Abhidhammattha Sangaha" Ch. VIII, section 4, on paññattis):

1. concept of continuity: (saṇṭhāna paññatti), corresponding to the continuity of things, such as land, mountain or tree, which concept is based on the rapid succession of the elements.
2. collective concept: (samūha paññatti), corresponding to modes of construction of materials, to a collection of things, such as a vehicle or a chariot.
3. conventional concept: (sammutti paññatti), such as person or individual, which is derived from the five khandhas.
4. local concept: (disā paññatti), a notion or idea derived from the revolving of the moon, such as the directions of east or west.
5. concept of time: (kāla paññatti), such as morning, evening.
6. concept of season: (māsa paññatti), notions corresponding to seasons and months. The months are designated by names, such as "Vesakha".
7. concept of space: (akāsa), such as a well or a cave. It is derived from space that is not contacted by the four Great Elements.
8. nimitta paññatti: the mental image which is acquired through the development of samatha, such as the nimitta of a kasiṇa.

We read in the "Abhidhammattha Sangaha":

> "All such different things, although they do not exist in the ultimate sense, become objects of thought in the form of shadows of (ultimate) things. They are called paññatti because they are thought of, reckoned, understood, expressed, and made known on account of, in consideration of, and with respect to, this or that mode. This paññatti is so called because it is made known. As it makes known, it is called 'paññatti'. It is described as 'name', 'name-made', etc."

Lobha-mūla-citta (consciousness with attachment) arises time and again through eyes, ears, nose, tongue, bodysense and mind-door. Even when lobha-mūla-citta is without wrong view (diṭṭhigata vippayutta), it is not merely attached to paramattha dhammas (realities) which appear through the six doors, but it is also attached to concepts. It is attached to the general appearance of things and to the details; it is attached to names and to subjects of thought.

We should ask ourselves, at this moment, what kinds of objects we usually experience in our daily life? The objects are mostly concepts and thus the characteristics of paramattha dhammas are hidden, they are not known as they are.

Questioner: When we touch grapes or a picture of grapes, softness and hardness[7] are paramattha dhammas, the flavour of grapes is a paramattha dhamma. Many realities that are joined together constitute a real grape and this we call a concept. Thus, I am inclined to think that a concept is real.

Sujin: The rūpa of flavour arises and then falls away; it can only last as long as seventeen moments of citta.[8] The rūpa that is the colour of grapes arises and then falls away very rapidly since it only lasts as long as seventeen moments of citta. Can we then say that grapes exist?

Questioner: They exist in our memory.

Sujin: There is a concept, a notion that there are grapes, but in reality there is only flavour which arises and then falls away, or hardness which arises and then falls away.

Questioner: A concept is formed because many paramattha dhammas are joined together into a mass or a whole.

Sujin: When one does not realize the arising and falling away of one reality at a time, one takes what appears to be a whole, for a thing which exists.

Questioner: Is a concept not real? A concept is constituted of many kinds of paramattha dhammas (realities): softness, hardness, heat, colour, odour or flavour. They are joined together; they are a whole, a thing that has such and such colour, this or that shape. There

[7]Softness and hardness are tangible objects, rūpas, which can be experienced through the bodysense.

[8]See Appendix.

is a concept of this or that person with such and such outward appearance. Thus, a concept is made up of paramattha dhammas.

Sujin: One will know that concepts are not paramattha dhammas if one learns to discern the characteristics of the different paramattha dhammas that arise together. One should be aware of one characteristic at a time as it appears through one doorway at a time. In order to know the truth we should realize the arising and falling away of rūpa, which appears through one doorway at a time.

Each rūpa lasts only as long as seventeen moments of citta and then it falls away. Therefore, rūpa that arises has no time to stand, walk, or do anything. During the time one lifts one's hand, already more than seventeen moments of citta have passed. One sees people walking or lifting their hands, but in reality the rūpas that arise fall away immediately and are succeeded by other rūpas. The rūpa which is visible object appears to cittas of the eye-door process and then, after there have been bhavanga-cittas in between, there are many mind-door processes of cittas. That is why one can see people walking or lifting their hands. Seventeen moments of citta pass away extremely rapidly. Thus, we should consider what happens in reality.

It should be known that the rūpa appearing at this moment through the eyes only lasts seventeen moments of citta and that it must fall away before sound can be experienced through ears. It seems that there can be hearing and seeing at the same time, but in between the moment of hearing and the moment of seeing there is an interval of more than seventeen moments of citta. The visible object, which appears through the eyes, and lasts seventeen moments of citta, must have fallen away before the citta that hears arises.

It seems that there can be hearing and seeing at the same time, but these are different moments of citta experiencing different objects. Rūpas arise and fall away and succeed one another.[9] Visible object appears through the eye-door and after there have been bhavanga-cittas in between, it appears through the mind-door. Then, there are many mind-door processes of cittas that think of concepts. That is why people who walk, lift their hands or move, can appear. When we see people

[9]Rūpas that fall away are immediately replaced by new rūpas so long as there are conditions for them. Rūpas of the body are produced by four factors: kamma, citta, temperature and nutrition.

lifting their hands or walking, there are countless nāma dhammas and rūpa dhammas arising and falling away all the time. So long as we don't realize the arising and falling away of nāma and rūpa, we cling to the idea that what appears are people, women, men, this or that thing. We cling to the concept of somebody or something.

When one studies paramattha dhammas, one should remember that they are real, that they are not beings, people or self; that they are not women, men, or different things. The dhammas that are true can be verified. One may have often heard the words that paramattha dhammas are real, that they are not beings, people or self, and one may have repeated these words oneself. However, paññā should be developed to the stage that the truth can be directly understood. Flavour and hardness are realities that appear and then, on account of these realities, there is a concept of grapes. The rūpas that arise and then fall away are real but there are, in the absolute sense, no grapes, no beings, or people. There are only rūpa dhammas and nāma dhammas that arise and fall away, succeeding one another very rapidly. Paramattha dhammas are real; they are not concepts.

From the beginning, the practice of the Dhamma should correspond to the theoretical knowledge acquired through listening and through study. The practice should be in accordance with the true characteristics of realities. We have, for example, learned that paramattha dhammas are anattā (not self), and thus we should try to understand the meaning of this, even on the theoretical level. We should consider it and develop paññā so that we can realize the truth in accordance with what we have learned before.

Questioner: Someone asked before whether concepts are real. There is, as you said, absolute truth (paramattha sacca) and conventional truth (sammutti sacca). Could one not say that concepts are real in the conventional sense?

Sujin: One can, but one should remember that concepts are not paramattha dhammas. The idea of grape has no flavour at all. Flavour is a reality and when it has appeared, we have a concept on account of it. We have a concept of flavour of grapes and we call it the flavour of grapes.

28
Concepts (III)

Lobha-mūla-citta (consciousness with attachment) without wrong view,[1] diṭṭhigata vippayutta, which arises in our daily life, is not only attached to visible object, sound, odour, flavour, tangible object and concepts, it is also attached to micchā samādhi, wrong concentration. Someone may, for example, apply himself to yoga exercises such as concentration on the breath in order to improve his bodily strength. Then, there is a kind of samādhi.

When the citta is not kusala, at such moments there is lobha-mūla-citta with micchā-samādhi, wrong concentration. There may only be attachment to samādhi with the aim of improving one's bodily health. There is not the wrong view that this is the way to realize the noble Truths. At that moment there is only attachment to concentration. Someone believes that he needs concentration for his bodily wellbeing. He has no wrong view that he should apply himself first to samādhi so

[1] Lobha-mūla-cittas can be accompanied by wrong view or they can be without wrong view. When they are accompanied by wrong view there is clinging to a distorted view of reality.

that he afterwards can consider nāma and rūpa and have right understanding of them more quickly, and that this is the way to realize the Noble Truths. If he has such wrong understanding, he will not know the characteristics of right mindfulness, sammā-sati. He will not know that sati is not self, anattā.

It is not true that when someone applies himself first to micchā-samādhi, it will help paññā to know the characteristics of nāma and rūpa. In order for sati to be sammā-sati, a factor of the Eightfold Path,[2] it must accompany sammā-diṭṭhi, right understanding, which understands the characteristics of the realities that are appearing. These are the objects sati should consider in the right way. It should be mindful of them so that right understanding can become more and more refined.

Right understanding of nāma and rūpa is accumulated as saṅkhāra-kkhandha[3] and thus conditions are being developed for the arising of direct awareness of the realities that are appearing. When there is seeing, one should know when the object is a paññatti, a concept, and when a paramattha dhamma. It is the same in the case of hearing, smelling, tasting, the experience of tangible object and the experience of an object through the mind-door.

When we watch television, a football game or tennis match, when we read a newspaper or look at pictures, we should know when the object is a concept and when a paramattha dhamma. If we do not know this, we may mistakenly think that only the story on television is a concept. In reality, however, there are concepts when we watch television and also when we do not watch television. Even the names of all of us here are nāma-paññattis; they are words of conventional language, which refer to citta, cetasika and rūpa which arise together and thus we know that there is this or that person.

Micchā-samādhi (wrong concentration) can accompany lobha-mūla-

[2]The sobhana cetasikas, beautiful cetasikas, which are the factors of the Eightfold Path are: right understanding, right thinking, right speech, right action, right livelihood, right effort, right mindfulness and right concentration. The development of the Eightfold Path is actually the development of right understanding of nāma and rūpa that appear at the present moment.

[3]This is the khandha or aggregate that includes all cetasikas except vedanā, feeling, and saññā, remembrance or perception. Paññā and all sobhana cetasikas are included in saṅkhārakkhanda and together they can become the accumulated condition for the growth of paññā, eventually leading to enlightenment.

citta without wrong view or with wrong view. In the latter case one believes that this kind of samādhi is the way to realize the four noble Truths. There is micchā-samādhi all over the world. While people apply themselves to concentration with citta which is not kusala citta accompanied by paññā, there is micchā-samādhi. When they believe that this is a faster way leading to mindfulness of the characteristics of nāma and rūpa, there is wrong understanding. Sammā-sati of the Eightfold Path can be mindful in the right way of the realities that appear if first the difference between the characteristics of nāma and rūpa is understood. Micchā-samādhi cannot condition right mindfulness.

Questioner: It is said that samādhi (concentration) is the proximate cause of vipassanā.

Sujin: What kind of samādhi is meant?

Questioner: It must be sammā-samādhi (right concentration) which is the proximate cause.

Sujin: It must be sammā-samādhi which arises together with sammā-sati, sammā-diṭṭhi (right understanding), sammā saṅkappa (right thinking) and sammā-vāyāma (right effort).

Concepts are the object of citta in daily life, at the moments that it does not have paramattha dhammas as object. We should find out ourselves how often we have concepts as object. There is seeing and then we think of a story about what appears through the eyes. There is hearing and then we think about what appears through the ears. It is the same with regard to the other sense-doors. The cittas that arise in a mind-door process experience visible object, sound, odour, flavour and tangible object, and they think in many different ways about all these objects.

Can there be other kinds of objects in our daily life, apart from paramattha dhammas or concepts? There can be either paramattha dhammas or concepts as objects in this life, in previous lives, or in future lives, in whatever plane or world one is living. There cannot be other kinds of objects. There are only six classes of objects (the objects which are experienced through the eyes, ears, nose, tongue, body and mind) and in these classes paramattha dhammas as well as concepts are included.

We may wonder whether the Buddha experienced objects that were concepts. Let us first speak about the daily life of ordinary people.

When the cittas of an eye-door process have fallen away and there have been bhavanga-cittas that arise in between, there is one series of mind-door process cittas that have as object the same paramattha dhamma as the eye-door process cittas that have just fallen away. After bhavanga-cittas that arise in between, there can be mind-door process cittas that think of the shape and form of what appeared. What appears through the eyes is a kind of rūpa, visible object, and this arises together with the four Great Elements of earth, water, fire and wind.[4]

We cannot separate colour from these four Great Elements. Wherever the four Great Elements are, the rūpas that are colour, odour, flavour and nutritive essence also have to be together with them. These eight rūpas cannot be separated from each other.[5] Thus, since we cannot take colour away from the four Great Elements, there can, after we have seen colour through the eyesense, be a concept on account of colour. Saññā remembers the meaning of the shape and form; we can have a concept of a whole, we can know that there is this or that thing, this or that person. Seeing conditions thinking of concepts. If there were no colour impinging on the eyesense and no seeing, could we then notice people, beings and different things?

The Buddha certainly had concepts as objects. When we listen to the Dhamma, we should also consider which cause leads to which effect. There are paramattha dhammas as well as concepts that can be the object of citta. At the moment a paramattha dhamma is not the object, a concept must be the object. The fact that this has been repeated time and again is a supporting condition for sati to be aware of the characteristics of the realities that appear.

Thus, it can be understood correctly that what appears through the eyes are only different colours. Since colour arises together with the four Great Elements and cannot be separated from them, different concepts are conceived on account of the colour that was seen. If satipaṭṭhāna arises, it can distinguish visible object, it can consider it and be aware of it, so that it can be correctly known that what appears are just different

[4]The four Great Elements of earth, water, fire and wind are conventional terms that refer to characteristics of rūpa such as solidity, cohesion, temperature and motion or pressure.

[5]Rūpas do not arise singly; they arise in groups, each of which consists of at least eight rūpas.

colours. Colour can be realized as only a kind of reality appearing through the eyes. It can be correctly understood that when one knows what different things are, there are, at the same time, mind-door process cittas that know concepts.

When we have studied the Dhamma and considered it, we shall see that the cittas of all beings, which arise in daily life, sometimes have a paramattha dhamma and sometimes a concept as object. There are not only cittas of the eye-door process that have colour as object. When the cittas of the eye-door process have fallen away and there have been bhavanga-cittas in between, mind-door process cittas arise experiencing the colour that was just before experienced by the eye-door process cittas. After the mind-door process cittas have fallen away and there have been bhavanga-cittas in between, there can be another series of mind-door process cittas that have a concept as object. If we do not know concepts, how can we lead our daily lives? If one didn't know what different things are, such as a table, a chair, food, a bowl, a plate or a spoon, one could not lead one's daily life. Also, animals must have concepts as objects, otherwise they could not stay alive. They must be able to know what is food and what is not.

Is there a difference in the way different people experience concepts, namely in the way the Buddha, the arahat, the anāgāmī, the sakadāgāmī, the sotāpanna[6] and the ordinary person experience them? There is a difference between ariyans and non-ariyans as to the way they experience concepts. Ordinary people who do not know anything about paramattha dhammas take concepts for things that are real. The ariyans who have realized the noble Truths know that all dhammas are anattā. The realities that arise and appear through eyes, ears, nose, tongue, bodysense and mind-door are impermanent, whereas concepts are not realities with the characteristics of impermanence and anattā. Concepts are not realities but they are the means to make things known. Concepts are the object of citta and cetasika when we know the meaning of the things that appear, when we know what different things are.

We should carefully consider phenomena and the conditions for their

[6]The arahat is fully enlightened; he has extinguished all defilements. The sotāpanna (first stage of enlightenment) has uprooted wrong view but still has other defilements. The sakadāgāmī and anāgāmī are at the second and third stage of enlightenment, respectively. All four are called ariyan, noble.

appearing; we should consider which cause leads to which effect. If there were no citta and cetasika, could there be concepts? That would be impossible. If there were only rūpas but no nāmas, no cittas and cetasikas, there could not be concepts. Rūpa is the reality that does not know an object, whereas citta and cetasika are the realities that know an object. Therefore, if citta and cetasika would not arise, concepts could not be known. Ariyans as well as non-ariyans have concepts as object, but there is a difference. Non-ariyans take concepts for realities whereas ariyans know when citta has a paramattha dhamma as object and when it has a concept as object.

When citta has a concept as object, is there wrong view, micchā-diṭṭhi? It depends on the kind of citta that has a concept as object. All ariyans have concepts as object but they do not have wrong view; they have completely eradicated the cetasika that is wrong view, micchā-diṭṭhi. If we do not carefully consider realities, we will not know the difference between lobha-mūla-citta with wrong view and lobha-mūla-citta without wrong view.

Lobha-mūla-citta without wrong view is attached to all objects. It is attached to what appears through the eyes and to the concept conceived on account of it. It is attached to sound that appears through the ears, and to a concept on account of the sound. It is the same in the case of the objects appearing through the other doorways. This is our ordinary daily life. Thus, lobha-mūla-citta can be attached to all objects without wrong view about them.

The sotāpanna and the sakadāgāmī have lobha-mūla-citta (consciousness with attachment) without wrong view, and this citta can be attached to all six classes of objects. The anāgāmī has lobha-mūla-citta without wrong view that is attached to the class of objects that are dhammārammaṇa, objects that can only be experienced through the mind-door. He has eradicated attachment to the sense objects that are visible object, sound, odour, flavour and tangible object. The arahat has neither kusala dhammas nor akusala dhammas on account of the six classes of objects. He has completely eradicated all defilements and akusala dhammas.

The person who is not an arahat may understand the characteristics of the objects as they are, he may know when the object is a paramattha dhamma and when a concept. However, so long as one has not eradicated all defilements, there are conditions for their arising. There can be happiness or sadness, like or dislike on account of the object, be they paramattha dhammas or concepts. To what extent defilements arise for the non-arahat depends on the degree of understanding that has been developed; it depends on whether a person is a non-ariyan or an ariyan who is a sotāpanna, a sakadāgāmī or an anāgāmī.

We should carefully consider when there is sakkāya-diṭṭhi, personality belief. Although concepts are not realities, paramattha dhammas, we may take them for things that really exist, and then there is wrong view. When someone clings to the concept of self, being, person or different things and really believes that they exist, there is the wrong view of sakkāya-diṭṭhi (personality belief). So long as sakkāya-diṭṭhi has not been eradicated, there are conditions for the arising of many other kinds of wrong view as well. There may be the wrong view that there is no kamma, no result of kamma. There may be the belief in an almighty god, the creator of the world and of all beings and all people. When we do not know the conditions for the arising of all saṅkhāra dhammas, conditioned dhammas, there can be different kinds of wrong view. However, clinging to wrong view does not occur each time citta has a concept as object.

Can concepts be the object of akusala citta? They can, and they are, in fact, usually the objects of akusala citta. There can be lobha-mūla-citta which is attached to a concept. Or, there can be dosa-mūla-citta which has aversion towards a concept. When one does not like this or that person, does one realize what the object is? At such moments a concept is the object of citta. Thus, we see that a concept can be the object of any kind of akusala citta.

Can a concept be the object of kusala citta? It can be the object of kusala citta. Concepts belong to our daily life and thus they are the objects of all kinds of cittas arising in our daily life. If we want to perform dāna (giving) but we don't know concepts, we wouldn't know what the gift is in conventional sense. In such a case, there could not be kusala citta that performs dāna. There cannot be abstention (virati) from wrong deeds or speech if one does not know what is there in conventional sense, if one does not know that there is a being or a person.

When someone develops samatha, can concepts be the object of citta? Someone may think that it is difficult to answer this question when he has not studied in detail the way of development of samatha and the subjects of calm. However, it is important to remember that when a dhamma is not the object of citta, a concept must be the object. Thus, also in samatha a concept can be the object of citta. All cittas, except the cittas that develop satipaṭṭhāna and the sense-door process cittas, can have concepts as object.

Only if we develop satipaṭṭhāna can we know whether a phenomenon is a paramattha dhamma. When satipaṭṭhāna does not arise, at such moments there is no awareness, no study and no investigation of the characteristics of paramattha dhammas. In our daily life, the object of citta is sometimes a paramattha dhamma and sometimes a concept. The development of satipaṭṭhāna is very intricate, because paññā must become very refined in order that it can see all the realities that appear as they are.

Questioner: Satipaṭṭhāna cannot have concepts as object and therefore, when we develop satipaṭṭhāna should we try to prevent citta from having a concept as object?

Sujin: That is not right because then we could not lead our ordinary daily life. We cannot prevent citta from having concepts as object. However, paññā can be developed so that it can be known that when a concept is the object, it is citta, a type of nāma that knows that concept. A concept could not be the object at that moment if there were no citta that knows it. When we develop satipaṭṭhāna, we should not force ourselves not to think of concepts. We should not try to stop knowing the different things that we normally see and recognize in daily life. If we did, we would not be able to know the characteristic of nāma dhamma, the reality that knows something. When a concept is the object, one should realize that citta and cetasika, which are nāma dhammas, have arisen and that, at that moment, they know an object that is a concept.

Satipaṭṭhāna can study and consider realities and be aware of them. Thus, it can be known that, when there is thinking, it is nāma which thinks, an element, a reality which experiences, not a self, a being or person. We should know that all dhammas are non-self, anattā, and that we cannot prevent citta from thinking of different things. Paññā should penetrate the characteristics of the different nāmas that experience different objects through the six doors. Then doubt about the characteristics of nāma dhammas can be eliminated. Nobody can prevent the arising of the phenomena of our daily life. It is because of ignorance that one tries not to think or not to know the concepts conceived on account of the things that appear. If someone tries to avoid thinking of concepts, paññā cannot be developed.

We should consider our way of practice. One may follow a kind of practice which is not the development of paññā (wisdom) which studies, notices, and considers the characteristics of nāma dhammas and rūpa dhammas. People don't lead their usual daily lives when they try to follow a particular practice. Then they develop the wrong path, micchā-magga, which is wrong understanding, wrong thinking, wrong speech, wrong action, wrong livelihood, wrong effort, wrong mindfulness, wrong concentration. That is not the right path, which is the development of satipaṭṭhāna and vipassanā.

If someone does not know as they are the characteristics of the realities that appear, and if he does not understand which cause leads to which effect, there will be wrong understanding. He will cling to wrong view; he will search for a way of practice that is the wrong path. There will be ignorance while he sees different colours and perceives different things.

We read in the "Kindred Sayings" (V, Mahā-Vagga, Book XLV, Kindred Sayings on the Way, Ch. 1, §4, The Brahmin):

> "Sāvatthī was the location for this discourse... Then the venerable Ānanda, robing himself in the forenoon and taking bowl and outer robe, entered Sāvatthī on his begging round. Now, the venerable Ānanda saw Jānussoṇi, the brahmin, driving out of Sāvatthī in his carriage, drawn by pure white mares. White were the steeds harnessed thereto and white the trappings, white the carriage. White were the fittings, white the reins, the goad, the canopy, his turban, his clothes and sandals, and by a white fan was he fanned. And when the people saw it they cried out, 'Ah! There is the best of carriages! There is the best of carriages for beauty!',"

Someone may just see white colour and then there can be wrong understanding if he does not know realities and if he does not know the way to realize the truth of not self. He may look for another way to know the truth. He may have the wrong understanding that a white carriage is the best. We read further on that the venerable Ānanda, after going on his begging round, came back, ate his meal and visited the Exalted One. He told him that he had seen Jānussoṇi in his white carriage and that the people had cried out that it was the best of carriages. Ānanda asked the Buddha whether he could point out the best of carriages in the Dhamma and Discipline. The Buddha explained that the defilements could be eradicated through the development of the Eightfold Path, not by seeing a white carriage with white trappings. The best of carriages is the ariyan eightfold Path. The Dhamma carriage is unsurpassed for its conquest in the fight.[7] The Buddha then said the following verse:

```
Whoso has confidence (saddhā) and wisdom, these two states,
Forever yoked together lead him on:
Conscience (hiri) the pole, and mind the yoke thereof,
And heedfulness (sati) his watchful charioteer.
The carriage is furnished with righteousness (sīla),
Rapture its axle, energy its wheels,
And calm, yoke fellow of the balanced mind,
Desirelessness the drapery thereof,
Goodwill and harmlessness his weapons are,
Together with detachment of the mind.
Endurance is his leathern coat of mail:
And to attain the peace this carriage rolls on.
It is built by oneself, and thus it becomes
The best of carriages, unconquerable in battle.
Seated therein the sages leave the world,
And verily they win the victory.
```

Thus, we can see that the white carriage and all the white paraphernalia, believed to be an auspicious sign, have nothing to do with the 'carriage' (yāna) which is the ariyan wisdom (ñāṇa).

In the commentary to this sutta, the "Sāratthappakāsinī", it is said that when the Brahmin Jānussoṇi drove around town, he had people

[7] In Pāli, there is a word association of yana, carriage, and ñāṇa, wisdom.

announce his coming ahead of time. When people had something to do outside of town, they would not leave, in order to see Jānussoṇi driving out. If people had already left town, they would return in order to see him. They believed it to be an auspicious sign to see the treasures and wealth of someone like Jānussoṇi. When the Brahmin Jānussoṇi was going to drive around the whole day, the people in town swept the roads from early morning on. They made them smooth with sand and scattered flowers all over. They helped each other to put up flags and banners and they caused the whole town to be filled with the smell of incense.

Jānussoṇi rode through the town in a white carriage with white paraphernalia, pulled by four white horses. The wheels and fittings of the carriage were made of silver. Jānussoṇi had two carriages, one for battle and one for all his paraphernalia. The battle carriage was four-sided and not so big; it could only take two or three people. But the carriage for all his paraphernalia was very large. There was room for eight to ten people who carried the canopy, the fan and palm leaves. These people could stand or comfortably lie down. The horses that pulled the carriage were all white and their ornaments were made of silver. The carriage looked white because its coverings were made of silver and it was decorated with ivory. The coverings of the other carriages were lion and tiger skins or yellow cloth. However, Jānussoṇi's carriage was covered by very precious cloth. The reins, and even the bridles were covered with silver. The canopy erected in the middle of the carriage was white.

Jānussoṇi's turban was seven inches wide and made of silver. His clothes were white, the colour of a lump of foam. His clothes and the coverings of his carriage were all of very expensive materials. His sandals, unlike the sandals of those that travel or go into the forest, were meant to be worn when he went in his carriage, and they were ornamented with silver. His fan was white with a handle of crystal.

He was the only person whose adornments were completely white. He used white face powder and white flowers to adorn himself. His jewellery, including the rings on his ten fingers and in his ears, was made of silver. His retinue consisted of ten thousand people and they were dressed in white clothes and adorned with white flowers and white jewellery.

Jānussoṇi enjoyed his wealth and dignity from the early morning, while he took his breakfast, applied perfumes and dressed himself in white. He went outside his palace and took off in his carriage. The brahmins of his retinue, who were also dressed in white, adorned with white cosmetics and white flowers, surrounded him while they carried his white canopy. Then, coins were scattered about for the children, and the people of the town would gather and cheer, tossing pieces of cloth. Jānussoṇi went around town to display his wealth. Thus, he would give people who wanted to have auspicious signs and blessings for good luck, an opportunity to see him. Those who were fortunate were able to enter the palace and go up to the first floor, open the windows and look down for a good view. When people saw the carriage of Jānussoṇi, they exclaimed that this was the best of carriages.

The Buddha said to Ānanda that people want to be praised because of beauty and wealth. However, just by being praised, one will not necessarily be beautiful and rich. Although the people who saw Jānussoṇi's carriage praised it as the best of carriages, it would not be the best just because people praised it as such. The Buddha said that in reality, Jānussoṇi's carriage was a miserable, ugly thing.

The Buddha further said to Ānanda that the best of carriages is a term that may be applied to the eightfold Path. This is an excellent way because it liberates one from all that is wrong. By the noble eightfold Path one can become an ariyan and attain nibbāna. The wisdom carriage, the Dhamma carriage, is the best vehicle, the best battle carriage. Nothing can surpass this carriage, and with it, the defilements can be conquered.

Thus, we see the difference between the carriage of Jānussoṇi and that of the Dhamma. There can be wrong view and wrong practice just because of seeing something. Some people may believe that white is an auspicious colour that conditions them to become pure, and without defilements. However, the Buddha said that in reality, Jānussoṇi's carriage was a miserable, ugly thing because it caused people to have wrong view. They had thought it was the best of carriages. The understanding of things as they are has nothing to do with the colour of someone's clothes or ornaments. When satipaṭṭhāna arises and is aware of the characteristics of the realities that appear, it can be said that it is the vehicle of paññā that leads to the eradication of defilements.

Part IV

The Development of Samatha

29
Development of Samatha

Samatha, or tranquil meditation, is not developed merely by concentration, samādhi. Samādhi is the dhamma that focuses on an object, it is ekaggatā cetasika accompanying each citta. When the citta is absorbed in an object for a long time, the characteristic of ekaggatā cetasika manifests itself as samādhi, concentration. It is firmly fixed on only one object. Ekaggatā cetasika that accompanies akusala citta is wrong concentration, micchā-samādhi, and ekaggatā cetasika that accompanies kusala citta is right concentration, sammā-samādhi.

If one tries to concentrate by focusing the citta for a long time on one object, and the citta is not accompanied by paññā, there is wrong concentration, micchā-samādhi. At such moments, one is attached to having the citta firmly fixed on one object. If there is no paññā, one cannot know the difference between lobha-mūla-citta, citta rooted in attachment, and kusala citta. Lobha-mūla-citta and kāmāvacara kusala citta (of the sense sphere) can be accompanied by the same types of feeling. Of the eight types of lobha-mūla-citta, four are accompanied by indifferent feeling and four by pleasant feeling. As to kāmāvacara kusala citta, four types are accompanied by indifferent feeling and four by pleasant feeling. In the case of indifferent feeling, the citta is neither happy nor unhappy, it is undisturbed, and in the case of pleasant feeling the citta is happy and delighted. When indifferent feeling or pleasant feeling arises, it is difficult to know whether there is lobha-mūla-citta or kusala citta.

Lobha-mūla-citta and mahā-kusala citta are entirely different types of citta: the eight types of lobha-mūla-citta are accompanied by akusala cetasikas whereas the eight types of mahā-kusala citta (kāmāvacara kusala citta) are accompanied by sobhana cetasikas. The akusala cetasika that is wrong view, micchā-diṭṭhi, can accompany lobha-mūla-citta; it accompanies four of the eight types of lobha-mūla-citta. The sobhana cetasika that is right view, sammā-diṭṭhi or paññā, can accompany mahā-kusala citta; it accompanies four of the eight types of mahā-kusala citta. When the characteristic of wrong view appears, it is evident that there is lobha-mūla-citta, not mahā-kusala citta, and when the characteristic of paññā appears, it is evident that there is mahā-kusala citta, not lobha-mūla-citta. Thus, the characteristic of wrong view and the characteristic of paññā show the distinction between lobha-mūla-citta and mahā-kusala citta. Someone who wants to develop samatha should know the difference between lobha-mūla-citta and kusala citta, otherwise he could be attached to having concentration. In that case, there would be micchā-samādhi, wrong concentration, which is without paññā.

Generally, people who try to concentrate on an object want the citta to be without disturbance, anxiety or worry about different matters and events in their daily life. They are satisfied if the citta can be firmly fixed on an object and they do not realize that at the moments they wish to concentrate on a specific subject, there is no mahā-kusala citta accompanied by paññā.

The development of samatha is actually the development of mahā-kusala accompanied by paññā. Someone who wants to develop samatha must have paññā that sees the danger of akusala, of lobha and dosa, aversion. He should not merely see the disadvantage of dosa, arising when there is worry or anxiety. If one does not know one's defilements and one does not see the danger of lobha, one will not be able to develop samatha. The person who develops samatha should be truthful, he should have paññā that sees the danger of lobha; he should have sati-sampajañña;[1] he should know the difference between lobha-mūla-citta and mahā-kusala citta accompanied by paññā. Then he can develop mahā-kusala accompanied by paññā, so that there are no longer akusala cittas arising in between the moments of developing calm, and he can reach the degree of samādhi which is access concentration, upacāra samādhi, and attainment concentration, appanā samādhi, arising at the moment of jhāna, absorption. The kusala jhānacitta of the first stage of jhāna is accompanied by the five jhāna factors of vitakka, applied thinking, vicāra, sustained thinking, pīti, rapture, sukha, happy feeling and ekaggatā, concentration.

It is not easy to develop mahā-kusala citta accompanied by paññā to such degree that it can be the foundation of kusala jhānacitta of the first stage, which is rūpāvacara kusala citta. Someone who wants to attain jhāna should not have the impediments that cause him to be unable to do so.[2] Such a person cannot attain jhāna or enlightenment, even if he cultivates samatha or vipassanā. For the person who can develop samatha and attain jhāna or develop vipassanā and attain enlightenment, there are the following requirements:[3]

1. He should not have vipāka that is an impediment, that is, he should be born with rebirth-consciousness accompanied by paññā, thus, tihetuka, accompanied by three sobhana hetus.

2. He should be without the impediment of kamma, that is, he should not have committed one of the five ānantariya kammas, weighty kammas. These kammas prevent rebirth in heaven and the arising of magga-citta and phala-citta. These five kinds of kamma are: patricide, matricide, killing of an arahat, wounding a Buddha and

[1] Sampajañña is often translated as clear comprehension. In this context, the person who develops samatha should not merely have theoretical knowledge of the difference between lobha-mūla-citta and mahā-kusala citta, but he should be able to distinguish between their characteristics when they appear.

[2] Abhabba puggala, a person who is unable of progress. He is not born with rebirth-consciousness accompanied by paññā, or he has committed ānantariya kamma, very serious akusala kamma that produces an immediate result at rebirth, or he has the kinds of wrong view which are of the degree of akusala kamma patha.

[3] He is a bhabba puggala, a person who is able to make progress. See "Gradual Sayings", Book of the Sixes, Ch IX, § 2 and 3.

creating a schism in the Order of monks, by not living in harmony with the Order.

3. He should be without the impediment of the kinds of wrong view classified as "wrong views with fixed destiny" (niyata micchādiṭṭhi). These are the wrong views of natthika-diṭṭhi (denial of the result of kamma), of ahetuka-diṭṭhi (denial of both kamma and result) and of akiriya-diṭṭhi (denial of the efficacy of kamma).[4]

Someone may be born with a paṭisandhi-citta, rebirth-consciousness, which is tihetuka, thus, accompanied by paññā, but he may be attached to visible object, sound, odour, flavour and tangible object and he may not see the danger of these sense objects. Then he will not be inclined to eliminate his infatuation with sense objects by observing sīla and developing samatha. Thus, the development of samatha to the degree of access concentration, upacāra samādhi and attainment concentration, appanā samādhi, is not at all easy. If someone takes lobha-mūla-citta for mahā-kusala citta, he may erroneously believe, when the citta conditions visions of hell, heaven, different places and events, that he has attained upacāra samādhi and appanā samādhi of the different stages of jhāna.

The development of samatha is a most intricate matter that should be studied carefully, so that there can be right understanding of it.

When we in our daily life are seeing, hearing, smelling, tasting, experiencing tangible objects or thinking, we should realize that akusala cittas are likely to arise more often than kusala cittas. In a day or in a month there are only very few moments of kusala cittas that have as objective dāna or sīla. Someone who sees the danger of akusala will be inclined to develop kusala citta. When there is no opportunity for dāna or sīla, one can develop the calm that is freedom from akusala in one's daily life, and that is kusala of the degree of samatha. It is beneficial to develop calm in daily life, even if one cannot attain access concentration or attainment concentration. However, if one wants to subdue defilements, so that the citta is calm, free from akusala, one needs to have paññā that knows how the citta can become calm, free from defilements, when one experiences sense objects or thinks. If that is not the case, kusala citta cannot arise.

---

[4]See Appendix to Citta, under akusala citta.

For the development of samatha, the development of kusala citta with calm, which is freedom from akusala, there are forty specific subjects that can condition calm. These subjects are: ten kasinas, ten meditations on foulness (asubha), ten recollections (anussati), the meditation on the repulsiveness of food (āhāre paṭikkūla saññā), defining of the four elements (catudhātu vavatthāna), the four divine abidings (brahmavihāras) and the four subjects of arūpa-jhāna.

The Ten Kasinas

The ten kasinas are the following:[5]

1. Earth kasina (paṭhavī kasiṇa), by means of which one meditates only on earth;
2. Water kasina (āpo kasiṇa), by means of which one meditates only on water;
3. Fire kasina (tejo kasiṇa), by means of which one meditates only on fire;
4. Air kasina (vāyo kasiṇa), by means of which one meditates only on air or wind;
5. Blue kasina (nīla kasiṇa), by means of which one meditates only on the colour blue;
6. Yellow kasina (pīta kasiṇa), by means of which one meditates only on the colour yellow;
7. Red kasina (lohita kasiṇa), by means of which one meditates only on the colour red;
8. White kasina (odāta kasiṇa), by means of which one meditates only on the colour white;

[5] A kasina is a concrete device, such as a disc of earth or a coloured disc, which can condition calmness. If one looks at it with right concentration one can acquire a mental image of it. Kasiṇa means whole, entire. If the earth kasina is one's meditation subject, all things can be seen as just "earth," and it is the same in the case of the other kasinas. The image conceived in this way can be extended without limitation.

9. Light kasina (āloka kasiṇa), by means of which one meditates only on light;

10. Space kasina (ākāsa kasiṇa), by means of which one meditates only on space.

Is the citta that pays attention to only earth kusala or akusala? If paññā does not arise while paying attention to earth, there is akusala citta that desires to think of earth or to focus on earth.

When paññā arises, the citta that meditates on earth is kusala. It can be realized that all material phenomena that appear cannot be without the element of earth[6] and that all the things one is attached to or desires are only earth. When one realizes that all the things in the world one used to be attached to are in essence only earth, it is a condition for subduing attachment to them.

It is difficult to have kusala citta that meditates on only earth, because when an object impinges on one of the senses or the mind-door, one is immediately taken in by that object. Therefore, if someone wants to develop samatha so that kusala citta becomes more and more established in calm, in freedom from akusala, he needs to be in a quiet place, where he is not disturbed by the noise of people. One should make the earth kasina of smooth clay in the form of a circle, without flaws and imperfections, so that it is suitable for meditation. Otherwise, the citta would be inclined to delight in and have attachment to the outward appearance of it.[7] When the person who develops the earth kasina looks at it and contemplates it with right understanding, there is kusala citta accompanied by paññā, and there is true calm. He should look at the earth kasina in order to remind himself to pay attention to only earth, all the time, and not to other objects.

It is most difficult to pay attention all the time to only earth with kusala citta that is calm, free from akusala. As the "Visuddhimagga" states, the kasina should not be too small, nor too large, it should not be too far away nor too near, it should not be placed too high nor too low. Vitakka cetasika, applied thinking, is one of the jhāna factors[8]

[6] Earth is one of the Four Great Elements present with all materiality.

[7] For details, see "Visuddhimagga" IV, 21-31.

[8] The jhāna-factors are specific cetasikas developed in samatha. These will be dealt with further on.

that is indispensable. Vitakka cetasika arising with mahā-kusala citta accompanied by paññā should "touch" or "strike at" the earth kasina. The citta should be free from akusala when one's eyes are closed as well as when they are open, so that a visualized image (uggaha-nimitta or acquired image) of the earth kasina can appear through the mind-door. This mental image is just as clear as when the person who develops the earth kasina was looking at it with his eyes open. Even if people are born with three hetus, thus, with paññā, they may not be able to acquire this mental image. It can appear when mahā-kusala citta accompanied by paññā is firmly established in calm with the earth kasina. When this mental image appears, one has not yet attained access concentration, upacāra samādhi.

It is not at all easy to guard this mental image and thereby have calm increased, while developing mahā-kusala citta accompanied by paññā. According to the "Visuddhimagga" (IV, 31), when the "hindrances"(nīvaraṇa dhammas, akusala dhammas which disturb and oppress the citta) have been successively suppressed, the citta is more established in calm and then a counter-image (paṭibhāga-nimitta) of the earth kasina appears. This image is clearer and more purified than the "acquired image" which appeared before. At that moment, the mahā-kusala citta accompanied by paññā has become more established in calm so that access concentration, upacāra samādhi, is reached. This kind of concentration is called access concentration, because it is close to attainment-concentration, which is firmly fixed on the object, at the moment the jhānacitta of the first stage arises.

The meditator should guard the counter-image by developing the mahā-kusala citta accompanied by paññā that has attained the degree of access concentration, so that calm increases all the time. In that way calm to the degree of attainment-concentration, appanā samādhi, can be reached, and the jhānacitta of the first stage can arise, which is of the level of rūpāvacara citta. However, in order to reach this stage, he should guard the counter-image as if it were the unborn child of a "Wheel-Turning Monarch."[9] He should avoid conditions not beneficial for the development of calm[10] and these are the following:

[9] World Ruler.

[10] See "Visuddhimagga" IV, 34-42.

1. He should avoid a dwelling where the mental image that has not yet arisen does not arise, and the mental image that has arisen is lost.

2. He should not be too far from an alms-resort or too near, and he should not be in a place where it is difficult to obtain almsfood or where almsfood is not plentiful.

3. He should avoid unsuitable speech, speech included in the kinds of "animal talk." Such speech is not beneficial for the development of paññā, and it leads to the disappearance of the mental image that has arisen.

4. He should avoid people who are full of defilements, who are engaged with what is unwholesome, because that causes him to be disturbed by impure cittas.

5. He should avoid unsuitable food, because that would make him ill.

6. He should avoid an unsuitable climate, because that would make him ill.

7. He should avoid postures that are unsuitable for his concentration.

If he avoids what is unsuitable and cultivates what is suitable, but appanā samādhi does not yet arise, he should have recourse to ten kinds of skill in absorption, dhammas beneficial for the arising of jhānacitta:[11]

1. He should make the basis (vatthu) clean, that is the internal basis, which is his body, and the external basis, which are his clothing and his dwelling. Otherwise, the citta will not be purified.

2. He should balance the faculties, indriyas.[12] For example, confidence and understanding should be balanced, energy and concentration should be balanced. They are balanced through mindfulness.

[11]See "Visuddhimagga" IV, 42-67.

[12]There are five indriyas, spiritual faculties, which should be developed, namely, confidence, energy, mindfulness, concentration and understanding.

3. He needs to have skill in protecting the mental image.
4. He should exert the citta when it should be exerted.
5. He should restrain the citta when it should be restrained.
6. He should encourage the citta when it should be encouraged.
7. He should regard the citta with equanimity when it should be regarded with equanimity.
8. He should avoid unconcentrated persons.
9. He should cultivate concentrated persons.
10. He should be inclined to and resolute upon those things that lead to concentration.

If he does not have those ten skills in absorption, mahā-kusala citta accompanied by paññā cannot become more firmly established in calm to the degree of being the foundation for appanā-samādhi, for the arising of rūpāvacara citta that is the jhānacitta of the first stage. But if he is equipped with these skills, jhānacitta can arise.

The jhānacitta is of a higher level of citta, it is of a plane of citta that is free from the sense sphere (kāmāvacara citta). In the mind-door process during which jhāna is attained, there are the following cittas arising in succession:

- bhavanga-citta, which is mahā-vipāka ñāṇa-sampayutta;[13]
- bhavanga calana (vibrating bhavanga), which is mahā-vipāka, ñāṇa-sampayutta;
- bhavangupaccheda (arrest bhavanga), which is mahā-vipāka, ñāṇa-sampayutta;
- manodvārāvajjana-citta, which is ahetuka kiriyacitta;
- parikamma (preparatory citta) which is mahā-kusala citta, ñāṇa-sampayutta;

[13]If one is not born with paññā, one cannot attain jhāna. If one is tihetuka, born with paññā, all bhavanga-cittas are accompanied by paññā.

- upacāra (access) which is mahā-kusala citta, ñāṇa-sampayutta (of the same type as parikamma);
- anuloma (adaptation) which is mahā-kusala citta, ñāṇa-sampayutta (of the same type as parikamma);
- gotrabhū (change of lineage) which is mahā-kusala citta, ñāṇa-sampayutta (of the same type as parikamma);
- kusala citta of the first stage of jhāna, which is rūpāvacara kusala citta;
- bhavanga-citta, which is mahā-vipākacitta, ñāṇa sampayutta.

When jhāna is attained for the first time, there is only one moment of rūpāvacara kusala citta, whereas, later on, when one's skill has increased, there can be more jhānacittas arising in succession without the arising of bhavanga-cittas in between. Such a process of jhānacittas is called "jhāna-samāpatti," jhāna attainment. It is the attainment to the citta that is calm and firmly concentrated on the object of jhāna. Then jhānacittas arise successively during the length of time determined upon by the meditator.

Before jhāna vīthi-cittas arise there must be mahā-kusala cittas accompanied by paññā each time. The first mahā-kusala javana-citta is parikamma, preparatory citta; it prepares appanā-samādhi, it is the condition for the attainment of absorption, appanā. If the mahā-kusala citta that is parikamma does not arise, the following cittas and appanā-samādhi that accompanies jhānacitta cannot arise.

The second mahā-kusala javana-citta is upacāra, access, because it is close to appanā-samādhi.

The third mahā-kusala javana-citta is anuloma, adaptation, because it is favourable (anukūla) to appanā-samādhi.

The fourth mahā-kusala javana-citta is gotrabhū, change of lineage, because it transcends the sensuous plane (kamāvacara bhūmi) so that the fine-material plane (rupāvacara bhūmi) can be reached.

When the fourth mahā-kusala javana-citta has fallen away, the following javana-citta is rūpāvacara kusala citta of the first stage of jhāna.

The development of five cetasikas that are the jhāna-factors condition the arising of rūpāvacara kusala citta of the first stage of jhāna. These factors accompanying the jhānacitta are:

- applied thinking (vitakka);
- sustained thinking (vicāra);
- rapture (pīti);
- happy feeling (sukha);
- concentration (ekaggatā).

Among the sobhana cetasikas accompanying the jhāna-citta these five factors are specifically counteractive to the "hindrances," the nīvaraṇa dhammas. The five hindrances are akusala dhammas that disturb the citta and prevent it from the development of calm. They are the following:

- kāmacchanda, sensuous desire, which is attachment to visible objects, sound, odour, flavour and tangible object;
- vyāpāda, ill-will or displeasure;
- thīna-middha, sloth and torpor, which are listlessness and dejectedness, inertness and drowsiness;
- uddhacca-kukkucca, restlessness and worry;
- vicikicchā, doubt about realities, doubt about cause and result.

The five jhāna-factors are opposed to the five hindrances. Vitakka cetasika applies itself to the object, it "touches" it, so that the citta is calm. Vicāra cetasika continually occupies itself with the object vitakka touches, so that the citta does not become restless and takes another object. Pīti cetasika is satisfied with and takes delight in the meditation subject and sukha vedanā, happy feeling, increases this satisfaction. Ekaggatā cetasika that supports the other jhāna-factors is firmly concentrated on the object of the jhāna-citta of the first stage.

The five jhāna-factors are opposed to, counteractive to the five hindrances in the following way ("Visuddhimagga" IV, 86):

1. Vitakka cetasika is opposed to thīna-middha, sloth and torpor. When vitakka "thinks" only of the meditation subject, touches it time and again, dejectedness, listlessness and drowsiness cannot arise.

2. Vicāra cetasika is opposed to vicikicchā, doubt. When vicāra cetasika is continually occupied with the object which vitakka touches, doubt about realities and doubt about cause and result cannot arise.

3. Pīti cetasika is opposed to vyāpāda, ill-will. When calm with the meditation subject increases, there will also be more rapture and delight with the subject of calm and then ill-will and displeasure cannot arise in between.

4. Sukha, happy feeling, is opposed to uddhacca-kukkucca, restlessness and worry. When there is happy feeling about the meditation subject, restlessness and worry that could turn to another object cannot arise.

5. Ekaggatā cetasika is opposed to kāmacchanda, sensuous desire. When samādhi is firmly concentrated on the meditation subject, there cannot be attachment to sense objects.

When rūpāvacara kusala citta of the first stage of jhāna accompanied by five jhāna-factors arises, attainment-concentration, appanā-samādhi, is firmly concentrated on the object. This jhānacitta that arises for the first time is not succeeded by other jhāna-cittas; it arises only once. After several bhavanga-cittas have arisen and fallen away in between, there is a mind-door process of cittas. The mind-door adverting-consciousness adverts to the jhānacitta and after it has fallen away it is succeeded by seven mahā-kusala cittas accompanied by paññā which considers the jhāna-factors; and then there will be bhavanga-cittas arising in between, to be followed by other mind-door processes. Only one of the jhāna-factors at a time is considered during one process of cittas. The mind-door processes of cittas which consider the jhāna-factors one at a time are called the processes of reviewing, paccavekkhaṇa vīthi, and these have to arise each time after jhāna has been attained.

The paññā of the person who attains rūpa-jhāna has to know the different characteristics of the five jhāna-factors. Thus, paññā must know the difference between vitakka cetasika, applied thinking, and vicāra cetasika, sustained thinking, it must know the difference between pīti, rapture, and sukha, happy feeling, and it must also know the characteristic of ekaggatā cetasika which is of the degree of appanā samādhi.

The person who develops samatha should have sati-sampajañña in his daily life, he should have right understanding of the characteristic of kusala citta and of akusala citta that may follow one upon the other very rapidly. If this is not known, he may erroneously believe that lobha-mūla-citta accompanied by pleasant feeling is calm which is kusala.

The person who develops samatha does not have extraordinary experiences. The development of samatha is the development of kusala through the mind-door. When the citta has become calm only the mental image of the meditation subject appears and this is the condition for the citta to become more firmly established in kusala. The person who, for example, develops the meditation subject of the water kasina has the mental image of this kasina as object, and he does not have visions of hell, of heaven or of different happenings. If someone tries to concentrate and believes to have all kinds of visions, he does not develop samatha.

In the development of samatha there must be mahā-kusala citta accompanied by paññā that attains calm by meditation on one of the forty meditation subjects of samatha. Lobha-mūla-citta or mahā-kusala citta which is unaccompanied by paññā may have as object one of these forty meditation subjects, but then there is no development of samatha. A child, or even a grown up, may recite the word "Buddha," without pondering on his virtues, but then there is no mahā-kusala citta accompanied by paññā, and thus no development of true calm by means of the recollection of the Buddha. Someone who sees a corpse may be frightened and then there is dosa-mūla-citta, not mahā-kusala citta accompanied by paññā. If a person tries to concentrate on his breathing without knowing in which way there can be true calm, freedom from defilements, there is no mahā-kusala citta accompanied by paññā. All meditation subjects of samatha should be developed by mahā-kusala citta accompanied by paññā, which has right understanding of the way to become calm. They should be developed in the same way as the earth kasina, as explained above.

The person who has attained the first stage of jhāna may see the disadvantage of vitakka cetasika, the cetasika that touches or "strikes" at the object. Vitakka which usually touches the sense objects that are visible object, sound, odour, flavour and tangible object is gross since on account of these objects akusala dhammas could easily arise. The jhānacitta could become calmer and more refined if it would be without vitakka and only accompanied by vicāra, pīti, sukha and ekaggatā. Therefore, he makes an effort to meditate on the object of the first stage of jhāna he attained and to develop more calm with that object without vitakka having to touch it. He can accomplish this if he acquires five "masteries" or skills, vasī, in jhāna. These are the following:

1. Mastery in adverting (āvajjana vasī), skill in adverting to the first jhāna wherever and whenever he wishes to.
2. Mastery in attaining (samāpacchana vasī), skill in entering into jhāna, that is causing the arising of jhānacitta, wherever and whenever he wishes to.
3. Mastery in resolving (adiṭṭhāna vasī), skill in resolving the duration of the series of jhānacittas that arise and fall away in succession, wherever and whenever he wishes to.
4. Mastery in emerging (vuṭṭhāna vasī), skill in emerging from jhāna, wherever and whenever he wishes to.
5. Mastery in reviewing (pacchavekkhaṇa vasī), skill in reviewing each of the jhāna-factors, one at a time, wherever and whenever he wishes to.

If someone wishes to attain higher stages of jhāna, he should see the disadvantages of the jhāna-factors of the lower stages and he should abandon those successively. The jhāna-factors are abandoned at different stages in the following way:

- When the jhānacitta of the second stage (dutiya jhāna) arises, vitakka (applied thinking) has been abandoned, and, thus, it is without vitakka and accompanied by the four factors of vicāra

(sustained thinking), pīti (rapture), sukha (happy feeling) and ekaggatā (concentration).

- The jhānacitta of the third stage (tatiya jhāna) is without vicāra and accompanied by the three factors of pīti, sukha and ekaggatā.

- The jhānacitta of the fourth stage (catuta jhāna) is without pīti and accompanied by the two factors of sukha and ekaggatā.

- The jhānacitta of the fifth stage (pañcama jhāna) is without sukha and accompanied by the two factors of upekkhā and ekaggatā.

As explained above, the jhāna-factors are abandoned in accordance with the fivefold system of jhāna. For some people paññā can abandon both vitakka and vicāra at the same time, and then the second stage of jhāna is without vitakka and vicāra. In that case, the stages of jhāna are reckoned according to the fourfold system and that means that the second, third and fourth stage of jhāna of the fourfold system are respectively like the third, fourth and fifth stage of the fivefold system.

If someone lacks the skills that are the "masteries," vasīs, it is impossible for him to abandon jhāna-factors of a lower stage so that he could attain higher stages of jhāna.

Whenever the jhānacittas have fallen away there have to be processes of cittas that review the jhāna-factors.

By the development of samatha defilements are subdued, they are not eradicated completely. Therefore, it may happen that jhānacitta declines, that it does not arise quickly, that one loses the skill one used to have, or even that jhānacitta does not arise again. If one wants to maintain one's skill in jhāna, one should apply oneself to the "masteries" each time one of the stages of jhāna has been attained.

With regard to the forty meditation subjects of samatha, some objects condition the citta to be calm, but not to the degree of upacāra samādhi, access concentration, and some objects condition calm to the degree of upacāra samādhi. Some objects condition calm only to the degree of the first jhāna, some to the degree of the fourth stage of jhāna according to the fivefold system, and some to the degree of the fifth jhāna. Some meditation subjects can exclusively be the object of the fifth jhāna.

There are six recollections (anussati) which can condition calm, but if one is not an ariyan, they cannot condition calm to the degree of upacāra samādhi. These recollections are: recollection of the Buddha (Buddhānussati), recollection of the Dhamma (Dhammānussati), recollection of the Sangha (Sanghānussati), recollection of generosity (cāgānussati), recollection of morality (sīlānussati), and recollection of devas (devatānussati). For those who are ariyans, these recollections can condition calm to the degree of upacāra samādhi, but not to the degree of appanā samādhi, attainment concentration.

The recollection of death (maraṇānussati) can condition calm only to the degree of upacāra samādhi. The recollection of peace (upasamānussati) is the meditation on nibbāna, which can be developed exclusively by ariyans, and this subject can condition calm only to the degree of upacāra samādhi.

The perception of repulsiveness in food (āhāre paṭikkūla saññā) is a meditation subject that can condition calm to the degree of upacāra samādhi.

The analysis of the four Elements (catu dhātu vavatthāna), a meditation subject on the Elements of Earth, Water, Fire and Wind, which are present in the body, can condition calm to the degree of upacāra samādhi.

The ten impurities (asubhā) are ten cemetery contemplations that can condition calm to the degree of the first jhāna.

Mindfulness of the body, kāyagatāsati, is a meditation on the loathsomeness of the body. It is a reflection on each of the thirty-two parts of the body, such as hair of the head, hair of the body, nails, teeth and skin. This meditation subject can condition calm to the degree of the first jhāna.

Mindfulness of breathing, ānāpāna sati, can condition calm to the degree of the fifth stage of jhāna.

The ten kasinas can condition calm to the degree of the fifth jhāna.

Three brahmavihāras (divine abidings), namely, loving-kindness, mettā, compassion, karuṇā, and sympathetic joy, muditā, can condition calm to the degree of the fourth jhāna of the fivefold system (and the third jhāna of the fourfold system).

The fourth brahmavihāra is equanimity, upekkhā. When someone has attained calm with the other three brahmavihāras to the degree of the fourth stage of jhāna, he can develop the brahmavihāra of upekkhā and this is exclusively the object of the jhāna of the fifth stage.

There are four stages of arūpa-jhāna, immaterial jhāna. The jhānacitta of these stages is of the same type as the jhānacitta of the fifth stage of rūpa-jhāna, but it does not have an object connected with rūpa. Someone who wants to develop arūpa-jhāna should first attain the fifth stage of rūpa-jhāna. Then he may see the disadvantage of this stage. Although it is the highest stage of rūpa-jhāna, the jhānacitta still has an object connected with rūpa, and therefore, he sees the danger of easily becoming infatuated with sense objects. Thus, he withdraws from rūpa as object and inclines to objects that are not rūpa, which are more subtle and more refined. If he abandons rūpa and takes as object arūpa that is boundless until appanā samādhi arises, he attains arūpa-jhāna kusala citta. Then the cittas arise and fall away in succession in a mind-door process, just as in the case of the attainment of rūpa-jhāna. He has to be equipped with the five "masteries," vasīs, so that he can attain higher stages of arūpa-jhāna.

There are four stages of arūpa-jhāna, and the jhānacitta of all four stages is of the same type as the jhānacitta of the fifth stage of rūpa-jhāna, but the objects are different and they become successively more subtle.

The first stage of arūpa-jhāna is the jhānacitta that has as object infinity of space, it is ākāsanañcāyatana jhānacitta.[14]

The second stage of arūpa-jhāna is the jhānacitta that has as object infinity of consciousness, it is viññāṇañcāyatana jhānacitta.[15] This citta has as object the jhānacitta of the first stage of arūpa-jhāna that experiences infinity of space. The person who cultivates this stage of arūpa-jhāna sees that the object of infinity of space is not as subtle as the object that is the jhānacitta experiencing infinity of space. Therefore, he transcends the object of infinity of space and takes as object the jhānacitta which experiences infinity of space, until appanā samādhi arises and he attains the second stage of arūpa-jhāna, of infinity of consciousness.

[14] Ākāsa means space, ananta means: infinite, and āyatana means: sphere.

[15] This term includes the words viññāṇa and ananta, meaning: consciousness which is infinite.

The third stage of arūpa-jhāna is the jhānacitta that has as object "there is nothing," it is ākiñcaññāyatana jhānacitta.[16] When the person who cultivates this stage sees that the object of the second stage, the infinity of consciousness, is not as subtle and refined as the object of nothingness, he transcends the object of the second stage and turns to the object of nothingness, which conditions more calm. He cultivates the object of nothingness until appanā samādhi arises and he attains the third stage of arūpa jhāna. The jhānacitta of this stage has nothingness as object, because it has no longer as object the jhānacitta experiencing infinity of space, which citta is the object of the second stage.

The fourth stage of arūpa jhāna is "neither-perception-nor-non-perception," the n'evasaññā-n'āsaññāyatana jhānacitta. This is the jhānacitta that has as object the jhānacitta of the third stage experiencing nothingness. The person who cultivates this stage sees that the jhānacitta which experiences nothingness is of a most subtle nature. Therefore, he takes this jhānacitta as object, so that appanā-samādhi arises, and he attains the fourth stage of arūpa-jhāna. Saññā and the accompanying dhammas at this stage of jhāna are so subtle that it cannot be said that they are present nor that they are not present; they are present in a residual way and cannot effectively perform their functions.[17] The arūpa-jhāna of the fourth stage, the "sphere of neither-perception-nor-non-perception" is so called, because it cannot be said that there is perception, saññā, nor can it be said that there is not.

The development of samatha, the calm that is freedom from defilements, up to the degree of arūpa-jhāna, can only be accomplished by a powerful citta. When someone has achieved this, he can train himself to reach the benefit of the special supernatural powers he has set as his goal. These are, for example, recollection of one's former lives, the resolution to have the "divine eye" by which one sees things that are far off, or that are obstructed, the resolution to have the "divine ear" by which one hears sounds far or near, the resolution to perform magical powers (iddhi pāṭihāriya) such as walking on water, diving into the earth, floating through the air, or the creation of different forms. However, if someone wants to train himself to have such special qualities he must

[16] Ākiñcañña means: there is nothing.

[17] See "Atthasālinī" I, Book I, Part VI. 207-209. There is a subtle residuum not only of saññā but also of the citta and the other accompanying dhammas.

have the highest skill in all kasinas and in the eight attainments that are the four stages of rūpa-jhāna and the four stages of arūpa-jhāna.

The "Visuddhimagga" describes fourteen ways of training to achieve supernatural powers (XII, 3-8). Someone who wishes to train himself to reach this goal should, for example, be able to attain jhāna with the kasinas in conformity with the order of the kasinas, that is, first with the earth kasina, after that with the water kasina, and so on. Or he should be able to attain jhāna with the kasinas in reverse order, or to skip jhānas of the different stages without skipping the successive kasinas, or to skip kasinas without skipping the successive stages of jhāna. Thus, he should know the right conditions for perfect control of his attainments.

It may seem that a person has such perfect control and that he can perform miracles, but, if he has not cultivated the right cause leading to the right effect, he does not really have the special qualities that are supernatural powers. The "Visuddhimagga" (IV, 8) explains that the development of the different stages of jhāna and the acquirement of supernatural powers is most difficult:

"It is not possible for a meditator to begin to accomplish transformation by supernormal powers unless he has previously completed his development by controlling his mind in these fourteen ways. Now the kasina preliminary work is difficult for a beginner and only one in a hundred or a thousand can do it. The arousing of the (acquired) mental image is difficult for one who has done the preliminary work and only one in a hundred or a thousand can do it. To extend the sign when it has arisen[18] and to reach absorption is difficult and only one in a hundred or a thousand can do it. To tame one's mind in fourteen ways after reaching absorption is difficult and only one in a hundred or a thousand can do it. The transformation by supernatural power after training one's mind in the fourteen ways is difficult and only one in a hundred or a thousand can do it. Rapid response after attaining transformation is difficult and only one in a hundred or a thousand can do it..."

It is the same in the case of remembering one's former lives, it is most difficult. Who could attain upacāra samādhi, access concentration, if the citta is not mahā-kusala citta accompanied by paññā? Who could claim to have attained appanā samādhi that arises at the moment of the first

[18]Extension of the sign means that the mental image can be extended until it is boundless.

stage of jhāna? Who could claim to have attained the second, third, fourth and fifth stage of jhāna, or arūpa-jhāna? Who could claim to remember his past lives if he cannot revert in memory from now to this morning? Can he remember each moment? Can he revert to yesterday evening, to yesterday morning, or can he, with a citta firmly established in calm, remember each moment reverting to the rebirth-consciousness, or even to the last moment of the last day of his past life and revert successively to past lives? This can only be achieved if the jhānacitta has become powerful, and if one has trained oneself in all the skills necessary for supernatural powers. If that is the case, one can cause mahā-kusala citta accompanied by paññā to arise and remembrance of past lives can be accomplished while reverting from a specific moment on to the past.

If one studies in detail and understands the right conditions for the special qualities which are the supernatural powers, one will know whether a certain achievement is truly due to those special qualities or not.

By the development of samatha defilements are not eradicated. In samatha the paññā is not developed which penetrates the characteristics of impermanence, dukkha and anattā, which knows the true nature of realities. Only this kind of paññā can eradicate defilements. If jhāna does not decline and jhānacitta can arise in the process just before the dying-consciousness, the jhānacitta is kamma-condition for the arising of jhāna vipākacitta that is the rebirth-consciousness in one of the brahma planes. However, when that person's lifespan has come to an end in such a plane, he will again revert to life in this world with clinging to self, to visible object, sound, odour, flavour and tangible object.

The development of samatha in past lives can be accumulated in the cycle of birth and death. It can be a condition for some people to have a presentiment of events that may take place. Someone who has developed concentration may be able to see omens and have a presentiment of events in the future. However, it should be remembered that for the accomplishment of supernatural powers samatha must be developed by mahā-kusala citta accompanied by paññā, so that calm grows and concentration on the meditation subject becomes firmly established, to the degree that the stages of jhāna can successively arise. It should be noted that all this is most difficult. A person who has developed concentration may have visions of future events, and some of his presentiments may come true whereas some may be wrong. His visions may be a result of his development of concentration, but they are not supernatural powers, the special qualities that are the result of the development of samatha.

If one develops samatha, it is already most difficult to attain even upacāra samādhi, access concentration. The reason is that when an object impinges on one of the senses or the mind-door, we usually turn to such an object with lobha, dosa or moha. Kusala citta of the level of dāna, sīla or mental development arises very rarely in our daily life. The moments of kusala citta are very rare when compared to the moments of akusala cittas that usually arise very rapidly, on account of the objects impinging on the senses and the mind-door. Defilements cannot be eradicated by the development of samatha. When defilements arise and overwhelm the citta, even samatha that has been developed to the degree of miraculous powers can decline.

Before the Buddha's enlightenment, there were people who accomplished the development of samatha to the highest degree of arūpa-jhāna, the sphere of neither-perception-nor-non-perception, and who could train themselves to attain supernatural powers, such as the divine eye, the divine ear, the remembrance of former lives and miraculous powers. However, in spite of this, they could not penetrate the four noble Truths, since they had not cultivated the right cause for this result. The right cause is the development of vipassanā, insight, to the degree that it becomes the right condition for the realization of the four noble Truths. Some people at that time had wrong understanding of the way leading to the realization of the four noble Truths; they followed the wrong practice. After the Buddha had attained enlightenment and taught the Dhamma, some of the ariyan disciples who had realized the four noble Truths had cultivated jhāna and some had not cultivated jhāna. The ariyans who had become enlightened without having attained jhāna were greater in number than those who had attained enlightenment with lokuttara cittas accompanied by jhāna-factors of different stages.[19] This shows us again that the development of samatha in the right way is extremely difficult and most intricate.

---

[19] See "Kindred Sayings" I, Ch VIII, The Vangīsa Suttas, §7, Invitation.

Part V

The Development of Insight

30

Factors Leading to Enlightenment

Defilements can be classified according to different degrees; they can be subtle, medium or coarse defilements.

The coarse defilements, vītikkama kilesas,[1] are the defilements that are the condition for committing akusala kamma through the body or through speech. One can abstain from vītikkama kilesa by the observance of sīla.

The medium defilements, pariyuṭṭhāna kilesas,[2] arise with the akusala citta that is not of the degree of akusala kamma. They can be temporarily subdued by kusala jhānacitta, and that is elimination by suppression, (vikkhambhana pahāna)[3].

The subtle defilements are the inherent tendencies, anusaya kilesas.[4] So long as defilements have not been completely eradicated, the anusaya kilesas lie dormant in the cittas that arise and fall away in succession.

[1] Vītikkama means transgression and kilesa means defilement.

[2] Pariyuṭṭhāna is derived from pariyuṭṭhāti, to arise, to pervade.

[3] Vikkhambhana means suppression, and pahāna means giving up, elimination.

[4] Anusayati means to lie dormant.

They are like germs that condition the arising of the medium defilements. Defilements cannot arise again when they have been completely eradicated (samuccheda pahāna)[5]. When the lokuttara magga-citta realizes the noble Truths and experiences nibbāna, anusaya kilesas are eradicated in accordance with the stage of enlightenment that has been attained. They are successively eradicated at the different stages of enlightenment.

Before the Buddha's enlightenment, people abstained from akusala by the observance of sīla and they could, by the development of samatha, temporarily subdue defilements (vikkhambhana pahāna). They could cultivate samatha even to the highest stage of arūpa-jhāna, the stage of "neither-perception-nor-non-perception." However, nobody could eradicate the inherent tendencies, the anusaya kilesas. The Buddha, after he had accumulated the perfections (pāramīs) for four incalculable periods of time and a hundred thousand aeons, attained Buddhahood and thereby became the Sammāsambuddha, who is unsurpassed in wisdom. He taught the way that should be followed to realize the ariyan Truths.

There were many disciples who could realize the noble Truths and eradicate defilements and thus, the ariyan Sangha[6] came into being. From that time on, people could study and apply the Dhamma, which the Buddha had realized when he attained enlightenment, and which he taught in all details for forty-five years. The Dhamma the Buddha taught is subtle, intricate and deep in meaning. The Buddha taught the characteristics of all realities he had penetrated at the time of his enlightenment. One should study and investigate the Dhamma the Buddha taught in detail so as to have right understanding of it. Otherwise, it will be impossible to develop the paññā that can penetrate the true nature of realities and eradicate defilements.

One should have right understanding of the Dhamma from the beginning so that paññā can be developed which knows the characteristics of realities as they are. From the beginning it should be known precisely which dhammas paññā can penetrate: all that is reality and that appears right now through the eyes, the ears, the nose, the tongue, the bodysense and the mind-door.

---

[5]Samuccheda means extirpation.

[6]The Sangha is the order of monks, and the ariyan Sangha are all those who have attained enlightenment, be they monks or lay followers.

Each moment when one sees, hears, smells, tastes, experiences tangible object or thinks, there is bound to be ignorance of the true nature of realities. The Buddha taught in all details about the dhammas that arise and appear all day long, at each moment, through the sense-doors and the mind-door. He taught the Dhamma so that we could see the disadvantages of defilements and the danger of being in the cycle of birth and death. So long as one does not see the danger of being in the cycle of birth and death, there is no sense of urgency, no energy to develop insight, vipassanā. Paññā developed in vipassanā sees the characteristics of realities as they are naturally appearing in daily life, and this kind of paññā can eradicate defilements.

The development of samatha and the development of vipassanā are different with different objectives and they are also different as to the degree of paññā that develops them. In samatha, mahā-kusala citta accompanied by paññā meditates on specific subjects so that calm can be obtained and the citta is firmly concentrated on the meditation subject. In vipassanā ultimate realities, paramattha dhammas, are the objects of paññā. These are the nāma dhammas and rūpa dhammas that arise and appear and then fall away. Mahā-kusala citta accompanied by paññā can begin to notice and investigate one reality at a time, over and over again. In that way it can gradually be realized that dhammas are not a being, person or self. The result of the development of samatha is rebirth in one of the brahma-planes. The result of the development of vipassanā is paññā that knows realities as they are and eradicates defilements. The lokuttara magga-citta has nibbāna as object and eradicates defilements in accordance with the stage of enlightenment that has been attained. When the stage of the arahat is attained, all defilements are eradicated completely by the magga-citta; that means the end to the cycle of birth and death, no more rebirth.

The person who develops vipassanā should be truthful with regard to himself. He should realize that he still has all kinds of defilements and he should not erroneously believe that lobha has to be eradicated first of all; this would be impossible. Someone who is still an ordinary person cannot pass over stages of development of understanding and become an arahat immediately. First of all, the clinging to "personality view" (sakkāya-diṭṭhi), by which one takes realities for a "whole," for self, being or person, should be completely eradicated. After that, other defilements can be eradicated stage by stage. If someone does not know that, while he is seeing, there is no self, being or person, how could he eradicate defilements such as attachment or aversion? It is the same with regard to the other doorways. So long as there is personality view, defilements cannot be eradicated.

Each reality that arises falls away very rapidly; it vanishes completely. Realities arise and fall away all the time. The Buddha taught the way to develop the paññā that knows the characteristics of realities as they are. The development of the eightfold Path is the one and only way to realize the truth. The factors of the eightfold Path are the following cetasikas: right understanding (sammā-diṭṭhi, paññā cetasika), right thinking (sammā-sankappa, vitakka cetasika), right speech (sammā-vāca cetasika), right action (sammā-kammanta cetasika), right livelihood (sammā-ājīva cetasika), right effort (sammā-vāyāma, viriya cetasika), right mindfulness (sammā-sati, sati cetasika) and right concentration (sammā-samādhi, ekaggatā cetasika).

In the beginning, when lokuttara citta has not yet arisen, the Path is still "worldly", lokiya, not lokuttara. Then there are usually five Path-factors performing their functions together, which means that the citta is not accompanied by the three abstentions, virati cetasikas, of right speech, right action and right livelihood. When there is an opportunity to abstain from akusala, only one type of virati arises at a time. Only at the moment of lokuttara citta the three virati cetasikas arise together. The five Path-factors (apart from the virati cetasikas) perform their functions together when there is awareness of a characteristic of nāma or rūpa appearing through one of the six doors. Paññā cetasika that arises together with sammā-sati gradually begins to consider and to investigate the characteristics of nāma and rūpa. Paññā has to consider realities very often, over and over again, so that it can clearly discern whether it is a nāma or a rūpa that appears.

The realities, which appear through the eyes, the ears, the nose, the tongue, the bodysense or the mind-door, can be classified as the four Applications of Mindfulness, Satipaṭṭhānas. They are the following:

1. Application of mindfulness of the body, kāyānupassanā[7] satipaṭṭhāna.

[7] Anupassanā means consideration, contemplation. It is derived from passati, to see, to understand.

When sati arises and is aware of a characteristic of a rūpa of the body, there is at such a moment kāyānupassanā satipaṭṭhāna.

2. Application of mindfulness of feeling, vedanānupassanā satipaṭṭhāna. When sati arises and is aware of a characteristic of feeling that appears, there is at such a moment vedanānupassanā satipaṭṭhāna.

3. Application of mindfulness of citta, cittānupassanā satipaṭṭhāna. When sati arises and is aware of a characteristic of one of the different types of citta, there is at such a moment cittanupassanā satipaṭṭhāna.

4. Application of mindfulness of dhammas, dhammānupassanā satipaṭṭhāna. This application of mindfulness includes the realities classified under aspects other than those of the first three applications of mindfulness.[8] When sati arises and is aware of a dhamma included in this application of mindfulness, there is at such a moment dhammānupassanā satipaṭṭhāna.

The word satipaṭṭhāna has three meanings:

1. The objects sati is aware of, thus, a paramattha dhamma, a nāma dhamma or a rūpa dhamma. These are classified as the four satipaṭṭhānas.

2. Sati cetasika that arises together with kāmāvacara citta accompanied by paññā (ñāṇa-sampayutta), and which is aware of the objects of mindfulness, the four satipaṭṭhānas.

3. The Teacher's threefold surpassing of delight and aversion with regard to the disciples who apply his teaching, with regard to those who do not apply it, and with regard to those people some of whom apply it and some do not. This is the Path the Sammāsambuddha and the ariyan disciples have developed.[9]

---

[8] Nāma and rūpa, which are included in the fourth application of mindfulness, are classified under different aspects, such as the "hindrances," the five khandhas, the āyatanas.

[9] An ariyan who practises this is fit to instruct others (M III, 221).

The development of the ariyan eightfold Path is actually the development of the four satipaṭṭhānas. It is the development of awareness and right understanding of the characteristics of realities, as they appear one at a time in our daily life, through the sense-doors and through the mind-door. Mindfulness is not easy and in the beginning it cannot often arise. The reason is that ignorance, clinging and all the other akusala dhammas have been accumulated for an endlessly long time in the cycle of birth and death. And also in this life, from the time we were born, defilements have been accumulated each day. The person who correctly understands cause and result of realities knows that he needs great patience and perseverance so that he is able to listen to the Dhamma, to study it carefully and to consider it. Only thus can one have understanding of the realities that appear through the eyes, the ears, the nose, the tongue, the bodysense and the mind-door.

By listening and considering, the right conditions are being accumulated for the arising of satipaṭṭhāna, awareness and investigation of the characteristics of the realities that are appearing. In this way, realities can be known as they are. Through awareness of realities, one will directly understand the truth in conformity with what one has learnt and understood intellectually, namely, that all dhammas, including satipaṭṭhāna and the factors of the eightfold Path, are anattā, non-self. Satipaṭṭhāna can arise when there are the right conditions, that is, when mahā-kusala citta accompanied by paññā has arisen time and again, and paññā has thus been accumulated. Then people will not deviate anymore from the right Path. They will not follow a practice other than being aware of, noticing and considering the nāma dhammas and the rūpa dhammas appearing through the six doors.

The person who develops paññā is truthful, sincere with regard to his own development. When satipaṭṭhāna arises, he knows that that moment is different from forgetfulness of realities. When satipaṭṭhāna arises, there cannot yet immediately be clear understanding of the characteristics of nāma and rūpa. Paññā develops only very gradually.

When sati of satipaṭṭhāna notices and considers the characteristics of the nāmas and rūpas that appear, there is also right effort arising together with sati. Right effort can be classified as fourfold, as four sammāppadhānas, right efforts: the effort to avoid, saṃvara-padhāna, the effort to overcome, pahāna-padhāna, the effort to develop, bhāvanā-padhāna, and the effort to maintain, anurakkhaṇa-padhāna.

Saṃvara-padhāna is the effort to avoid the arising of akusala dhammas that have not arisen yet.

Pahāna-padhāna is the effort to overcome or eliminate the akusala dhammas that have arisen.

Bhāvanā-padhāna is the effort to develop the kusala dhammas that have not yet arisen.

Anurakkhaṇa-padhāna is the effort to maintain the kusala dhammas that have arisen so that they will reach completion.

These four right efforts are the foundation for the accomplishment of result, but there are other sobhana dhammas that have to accompany them in order to reach the goal and among these are the four "Roads to Power" or "Bases of Success," iddhi-pādas.[10] These are the following:

- The Basis of Success of chanda. This is chanda cetasika or wish-to-do. Chanda wishes to consider and to be aware of the characteristics of the nāmas and rūpas that are appearing, so that they can be known as they are. Chanda is compared to a royal attendant who is diligent in his service to the King. Even so is chanda a basis of accomplishment so that the right result can be reached.[11]

- The Basis of Success of viriya. This is viriya cetasika or energy, energy to notice and consider the characteristics of the nāmas and rūpas that are appearing. By dependence on energy, the right result can be accomplished. Viriya is compared to a royal attendant who assists the King by his courage in the performance of his task.

- The Basis of Success of citta. Through citta the right result can be achieved. Citta is compared to a royal attendant who gives assistance to the King by accomplishing his task well because of his natural good qualities.

- The Basis of Success of vimaṃsā, investigation. This is paññā cetasika that carefully considers and investigates the characteris-

[10]Iddhi means power or success and pāda is foot or step. The iddhi-pādas in vipassanā are a basis for reaching enlightenment. They are among the thirty-seven factors pertaining to enlightenment, bodhipakkhiya dhammas

[11]See the "Dispeller of Delusion", "Sammohavinodanī", commentary to the Book of Analysis, in the section on Iddhi-pādas (II, Ch 9).

tics of realities. By dependence on paññā, the right result can be achieved. Vimaṃsā is compared to a royal attendant who gives assistance to the King by his wisdom.

Each of these royal attendants can, because of his own natural capability, be a dependable support in the accomplishment of the goal. Even so, the Bases of Success are a dependable support to reach the right result.

The four Bases of Success have to depend on the five "spiritual faculties," indriyas, so that they can perform their functions. These faculties have to be developed so that they can have a leading function with regard to the development of the right Path. They are the following:

- The faculty of confidence, which is saddhā cetasika. This is a leader when there is confidence in awareness of the characteristics of realities that are appearing.

- The faculty of energy, which is viriya cetasika. This is a leader when there is energy and courage that prevents laziness and being disheartened with regard to awareness right now. It is energy for awareness of the characteristics of realities that are appearing.

- The faculty of mindfulness, which is sati cetasika. It is a leader that prevents forgetfulness, it is mindful of the characteristics of realities which are appearing.

- The faculty of concentration, samādhi, which is ekaggatā cetasika. It is a leader in focusing on the object that is appearing.

- The faculty of wisdom, which is paññā cetasika. It is a leader in careful consideration, investigation and study of the characteristics of the realities that appear.

When the five faculties have been developed, they become powerful and unshakable. They do not vacillate with regard to their task of considering whatever object appears. Then they can become "powers," balas. They are the following:

- The power of confidence, saddhā, which cannot be shaken by lack of confidence.

- The power of energy, viriya, which cannot be shaken by discouragement.
- The power of mindfulness, sati, which cannot be shaken by forgetfulness of the realities that appear.
- The power of concentration, samādhi, which cannot be shaken by distraction with regard to the object that appears.
- The power of wisdom, paññā, which cannot be shaken by ignorance.

Saddhā, viriya, sati and samādhi can become strong when paññā has become a power. When paññā thoroughly understands the characteristics of nāma and rūpa, it has become unshakable; it does not vacillate. When seeing appears, paññā can realize its characteristic as nāma, the reality, the element that experiences. It is the same with regard to hearing, smelling, tasting, the experience of tangible object and thinking; these can be realized as nāma.

When paññā accompanied by sati considers the characteristics of nāma and rūpa over and over again, it becomes more accomplished, so that different stages of insight, vipassanā ñāṇas, can be reached. Then paññā is accompanied by the seven factors of enlightenment, bojjhangas. These factors, which lead to the realization of the noble Truths, are the following:

1. The enlightenment factor of mindfulness, sati cetasika.
2. The enlightenment factor of investigation of Dhamma, dhammavicaya. This is paññā cetasika.
3. The enlightenment factor of energy, viriya cetasika.
4. The enlightenment factor of rapture, pīti cetasika.
5. The enlightenment factor of calm, passaddhi. These are the cetasikas that are calm of cetasikas, kāya-passaddhi, and calm of citta, citta-passaddhi.
6. The enlightenment factor of concentration, which is samādhi, ekaggatā cetasika.

7. The enlightenment factor of equanimity, upekkhā, which is tatramajjhattatā cetasika.

When paññā has become accomplished to the degree that it can realize the noble Truths, it is accompanied by these seven factors of enlightenment. Paññā reaches accomplishment by means of thirty-seven dhammas pertaining to enlightenment, the bodhipakkhiya dhammas. These are: the four applications of mindfulness, the four right efforts, the four bases of success, the five faculties, the five powers, the seven factors of enlightenment and the eight Path-factors.[12]

The lokuttara citta is accompanied by all eight Path-factors. These are the following cetasikas: sammā-diṭṭhi, right view, sammā-sankappa, right thinking, sammā-vāca, right speech, sammā-kammanta, right action, sammā-ājīva, right livelihood, sammā-vāyāma, right effort, sammā-sati, right mindfulness, and sammā-samādhi, right concentration. The lokuttara citta is accompanied by all the dhammas pertaining to enlightenment, bodhipakkhiya dhammas, when enlightenment is attained and nibbāna is experienced in a mind-door process. That process runs as follows:

bhavanga-cittas:

bhavanga-cittas, vipākacittas which are ñāṇa-sampayutta1 bhavanga-calana, vibrating bhavanga, vipākacitta which is ñāṇa-sampayutta bhavangupaccheda, arrest bhavanga, which is vipākacitta ñāṇa-sampayutta

mind-door adverting-citta:

manodvārāvajjana-citta which is kiriyacitta

javana-cittas:

parikamma (preparatory), mahā-kusala which is ñāṇa-sampayutta upacāra (proximatory), mahā-kusala which is ñāṇa-sampayutta (of the same type as parikamma) anuloma (adaptation), mahā-kusala which is ñāṇa-sampayutta (of the same type as parikamma) gotrabhū (change-of-lineage)1, mahā-kusala which is ñāṇa-sampayutta (of the same type as parikamma) sotapatti magga-citta, lokuttara kusala citta sotapatti phala-citta, lokuttara vipākacitta sotapatti phala-citta, lokuttara vipākacitta

[12]In the classification of these thirty-seven dhammas, the same cetasikas occur several times, but they have been classified under different aspects and with different intensities. This shows how many qualities have to be developed so that there are conditions for the attainment of enlightenment.

bhavanga-citta:

bhavanga-citta, which is vipākacitta ñāṇa-sampayutta.

In the case of lokuttara jhāna,[13] the lokuttara jhānacitta is accompanied by the jhāna-factors of the stage of jhāna that was attained just before enlightenment. Thus, if there is lokuttara jhānacitta accompanied by the factors of the second stage of jhāna, vitakka cetasika, sammā-sankappa (right thinking) does not arise.[14] If there is lokuttara jhānacitta accompanied by the factors of the third stage of jhāna, vicāra cetasika (sustained thinking) does not arise. If there is lokuttara jhānacitta accompanied by the factors of the fourth stage of jhāna, pīti cetasika (rapture) does not arise. If there is lokuttara jhānacitta accompanied by the factors of the fifth stage of jhāna, there is upekkhā vedanā (indifferent feeling), instead of somanassa (pleasant feeling).

A person who is keen (tikkha puggala) and realizes the noble Truths rapidly, does not need parikamma (preparatory consciousness) in the process during which magga-citta arises. Thus, in that process there are upacāra (proximatory consciousness), anuloma (adaptation), gotrabhū (change-of-lineage), magga-citta, and then, instead of two moments of phala-citta, there are three moments of phala-citta.[15]

When the magga-vīthi-cittas have fallen away, there are bhavanga-cittas arising and falling away, and then there are processes of cittas reviewing the enlightenment that was attained (paccavekkhaṇa vīthi). There are five different processes of reviewing ocurring one after the other: the reviewing of the magga-citta, of the phala-citta, of nibbāna, of the defilements that have been eradicated and of the defilements that have not yet been eradicated.

When the magga-vīthi-cittas of the different stages of enlightenment have fallen away, they must be followed by processes of reviewing. Thus, the ariyan does not have wrong understanding with regard to his stage of enlightenment. The sotāpanna does not erroneously believe that he is a sakadāgāmī (once-returner, who has attained the second stage of enlightenment), and it is the same for the sakadāgāmī, the anāgāmī (non-returner, who has attained the third stage of enlightenment) and the arahat.

---

[13] For those who have developed samatha and vipassanā. See Appendix to Citta.

[14] See the section on Samatha.

[15] Thus, altogether there are seven javana-cittas.

At the higher stages of enlightenment, following upon the stage of the sotāpanna, there is in the process of enlightenment instead of change-of-lineage, gotrabhū, "purification," vodāna. The reason is that the person who attains a higher stage of enlightenment is no longer an ordinary person.

31
The Stages of Vipassanā

Before enlightenment can be attained, mahā-kusala citta which is ñāṇa-sampayutta (accompanied by paññā), has to consider and investigate the characteristics of all kinds of nāma and rūpa over and over again, life after life. In this way, understanding of realities can grow. When paññā has become keener and more accomplished, mahā-kusala citta accompanied by paññā that is vipassanā ñāṇa, insight wisdom, can arise. The kind of paññā that is vipassanā ñāṇa can clearly realize the characteristics of nāma and rūpa through the mind-door, in accordance with the stages of insight that are successively reached. There are several stages of insight that have to be reached before enlightenment can be attained.

The first stage of insight is Knowledge of the difference between nāma and rūpa, nāma-rūpa-pariccheda-ñāṇa.[1]

Mahā-kusala citta ñāṇa-sampayutta arises and clearly distinguishes the difference between the characteristic of nāma and the characteristic

[1] See "Visuddhimagga" Ch XVIII. Pariccheda is derived from paricchindati, to mark out, limit or define.

of rūpa as they appear one at a time. The objects constituting "the world" appear as devoid of self. At that moment there is no attā-saññā, wrong remembrance of self, which used to remember or perceive realities as a "whole", conceived as "the world". This is the beginning of right remembrance of the realities which appear as anattā. Satipaṭṭhāna should continue to be aware of all kinds of nāma and rūpa, in addition to those realized at the moment of vipassanā ñāṇa. When there is awareness of realities, paññā should consider again and again anattā-saññā penetrated at the moment of vipassanā ñāṇa. Otherwise attā-saññā, which has been accumulated for a long time in the cycle of birth and death, cannot be eradicated.

The second stage of vipassanā ñāṇa is Discerning conditions for nāma and rūpa, paccaya-pariggaha-ñāṇa.[2]

When the moments of vipassanā ñāṇa have fallen away, the world appears as it used to appear, as a "whole". The person who develops satipaṭṭhāna clearly knows the difference between the moment of vipassanā ñāṇa and the moment that is not vipassanā ñāṇa. When vipassanā ñāṇa has fallen away, ignorance and doubt about realities can arise again, since these defilements have not been eradicated. When the first stage of insight has been reached, there is full comprehension of what has been known, ñāta pariññā.[3] Paññā realizes as they are the characteristics of realities that appear at the moments of vipassanā ñāṇa. Then there is no ignorance and doubt about those realities. The first stage of insight is only a beginning stage that can lead to the following stages of insight, which penetrates the characteristics of nāma and rūpa more and more.

When satipaṭṭhāna continues to be mindful of the realities that appear and investigates their characteristics, there can be more understanding of their conditions. When one object appears at a time, paññā can realize that nāma, the element that experiences, arises because of conditions, that it is conditioned by that object. If there were no object appearing, nāma could not arise. Thus, whenever there is nāma, there must be an object experienced by nāma. When one object at

[2]See "Visuddhimagga" Ch XIX. Pariggaha is derived from pariganhāti, to examine, take possession of or comprehend.

[3]Pariññā means comprehension, or full understanding. There are three kinds of pariññā and these will be explained further on.

a time appears, paññā can understand that the dhammas that arise are dependent on conditions. In this way, paññā can see more clearly the nature of anattā of all dhammas and thus there will gradually be more detachment from the inclination to take objects for self. When the factors of the Eightfold Path, cetasikas included in saṅkhārakkhandha, have been developed to a higher degree, they can condition the arising of the second vipassanā ñāṇa. This is paccaya-pariggaha-ñāṇa, which directly understands the dependency on conditions of nāma and rūpa at the moment they arise. Thus, there is awareness and direct understanding of the arising of realities such as hearing, sound, pleasant feeling, unpleasant feeling or thinking. All these dhammas, each arising because of its own conditions, are realized one at a time, as clearly distinct from each other. They are realized as devoid of self.

Vipassanā ñāṇa clearly knows the characteristics of the realities that naturally appear and it knows them through the mind-door. Vipassanā ñāṇa discerns the characteristics of the different objects as clearly distinct from each other and it realizes them as non-self. When vipassanā ñāṇa has fallen away, the world appears as it used to appear, as a "whole".

The third vipassanā ñāṇa is Comprehension by groups, sammasana ñāṇa.[4]

This is the paññā that clearly realizes the rapid succession of nāmas and rūpas as they arise and fall away. When this stage of insight has not yet arisen, one knows that nāma and rūpa arise and fall away very rapidly, but the rapid succession of nāmas and rūpas as they arise and fall away does not appear. At the first stage and at the second stage of insight, paññā penetrates the characteristics of nāma and of rūpa, one at a time, as distinct from each other, but it does not yet realize their rapid succession as they arise and fall away.

The first, the second and the third stages of insight are only beginning stages, they are called "tender insight", taruṇa vipassanā. They are not "insight as power", balava[5] vipassanā, that is, insight which has become more powerful at the higher stages. At the stages of tender insight, there is still thinking of the nāmas and rūpas that are realized.

[4]See "Visuddhimagga" Ch XX, 6 and following. Sammasana is derived from sammasati, to grasp, to know thoroughly.

[5]Bala means power.

However, although there is thinking, different dhammas are not joined together into a "whole", into "the whole world," as one was used to doing.

Since there is still thinking of the nāma and rūpa at the three beginning stages of vipassanā, paññā is called "cintā ñāṇa", "cintā" meaning thinking or consideration. Some people may have misunderstandings about the stages of insight where there is still thinking. They may believe that there is already "tender insight" when one considers and notices characteristics of nāma and rūpa and has more understanding of them. However, so long as vipassanā ñāṇa has not arisen yet, one cannot penetrate the nature of anattā of vipassanā ñāṇa. One cannot understand that vipassanā ñāṇa, which clearly realizes the characteristics of nāma and rūpa through the mind-door, can arise at any place, at any time, and that it can take as object whatever reality appears.

Someone may erroneously believe, when he is aware, when he is considering and noticing the characteristics of nāma and rūpa, that he has clear understanding of them and that he has already reached the first stage of insight, knowledge of the difference between nāma and rūpa, nāma-rūpa-pariccheda-ñāṇa. A person can have such misunderstanding because he does not yet know that vipassanā ñāṇa must appear as anattā, as not self, just as the other types of nāma that appear. When vipassanā ñāṇa arises, characteristics of nāma and rūpa appear through the mind-door.[6] The rūpas that are sense-objects are experienced through the corresponding sense-doors and after each sense-door process, the object is experienced through the mind-door. However, when there is no vipassanā ñāṇa, the mind-door process does not appear; it is, as it were, concealed by the cittas that experience sense objects in the sense-door processes. At the moments of vipassanā ñāṇa, rūpas appear very clearly through the mind-door, and at that moment the mind-door conceals, as it were, the sense-doors. Then the situation is opposite to the moments when there is no vipassanā ñāṇa.

Some people believe, when they consider nāma and rūpa and know that this nāma is conditioned by that rūpa and this rūpa is conditioned by that nāma, that the second stage of insight has already arisen, namely the direct understanding of conditionality, paccaya-pariggaha-

[6] Vipassanā ñāṇa arises in a mind-door process.

ñāṇa. However, when the first stage of insight, nāma-rūpa-pariccheda-ñāṇa, has not arisen yet, the following stages of insight cannot arise either. When the first stage of insight has arisen, one will not erroneously believe that there is vipassanā ñāṇa when there is no vipassanā ñāṇa. When vipassanā ñāṇa has arisen, one understands its nature of anattā. One realizes that it has arisen because of the right conditions; one knows that the factors of the eightfold Path were developed to such degree that that stage of insight could arise. Vipassanā ñāṇa can only arise when the right conditions have been cultivated, that is, the development of satipaṭṭhāna, which studies, investigates and notices the characteristics of nāma and rūpa as they naturally appear in daily life over and over again, so that paññā can become keener.

Someone who does not even know the difference between the characteristics of nama and rupa may mistakenly believe that he has reached the third stage of insight, the stage of comprehension by groups, sammasana ñāṇa. He may think that he can experience the arising and falling away of nāmas, one after the other, and that that is the third stage of insight. However, if someone has not developed satipaṭṭhāna and has not been aware of the characteristics of different kinds of nāma that appear, he does not realize nāma as the element which experiences. He may believe that he experiences the arising and falling away of nāma, but he does not clearly know what nāma is. He confuses nāma and rūpa, he does not know that nāma is entirely different from rūpa.

A person who is impatient wishes vipassanā ñāṇa to arise soon. He will try to do something other than being aware of the characteristics of nāma and rūpa that naturally appear and have arisen because of appropriate conditions. It is impossible to hasten the development of paññā. Paññā can only grow gradually and there is no other condition for its growth but the development of satipaṭṭhāna in our ordinary daily life. If someone tries to do something else, he will go the wrong way and the wrong cause cannot bring the right result. If someone hopes for a quick result of his practice, it is the wrong path; he does not understand what the right Path is. Lobha-mūla-citta accompanied by wrong view motivates the development of the wrong path and this will lead to the wrong release,[7] not the right release that is freedom from defilements.

[7] Micchā-vimutti.

The fourth vipassanā ñāṇa is Knowledge of the arising and falling away of nāma and rūpa, udayabbaya ñāṇa.[8]

Vipassanā ñāṇa of the third stage realizes the rapid succession of nāmas and rūpas as they arise and fall away. However, at this stage paññā is not yet keen enough to see the danger and disadvantages of the arising and falling away, so that there can be detachment from them. The immediate arising of a new dhamma after the falling away of the former dhamma covers up the danger of the arising and falling away. Paññā should become keener so that the following stages of insight can be reached. At the fourth stage, paññā can penetrate more clearly the arising and falling away of each kind of nāma and each kind of rūpa separately. One should not try to do something else but continue to consider the characteristics of nāma and rūpa. One should be steadfast in the development of paññā.

All kinds of nāma and rūpa can be object of understanding, no matter whether they are kusala dhammas or akusala dhammas, no matter of what degree of kusala or akusala they are or through which doorway they appear. The fourth stage of vipassanā ñāṇa, udayabbaya ñāṇa, knows more precisely the arising and falling away of each kind of nāma and of rūpa as it appears one at a time. This stage of insight can arise when "full understanding of investigation," tīraṇa pariññā, has become more accomplished.[9] Full understanding of investigation is the kind of paññā that considers and clearly understands the characteristics of all kinds of nāma and rūpa as they appear through the six doors. So long as this is not the case, there are no conditions for the arising of udayabbaya ñāṇa.

The person who develops the right Path knows that nibbāna, the reality that eradicates defilements, cannot be realized if understanding of conditioned realities has not been fully developed. First, the paññā should be developed which clearly understands the characteristics of

[8]See "Visuddhimagga" Ch XXI, for this stage and the following stages, which are mahā-vipassanā ñāṇa, principal insight. Udaya is rise and baya is fall.

[9]There are three pariññās: full understanding of the known, ñāta pariññā, full understanding of investigation, tīraṇa pariññā, and full understanding of abandoning, pahāna pariññā. When a stage of insight has been reached, the knowledge gained at such moments should be applied. The three pariññās are degrees of paññā that applies insight knowledge by considering again and again nāma and rūpa. This will be explained more further on.

nāma and rūpa as they naturally appear in daily life. It is impossible to realize nibbāna if paññā does not penetrate thoroughly and precisely the characteristics of all kinds of nāma and rūpa that appear through the six doors.

The characteristics of nāma and rūpa that appear through each of the six doorways are different from each other. If paññā does not precisely understand the difference between the characteristics of nāma and rūpa as they appear through the six doorways, the arising and falling away of nāma and rūpa cannot be realized. Then, ignorance, doubt and wrong view about realities cannot be eradicated.

The fifth stage of vipassanā ñāṇa is Knowledge of dissolution, bhaṅga ñāṇa.[10]

Even though the fourth stage of vipassanā ñāṇa clearly realizes the arising and falling away of one characteristic of nama and of rupa at a time, clinging to them is still very persistent. Clinging to all realities has been accumulated for an endlessly long time in the cycle of birth and death. Ignorance and clinging to the concept of self are like firmly implanted roots that are hard to pull up. Paññā has to be developed more thoroughly through satipaṭṭhāna. There must be awareness and investigation again and again of the arising and falling away of nāma and rūpa which was already realized at the fourth stage of insight. Paññā should investigate more thoroughly the falling away of the nāmas and rūpas that appear. Then it can be seen that dhammas that fall away cannot be any refuge. Through the development of satipaṭṭhāna, paññā becomes keener and more accomplished so that there are the right conditions for the fifth stage of vipassanā ñāṇa, knowledge of dissolution, bhaṅga ñāṇa. This stage of vipassanā clearly realizes that nāma and rūpa that arise and fall away cannot be any refuge, that they cannot give any security. Then there is the beginning of the third pariññā, "full understanding of abandoning," pahāna pariññā. This pariññā can lead to higher stages of paññā, to paññā that begins to detach from clinging to the idea of self, being or person.

The sixth stage of insight is Knowledge of terror, bhaya ñāṇa.

When the knowledge of dissolution, bhaṅga ñāṇa, has fallen away, the person who develops vipassanā realizes that defilements are still

[10]Bhaṅga means dissolution or breaking up.

strong, that there are conditions for their arising to the extent they have been accumulated. He carefully considers the characteristic of dissolution of nāma and rūpa, but the clinging to the concept of self is still firmly accumulated. This kind of clinging can be eliminated by seeing the danger and unsatisfactoriness of the dissolution of nāma and rūpa. Paññā should continue to consider the characteristics of nāma and rūpa and thereby realize more and more the danger and disadvantage of the dissolution of realities. When paññā has become more accomplished there can be the right conditions for the arising of the sixth stage of insight, knowledge of terror. This knowledge sees the danger of nāma and rūpa while it clearly realizes at that moment the arising and falling away of nāma and rūpa.

The seventh stage of insight is Knowledge of danger, ādīnava ñāṇa.

Knowledge of terror, bhaya ñāṇa, sees the disadvantage of the arising and falling away of nāma and rūpa, but when this knowledge has fallen away, clinging to the concept of self can still arise; it has not been eradicated. The person who develops satipaṭṭhāna understands that the danger and disadvantage of nāma and rūpa that arise and fall away should be realized more deeply and under various aspects. In that way the inclination to take nāma and rūpa for self will decrease. When sati is aware of the characteristics of the realities that arise and fall away, paññā becomes keener and sees more clearly the disadvantage of the arising and falling away of nāma and rūpa. Paññā becomes accomplished to the degree that it conditions the arising of knowledge of danger, ādīnava ñāṇa. When this knowledge arises, it clearly realizes the danger and disadvantage of nāma and rūpa that arise and fall away.

The eighth stage of vipassanā ñāṇa is Knowledge of dispassion, nibbidā ñāṇa.

When the danger of all conditioned realities is realized, they seem to be like a building that has caught fire. The clinging to life becomes less when one clearly sees the futility of the nāma and rūpa that appear. Then there is knowledge of dispassion, nibbidā ñāṇa.

The ninth stage of vipassanā ñāṇa is Knowledge of desire for deliverance, muccitukamyatā ñāṇa.[11]

When paññā realizes more and more clearly the futility of the nāma

[11] Muccati means to become free and kamyatā means wish.

and rūpa that appear, and it becomes more detached from them, paññā wants to become liberated from nāma and rūpa that arise and fall away. The paññā that wants to be liberated is knowledge of desire for deliverance, mucitukamyatā ñāṇa.

The tenth stage of vipassanā ñāṇa is Knowledge of reflection, paṭisaṅkhā ñāṇa.[12]

When desire for deliverance has become stronger, paññā will be inclined to consider over and over again the three general characteristics of conditioned dhammas: impermanence, dukkha and anattā. When paññā clearly realizes the characteristic of impermanence of all conditioned dhammas that arise and fall away, it sees them as completely devoid of any security, as fleeting, unenduring, changeable, unstable and as no refuge. When paññā clearly realizes the characteristic of dukkha of all conditioned realities that arise and fall away, it sees them as continually oppressive, as something threatening from which there is no escape, as something incurable, as danger, as something unattractive, not worth clinging to. When paññā clearly realizes the characteristic of anattā of all conditioned realities that arise and fall away, it sees them as empty, void, as something that cannot be owned, as beyond control. The paññā that clearly realizes the three characteristics of all conditioned dhammas, saṅkhāra dhammas, is knowledge of reflection, paṭisaṅkhā ñāṇa.

The eleventh stage of vipassanā ñāṇa is Knowledge of equanimity about conditioned dhammas, saṅkhārupekkhā ñāṇa.

When the paññā that clearly realizes the three general characteristics of all conditioned dhammas has become more accomplished, there will be less inclination to take conditioned dhammas for permanent, for happiness or for self. Thus, there can be more equanimity towards conditioned dhammas. The person who develops vipassanā knows that so long as nibbāna does not appear and paññā can, therefore, not penetrate its characteristic, he should continue to investigate whichever of the three general characteristics of conditioned realities appears as object. The paññā that leads to equanimity towards the conditioned dhammas that arise and fall away is knowledge of equanimity about conditioned dhammas, saṅkhārupekkhā ñāṇa. This knowledge is the insight that

[12]Paṭisaṅkhāna means discrimination.

leads to attainment of what is supreme; it leads to emergence.[13] It is the paññā which conditions someone to leave the state of an ordinary person, and this occurs when the magga-citta, path-consciousness, arises.

The twelfth stage of vipassanā ñāṇa is Adaptation knowledge, anuloma ñāṇa.

Adaptation knowledge, or conformity knowledge, is the vipassanā ñāṇa that arises in the process during which enlightenment is attained, the magga-vīthi. This kind of knowledge conforms to the clear understanding of the noble Truths.[14] Adaptation knowledge is the three moments of mahā-kusala cittas accompanied by paññā arising in the magga-vīthi. They are: parikamma or preparatory consciousness, upacāra or access and anuloma or adaptation. These three cittas have as their object one of the three general characteristics.[15] They realize the conditioned dhamma appearing at that moment either as impermanent, or as dukkha or as anattā. Adaptation knowledge adapts or conforms to detachment from the objects that are conditioned dhammas.

For the person who is keen (tikkha puggala), that is, who has keen paññā and can realize the Noble Truths rapidly, there are two moments of adaptation knowledge, because he does not need preparatory consciousness, parikamma.

The thirteenth stage of vipassanā ñāṇa is Change-of-lineage knowledge, gotrabhū ñāṇa.

This knowledge succeeds the anuloma ñāṇa, which includes three moments of citta for the person who realizes the Noble Truths more slowly than a person with keen paññā, and two moments for a person with keen paññā.[16] Change-of-lineage knowledge is mahā-kusala citta ñāṇa-sampayutta and this citta has nibbāna as object. It is repetition-

[13] In Pāli: vuṭṭhāna gaminī paññā. Vuṭṭhāna means rising up and gaminī means going.

[14] The "Visuddhimagga" (XXI, 130) states that anuloma ñāṇa conforms to what precedes and to what follows. It conforms to the eight preceding kinds of insight knowledge and to the thirty-seven enlightenment factors that partake of enlightenment which will follow.

[15] The third citta is anuloma, adaptation, but all three cittas preceding gotrabhū are adaptation knowledge.

[16] A person who is slow is called in Pāli: manda puggala, and a person who is keen is called: tikkha puggala.

condition, asevana-paccaya,[17] for the succeeding magga-citta of the stage of the sotāpanna, which is lokuttara kusala citta. The magga-citta has nibbāna as object and eradicates defilements.

In the process of cittas, all seven javana-cittas usually have the same object, but it is different in the case of the magga-vīthi. The cittas that are parikamma, preparatory consciousness, upacāra, access, and anuloma, adaptation, have as object one of the three general characteristics of conditioned realities. The following cittas in that process, the gotrabhū, change-of-lineage, the magga-citta and the moments of phala-citta (two or three moments), have nibbāna as object. Gotrabhū is mahā-kusala citta that has for the first time nibbāna as object. It is, as it were, "adverting" to the magga-citta of the stage of the sotāpanna that succeeds the gotrabhū and has nibbāna as object. The "Visuddhimagga" (XXII, 11) states that this citta, since it can only realize nibbāna but not dispel defilements, is called "adverting to the Path." We read:

> "For although it is not adverting (āvajjana)[18], it occupies the position of adverting; and then, after as it were giving a sign to the path to come into being, it ceases."

The path-consciousness that succeeds it can then, while it experiences nibbāna, eradicate defilements.

The "Atthasālinī" (II, Book I, Part VII, Ch I, the first Path, 232, 233) and the "Visuddhimagga" (XXII, 8-10) use a simile for anuloma ñāṇa and gotrabhū ñāṇa. A man went out at night in order to look at the moon. The moon did not appear because it was concealed by clouds. Then a wind blew away the thick clouds, another wind blew away the medium clouds and another wind blew away the fine clouds. Then that man could see the moon free of clouds. Nibbāna is like the moon. The three moments of anuloma ñāna, adaptation knowledge, are like the three winds. Gotrabhū ñāṇa is like the man who sees the clear moon in the sky, free of clouds.

[17] The preceding javana-citta conditions the succeeding one by way of repetition-condition.

[18] It does not perform the function of adverting, āvajjana, such as is performed by the first citta arising in a sense-door process or in the mind-door process.

As the three winds are able only to disperse the clouds covering the moon and do not see the moon, even so the three moments of anuloma ñāṇa are able only to dispel the murk that conceals the Noble Truths but they cannot experience nibbāna. Just as the man can only see the moon but cannot blow away the clouds, so gotrabhū ñāṇa can only experience nibbāna but cannot dispel defilements.

The fourteenth stage of vipassanā ñāṇa is Path knowledge, magga ñāṇa.

When gotrabhū has fallen away, it is succeeded by the path-consciousness of the sotāpanna and this citta transcends the state of the ordinary person and reaches the state of the noble person, the ariyan. This citta eradicates defilements in accordance with the stage of enlightenment that has been reached.

The fifteenth stage of vipassanā ñāṇa is Fruition knowledge, phala ñāṇa.

When the magga-citta of the sotāpanna has fallen away, it conditions the arising of the succeeding citta, the phala-citta. The phala-citta, which is lokuttara vipākacitta, immediately succeeds the magga-citta without any interval. Lokuttara kusala citta is kamma-condition for the vipākacitta which follows without delay, without there being other cittas in between, and therefore it is called "without delay," akāliko.[19] Thus, lokuttara vipākacitta is different from other kinds of vipākacitta. The lokuttara vipākacittas, which are two or three moments of citta arising in the magga-vīthi and succeeding the magga-citta, perform the function of javana. Thus, they perform a function different from the functions performed by other types of vipākacitta.

The sixteenth stage of vipassanā ñāṇa is Reviewing knowledge, paccavekkhaṇa ñāṇa.

When the magga-vīthi-cittas have fallen away, they are succeeded by bhavanga-cittas and then mind-door process cittas arise. These cittas review the enlightenment that was attained. In one process cittas review the magga-citta, in one process the phala-citta, in one process the defilements that have been eradicated, in another process the defilements which are still remaining and in another process again nibbāna.

[19] Kāla means moment, and "a" denotes a negation. See "Visuddhimagga", Ch VII, 80, under Recollection of the Dhamma. The Dhamma is sandiṭṭhiko, visible here and now, and akāliko, without delay.

The person for whom the magga-citta and the phala-citta of the stage of the arahat have arisen, does not have to review the remaining defilements since the magga-citta of the arahat has completely eradicated all defilements.

Summarizing the vipassanā ñāṇas, they are:

- Knowledge of the difference between nāma and rūpa, nāma-rūpa-pariccheda-ñāṇa,
- Discerning conditions for nāma and rūpa, paccaya-pariggaha-ñāṇa,
- Comprehension by groups, sammasana ñāṇa,
- Knowledge of arising and falling away, udayabbaya ñāṇa,
- Knowledge of dissolution, bhaṅga ñāṇa,
- Knowledge of terror, bhaya ñāṇa,
- Knowledge of danger, ādīnava ñāṇa,
- Knowledge of dispassion, nibbidā ñāṇa,
- Knowledge of desire for deliverance, mucitukamyatā ñāṇa,
- Knowledge of reflexion, paṭisankhā ñaṇa,
- Knowledge of equanimity about conditioned dhamma, saṅkhārupekkhā ñāṇa,
- Adaptation or conformity knowledge, anuloma ñāṇa,
- Change-of-lineage knowledge, gotrabhū ñāṇa,
- Path knowledge, magga ñāṇa,
- Fruition knowledge, phala ñāṇa,
- Reviewing knowledge, paccavekkhaṇa ñāṇa.

Vipassanā ñāṇas have been classified here as sixteen. However, in some texts they are classified as nine, that is, when the classification begins with the first principal insight (mahā-vipassanā), Knowledge of the arising and falling away (uddayabbaya ñāṇa) and ends with Adaptation knowledge (anuloma ñāṇa). These nine stages of vipassanā ñāṇa which do not include the three beginning stages of "tender insight" are "vipassanā as power," balava vipassanā.

Sometimes vipassanā ñāṇas are classified as ten, when the classification begins with the third stage of tender insight, Comprehension by groups (sammasana ñāṇa) and ends with Adaptation knowledge.

The exposition of all the different stages of insight, from the first stage up to adaptation knowledge, arising before the attainment of enlightenment, shows that the development of insight is a long process. Very gradually, insight can become keener and more accomplished, so that adaptation knowledge can arise and conform to the realization of nibbāna.

32

Different Kinds of Purity

Paññā developed in satipaṭṭhāna becomes keener and purer as successive stages of vipassanā are reached. In the development of satipaṭṭhāna there are different kinds of purity, visuddhi, and these can be classified as sevenfold.

The first purity is purity of sīla, sīla visuddhi. Sīla arising together with satipaṭṭhāna that is aware of the characteristics of nāma and rūpa is sīla visuddhi. At that moment, there is purification from ignorance about the characteristics of paramattha dhammas that are non-self. When satipaṭṭhāna does not arise, one is bound to take sīla for self, and, thus, sīla is not sīla visuddhi.

The second purity is purity of citta, citta visuddhi. This is actually different degrees of samādhi, concentration. When sati is aware of the characteristics of nāma and rūpa and when jhānacitta is the object of satipaṭṭhāna, jhānacitta is citta visuddhi. At that moment, one does not take jhānacitta for self.

The third purity is purity of view, diṭṭhi visuddhi. This is the stage of insight that is nāma-rūpa-pariccheda-ñāṇa, the paññā that clearly discerns the difference between the characteristics of nāma and rūpa. At that moment, one does not take any reality, including insight knowledge, for self. There is purity of view, diṭṭhi visuddhi, because there was never before such clear realization of the different characteristics of nāma and rūpa as non-self.

The fourth purity is purity by overcoming doubt, kaṅkhāvitaraṇa visuddhi.[1]

When purity of view has arisen, paññā developed through satipaṭṭhāna sees the characteristics of dhammas as they really are.[2] Paññā sees realities as they are while sati is aware of the characteristics of realities as they appear through the eyes, the ears, the nose, the tongue, the body-sense and the mind-door. In that way, paññā becomes accomplished to the degree that the second stage of insight can arise: Knowledge of discerning conditions of nāma and rūpa, paccaya-pariggaha-ñāṇa. When one directly understands that realities arise because of their appropriate conditions, doubt about their conditional arising is eliminated. Then there is the purity by overcoming doubt.

The fifth purity is purity by knowledge and vision of what is the path and what is not the path, maggāmagga-ñāṇadassana visuddhi.[3]

When purity by overcoming doubt has arisen, paññā becomes more accomplished through satipaṭṭhāna, which is aware of the characteristics of nāma and rūpa. Paññā becomes more familiar with their characteristics and comes to know them more clearly. Paññā realizes that realities are equal in the sense that all of them are only conditioned dhammas, and thus there is more equanimity with regard to them. This means that there is more detachment, less inclination to cling to any particular nāma or rūpa. Paññā is more inclined to investigate the arising and falling away of the nāma and rūpa which appear, their characteristics of impermanence, dukkha and anattā. Thus, paññā can realize the arising and falling away of dhammas in succession, at the stage of insight which is comprehension by groups, sammasana ñāṇa. After that stage

[1] Kaṅkhā means doubt and vitaraṇa means overcoming.

[2] There is knowledge and vision in conformity with the truth, in Pāli: yathābhūta ñāṇa dassana. Yathābhūta means: as it really is; ñāṇa means knowledge and dassana means seeing or vision.

[3] See "Visuddhimagga" Ch XXII. Amagga means: not the path, "a" being a negation.

there can be the fourth stage of insight that is Knowledge of the arising and falling away of realities, udayabbaya ñāṇa. This is a more precise knowledge of the arising and falling away of one kind of nāma and one kind of rūpa at a time.

After the fourth stage of insight has fallen away, defilements can arise. Since they have not been eradicated, they can condition the arising of one or more "imperfections of insight," vipassanūpakkilesas ("Visuddhimagga" Ch XX, 105-129). There are ten imperfections of insight, arising on account of the following factors:

- illumination, obhāsa,
- insight knowledge, vipassanā ñāṇa,
- rapture, pīti,
- tranquility, passaddhi,
- happiness, sukha,
- resolution, adhimokkha,
- exertion, paggāha,
- assurance, upaṭṭhāna,
- equanimity, upekkhā,
- delight, nikanti.

As to the first imperfection arising on account of illumination, this can occur when the fourth stage of insight, Knowledge of the arising and falling away of nāma and rūpa, has fallen away. The citta may have reached such a degree of calm that it conditions the arising of illumination.[4] When attachment to this arises, it is an imperfection of insight. This imperfection causes the interruption of the development of insight. One does not investigate the arising and falling away of realities

[4]Brightness, emanating from one's body, Vis. XXII, 107, footnote 34. The "Visuddhimagga" states that this imperfection usually arises in someone who has developed calm and insight.

anymore and does not attend to their characteristics of impermanence, dukkha and anattā.

The second imperfection is attachment to paññā that clearly realizes the characteristics of nāma and rūpa as they arise and fall away very rapidly. One is attached to the knowledge that is keen and that arises in him like a lightning flash. Due to this imperfection, one does not continue to investigate the arising and falling away of realities and to develop understanding of the three general characteristics.

The third imperfection is attachment to rapture and satisfaction about the direct understanding of the arising and falling away of dhammas.

The fourth imperfection is attachment to tranquillity, to freedom from restlessness, heaviness, rigidity, crookedness or unwieldiness.

The fifth imperfection is attachment to the happy feeling which is very intense and which arises owing to insight.

The sixth imperfection is clinging to the resolution, steadfastness and strong confidence that arise due to insight.

The seventh imperfection is clinging to well-exerted energy which is neither too strained nor too lax, and which arises due to insight.

The eighth imperfection is clinging to well-established mindfulness and assurance that arises in association with insight.

The ninth imperfection is clinging to equanimity and impartiality towards all conditioned dhammas, which occurs in association with insight. One may cling when paññā is as keen and fast as a flash of lightning while it realizes the arising and falling away of the objects that appear.

The tenth imperfection of insight occurs when someone delights in insight that clearly realizes the characteristics of nāma and rūpa as they are.

When paññā has become keener, it realizes the intricacy and subtlety of the imperfections of vipassanā and it knows that these must be eliminated. Paññā realizes that, so long as they arise, the right Path leading to elimination of even the more subtle attachment to realities is not developed. That is purity by knowledge and vision of what is the path and what is not the path, maggāmagga-ñāṇadassana-visuddhi. Then there can be insight knowledge of the fourth stage, Knowledge of the arising and falling away of nāma and rūpa, while the person who develops insight is now free from the imperfections of insight.[5]

The sixth purity is purity by knowledge and vision of the path, paṭipadā-ñāṇadassana-visuddhi.[6]

When the imperfections of insight have been overcome, paññā becomes more accomplished as the development of satipaṭṭhāna continues, and then there is purity by knowledge and vision of the path. While the person who develops insight is now free from the imperfections of insight, there is this purity from the fourth stage of insight on, which is Knowledge of the arising and falling away of realities, and it continues up to Adaptation knowledge, anuloma ñāṇa. Adaptation knowledge are the three moments of citta arising in the magga-vīthi: parikamma or preparatory citta, upacāra or access and anuloma or adaptation.

The seventh purity is purity by knowledge and vision, ñāṇadassana-visuddhi.[7]

When the three moments of Adaptation knowledge have fallen away, Change-of-lineage knowledge, gotrabhū ñāṇa, arises. It has the characteristic of adverting to lokuttara citta, and it neither belongs to the sixth purity, purity by knowledge and vision of the path, nor to the seventh purity, purity by knowledge and vision; it is intermediate between these two kinds of purities. Still, it is reckoned as insight knowledge, because it follows the course of insight (Vis. XXII, 1). When change-of-lineage has fallen away, magga-citta arises and then there is purity by knowledge and vision. Thus, there are seven purities in all.

[5]The "Visuddhimagga" Ch XXI, 2, explains why the Knowledge of arising and falling away of realities should be pursued again. The person who develops insight could not realize clearly the three general characteristics of realities so long as he was disabled by the imperfections. When the imperfections have been overcome, he should pursue the Knowledge of arising and falling away of realities again in order to realize the three characteristics more clearly.

[6]See "Visuddhimagga" Ch XXI.

[7]See "Visuddhimagga" Ch XXII.

33

The Three Kinds of Full Understanding

The development of satipaṭṭhāna is the development of paññā leading to the realization of the noble Truths. In the course of the development of insight, three degrees of full understanding, pariññā, can be discerned: full understanding of the known, ñāta pariññā,[1] full understanding as investigation, tīraṇa pariññā,[2] and full understanding as abandoning, pahāna pariññā.[3]

Full understanding of the known, ñāta pariññā, is paññā realizing the characteristics of nāma and rūpa that appear as non-self. Insight of the first stage, which clearly discerns the difference between the characteristics of nāma and of rūpa, nāma-rūpa-pariccheda-ñāṇa, is the basis for the further development of paññā. Full understanding of the known is paññā that applies the knowledge gained at the moment of this stage of insight, and it begins at this stage. Paññā should continue to investigate over and over again the characteristics of other kinds of nāma

[1]Ñāta means what has been known and pariññā means full understanding.

[2]Tīraṇa means judgement, investigation.

[3]Pahāna means abandoning.

and rūpa, in addition to those realized at the moment the first stage of insight knowledge arose. Only then can nāma and rūpa be clearly understood as they are.

Full understanding as investigation, tīraṇa pariññā, is paññā that thoroughly investigates nāma and rūpa, without preference for any particular nāma or rūpa, without selection of them. Paññā realizes the characteristics of realities as they appear through all six doors and thus it can see them as only dhammas. When paññā clearly realizes that all nāma and rūpa are equal, in as far as they are only dhammas, it becomes more accomplished. Thus it can realize the fourth stage of insight, knowledge of the arising and falling away of nāma and rūpa.[4] Full understanding of investigation begins at this stage.

The third kind of full understanding is full understanding of abandoning, pahāna pariññā. When paññā investigates the dissolution of nāma and rūpa and it can clearly realize this, the stage of insight can be reached which is Knowledge of dissolution, bhaṅga ñāṇa. From then on, paññā begins to become more detached from nāma and rūpa. Paññā becomes detached because it sees more clearly the disadvantage and danger of nāma and rūpa. Full understanding of abandoning begins at the stage of Knowledge of dissolution and continues up to Path knowledge, magga ñāṇa, when enlightenment is attained.

In our daily life, there are more conditions for akusala dhammas than for awareness and understanding of the characteristics of the dhammas that naturally appear. Akusala dhammas arise very often and therefore it is necessary to cultivate the thirty-seven factors leading to enlightenment, bodhipakkhiya-dhammas. These factors which lead to the realization of the four noble Truths are, as we have seen, the four satipaṭṭhānas, the four right efforts (sammappadhānas), the four bases of success (iddhi-pādas), the five spiritual faculties (indriyas), the five powers (balas),the seven factors of enlightenment (bojjhangas) and the eight factors of the noble eightfold Path.

The factors that lead to enlightenment should be developed over and over again for a long time; they can only be gradually accumulated. Nobody can cause the arising of paññā just by a particular way of behaviour or by particular activities. Paññā can be developed naturally, in one's

[4]The first stage of mahā-vipassanā ñāṇa.

daily life, by awareness of the characteristics of realities, which are non-self, which arise because of their appropriate conditions and then fall away very rapidly. There can be awareness of what appears at this very moment through the eyes, the ears, the nose, the tongue, the bodysense or the mind-door. Does one know at this moment what satipaṭṭhāna exactly is? Does one know that what is appearing now through the senses or the mind-door is a paramattha dhamma, non-self? If this is not known, paññā of the level of intellectual understanding should first be developed. It is necessary to listen to the Dhamma the Buddha taught so that people would have right understanding of the characteristics of realities that appear. The Buddha taught the Dhamma so that people would have right understanding in conformity with the truth that he had realized when he attained Buddhahood. One should have correct understanding of the practice, which is the development of paññā. Only the right cause can bring the right result, that is, paññā that sees realities as they are, as impermanent, dukkha and anattā. Paññā should realize that realities that arise and fall away are dukkha, unsatisfactory, not leading to happiness, and paññā should penetrate the nature of anattā of the realities appearing at this moment. There is no other way to know realities as they are but satipaṭṭhāna, which time and again is aware, studies and investigates the characteristics of the dhammas appearing right now. In this way, wholesome qualities, sobhana cetasikas, are accumulated and can thus be a condition for paññā to become more accomplished, so that the different stages of insight can be reached.

The Sammāsambuddha had accumulated the perfections for four incalculable periods and hundred thousand aeons. From the time the Buddha Dīpaṅkara proclaimed him to be a Sammāsambuddha in the future, he developed all the perfections from life to life. He came to see and listened to twenty-four former Buddhas during his past lives before he attained Buddhahood. In his last life, while sitting under the Bodhi tree, he penetrated the four noble Truths and attained successively the stages of enlightenment of the sotāpanna, the sakadāgāmī, the anāgāmī and finally the stage of the arahat, and thereby became the Sammāsambuddha with incomparable wisdom. He attained Buddhahood in the last vigil of the night of the full moon, in the month of Vesākha.

The Buddha's chief disciples were the venerable Sāriputta who was pre-eminent in wisdom and the venerable Moggallāna who was pre-eminent in supernatural powers. They had developed paññā during one incalculable period of time and hundred thousand aeons. In his last life, Sāriputta attained the stage of the sotāpanna after he had listened to the Dhamma which Assaji explained to him. When Sāriputta explained to Moggallāna the Dhamma he had heard from Assaji, Moggallāna attained the stage of the sotāpanna. Later on, they both became arahats. The disciples who were pre-eminent in different ways, such as Kassapa, Ānanda, Upāli and Ānuruddha, had cultivated paññā for hundred thousand aeons. In the Buddha's time, there were many people who had cultivated paññā to the degree that they could penetrate the four noble Truths and attain enlightenment. The time just before the Buddha had passed away was the most favourable time for the development of paññā. The period from his parinibbāna until the present time is not all that long, but still, the present time is less favourable for the realization of the noble Truths. For the realization of the noble Truths the right conditions have to be present, which are study and understanding of the Dhamma and the right way of practice. Only the right cause, the development of paññā, can bring the right result.

Before the Buddha's enlightenment, people could develop samatha even to the degree of realizing supernatural powers. They could perform miracles but they could not eradicate defilements. When the Buddha attained supreme enlightenment and taught the Dhamma he had penetrated, many people could realize the noble Truths. People who had formerly developed samatha to the degree of jhāna could, if they also had developed satipaṭṭhāna, realize the noble Truths. Thus, two kinds of ariyans can be discerned: those who had not developed jhāna, who were "sukkha vipassaka",[5] and those who had developed jhāna.

The ariyan with "mere insight," who is sukkha vipassaka, attains enlightenment without jhānacitta as basis or proximate cause. For him jhānacitta cannot serve as object of insight since he has not attained jhāna. It is true that the lokuttara citta which clearly realizes nibbāna is firmly established on nibbāna with strong concentration, just like the attainment concentration, appanā samādhi, which is firmly fixed on the object of the different stages of jhānacitta. However, the ariyan who

[5] Sukkha vipassanā, mere insight, is also translated as "dry insight."

is sukkha vipassaka does not have proficiency in jhāna and he cannot attain it. When cittas are counted as eighty-nine, the lokuttara cittas of those who did not develop jhāna, who are sukkha vipassaka, are taken into account.

The ariyan who has developed jhāna can attain magga-citta and phala-citta with jhāna as basis or proximate cause but he must acquire "masteries," vasīs, of jhāna.[6] In that case, jhānacitta can be the object of mahā-kusala citta accompanied by paññā that investigates and realizes its true nature, and then enlightenment can be attained. The ariyan who attains enlightenment with magga-citta and phala-citta accompanied by jhāna factors of the different stages of jhāna is delivered from defilements by paññā and by calm associated with the different stages of jhāna. When cittas are counted as one hundred twenty-eight, the lokuttara cittas of the ariyan who has developed jhāna are included.[7]

[6] See the section on Samatha.

[7] Instead of eight lokuttara cittas, magga-citta and phala-citta of the four stages of enlighten-ment, there are forty lokuttara cittas: five times eight lokuttara cittas when taking into account the factors of the five stages of jhāna.

34
The Three Attainments

There are three attainments or samāpattis:[1]

- attainment of jhāna, jhāna-samāpatti,
- fruition attainment, phala-samāpatti,
- attainment of extinction, nirodha-samāpatti.

An ordinary person who is not an ariyan may attain jhāna and acquire the skills, vasīs, in jhāna, such as attaining jhāna and emerging from it in the order of the successive stages of jhāna. Someone who is proficient in jhāna[2] can

have jhāna-samāpatti, that is, jhānacittas arising in succession in a mind-door process without bhavanga-cittas in between, for a period lasting as long as he has determined. During that time, he is free from

[1] Samāpajjati means to enter upon.

[2] In Pāli: jhāna-lābhī. Lābha means gain or acquisition, and lābhī means the person who acquires something.

pain and unhappiness. This is because he is free from the sense objects and experiences only the meditation subject of jhāna, which conditions the happiness of true calm.

The ariyan who has developed jhāna and attained enlightenment with lokuttara cittas accompanied by jhāna factors of the different stages of jhāna can, after these cittas have fallen away, attain fruition-attainment, phala-samāpatti, again during his life. For him there can be other processes where phalacittas accompanied by jhāna factors of the first, second, third, fourth or fifth stage of jhāna experience nibbāna again. It depends on the stage of enlightenment he has attained what type of phala-citta arises accompanied by jhāna factors of one of the stages of jhāna. When there is fruition-attainment, phala-cittas can arise in succession without bhavanga-cittas in between, for a period lasting as long as he has determined.

In the mind-door process of cittas with fruition-attainment, the kāmāvacara cittas (cittas of the sense sphere) that arise first are not parikamma, preparatory consciousness, and upacāra, access, but there are three moments of adaptation or conformity, anuloma, because these cittas adapt or conform to the phalacitta, which is lokuttara jhānacitta and which arises again, experiencing nibbāna. These moments are different from parikamma, upacāra and anuloma which arose in the magga-vīthi where the magga-citta arose and eradicated defilements. In the case of fruition attainment phala-citta arises and experiences nibbāna for a period lasting as long as that person has determined.

The anāgāmī and the arahat who have attained the fourth arūpa-jhāna, the stage of neither-perception-nor-non-perception,[3] can attain cessation, nirodha-samāpatti. This is the attainment of the temporary cessation of citta and cetasikas. They do not arise anymore, but this stage cannot last longer than seven days. The reason is that food that has been taken cannot support the body longer than seven days. The temporary cessation of citta and cetasika is conditioned by two powers: by samatha and by vipassanā. The anāgāmī and the arahat who have not attained calm to the degree of the fourth arūpa-jhāna cannot attain cessation. Neither can the sotāpanna and the sakadāgāmī attain

[3]See the section on Samatha. At this stage, there are still citta and cetasikas, but they are very subtle, they are present in a residual way.

cessation, even if they have reached the fourth stage of arūpa-jhāna.[4]

Those who are able to attain cessation should first attain successively all the stages of rūpa-jhāna. They should emerge from each stage and then investigate with insight saṅkhāra dhammas, conditioned dhammas, as impermanent, dukkha and anattā, before they attain the following stage of jhāna. When they have emerged from the third stage of arūpa-jhāna, the sphere of nothingness, however, they should first advert to a fourfold preparatory task ("Visuddhimagga" Ch XXIII, 34): non-damage to others' property; the community's waiting; the Master's summons; the limit of duration.

As regards non-damage to others' property, this refers to what a bhikkhu uses or keeps, and what are not his personal property but the property of others, such as bowl, robes, bed and dwelling. He should resolve that such property will not be damaged, that it will not be destroyed by fire, water, wind, thieves and so on within the period of cessation-attainment, which lasts no longer than seven days. He does not have to make a specific resolution with regard to his personal property, such as his inner robes and outer robes, or his seat. These are protected from damage or loss by the attainment of cessation itself.

As regards the Master's summons, he should resolve to emerge from cessation when the Buddha requires his presence.

As regards the limit of duration, he should know whether his life will last longer than seven days or not. During the period of cessation, the dying-consciousness cannot arise. Thus, when his lifespan is not due to end within seven days he can enter cessation.

When a bhikkhu has done the fourfold preparatory task, he can attain the fourth stage of arūpa-jhāna. After two moments of arūpa-jhānacittas of that stage, which arise in that process, he achieves cessation of citta and cetasika. They do not arise anymore and this state can last for seven days. When he emerges from cessation, one moment of phala-citta arises, to be followed by bhavanga-cittas. The attainment of cessation can occur only in the planes where there are five khandhas.

[4]Both the power of samatha and the power of vipassanā are necessary. The sotāpanna and the sakadāgāmī, even if they have attained the highest stage of arūpa-jhāna, do not have the same degree of paññā as the anāgāmī and the arahat; thus, in their case paññā is not powerful enough to be able to condition cessation.

It cannot occur in the arūpa-brahma planes where rūpa-jhānacitta does not arise.[5]

[5]As we have seen, the person who will attain cessation has to attain all stages of rūpa-jhāna and arūpa-jhāna. In the arūpa-brahma planes there are no conditions for rūpa-jhāna. Birth in those planes is the result of arūpa-jhāna.

Part VI

Dialogue on Vipassanā

35

The Natural Way of Development

Questioner: Among the forty kinds of meditation subjects of samatha, I prefer "Mindfulness of Breathing." However, I understand that by means of this subject, I cannot eradicate defilements, that I cannot realize the noble Truths and reach nibbāna.

Sujin: Through samatha defilements cannot be eradicated, nor can the noble Truths be realized and nibbāna be attained.

Questioner: I think that people's aim is eradicating defilements and attaining nibbāna. However, they do not understand what the cause of clinging is in daily life. They do not know when there is lobha. If someone just wishes to eradicate defilements without knowing them as they are, there is clinging to a result. Is it then possible for them to develop satipaṭṭhāna?

Sujin: No, it is impossible.

Questioner: Can we develop both samatha and vipassanā?

Sujin: People will know for themselves whether they are developing samatha or vipassanā. However, if there is no right understanding of these different ways of development, neither samatha nor vipassanā can be developed.

Questioner: Could you please give some directions for the development of vipassanā?

Sujin: Nobody can hasten the development of satipaṭṭhāna. The goal of satipaṭṭhāna is the eradication of defilements. However, a person who does not know his defilements is not motivated to follow the way leading to their eradication. If someone would line up children who are ignorant of their defilements and tell them to eradicate defilements by the development of satipaṭṭhāna, they would not want to eradicate defilements. How could they then develop satipaṭṭhāna?

All people, children and adults alike, have many defilements. If one would ask them whether they would wish to get rid of them, most of them would answer that they do not wish to. Therefore, one should not try to force others to develop satipaṭṭhāna.

Some people, when they hear about defilements, may not like to have them, but do they really know their defilements? Attachment, lobha, is a defilement. Do people want to have lobha? They may not like the idea of having lobha, but actually, people like lobha each and every moment. This shows that one does not understand the characteristic of the defilement of lobha. We can find out whether we really understand lobha as a defilement or not. Is the food delicious? Are our clothes and the things with which we beautify ourselves nice? Is this music pleasing, that odour fragrant, and is the chair soft and comfortable? Is what we touch agreeable? Although some people do not like the idea of having lobha and think that they should not have it, they can find out that citta needs lobha all the time.

The development of satipaṭṭhāna is the development of sati and paññā. It is not trying to have concentration, samādhi.

Question: What is attā-saññā, remembrance of self?

Sujin: Attā-saññā is remembrance (saññā) with clinging to the concept of self (attā), thus, wrong perception of self. We do not have doubts about attā-saññā because we all are familiar with it. When a person has realized the noble Truths at the attainment of the first stage of enlightenment, the stage of the stream-winner (sotāpanna), the wrong view is eradicated which takes realities for self, for beings or for people. However, there is bound to be attā-saññā if one has not developed satipaṭṭhāna. There is bound to be ignorance and wrong view if sati does not arise, if there is no awareness of the characteristics of realities as they naturally appear through one doorway at a time. Wrong view takes the realities that appear for a compound, a "whole," for something that lasts, for attā, self. If people at this moment do not know realities as they are, there is bound to be attā-saññā, the remembrance or perception that it is "I" who is seeing, and that what is seen is a being, a person, a self.

When someone has only theoretical understanding of realities that is the result of listening to the Dhamma, he is not able to directly understand nāma and rūpa as they are. He does not realize that what he sees and conceives as people and beings, is in reality only that which appears through the eyes. Therefore, we should time and again investigate the Dhamma we hear and study, we should ponder over it in all details. Only in this way the meaning of the words that designate characteristics of realities can be fully understood.

The wording "that which appears through the eyes" describing the characteristic of visible object is altogether appropriate. It explains that visible object is only an element (dhātu) appearing through the eyes so that it can be seen. No matter what colour it is: red, green, blue, yellow or white, a bright or a dull colour, it must appear when it impinges on the rūpa that is eyesense. When someone, after having seen what appears through the eyesense, does not understand realities as they are, there is bound to be attā-saññā. He takes what was seen for people, beings or things. When people are absorbed in different colours, it causes them to think of a "whole", of shape and form, and, thus, there is remembrance (saññā) of the outward appearance of persons and things. When it seems that one sees people, beings or things, there are in reality only different colours that are seen, such as black, white, the colour of skin, red or yellow.

If people did not interpret different colours or "translate" them into shape and form, they would not conceive them as beings, people or things. Therefore, when we see and we are then absorbed in the shape and form, in the outward appearance (nimitta) and the details of things, we should know that this occurs only because colour appears. When colours appear, we think about them, interpret them and "translate" them into shape and form of different things.

When sati arises and is mindful of realities and paññā begins to study and investigate their characteristics, one will begin to understand that the outward appearance and all the details of things, all the different colours, are only what appears through the eyes, nothing else. Then paññā begins to penetrate the characteristics of realities as not a self, not a being, not a person. If sati arises and is aware time and again, one will understand the meaning of the Buddha's words explaining that, by the development of the understanding of the realities which naturally appear, one will not cling to the outward appearance and the details of things.

We read in the "Middle Length Sayings" (I, no. 27) in the "Lesser Discourse on the Simile of the Elephant's Footprint" that the Buddha spoke to the Brahmin Jāṇussoṇi about the monk's life. He spoke about the "restraint of the senses":

> "He, possessed of the ariyan body of moral habit, subjectively experiences unsullied well-being. Having seen visible object with the eye, he is not entranced by the general appearance, he is not entranced by the detail. If he dwells with this organ of sight uncontrolled, covetousness and dejection, evil unskilled states of mind might predominate. So he fares along controlling it; he guards the organ of sight, he comes to have control over the organ of sight..."
>
> (The same is said with regard to the other doorways.)

This kind of restraint can be achieved through the development of paññā that understands the realities that appear as they are. One will begin to let go of attā-saññā with regard to what appears through the eyes, the ears, the nose, the tongue, the bodysense and the mind-door, in accordance with the degree of paññā that has been reached.

We should remember that no matter which topic or which detail the teachings deal with, it all concerns the realities of daily life. Sati should be aware of the realities that appear so that paññā is able to clearly understand their characteristics. This leads to the complete eradication of defilements.

We should listen carefully to the Dhamma, we should study and investigate the dhammas that are already appearing, which are our ordinary daily life. We cannot yet immediately eradicate lobha, dosa, moha and the other defilements. People desire to eradicate defilements, but they should know that defilements can only be eradicated at the moment of enlightenment, when the magga-citta, path-consciousness, arises. First, "personality view", sakkāya-diṭṭhi, is eradicated, which takes the dhammas appearing through the six doors for self, being or person. Personality view is eradicated at the first stage of enlightenment, the stage of the stream-winner, sotāpanna.

After that stage has been attained, paññā should be developed further so that the following stages of enlightenment can be attained and defilements can successively be eradicated. These stages are the stages of the once-returner, sakadāgāmī, the non-returner, anāgāmī, and the arahat. Thus, paññā can be developed only gradually. One should not try to hasten its development, one should not believe that it is sufficient just to practise for a day, a month or a year, without even understanding the right conditions for sati. Actually, sati which is sammā-sati (right mindfulness) of the Eightfold Path can only arise if one first studies and understands the characteristics of realities as they appear through the senses and through the mind-door. Then sammā-sati can arise and be aware, and paññā can begin to investigate realities that naturally appear in daily life, so that they can be seen as they really are.

The development of satipaṭṭhāna is a threefold training (sikkhā): training in higher morality, adhisīla sikkhā, training in higher consciousness, adhicitta sikkhā, training in higher wisdom, adhipaññā sikkhā.

When sati is aware of the realities that are appearing, there is higher sīla, sīla that is more refined. Sati is aware of the characteristics of citta, cetasika and rūpa. It is aware of kusala dhammas and akusala dhammas before actions through the body or through speech arise.[1]

Satipaṭṭhāna is training in higher consciousness, which means concentration, samādhi or ekaggatā cetasika.[2] When sammā-sati arises, there is concentration on the nāma or rūpa that appears, on the dhamma that arises and falls away very rapidly.

Satipaṭṭhāna is training in higher wisdom, because paññā investigates and studies in detail the characteristics of realities as they are appearing in daily life, so that they can be known as they are.

[1] Sati guards the six doors and can prevent the commitment of akusala through body or speech.

[2] Sometimes citta stands for concentration.

Questioner: Everything you have explained is very beneficial for me at this moment. But, although I have some understanding of what I heard, my understanding is not yet sufficient. When I practise satipaṭṭhāna, I immediately cling to a concept of self who is making use of sati. I am only a beginner and, as far as I know myself, I have not even attained the first stage of insight that knows the difference between the characteristic of nāma and of rūpa, nāma-rūpa-pariccheda-ñāṇa. What should I do to have more understanding?

Sujin: If someone tries to do something special with the aim to develop insight, his life will be very complicated. How can he act in the right way if there is still a concept of self who will do particular things? If people wish to do particular things in order to have more understanding, they are clinging. They cling to the understanding of nāma and rūpa that have arisen already. Satipaṭṭhāna is the dhamma which is aware of whatever reality appears through one of the six doors, such as the dhamma appearing through the eyes, visible object, when there is seeing at this moment. Gradually satipaṭṭhāna can be aware naturally and paññā can begin to study and investigate the true nature of nāma and rūpa.

Question: How should we develop satipaṭṭhāna when we are seeing?

Sujin: When there is seeing, you can be aware and realize that what appears to seeing is a type of reality which only appears through the eyes. When we see hairs, a table, a chair, a pillar or a hall, we should know that what is seen is in reality only that which appears through the eyes. It does not appear through the ears, the nose, the tongue or the bodysense. When paññā has not been developed to the degree of knowing the difference between the characteristics of nāma and rūpa, this stage of insight cannot arise.

Questioner: When I receive a Dhamma book about the practice in daily life, I read it many times, because I want to be able to practise. However, all the time there is a concept of self, there is self who sees when there is seeing. I cannot realize that colour is rūpa, seeing is nāma. I keep on thinking about all that has been explained, but I cannot be aware of nāma and rūpa in the right way. Please, could you explain to me how to be aware?

Sujin: When there is seeing which experiences an object through the eyes, can you at that moment investigate the characteristic of the dhamma that naturally appears? It is essential to know how understanding should be developed, so that later on paññā can become accomplished to the degree of the first stage of insight, knowledge of the difference between nāma and rūpa. First of all, sati can be aware and study the different characteristics of nāma and rūpa which are naturally appearing through any doorway. Awareness is different from thinking about nāma and rūpa, from theoretical understanding that stems from listening to the Dhamma. Awareness of realities is not developed when you, while seeing, think about it with agitation, worry and nervousness. It is not developed if you think with agitation that what appears is rūpa and that seeing is nāma. At such a moment, there is no investigation, no study of a characteristic of rūpa or a characteristic of nāma. It is necessary to have first correct understanding of the characteristics of nāma and rūpa so that satipaṭṭhāna can arise and be directly aware of them. You should understand that the nāma that sees is a reality that experiences something, that it has no shape or form and that it is non-self. It is not necessary to assume a particular posture in order to know realities. It is not necessary to stand first and then see, or to sit or lie down first and then see, so that you would know seeing as it is.

Satipaṭṭhāna investigates precisely the characteristic of seeing as a type of reality that experiences something, not "I" or self, not a being or a person. When satipaṭṭhāna arises and it is aware of the characteristic of rūpa appearing through the eyes, that characteristic can be investigated. In this way it can be known as only a type of reality, not self, not a being or a person.

Questioner: The practice should be steadfast, not agitated, as you just said. Therefore, is it possible to use the method of satipaṭṭhāna of breathing (ānāpāna satipaṭṭhāna)? The subjects of satipaṭṭhāna are body, feeling, citta and dhamma, but we can combine these with ānāpāna sati, mindfulness of breathing. I myself have given the name of "ānāpāna satipaṭṭhāna" to this way of practice.

Sujin: It is mostly the desire for result that causes a person to look for a combination of several methods. He may not know how to develop understanding and tries therefore to use one method in combination with another one so that understanding (sampajañña) would become more accomplished. He believes that there is in that way no forgetfulness and that he can focus for a long time on one object. However, is that not clinging? People may well wish to focus citta for a long time on a particular object, but they cannot be mindful in the right way, they cannot be mindful, of what appears, for example, through the eyes or through the other doorways. When people try to make citta concentrate on one object they are actually combining several methods of development because of clinging to result. It is not the development of paññā.

For the person who develops satipaṭṭhāna naturally, the aim is to understand realities and thereby to become detached from them. However, if one has no understanding yet, one cannot become detached. Can you, while you try to make citta concentrate on one object, let go of desire? If you try to concentrate, you do not develop paññā with the aim of understanding realities and becoming detached. If people try to do something other than developing satipaṭṭhāna naturally, they will not know as they are the characteristics of realities that are appearing at this moment. Hearing is real, it appears naturally and so it is with thinking, happy feeling or unhappy feeling; they all appear naturally, they are all dhammas, realities. If sati does not arise and is not aware of realities, there is not the development of satipaṭṭhāna. What is the use of combining different methods of practice if there is no understanding of nāma and rūpa as they appear already through the six doors?

Questioner: When I combine different methods, I acquire more understanding of the three characteristics of impermanence, dukkha and anattā. They are explained in the textbooks I have read. I also have read about mindfulness of breathing and this helps me not to be distracted by other matters. If I have a problem that I cannot solve, I apply myself to mindfulness of breathing. But if I try to think, "seeing through the eyes is nāma, it is non-self," or, "hearing is non-self," I feel confused. There is still self all the time, self who is acting, who is thinking. I feel confused and worried about that.

Sujin: If you combine different ways of practice, you are bound to become worried, because there is no paññā which investigates and studies the characteristics of realities as they naturally appear. You said that the benefit derived from your way of practice is knowing the three general characteristics of realities: impermanence, dukkha and anattā. However, that is only textbook knowledge of the three characteristics. If you do not know nāma and rūpa as they appear, how can you know the three general characteristics of nāma and rūpa? They must be characteristics of the nāma and rūpa that appear, one at a time.

It is through insight knowledge, vipassanā ñāṇa, that the three general characteristics are penetrated. There cannot be vipassanā ñāṇa if one does not know the different characteristics of the nāmas and rūpas as they appear one at a time. If one does not know the difference between the characteristic of nāma and the characteristic of rūpa, the three general characteristics of realities cannot be penetrated.

Questioner: How should one be aware? I know that sati is aware, but how? Should there be profound consideration or a more superficial consideration of the three general characteristics of impermanence, dukkha and anattā? Or should there be awareness only of softness and hardness? I have understood what you taught about the practice, I listened for two or three years. However, I cannot practise. I learnt about nāma and rūpa, but what are they? How should I be aware of them? I feel confused about awareness of dhammas at the present moment. There must be a special method for this. A special method is important. Should there be profound awareness or awareness which is more superficial, awareness for a long time or for a short time? But I take everything for self.

Sujin: This way of acting leads to confusion. You may try to regulate sati, to have profound awareness or a more superficial awareness, to have a great deal of it or only a little, but, as regards the development of paññā, there is no special method or technique. The development of paññā begins with listening to the Dhamma, and studying the realities sati can be aware of, so that understanding can grow. These are conditions for the arising of sati that is directly aware of the characteristics of nāma and rūpa as they naturally appear. Since the nāma and rūpa that appear are real, paññā can come to know their true nature.

You should not try to regulate sati and try to make it strong or to make it decrease so that it is weak, or to make it superficial. If one acts in that way, one clings to the concept of self and does not investigate and study the characteristics of the dhammas that appear. What are the realities that appear? Someone who is not forgetful considers realities and he can be naturally aware of their characteristics. He begins to know very gradually the characteristics of nāma dhammas and rūpa dhammas. He does not try to make sati focus on an object so that it could consider that object more deeply, over and over again. Sati arises and falls away, and then there may be again forgetfulness, or sati may be aware again of another object. Thus, we can see that satipaṭṭhāna is anattā. People who understand that all realities, including satipaṭṭhāna, are anattā, will not be confused. If someone clings to the concept of self, he is inclined to regulate and direct sati, but he does not know the right way. If one's practice is not natural, it is complicated and creates confusion. If awareness is natural, if the characteristics of realities that appear are considered and investigated, there will be understanding, no confusion.

Questioner: I do not know yet the characteristic of satipaṭṭhāna. When I listen intently to your lecture, I understand the subject matter, the theory. There is also awareness while I have theoretical understanding, but I do not consider nāma and rūpa at this moment. I am not sure whether that is satipaṭṭhāna or not.

Sujin: If we do not know that our life is only nāma and rūpa, we are bound to take realities for self. We are full of the concept of self and this can only be eradicated completely by satipaṭṭhāna. Sati can be aware and begin to investigate the characteristics of nāma and rūpa that appear. In the beginning, when sati is aware, there cannot yet be clear understanding of the realities that appear as nāma and as rūpa. The understanding may be so weak that it is hardly noticeable. Understanding develops only gradually, it can eliminate ignorance stage by stage; ignorance cannot be immediately eradicated. It is just as in the case of the knife-handle someone holds each day and which wears off only a little at a time.

We read in the "Kindred Sayings" (III, Middle Fifty, Ch V, § 101, Adze-handle) that the Buddha, while he was in Sāvatthī, said to the monks that defilements can be eradicated by realizing the arising and falling away of the five khandhas. This cannot be achieved "by not knowing, by not seeing." If someone would just wish for the eradication of defilements and he would be neglectful of the development of understanding, defilements cannot be eradicated. Only by the development of understanding, defilements can gradually be eliminated. We read:

> "Just as if, monks, when a carpenter or carpenter's apprentice looks upon his adze-handle and sees thereon his thumb-mark and his finger-marks he does not thereby know: 'Thus

> and thus much of my adze-handle has been worn away today, thus much yesterday, thus much at other times.' But he knows the wearing away of it just by its wearing away. Even so, monks, the monk who dwells attentive to self-training has not this knowledge: 'Thus much and thus much of the āsavas has been worn away today, thus much yesterday, and thus much at other times.' But he knows the wearing away of them just by their wearing away."

Understanding has to be developed for an endlessly long time.[3] Some people dislike it that sati and paññā develop only very gradually, but there is no other way. If someone is impatient and tries to combine different ways of practice in order to hasten the development of paññā, he makes his life very complicated.

Questioner: What is the difference between the practice that is natural and the practice that is unnatural?

Sujin: At this moment, you are sitting in a natural way and you may be aware of realities which appear, such as softness or hardness, presenting themselves through the bodysense, or visible object appearing through the eyesense. All these dhammas appear naturally. However, someone's practice is unnatural if he believes, while he develops satipaṭṭhāna, that he should sit cross-legged, in the lotus position, and that he should concentrate on specific realities. There is desire when a person selects realities that have not arisen yet as objects of awareness. He neglects to be aware of realities that appear already, such as seeing, hearing, visible object, sound, odour, flavour, cold, heat, softness or hardness. Even if there is only a slight amount of wrong understanding, it conditions clinging and this hides the truth. In that case, paññā cannot arise and know the dhammas appearing at that moment.

People who develop satipaṭṭhāna should know precisely the difference between the moment of forgetfulness, when there is no sati, and the moment when there is sati. Otherwise, satipaṭṭhāna cannot be de-

[3]The "Cariyāpiṭaka", the "Basket of Conduct" deals with the perfections the Buddha had to develop as a Bodhisatta, for a hundred thousand aeons and four incalculable ages. The commentary, the "Paramatthadīpanī", states in the "Niddesa," the explanation at the beginning, that among the requisites of enlightenment is "the development for a long time," cira kāla bhāvanā. It adds, "the development time and again, for a long time."

veloped. If one is usually forgetful, one is bound to be forgetful again. Someone may wish to select an object in order to concentrate on it, but this is not the way to develop satipaṭṭhāna. We should have right understanding of the moment when there is forgetfulness, no sati, that is, when we do not know the characteristics of realities appearing in daily life, such as seeing or hearing. When there is sati, one can consider, study and understand the dhammas appearing through the six doors. When someone selects a particular object in order to focus on it, he will not know that sati is non-self. When sati arises, it can be aware of realities that naturally appear. When odour appears, there can be awareness of odour that presents itself through the nose. It can be known as only a type of reality that arises, that appears and then disappears. Or the nāma which experiences odour can be understood as only a type of reality that presents itself. After it has experienced odour, it falls away. It is not a being, a person or self.

Questioner: Is it true that the sotāpanna, the person who has attained the first stage of enlightenment, does not recognize his father or mother?

Sujin: The sotāpanna clearly realizes the dhamma that sees as a type of nāma. After seeing he knows what it is that was perceived, namely a person, a being or a thing he can think of. Thinking is another type of nāma that arises and then falls away. Is there anybody who sees and then does not know the meaning of what was seen? If that is the case, the Buddha would not have recognized Ānanda or Moggallāna, or anything at all. Then there would be only the nāma that sees and no other types of nāma that recognize what was seen. However, dhammas take their own natural course, they are what they are. Apart from the nāma that sees there is, after the seeing, also the nāma that knows the meaning of what was seen.

36

The Characteristic of Dukkha

Questioner: What should a layman do who wants to be free from dukkha? He may see that there is such a great deal of dukkha, that it is so terrible and that it occurs all the time, because people are born and they have to be born again and again. Is there a short way to become free from dukkha?

Sujin: When someone says that there is such a great deal of dukkha, that it is so terrible, there is bound to be wrong view that clings to the concept of self. Only if there is no wrong view of self can dukkha become less. The Buddha explained that all the different kinds of dukkha can be eliminated according as defilements are eradicated stage by stage. So long as defilements have not been eradicated, there have to be countless rebirths. So long as there is birth, there is dukkha. The sotāpanna who has attained the first stage of enlightenment and has eradicated defilements in accordance with that stage, will not be reborn more than seven times. We read in the "Kindred Sayings" (II, Nidāna vagga, Ch XIII, § 1, The Tip of the Nail):

> "Thus have I heard. On a certain occasion the Exalted One was staying near Sāvatthī at the Jeta Grove, in Anāthapiṇḍika's Park.
>
> Then the Exalted One took up a little pinch of dust on the tip of his finger-nail and said to the monks: 'What do you think, monks? Whether is this pinch of dust that I have taken up on my finger-nail the greater, or the mighty earth?'
>
> 'The latter, lord, the mighty earth is the greater. Infinitely small is this pinch of dust taken up by the Exalted One on his finger-nail, not by a hundredth part, nor by a thousandth part, not by a hundred thousandth part does it equal the mighty earth when set beside it – this pinch of dust taken up by the Exalted One on his finger-nail.'
>
> 'Even so, monks, for the ariyan disciple who has won vision, for the person who has understanding this is the greater dukkha, to wit, that which for him is wholly perished, wholly finished; little is the dukkha that remains, not worth the hundredth part, not worth the thousandth part, not worth the hundred thousandth part when measured with the former dukkha which for him is wholly perished, wholly finished, to wit, a term of seven times.[1]
>
> So great in good, monks, is it to be wise in the Dhamma; so great a good is it to have gained the eye of the Dhamma."'

Since the number of rebirths of ordinary people, who have not attained enlightenment, is countless, the dukkha that arises because of birth must be immeasurable.

Questioner: We all want to know what to do so that we can begin now with the practice of vipassanā.

Sujin: One should be aware of the characteristic of the reality that appears. When sati is aware of whatever reality appears, vitakka cetasika which is "right thinking", sammā-sankappa of the eightfold Path, touches or "hits" the characteristic of the object which is appearing. At that moment, paññā can begin to study and gradually to realize the true nature of that object. In that way paññā can develop.

[1] Seven rebirths.

Understanding can arise and develop when sati is aware of the characteristics of realities that appear and these are considered and investigated at that moment. The realities that arise and appear fall away very rapidly. Paññā may not be keen enough yet to consider and study those realities. For example, when there is hearing, sati may arise and be aware of hearing, just for a moment, but there may not be paññā yet that is sufficiently keen to investigate that characteristic in order to know it as only a nāma which experiences sound. The nāma that hears has completely fallen away. In the beginning there is not yet clear understanding of realities such as hearing, but this is quite normal. Nobody can investigate the true nature of sound and of the nāma that hears by trying to catch them or to get hold of them. However, the nāma that hears will surely arise again and if one develops sati and paññā, there can be awareness again of the nāma that hears.

Now, at this moment, sati can arise and be aware of one characteristic of nāma or rūpa at a time, as it appears through one of the six doorways. In this way paññā can gradually develop to the degree of clearly knowing the difference between the characteristic of nāma and the characteristic of rūpa. Paññā will, for example, be able to distinguish between the characteristics of the nāma that hears and of the rūpa that is sound. These are different characteristics and they should be known one at a time. Eventually one will become more familiar with the true nature of nāma and of rūpa and then the understanding of their characteristics will become more accomplished. No matter which type of nāma or rūpa appears, and no matter where, awareness and understanding of them can naturally arise, and that is the development of satipaṭṭhāna in daily life. When understanding develops and becomes more accomplished, ignorance can gradually be eliminated.

Questioner: After one has paid respect to the Buddha by chanting texts, one may wish to sit and concentrate on a meditation subject. How can one do that with wise attention, so that there is no attachment or aversion with regard to the meditation subject?

Sujin: When there is right mindfulness, sammā-sati, of the eightfold Path, there truly is wise attention. It is not necessary to sit and concentrate on a meditation subject. When someone believes that he should sit and concentrate with the purpose of having sati, he has the wrong understanding that there is a self who could make sati arise at a fixed time. However, sammā-sati does not have to wait until one has paid respect by chanting texts. Who is paying respect to the Buddha? If someone does not know that it is nāma and rūpa, he takes the realities at that moment for self. He has an idea of, "I am paying respect", he clings to an idea of self who chants texts. Sammā-sati can arise and be aware of any reality that appears when we are paying respect or chanting texts, or at other moments, no matter which posture we assume.

Bhikkhu: I have a question on satipaṭṭhāna. I have read that among the twenty-eight rūpas, there are rūpas that cannot be seen, rūpas that cannot impinge, subtle rūpas, rūpas that are far, and so on. Could you explain about this?

Sujin: There is only one rūpa among the twenty-eight rūpas that can be seen, and that is visible object that appears through the eyesense. Visible object can be seen and it is among the rūpas that impinge or contact (sappaṭigha rūpas)[2]. There are other rūpas that can impinge: the sense objects, apart from visible object, which are sound, odour, flavour and tangible object, consisting of solidity (appearing as hardness or softness), temperature (appearing as heat or cold) and motion (appearing as motion or pressure). Furthermore, there are the senses that can be contacted or impinged on, namely, eyesense, earsense, smelling-sense, tasting-sense and bodysense. These eleven rūpas can impinge or can be impinged on, but they cannot be seen, whereas visible object can impinge and can be seen.[3] The twelve rūpas that can impinge are coarse rūpas. They are also called rūpas that are "near", because they can be investigated and known.

The sixteen other rūpas among the twenty-eight rūpas are the subtle rūpas. They cannot be seen nor are they impinging. Subtle rūpas are "far", they cannot easily be discerned.

The dhammas the Buddha explained are true and people who develop satipaṭṭhāna can verify them; they can know the characteristics of the dhammas that naturally appear, just as they are. However, the Dhamma is subtle and deep. For example, when a person learns that visible object is the reality appearing through the eyes, he may think that it is not difficult to understand this. But theoretical understanding is not the same as understanding of the characteristic of seeing when

[2]Paṭigha means anger or collision. Sappaṭigha is with impact.

[3]See "Visuddhimagga" Ch XIV, 74.

he sees. If he does not develop satipaṭṭhāna so that paññā becomes keener, he cannot realize the characteristics of nāma and rūpa as they are. When one sees, visible object is experienced through the eyes, but what one sees one takes for people, beings and different things. Then doubt arises and people wonder what visible object is like, what characteristic it has.

Visible object is the reality that appears when our eyes are open and there is seeing, not yet thinking about anything. Then the characteristic of visible object can appear naturally, as it is. As paññā develops, one can become familiar with the fact that visible object which appears is not a being, person, self or anything else. Visible object is only the reality that appears through the eyes, that is its true nature. If people are not inclined to study and investigate the characteristic of visible object, it will be impossible for them to relinquish clinging to the idea they used to have of seeing people, beings or different things.

Questioner: What is the meaning of studying realities?

Sujin: There is this kind of study when sati is aware and considers the characteristic of whatever reality appears. That reality can be known as nāma, which experiences something, or as rūpa which does not experience anything. This is the study of the characteristic of non-self of the reality that appears and it is different from merely thinking of words or naming realities. When paññā has become more accomplished, it can penetrate the three general characteristics of nāma and rūpa: impermanence, dukkha and anattā.

Questioner: When my eyes are open I am seeing, but I do not pay attention to anything else. Is this correct?

Sujin: We cannot prevent the arising and falling away of cittas which succeed one another, that is their nature. When sati arises, it can be aware of whatever reality appears naturally, just as it is.

Questioner: For most people the aim of the development of satipaṭṭhāna is to become free from dukkha. When paññā has arisen, one is free from dukkha.

Sujin: Freedom from dukkha cannot be realized easily. Paññā should first be developed stage by stage, so that ignorance, doubt and wrong view that takes realities for self can be eliminated. If people develop sati and paññā naturally, they will know that paññā grows very gradually, because ignorance arises many more times a day than kusala. This was so in past lives and it is also like this in the present life.

Questioner: The problem is that when an object impinges on one of the doorways I am bound to be forgetful, I lack sati.

Sujin: That is quite normal. When sati is still weak, it cannot arise immediately.

Questioner: I have studied the texts the monks chant in the morning, about the khandhas of clinging, upadāna khandhas. There is clinging to the five khandhas and this is dukkha. What does this mean?

Sujin: The five khandhas of clinging are certainly dukkha. So long as there is ignorance of the true nature of the dhammas that appear, there is bound to be happiness and sorrow. The arising of happiness and sorrow is a kind of dukkha, because at such moments there is no calm, no freedom from defilements. When paññā does not arise, the difference between kusala citta and akusala citta is not known. We all enjoy having lobha. There is no end to the enjoyment of lobha, until paññā discerns the difference between the moment of kusala, when there is non-attachment, and the moment of lobha, when there is pleasure, amusement, desire, enjoyment or clinging.

When paññā does not arise, we enjoy defilements, we like to have lobha; it never is enough, no matter whether we experience an object through the eyes, the ears, the nose, the tongue, the bodysense or the mind-door. Generally, people do not know that such moments are dukkha, that they are harmful and dangerous. Thus, the five khandhas of clinging are dukkha.

Questioner: When we are heedful when objects are impinging, for example, when visible object contacts the eye or sound contacts the ear, there will be neither happiness nor sorrow.

Sujin: There is not "somebody" or a "self" who could be heedful or force the arising of sati. When sati arises, we can know the difference between the moment with sati and the moment without sati.

Questioner: The five khandhas of the ordinary person must be the same as those of the arahat, but the khandhas of the ordinary person are still objects of clinging and this causes the arising of dukkha. When we gradually learn to be heedful when sense objects such as visible object or sound are impinging on the relevant doorways, do we develop satipaṭṭhāna in the right way?

Sujin: One should remember that all dhammas are anattā, non-self, so that sati can be developed in the right way. One should know when there is sati and when there is no sati. When one has a concept of self who is heedful, satipaṭṭhāna is not developed.

Questioner: The word anattā is difficult to understand. We can translate the Pāli term attā as self and the term anattā as non-self, but we do not really understand the meaning of these terms. We may say that there is no self, but we still cling to the concept of self.

Sujin: What is the self?

Questioner: We may assume that we are the "self," but the Buddha states that there are only the five khandhas that arise together.

Sujin: The khandhas are not a person, not a self, but if we do not know that there are only the khandhas, we assume that there is a self.

Questioner: Although we know this, we still think, when we are seeing, that a self is seeing.

Sujin: That is so because we do not yet have clear comprehension of the true characteristics of the khandhas as realities which arise and fall away very rapidly. They can be classified in different ways, namely, as past, present and future; as coarse and subtle; as internal and external; as far and near, and so on. If one can discern the characteristics of the khandhas, one will know that each characteristic of reality that arises and falls away is only rūpakkhandha (physical phenomena), vedanākkhandha (feeling), saññākkhandha (remembrance or perception), saṅkhārakkhandha (formations or activities, all cetasikas other than vedanā and saññā) or viññāṇakkhandha (consciousness).

Questioner: I have heard that the postures conceal dukkha. Please, could you explain this?

Sujin: All conditioned realities have the characteristic of dukkha. They arise and fall away, they are impermanent and therefore, they cannot be a real refuge, they are dukkha. Thus, dukkha is not merely painful feeling. When it is said that the postures conceal dukkha, one should understand that this refers not just to painful feeling but to the characteristic of dukkha inherent in all conditioned realities. One may believe that there is no dukkha when, at this very moment, one is sitting, lying down, standing or walking without being stiff. The belief that the change of one posture into another one conceals dukkha is not paññā that clearly realizes the arising and falling away of nāma dhammas and rūpa dhammas. Nāma and rūpa arise together when one assumes different postures and dukkha is concealed so long as one does not know the characteristic of dukkha of one rūpa and of one nāma at a time, as they arise and fall away.

When one asks people who have just assumed a new posture whether there is dukkha, they will answer that there is not. If they confuse painful feeling with the truth of dukkha, how can they understand that the postures conceal dukkha? There must be dukkha, otherwise it cannot be said that the postures conceal dukkha. Any idea of a posture or of the whole body, no matter there is painful feeling or not, conceals the characteristic of dukkha. So long as one has not realized the arising and falling away of nāma and rūpa one does not understand the truth of dukkha.

If a person does not develop paññā in order to understand nāma and rūpa as they are, he has wrong understanding of dukkha. He may believe that he knows the truth of dukkha when he ponders over his painful feeling, dukkha vedanā, caused by stiffness, before he changes into a new posture in order to relieve his pain. He cannot know the truth of dukkha so long as he does not discern the characteristic of non-self of nāma and rūpa. This is the case if he does not know the nāma which sees and colour appearing through the eyes, the nāma which hears and sound appearing through the ears, the nāma which smells and odour, the nāma which tastes and flavour, the nāma which experiences tangible object and tangible object, the nāma which thinks, happiness, sorrow and other realities.

Also, the reality which thinks that it will change posture is not self, it should be realized as a type of nāma which arises and then falls away. If one does not know this, one will not be able to understand the characteristic of dukkha. Only if one is naturally aware of nāma and rūpa as they appear one at a time, paññā can develop stage by stage, so that the noble Truth of dukkha can be realized.

Questioner: When there is sati, it seems that only dukkha appears, but I cannot separate nāma and rūpa when I experience objects through the senses and through the mind-door. I just have theoretical knowledge of different realities that appear one at a time through the different doorways. I went to a meditation centre to gain more knowledge about the practice, but I did not study a great deal, I just practised.

Sujin: Are you satisfied with your understanding or not yet?

Questioner: I am still studying, thus, I cannot say that I am satisfied.

Sujin: You said that you went to a meditation centre in order to study and practise. However, when you went there you did not gain much understanding of realities. Is it then of any use to go there?

Questioner: It is useful. When we are at home, usually many akusala cittas arise. If we go to a meditation centre, we meet the right friend in Dhamma and we are in a quiet, peaceful place. Thus, there are conditions for the arising of many kusala cittas. I think that a meditation centre is useful.

Sujin: There are four factors necessary to attain the stage of the sotāpanna: meeting the right friend in Dhamma, hearing the Dhamma from that person, considering the Dhamma one heard with wise attention and the practice in conformity with the Dhamma. These factors are not related to a particular place where one should stay. We can compare the place where the Buddha stayed with the meditation centre at the present time. As to the place where the Buddha and the monks stayed in the past, they led their daily life, making their rounds to collect almsfood, discussing the Dhamma, and performing their different duties in accordance with the Vinaya. The Buddha exhorted people there to perform all kinds of wholesome deeds. Do people in the present time who go to a meditation centre practise in the same way as the Buddha's followers in the past or do they practise differently? If the cause, that is, the practice, is different, how could the result be the same? For example, Anāthapiṇḍika, a lay follower at the Buddha's time who had the Great Monastery (Mahā-vihāra) of the Jeta Grove constructed, did not have the wrong understanding that one could become enlightened only at that particular place. Layfollowers at that time attained enlightenment each in different places, depending on their daily life.

We read in the "Gradual Sayings"(III, Book of the Fives, Ch XIX, §1, Forest-gone) that the Buddha said to the monks:

> "Monks, these five are forest-gone. What five? One is forest-gone out of folly and blindness; one out of evil desires and longings; one foolish and mind-tossed; one at the thought: 'It is praised by Buddhas and their disciples'; and one is forest-gone just because his wants are little, just for contentment,

> just to mark (his own faults),[4] just for seclusion, just because it is the very thing.[5]
>
> Verily, monks, of these five who have gone to the forest, he who has gone just because his wants are little, for contentment, to mark (his own faults), for seclusion, just because it is the very thing–he of the five is topmost, best, foremost, highest, elect.
>
> Monks, just as from the cow comes milk, from milk cream, from cream butter, from butter ghee, from ghee the skim of ghee which is reckoned topmost; even so, monks, of these five forest-gone, he who has gone just because his wants are little, for contentment, to mark (his own faults), for seclusion, and just because it is the very thing–he of the five is topmost, best, foremost, highest, elect."

Why were some monks dwelling in the forest out of folly and blindness? Some people think that once they are in the forest they will be able to realize the four noble Truths. Are those who think thus not forest dwellers out of folly and blindness? If a person has right understanding of cause and effect, he will see that no way of life was more excellent than the life of the monk who had left the householder's life in order to go to the place where the Buddha dwelt. This is altogether different from someone's life in a meditation centre where he goes just for a short period, out of desire to attain enlightenment. Some people believe that staying in a centre for the practice of vipassanā, although it is not in conformity with their nature, will be the condition to realize the noble Truths. If that were true, then laypeople who practise vipassanā in a meditation centre should deserve more praise than the monks in the Buddha's time who were leading their ordinary daily life in accordance with the rules of the Vinaya, such as going on their alms rounds, listening to the Dhamma and discussing it, and performing the different duties of the Sangha.

Questioner: I understand that a certain way of life does not conform to a person's nature. If he would force himself to act against his nature that would not be right, is that not so?

---

[4]To eliminate them.

[5]He wants to practise what is beneficial.

Sujin: People should consider cause and effect in the right way. A great number of monks did not live in a forest. The Buddha did not force people to develop satipaṭṭhāna in a forest, in a specific room, or in any other place where they were free from the performing of their tasks. It is true that the Buddha praised the forest life, that he praised a secluded life or whatever else was a condition for the non-arising of lobha, dosa and moha. However, he did not force anybody, he did not establish rules for the development of paññā. The Buddha clearly knew the different accumulations of people and, thus, he preached the Dhamma in such a way that his followers would listen and develop right understanding naturally. Thus, they would be able to eliminate defilements. He taught people the development of satipaṭṭhāna in their daily life, in conformity with their status, no matter whether they were monk or layfollower.

When awareness arises and one begins to consider and study the characteristics of nāma and rūpa so that paññā becomes more accomplished, one's inclinations can gradually be changed. People will be less overcome by lobha, dosa and moha on account of the objects experienced through the sense-doors and through the mind-door. However, accumulated inclinations cannot be changed on the spur of the moment. Some people think that a meditation centre should not be repainted, because that would be a condition for lobha. However, when they return to their homes after they have stayed in the centre, they have their houses repainted, they plant trees and look after their flowers, thus, they follow their accumulated inclinations.

The Buddha taught true Dhamma (sacca Dhamma), so that people could have right understanding of cause and effect with regard to all realities. He taught the development of satipaṭṭhāna so that paññā could become accomplished to the degree of eradicating latent tendencies. Latent tendencies have been accumulated from past lives on to the present life in the cittas that arise and fall away in an uninterrupted succession. Ignorance (avijjā), not knowing the characteristics of nāma and rūpa, and wrong view, diṭṭhi, which takes nāma and rūpa for self, are latent tendencies.

One takes all kinds of realities for self, no matter whether one sees, hears, tastes, smells, experiences tangible object, thinks, feels happy or unhappy. The only way leading to the eradication of latent tendencies is the development of satipaṭṭhāna. This is awareness and investigation of the realities that appear so that they can be understood more clearly. Understanding is developed stage by stage. When paññā is developed to the degree of the first stage of insight, "the defining of nāma and rūpa" (nāma-rūpa-pariccheda-ñāṇa), paññā can clearly comprehend the difference between the characteristic of nāma and of rūpa appearing at that moment.

Paññā cannot be developed if one tries to make dukkha arise by sitting, lying down, standing or walking for a long time, so that one has painful feeling. Paññā can only be developed by considering and studying with awareness nāma and rūpa as they naturally appear through the senses and through the mind-door. They arise because of their own conditions, no matter where one is.

37

The Meaning of Anattā

Questioner: There are four Applications of Mindfulness: mindfulness of the body, of feeling, of citta and of dhammas. The commentator[1] compares these four subjects with four gateways of a city, one of which faces east, one west, one north and one south. People can go to the centre of the city by anyone of these four gates. Many teachers today say that just as one can use anyone of the gates to enter the city, it is sufficient to cultivate only one of the Four Applications of Mindfulness; one does not need all four. Only mindfulness of the body would be sufficient. Can one then in this way reach nibbāna?

Sujin: The development of paññā is very subtle. It is not so that anyone who reads the commentary can practise. Where is the gate? If people do not know where the gates are, through which gate can they enter?

Questioner: The gates are: body, feeling, citta and dhammas.

---

[1] See the Commentary to the Satipaṭṭhāna Sutta, Middle Length Sayings no. 10, the Papañcasūdanī, in "The Way of Mindfulness" by Soma Thera, B.P.S. Kandy, Sri Lanka.

Sujin: What do you know through the bodysense? One should really consider all realities in detail, no matter whether they are classified as khandhas, āyatanas,[2] dhātus (elements) or the noble Truths. They are not beings, people or self. Conditioned realities appearing in daily life are either nāma, the reality that experiences something, or rūpa, the reality that does not know anything. We may understand this in theory, but that is not the direct realization of the characteristic of non-self of nāma and rūpa. As far as the level of theoretical understanding is concerned which stems from listening to the Dhamma, one may have no doubt that rūpa is real, that the rūpa that arises and appears through the eyes are only different colours. One may have no doubt that sound is the rūpa which appears through the ears, odour the rūpa which appears through the nose, flavour the rūpa which appears through the tongue, and so on. People may have no doubt that nāma is real, that it arises and experiences different objects; they can have theoretical understanding of this. However, if there is no awareness of the characteristic of nāma, how can there be paññā that directly understands nāma as the reality which experiences an object, as the element, the nature that knows? Can the development of only awareness of the body be the condition to realize the characteristic of nāma?

The person who develops paññā should be aware of the characteristic of nāma while he is seeing. He can investigate and study that characteristic so that it can be realized as only a kind of experience. When there is hearing, there can be awareness of it and it can be understood as a reality which experiences sound. When someone develops satipaṭṭhāna he should study and investigate time and again the characteristic of the nāma which experiences an object through one of the six doorways, so that he can understand nāma as it really is. When paññā realizes that there are nāmas which are not yet known, it will also study and investigate these, and in this way the characteristic of nāma can clearly appear as only an element which experiences, only a reality, not a being, person or self.

Someone may make an effort to be aware just of the characteristic of the nāma that hears and he is not aware of the nāma that sees.

[2]The internal āyatanas are the five senses and mind-base, including all cittas, and the external āyatanas are the sense objects and dhammāyatana which includes: cetasikas, subtle rūpas and nibbāna.

How can he then understand the true characteristic of the element that experiences while he is seeing? People can verify for themselves that this is not the right way of development.

Paññā can develop by awareness that considers and studies the characteristics of the nāmas experiencing an object through the senses and through the mind-door. If paññā clearly understands all kinds of nāma that appear, if it understands these as the element which experiences an object, doubt about nāma can gradually be eliminated. Paññā can become keener and more accomplished as it develops in successive stages. However, if someone intends to know only one kind of nāma, it is evident that there is still ignorance and doubt with regard to the characteristics of the other kinds of nāma he has not been aware of. And thus, ignorance and doubt with regard to nāma as the element which experiences cannot be eliminated.

Questioner: People gain understanding from listening to the Dhamma. When they practise they can attain the first stage of vipassanā ñāṇa, "defining of nāma and rūpa." They pass that stage.

Sujin: How do they pass that stage?

Questioner: I do not know anything about that.

Sujin: People should not become excited when they are wondering whether others have passed a stage of insight knowledge. It is by a person's own understanding that he can know that paññā has been developed to the degree of the first vipassanā ñāṇa. He knows that insight knowledge realizes nāma and rūpa as they naturally appear, one characteristic at a time, in a mind-door process. At the moments of vipassanā ñāṇa, not merely one kind of nāma or one kind of rūpa has been penetrated.

Questioner: Someone may have practised insight unto to the fifth stage of mahā-vipassanā ñāṇa, the "knowledge of dispassion"(nibbidā ñāṇa). He watches the rūpa that sits, stands or walks, and he practises until he reaches the "knowledge of dispassion." I have doubts about how he watches the rūpa that sits, stands or walks. How should we practise so that we can attain that stage of vipassanā ñāṇa?

Sujin: What is the meaning of the first stage of insight, "defining of nāma and rūpa"? So long as one has not realized that stage yet, one cannot attain "knowledge of dispassion."

There is mindfulness of the body when sati is mindful of one characteristic at a time of rūpa paramattha, as it appears through the bodysense. It may be a rūpa such as cold, heat, softness, hardness, pressure or motion. Mindfulness of the body is not watching the postures of sitting, lying, standing or walking. When, for example, cold appears, there is only the characteristic of cold, there is no "I," it is not "mine," not self. If someone does not know the characteristic of rūpa as it appears through one doorway at a time, as only a kind of rūpa, he cannot even attain the first stage of insight knowledge, which discerns the difference between the characteristic of nāma and the characteristic of rūpa. How could paññā then realize the stage of "knowledge of dispassion," the fifth stage of "principal insight" (mahā-vipassanā)?

Questioner: In the section of "Clear Comprehension" (sampajañña) in the "Satipaṭṭhāna sutta," it is explained that when we are standing, we should know that we are standing, when walking, sitting, bending or stretching, we should know that we are doing so. We should know the characteristics of the different postures. When we know that we are walking while we are walking, is that the practice with regard to the rūpa that walks?

Sujin: If there would be no rūpa, could we walk?

Questioner: If there would be no rūpa, there would be only air and this cannot walk.

Sujin: When you are walking there is one characteristic of rūpa appearing at a time and it can be known as it appears through one doorway.

Questioner: Is it rūpa that walks?

Sujin: The rūpa which appears, no matter whether we are sitting, lying down, standing or walking, appears through the sense-doors or through the mind-door. It is anattā, it appears anyway because of the appropriate conditions; it is of no use trying to select a particular rūpa.

Questioner: As we have seen, in the commentary, the Papañcasūdanī, a simile is used of the four gateways leading to the centre of the city. A person who enters the city can enter through any one of these four gateways. Therefore, some people select a particular object; they develop only mindfulness of the body, not the other applications of mindfulness.

Sujin: When someone reads the commentary he ought to understand what paññā should know in order to eradicate wrong view, which takes realities for self.

There are two kinds of realities: nāma and rūpa. So long as people do not clearly know the characteristics of nāma and rūpa, they take them for self.

As regards the wording, "while walking, we should know that we are walking," in reality it is not "I" or self who is walking. When sati is aware of the characteristics of rūpas of the body that appear while walking, there is mindfulness of the body (kāyānupassanā satipaṭṭhāna)[3]. However, people cannot force sati to be aware all the time of rūpas appearing through the bodysense. Sati is anattā and it depends on conditions whether it will arise and be aware of a characteristic of nāma or rūpa. It can be aware of any characteristic of nāma or rūpa that arises and appears naturally, just as it is. The paññā that eradicates wrong view knows clearly the characteristics of nāma and rūpa as they appear through the six doors and it realizes them as non-self.

We read in the "Kindred Sayings" (IV, Saḷāyatana vagga, Kindred Sayings on Sense, Fourth Fifty, Ch III, § 193, Udāyin):

> "Once the venerable Ānanda and the venerable Udāyin were staying at Kosambī in Ghosita Park. Then the venerable Udāyin, rising at eventide from his solitude, went to visit the venerable Ānanda, and on coming to him... after the exchange of courtesies, sat down at one side. So seated the venerable Udāyin said to the venerable Ānanda: 'Is it possible, friend Ānanda, just as this body has in divers ways been defined, explained, set forth by the Exalted One, as being without the self, is it possible in the same way to describe the consciousness, to show it, make it plain, set it forth, make it clear, analyze and expound it as being also without the self?'
>
> 'Just as this body has in divers ways been defined, explained, set forth by the Exalted One, as being without the self, friend Udāyin, so also is it possible to describe this consciousness, to show it, make it plain, set it forth, make it clear, analyze and expound it as being also without the self. Owing to

[3] Anupassanā means consideration or contemplation.

the eye and visible object arises seeing-consciousness, does it not, friend?'

'Yes, friend.'

'Well, friend, it is by this method that the Exalted One has explained, opened up, and shown that this consciousness also is without the self.' "

(The same is said with regard to the other doorways).

If someone does not clearly know the reality that is nāma, doubt has not been eliminated yet. If there is still doubt, how can he realize the noble Truths? Through which gate will he enter? The gateways mentioned in the commentary refer to the moments before lokuttara citta arises and realizes nibbāna. In the process of attaining enlightenment, mahā-kusala kāmāvacara cittas (of the sense sphere) arise before lokuttara citta arises, and it depends on conditions which of the four satipaṭṭhānas this kāmāvacara citta takes as object.[4] However, this does not mean that someone could enter the city, that is, realizing nibbāna, without clearly knowing the characteristics of rūpakkhandha, vedanākkhandha, saññākkhandha, saṅkhārakkhandha and viññāṇakkhandha.

Before someone can understand that this body is anattā and that also this consciousness is anattā, the characteristics of nāma and rūpa appearing at this moment must be "described, shown, made plain, set forth, made clear, analysed and expounded", as we read in the sutta. Characteristics of nāma and rūpa appear at this moment, while we see, hear, smell, taste, experience tangible object or think.

It is not easy to be able to penetrate the meaning of anattā, to understand the true nature of all realities, to realize them as anattā. If Ānanda had not been a sotāpanna, he would not have known thoroughly the realities that are nāma and rūpa. Only paññā of that degree can eradicate wrong view that takes nāma and rūpa for self, being or person. If Ānanda had not been a sotāpanna, he could not have said to Udāyin that it is also possible to describe consciousness, to show it, make it plain, set it forth, make it clear, analyse it and expound it as being

[4]It can experience only one object at a time and it realizes that object as impermanent, dukkha or non-self.

anattā. Therefore, when someone realizes the true nature of a particular dhamma, then that dhamma will appear clearly to him.

At this moment, realities arise and then fall away very rapidly. If a person has not realized the true nature of realities, they do not appear to him as they are, even if he says that, while there is seeing or hearing, nāma is the element which experiences an object. Whereas, when realities have appeared to him as they are, it is evident that he clearly knows their true characteristics.

Ānanda had no doubt about the characteristics of nāma and rūpa, no matter through which doorway they appeared. If someone at the present time thinks that he should develop mindfulness of only one of the Four Applications of Mindfulness, such as mindfulness of the body, or that he should know only one type of nāma or rūpa, could he know the true characteristics of nāma and rūpa? If he would understand the truth of realities, why does he not know, while he is seeing, the nāma which experiences an object through the eyes, as the element which sees? Why does he not know, while he is hearing, the nāma that experiences an object through the ears, the element that hears? Why does he not realize, while thinking, that it is only nāma which knows concepts or words? If he would really understand what nāma is, he would be able to understand the true nature of the element that experiences an object.

There is a way to find out whether one knows the truth of realities or not. When a nāma or rūpa appears through one of the six doors and paññā can distinguish between the characteristic of nāma and the characteristic of rūpa, their characteristics are known as they are. Paññā should be able to discern the different characteristics of nāma and of rūpa when there is seeing, hearing, smelling, tasting, experiencing tangible object or thinking. In this way, the meaning of anattā can be penetrated; the nāma and rūpa that appear can be realized as anattā.

When Ānanda asked Udāyin whether seeing-consciousness arises owing to the eye and visible object, Udāyin had no doubt about eyesense and the rūpa appearing through the eyes, while seeing at that moment. We read further on in the Udāyin Sutta that Ānanda said:

> " 'Well, if the condition, if the cause of the arising of seeing-consciousness should altogether, in every way, utterly

> come to cease without remainder, would any seeing-consciousness be evident?'
>
> 'Surely not, friend.'
>
> 'Well, it is by this method that the Exalted One has explained, opened up, and shown that this consciousness also is without the self."'

If one really understands that while there is hearing, there is no seeing, one can know the characteristics of realities as they are. When there is thinking about different matters, there is no seeing, no hearing. There is only the nāma that thinks at such a moment about different subjects. In this way, the characteristics of realities can be understood as they are.

As Ānanda said to Udāyin, seeing arises dependent on eyesense and visible object which appears through the eyes, but, when eyesense and visible object which are impermanent have completely fallen away, how could there be seeing? Seeing must have fallen away.

If someone at this moment would clearly know the characteristic of the reality which experiences an object, as an element which experiences, he would have attained already the first stage of insight knowledge, the "defining of nāma and rūpa."[5] One cannot develop paññā immediately to the degree of insight that is the fifth stage of "principal insight," "knowledge of dispassion" (nibbidā ñāṇa). After the first stage of insight, paññā has to be developed further so that it can directly understand conditions for the realities that arise. The second stage of insight is "discerning conditions for nāma and rūpa" (paccaya-pariggaha-ñāṇa).

Then paññā can be developed further to the degree of realizing the arising and falling away of realities in succession. This is the third stage of insight, "comprehension by groups" (sammasana ñāṇa).

After that paññā should be developed to the degree of realizing the arising and falling away of one reality at a time, separately. This is the first stage of "principal insight" (mahā-vipassanā), "knowledge of the arising and falling away of nāma and rūpa" (udayabbaya ñāṇa).

After that paññā must be developed further so that it can penetrate more the impermanence of realities that fall away all the time. This is

[5] Then paññā knows precisely nāma as being different from rūpa, paññā knows nāma as nāma.

the second stage of principal insight, "knowledge of dissolution" (bhaṅga ñāṇa). Then paññā must be developed still further to the stage of seeing more clearly the danger and disadvantage of the falling away of realities. This is the third stage of principal insight, "knowledge of appearance as terror" (bhaya ñāṇa). After that the fourth stage can be realized, which is "knowledge of danger" (ādīnava ñāṇa). After that paññā, should be developed to the degree of the fifth stage of insight, "knowledge of dispassion" (nibbidā ñāṇa). After that several more stages of insight have to be reached before enlightenment can be attained.

Paññā should clearly understand the characteristics of realities. It is impossible to enter the gateway to nibbāna if the characteristic of nāma is not known, and if only the postures of sitting, lying down, standing or walking are known. If someone knows which posture he has assumed, he has only remembrance or perception of the rūpas that arise together and constitute a "whole" of a posture. He does not realize the characteristics of nāma and rūpa, one at a time, as they arise and appear naturally, just as they are, through the different doorways and then fall away.

As we read in the Udāyin Sutta, Ānanda said to Udāyin with reference to seeing-consciousness, that the Buddha had explained that this is also without the self. Ānanda said to Udāyin:

> " 'Owing to the eye and visible object arises seeing-consciousness, does it not, friend?"
>
> "Yes, friend."
>
> "Well, friend, it is by this method that the Exalted One has explained, opened up, and shown that this consciousness also is without the self."

He repeated the same about the other sense-cognitions and the consciousness that experiences objects through the mind-door.

This sutta shows how beneficial it is that the Buddha explained the Dhamma completely and in all details. He explained about all types of citta, which are nāma. If someone could realize the noble Truths by having only one kind of object of mindfulness, of what use would it be that the Buddha explained about all the other dhammas? He explained all about seeing, hearing, smelling, tasting, the experience of tangible object, thinking, pleasant and unpleasant feeling, remembrance and other dhammas. He did so in order to help people to be mindful of these realities, to consider, study and clearly comprehend them. That is the way leading to the complete eradication of doubt and wrong view about nāma and rūpa.

Someone may believe that, by knowing only one type of nāma or one type of rūpa, he can still realize the noble Truths. He pretends to be able to realize enlightenment, but he does not understand the characteristics of nāma and rūpa as they naturally appear, just as they are. Then he is sure to have doubt and uncertainty about the nāma and rūpa he believes he cannot know. It is evident that he in that way cannot attain enlightenment.

We read further on in the Udāyin Sutta about a simile Ānanda used. He said to Udāyin:

> "Suppose, friend, that a man should roam about in need of heart of wood, searching for heart of wood, looking for heart of wood, and, taking a sharp axe, should enter a forest. There he sees a mighty plantain-trunk, straight up, new-grown, of towering height. He cuts it down at the root. Having cut it down at the root, he chops it off at the top. Having done so he peels off the outer skin. But he would find no pith inside, much less would he find heart of wood.
>
> Even so, friend, a monk beholds no trace of the self nor of what pertains to the self in the sixfold sense-sphere. So beholding, he is not attached to anything in the world. Unattached he is not troubled. Untroubled, he is of himself utterly set free. So that he realizes, 'Destroyed is rebirth. Lived is the righteous life. Done is the task. For life in these conditions there is no hereafter.' "

We just read that Ānanda said that a man in search for heart of wood enters a forest and sees a mighty plantain-trunk, straight up, new-grown, of towering height. So long as it is a plantain-trunk, it still has the appearance of a "whole." Then we read, "Having cut it down at the root, he chops it off at the top. Having done so, he peels off the outer skin." We should eliminate clinging to what we are used to taking for a "whole", for a "thing", for self.

We then read, "But he would find no pith inside, much less would he find heart of wood." Thus, he becomes detached from the idea of plantain-trunk. It is the same as in the case of a cow that is still not cut up by a cattle butcher, as we read in the Papañcasūdānī, the commentary to the Satipaṭṭhānasutta. If the cattle butcher does not skin it and cut it up in different parts, he is bound to see it as a cow, he does not see it as different elements. So long as rūpas are still seen as joined together, one perceives them as a "whole," or as a whole posture such as the "sitting rūpa". People are bound to consider realities as a thing, a self, a being or person who is there. Only if someone knows nāma and rūpa as they are, he does not take them for beings or people anymore. It is just as after peeling off the skin of the plantain, any pith in it is not to be found, much less heart of wood. As we have read, Ānanda said: "Even so, friend, a monk beholds no trace of self nor what pertains to the self in the sixfold sense-sphere."

In the sixfold sense-sphere (phassāyatana)[6] there is no posture. Eyesense is an internal "āyatana", and visible object is rūpāyatana, an external āyatana, it is only what appears through the eyes. Someone may see a person who is sitting and cling to the idea of "person" or "self", although he says that there is no self. If he has only theoretical understanding, he may not realize that the truth of anattā can be understood only by awareness of seeing and other realities that appear. Paññā should know that seeing only sees what appears through the eyes. After having seen visible object, one thinks of and remembers the shape and form of what appears and knows what it is. Also at that moment there is a type of nāma that knows and remembers something, it is not a being, person or self who does so. When hearing arises which experiences sound through the ears, no remembrance remains of what was experienced through the eye-door, no remembrance of a perception of people sitting and talking to each other. When hearing presents itself, sati can be aware of the reality that hears, an element which experiences only sound. After that, citta thinks of words or concepts, on account of different sounds, low and high, which have been heard. Paññā can know, when words are understood, that only a type of nāma understands the meaning of words.

If different types of realities are known, one characteristic at a time, as nama and rupa, the wrong view that takes realities for self is elimi-

[6] Phassa is contact. There is contact due to the external āyatanas and the internal āyatanas.

nated. One will let go of the idea of realities as a "whole" or a posture. Then it can be understood what it means to have inward peace, because citta does not become involved in outward matters, such as self, people or beings. There is no longer the world one used to cling to, the world outside, which is full of people and different things. There is no longer what one used to take for a particular person, for a thing, for self, all permanent and lasting. Whenever sati arises paññā can at that moment understand realities clearly, and then there is inward peace, because there are no people, beings or things. Whereas, when there are many people, many concepts in one's life, there is no peace. If someone sees a person he is acquainted with or he has a particular relation with, he thinks, as soon as he has seen him even for a moment, a long "story" about him. If he sees a person he does not know, the "story" is short; he thinks only for a little while about him and then the "story" is over. He does not continue to think about him.

As a person develops paññā, he acquires more understanding of the excellent qualities of the Buddha and of the Dhamma he taught in all details. One can appreciate the teachings also at the level of restraint or "guarding" of the senses (saṃvara sīla) as contained in the Pāṭimokkha, the Disciplinary code for the monks. This is the conduct through body and speech befitting the "samana," the person who is a monk, who leads a peaceful life. We read in the "Visuddhimagga" (I, 50) about the restraint of the monk with regard to seeing:

> "What is proper resort as guarding? Here 'A bhikkhu, having entered inside a house, having gone into a street, goes with downcast eyes, seeing the length of a plough yoke, restrained, not looking at an elephant, not looking at a horse, a carriage, a pedestrian, a woman, a man, not looking up, not looking down, not staring this way and that.' This is called proper resort as guarding."

This was said to remind us not to continue the "story" after the seeing and dwell on it for a long time, thinking in various ways of this or that person or matter. When we have seen, we should know that it is only seeing. No matter whether one looks no further than the length of a plough yoke ahead or not, there is seeing and then it is gone. In that way, one will not be absorbed in the outward appearance and details.

Paññā can clearly understand that it is just because of thinking that we are used to seeing the outward world that is full of people. If we do not think, there is only seeing and then it is gone. Can there be many people at that moment? However, one is used to thinking for a long time, and thus one is bound to think time and again of many different subjects.

In what way someone thinks, depends on the conditions that have been accumulated. People may see the same thing, but each individual thinks differently. When people see, for example, a flower, one person may like it and think it beautiful, whereas someone else may dislike it. It all depends on the individual's thinking. Each person lives with his own thoughts, and thus, the world is in reality the world of thinking. When sati is aware of nāma and rūpa, it will be clearly known that it is only a type of nāma that thinks of different subjects. If the characteristic of the nāma that thinks is clearly known, it can be understood that someone's conception of people and beings is not real. When someone is sad and he worries, he should know that there is sadness just because of his thinking. It is the same in the case of happiness, it all occurs because of thinking. When someone sees on T.V. a story he likes, pleasant feeling arises because he thinks of the projected image he looks at. Thus, people live only in the world of thinking, no matter where they are.

The world of each moment is nāma that arises and experiences an object through one of the sense-doors and through the mind-door, and after that citta continues to think of different stories.

Questioner: You just said that happiness and sadness are only a matter of thinking. I do not understand this yet. Who likes to think of something that makes him unhappy? Nobody likes to be unhappy. In what way does a person think so that he is unhappy?

Sujin: It is not so that a person thinks in order to be unhappy. There are conditions for the arising of unhappiness due to the thinking.

Questioner: Does this mean that there are conditions for sadness when someone, for example, has to part with his possessions or when he has lost a horse-bet? He returns home and thinks of the horse-bet he has lost. Then the horse-bet may be a condition for his unhappiness.

Sujin: If he would not think about the horse which has lost the race, could there be sorrow about it?

Questioner: No, there would not.

Sujin: When there is seeing or hearing and after that thinking, paññā should know that thinking is only a type of nāma which thinks about different subjects and then falls away. When someone thinks about a horse, there is no horse at that moment. There is remembrance of an idea or concept of a horse and this causes the arising of unhappiness. Thus, unhappiness arises because a person thinks about something he does not like, and happiness arises because he thinks about something he likes.

The Dhamma we study, the whole Tipiṭaka, together with the commentaries and sub-commentaries, have been taught so that paññā can arise and understand the realities that are naturally appearing at this moment, just as they are. People may have listened and studied much, they may have had many Dhamma discussions and pondered over the Dhamma very often, but all their learning should lead to accumulating conditions, that are all good qualities included in saṅkhārakkhandha, for the arising of right awareness. Then sati can be aware, study and consider the characteristics of the realities appearing at this moment through the sense-doors and the mind-door. People may have heard this time and again, but they need to be reminded to investigate the dhammas that are real, one at a time. If sati is aware, there will be right understanding of dhammas and eventually they will be realized as anattā. Day in day out there are only nāma and rūpa, arising and falling away each moment. When they have fallen away, there is nothing left of them, they do not last even for a moment.

We should know that our enjoyment or sorrow that arose in the past have fallen away, that they are completely gone. Now there is just the present moment and it is only at this moment that we can study realities and understand them as not self, not a being or a person. Some people say that they do not wish to meet a particular person again in a next life. If they would have right understanding of the Dhamma, they would not have such thoughts. In a next life, there will not be this or that person one meets at the present, nor will there be "I". After death, the existence of someone as this particular person in this life has definitely come to an end. Only in this life there is this person and in a next life he is another person. Therefore, one should not worry nor have anxiety about meeting a particular person again. This is impossible, since the existence as this or that person does not continue on to the next life.

If someone has irritation or annoyance about another person, he should understand that in reality there is not that person. There are only dhammas, citta, cetasika and rūpa, which arise and then fall away. Life, in the ultimate sense, lasts only as long as one single moment of citta.

If we reflect time and again on death, it can support the development of satipaṭṭhāna. If we consider that we may die this afternoon or tomorrow, it can be a supporting condition for sati to be aware of the characteristics of nāma and rūpa that appear. For those who have not realized the noble Truths, thus, for those who are not ariyans, it is not certain whether, after the dying-consciousness has fallen away, the rebirth-consciousness will arise in a happy plane or in an unhappy plane of existence. It is not certain whether there will be again an opportunity to listen to the Dhamma and to develop satipaṭṭhāna.

At death, a person parts with everything in this life, it is all over. There is nothing left, not even remembrance. When a person is born into this life, he does not remember who he was, where he lived and what he did in his former life. His existence as a particular person in a former life has come to an end. Even so, in this life, everything comes to an end. A person performs kusala kamma and akusala kamma, he may have conceit about his race, family, possessions, honour and fame, all this comes to an end. There will be no ties left with all the things in this life. All that we find so important in this life, all that we are holding on to and take for self, will come to an end. If people realize the true characteristics of paramattha dhammas that arise because of their own conditions, they will eliminate the inclination to take them for beings, people or self.

Even remembrance that arises and falls away is only a type of nāma. If sati is aware of nāma and rūpa and paññā understands them clearly, one can let go of the wrong view of a self or person who exists in this life. Then one has realized the characteristic of "momentary death" (khaṇika maraṇa) of realities, their passing away at each moment. There are three kinds of death:[7]

- momentary death, khaṇika maraṇa, which is the arising and falling

[7] "Dispeller of Delusion," Commentary to the Book of Analysis, Classification of the Truths, 101.

away of all conditioned dhammas;

- conventional death, sammuti maraṇa, which is dying at the end of a lifespan;
- final death, samuccheda maraṇa,[8] which is parinibbāna, the final passing away of the arahat who does not have to be reborn.

[8] Samuccheda means destruction.

Part VII

Appendices

A
Citta

Cittas can be classified as 89 or 121 types.

89 types of citta:

kāmāvacara cittas (of the sense sphere): 54 types

rūpāvacara cittas (of rūpa-jhāna): 15 types

arūpāvacara cittas (of arūpa-jhāna): 12 types

lokuttara cittas (supramundane): 8 types

121 types of citta:

kāmāvacara cittas: 54 types

rūpāvacara cittas: 15 types

arūpāvacara cittas: 12 types

lokuttara cittas: 40 types

Kamāvacara cittas are cittas of the lowest level, and they usually arise and fall away in daily life, each moment, no matter whether we are asleep or awake. The sense objects, which are rūpa paramattha dhamma, are experienced by kāmāvacara cittas. Among the twenty-eight rūpa paramattha dhammas, seven kinds of rūpas appear as objects in daily life through the eyes, the ears, the nose, the tongue, the bodysense and the mind-door. These rūpas, which are the objects citta usually experiences, are called in Pāli: gocara visaya rūpas. Gocara means pasture and visaya means sphere, object. The gocara visaya rūpas are:

- visible object or colour, rūpārammaṇa or vaṇṇa, which appears when it impinges on the eyesense;
- sound, saddārammaṇa, which appears when it impinges on the earsense;
- odour, gandhārammaṇa, which appears when it impinges on the smelling-sense;
- flavour, rasārammaṇa, which appears when it impinges on the tasting-sense;
- tangible objects, phoṭṭhabbārammaṇa, the three rūpas of earth-element (softness or hardness), heat-element (cold or heat) and wind-element (pressure or motion), which appear when they impinge on the bodysense.

The cittas that arise and fall away all the time in daily life are usually of the level of kāmāvacara cittas. They are engaged in the seven kinds of sense objects; they experience these rūpas through the appropriate doorways or they think about them.

54 Types of Kāmāvacara Cittas:

ahetuka (rootless) cittas: 18 types

kāma-sobhana cittas (beautiful cittas of the sense sphere): 24 types

Akusala Cittas: 12 types

Akusala citta is the citta that is not wholesome, not beautiful, because it is accompanied by akusala cetasikas. The twelve types of akusala cittas are:

- lobha-mūla-cittas (cittas rooted in attachment): 8 types
- dosa-mūla-cittas (cittas rooted in aversion): 2 types
- moha-mūla-cittas (cittas rooted in ignorance): 2 types

Mūla means root. There are three cetasikas which are the cause or origin of akusala dhammas: lobha cetasika (attachment), dosa cetasika (aversion) and moha cetasika (ignorance). These three cetasikas are roots, mūla or hetu.

Lobha-mūla-citta: the citta accompanied by lobha cetasika, which is the condition for delight in and clinging to the object that appears. Lobha-mūla-cittas are classified as eight types:

1. Accompanied by pleasant feeling, with wrong view, unprompted (somanassa-sahagataṃ, diṭṭhigata-sampayuttaṃ, asaṅkhārikam-ekaṃ). This type is accompanied by pleasant feeling, a feeling of happiness, and it is associated with the cetasika diṭṭhi, wrong view about realities. It is unprompted, asaṅkhārika, which means that it has strength, it arises without being dependent on inducement.

2. Accompanied by pleasant feeling, with wrong view, prompted (somanassa-sahagataṃ, diṭṭhigata-sampayuttaṃ, sasaṅkhārikam ekaṃ). This type is accompanied by pleasant feeling and it is associated with wrong view. It is prompted, sasaṅkhārika, which means that it is weak, it arises by being dependent on inducement.

3. Accompanied by pleasant feeling, without wrong view, unprompted (somanassa-sahagataṃ, diṭṭhigata-vippayuttaṃ, asaṅkhārikam ekaṃ). This type is accompanied by pleasant feeling and it is without wrong view; it is not accompanied by diṭṭhi cetasika. It has strength, it arises without being dependent on inducement.

4. Accompanied by pleasant feeling, without wrong view, prompted (somanassa-sahagataṃ, diṭṭhigata-vippayuttaṃ, sasaṅkhārikam ekaṃ). This type is accompanied by pleasant feeling and it is without wrong view. It is weak, it arises by being dependent on inducement.

5. Accompanied by indifferent feeling, with wrong view, unprompted (upekkhā-sahagataṃ, diṭṭhigata-sampayuttaṃ, asaṅkhārikam ekaṃ). This type is accompanied by indifferent feeling, feeling which is neither pleasant nor unpleasant. It is associated with wrong view. It has strength, it arises without being dependent on inducement.

6. Accompanied by indifferent feeling, with wrong view, prompted (upekkhā-sahagataṃ, diṭṭhigata-sampayuttaṃ, sasaṅkhārikam ekaṃ). This type is accompanied by indifferent feeling. It is associated with wrong view. It is weak, it arises by being dependent on inducement.

7. Accompanied by indifferent feeling, without wrong view, unprompted (upekkhā-sahagataṃ, diṭṭhigata-vippayuttaṃ, asaṅkhārikam ekaṃ). This type is accompanied by indifferent feeling. It is without wrong view. It has strength, it arises without being dependent on inducement.

8. Accompanied by indifferent feeling, without wrong view, prompted (upekkhā-sahagataṃ, diṭṭhigata-vippayuttaṃ, sasaṅkhārikam ekaṃ). This type is accompanied by indifferent feeling. It is without wrong view. It is weak, it arises by being dependent on inducement.

Dosa-mūla-citta: the citta accompanied by dosa cetasika, the dhamma that is coarse and harsh, which dislikes the object it experiences. There are two types of dosa-mūla-citta:

1. Accompanied by unpleasant feeling, with anger, unprompted (domanassa-sahagataṃ, paṭigha-sampayuttaṃ, asaṅkhārikam ekaṃ). This type, which is accompanied by unhappy feeling, arises together with paṭigha, dosa cetasika, the dhamma that is coarse and harsh. It has strength, it arises without being dependent on inducement.

2. Accompanied by unpleasant feeling, with anger, prompted (domanassa-sahagataṃ, paṭigha-sampayuttaṃ, sasaṅkhārikam ekaṃ). This type is different from the first type in as far as it is weak: it arises by being dependent on inducement.

Moha-mūla-citta: the citta accompanied by moha cetasika, the dhamma that is deluded, which does not know the truth of realities. There are two types of moha-mūla-citta:

1. Arising with indifferent feeling, accompanied by doubt (upekkhā-sahagataṃ, vicikicchā-sampayuttaṃ). Moha-mūla-citta arises together with indifferent feeling and this type is accompanied by doubt, vicikicchā cetasika, which is doubt about the truth of realities.

2. Arising with indifferent feeling, accompanied by restlessness (upekkhā-sahagataṃ, uddhacca-sampayuttaṃ). This type, which arises also with indifferent feeling, is accompanied by restlessness or agitation (uddhacca cetasika).

Each citta is accompanied by several types of cetasikas. Cittas are accompanied by a different number of cetasikas depending on the type of citta concerned. Each citta is accompanied by feeling, vedanā cetasika, which is different depending on the type of citta.

Each type of akusala citta is accompanied by four akusala cetasikas (akusala sādhāraṇa[1] cetasikas) which are: moha cetasika; shamelessness, ahirika cetasika, which has no shame of evil; lack of moral dread, anottappa cetasika, which does not fear the danger of akusala; restlessness or agitation, uddhacca cetasika, which is involved with akusala dhammas.

The twelve akusala cittas can be differentiated with regard to their roots (mūla, the three akusala hetus of lobha, dosa and moha), and then they are classified as follows:

- moha-mūla-citta, which is not accompanied by lobha cetasika nor by dosa cetasika,

[1] Sādhāraṇa means common or general. The cetasikas that are common to all akusala cittas.

- dosa-mūla-citta, which is not accompanied by lobha cetasika,
- lobha-mūla-citta, which is not accompanied by dosa cetasika.

The twelve akusala cittas can be differentiated with regard to three accompanying feelings, namely, indifferent feeling, pleasant feeling and unpleasant feeling:

- Indifferent feeling, upekkhā vedanā cetasika, accompanies lobha-mūla-citta and moha-mūla-citta. It does not accompany dosa-mūla-citta.
- Pleasant feeling, somanassa vedanā cetasika, accompanies lobha-mūla-citta. It does not accompany dosa-mūla-citta and moha-mūla-citta.
- Unpleasant feeling, domanassa vedanā cetasika, only accompanies the two types of dosa-mūla-citta. It does not accompany any other type of citta.

With regard to the second type of moha-mūla-citta, which arises with indifferent feeling and is accompanied by restlessness (upekkhā-sahagataṃ, uddhacca-sampayuttaṃ), this type is not accompanied by doubt (vicikicchā), but it is akusala citta since it is accompanied by akusala cetasikas. When there is akusala citta that is not one of the eight types of lobha-mūla-citta, one of the two types of dosa-mūla-citta or moha-mūla-citta accompanied by doubt, it is moha-mūla-citta accompanied by restlessness.

When akusala citta is strong, there is a condition for the accompanying cetanā (volition or intention) to commit one of the ten evil courses of action, kamma-patha. The ten akusala kamma-pathas are the following:

- Three kinds of bodily action (kāyakamma): the killing of living beings (pāṇātipāto), stealing, which is taking what has not been given (adinnādānaṃ), and sexual misconduct (kāmesu micchācāro).
- Four kinds of verbal action (vacīkamma): lying (musāvādo), rough speech (pharusavācā), slandering (pisuṇavācā) and idle talk (samphappalāpo).

- Three kinds of mental action (manokamma): covetousness or planning to take away someone else's property (abhijjhā), ill will or wishing to hurt or harm someone else (vyāpādo) and wrong view (micchādiṭṭhi). Not every kind of wrong view is akusala kamma-patha. Wrong view that is akusala kamma-patha are the three following views:

1. Natthika[2] diṭṭhi, denial of the result of kamma; any result that arises does not originate from kamma.[3]
2. Ahetuka diṭṭhi, denial of both kamma and result. Kamma does not produce result, whatever arises has no condition, no cause.[4]
3. Akiriya diṭṭhi, denial of the efficacy of kamma. Kamma, action, is merely a behaviour by way of the body; there are no good and bad actions that produce results.[5]

When the akusala citta that motivates akusala kamma-patha has fallen away, the cetanā cetasika (volition), which arose and fell away together with the akusala citta, is kamma-condition, kamma-paccaya, for the arising of akusala vipākacitta. There are seven types of akusala vipākacittas which are the results of kamma and which arise when it is the appropriate time.

18 Types of Ahetuka Cittas:

Ahetuka cittas are not accompanied by cetasikas that are roots, hetus. There are six hetus: three are akusala and three are sobhana. The three akusala hetus are the cetasikas of lobha, dosa and moha. These arise, as the case demands, with twelve akusala cittas, they do not accompany other types of citta. The three sobhana hetus are the

---

[2] Natthi means: there is not.

[3] As taught by Ajita Kesakambali ("Dialogues of the Buddha" I, no 2, Fruits of the Life of a Recluse, § 55). He taught that after death there is no next life but annihilation.

[4] Ahetuka means: without cause. Makkhali Gosāla taught that there is no condition or cause for the corruption and purity of beings, that everything is predestined by fate (D. I, no 2, § 53).

[5] As taught by Pūraṇa Kassapa (D. I, no. 2, § 53.) Kamma literally means action, it is derived from karoti, to do.

cetasikas of alobha, adosa and amoha or paññā. The citta that is accompanied by sobhana hetus is sobhana citta, the citta that is beautiful or wholesome.

Eighteen types of cittas are not accompanied by these six hetus. They are ahetuka cittas and also asobhana cittas. The other seventy-one cittas, out of the eighty-nine cittas, are accompanied by hetus, they are sahetuka cittas ("sa" means: "with").

Among the eighteen ahetuka cittas, seven types are akusala vipākacittas, eight types are ahetuka kusala vipākacittas and three types are ahetuka kiriyacittas. These ahetuka cittas are classified as follows:

7 Types of Akusala Vipākacittas:

Among these are the five sense-cognitions that are akusala vipākacittas, experiencing each their relevant object that is unpleasant. They are:

- seeing, experiencing colour, accompanied by indifferent feeling (upekkhā sahagataṃ cakkhuviññāṇaṃ);
- hearing, experiencing sound, accompanied by indifferent feeling (upekkhā sahagataṃ sotaviññānaṃ);
- smelling, experiencing odour, accompanied by indifferent feeling (upekkhā sahagataṃ ghāṇaviññāṇaṃ);
- tasting, experiencing flavour, accompanied by indifferent feeling (upekkhā sahagataṃ jivhāviññāṇaṃ);
- body-consciousness, experiencing tangible object, accompanied by painful feeling (dukkha sahagataṃ kāyaviññānaṃ).

Furthermore there are:

- receiving-consciousness accompanied by indifferent feeling (upekkhā sahagataṃ sampaṭicchanaṃ);
- investigating-consciousness accompanied by indifferent feeling (upekkhā sahagataṃ santīraṇaṃ).

The receiving-consciousness which is akusala vipākacitta arises after each of the five sense-cognitions that are akusala vipākacittas and it receives the relevant object. The investigating-consciousness that arises after the receiving-consciousness is akusala vipākacitta and it considers that object.

All these akusala vipākacittas are the results of akusala kamma and they experience an unpleasant object (aniṭṭhārammaṇa).

8 Types of Ahetuka Kusala Vipākacittas:

These types of cittas are the results of eight types of kāmāvacara kusala cittas accompanied by cetanā (volition) that accomplishes one of the ten meritorious deeds (puñña kiriya vatthu). These are included in generosity, dāna, morality, sīla, and mental development, bhāvanā. When kusala cetanā has arisen and accomplishes kusala kamma, kusala cetanā is kamma-paccaya, kamma-condition, for the arising of result later on. The result can be sixteen types of kāmāvacara kusala vipākacittas, namely: eight types of kāmāvacara sahetuka kusala vipākacittas (with roots) and eight types of ahetuka kusala vipākacittas (without roots).

Among the eight types of ahetuka kusala vipākacittas are the five sense-cognitions that are kusala vipākacittas, experiencing each their relevant object, and this object is pleasant (iṭṭhārammaṇa). They are:

- seeing, experiencing colour, accompanied by indifferent feeling (upekkhā sahagataṃ cakkhuviññāṇaṃ);
- hearing, experiencing sound, accompanied by indifferent feeling (upekkhā sahagataṃ sotaviññānaṃ);
- smelling, experiencing odour, accompanied by indifferent feeling (upekkhā sahagataṃ ghāṇaviññāṇaṃ);
- tasting, experiencing flavour, accompanied by indifferent feeling (upekkhā sahagataṃ jivhāviññāṇaṃ);
- body-consciousness, experiencing tangible object, accompanied by pleasant bodily feeling (sukha sahagataṃ kāyaviññānaṃ).

Furthermore there are:

- receiving-consciousness accompanied by indifferent feeling (upekkhā sahagataṃ sampaṭicchanaṃ);
- investigating-consciousness accompanied by indifferent feeling (upekkhā sahagataṃ santīraṇaṃ);

- investigating-consciousness accompanied by pleasant feeling (somanassa sahagataṃ santīraṇaṃ).

The receiving-consciousness arises after each of the five sense-cognitions that are kusala vipākacittas and it receives the relevant object. The investigating-consciousness, which arises after the receiving-consciousness and considers the object, can be accompanied by indifferent feeling or by pleasant feeling. When it is accompanied by pleasant feeling, the object is extraordinarily pleasant.

A pleasant object (iṭṭhārammaṇa) can have different degrees of pleasantness. It can be just a pleasant object or an extraordinarily pleasant object (adiṭṭhārammaṇa). If kusala vipākacitta is the result of kusala kamma of great purity and accompanied by pleasant feeling, it experiences an extraordinarily pleasant object, and in that case the investigation-consciousness, the santīraṇa-citta, which arises in a sense-door process and considers that object, is accompanied by pleasant feeling. If the object experienced by the kusala vipākacittas in a sense-door process is an object that is pleasant but not extraordinarily pleasant, the investigating-consciousness is accompanied by indifferent feeling.

3 Types of Ahetuka Kiriyacittas:

Kiriyacitta is the citta that is not kusala citta nor akusala citta, cittas that are cause, and it is not vipākacitta, citta that is result. Ahetuka kiriyacitta is the kiriyacitta not accompanied by the cetasikas that are hetus. There are three types of ahetuka kiriyacittas:

- five-sense-door adverting-consciousness, accompanied by indifferent feeling (upekkhā sahagataṃ pañcadvārāvajjana cittaṃ);
- mind-door adverting-consciousness, accompanied by indifferent feeling (upekkhā sahagataṃ manodvārāvajjana cittaṃ);
- smile-producing consciousness, accompanied by pleasant feeling (somanassa sahagataṃ hasituppāda cittaṃ).

The five-sense-door adverting-consciousness, pañcadvārāvajjana-citta,[6] is the first vīthi-citta, citta arising in a process, which experiences the object impinging on the eye, ear, nose, tongue or bodysense. Kiriyacitta

[6] Pañca means five, dvāra means door and āvajjana means adverting.

is different from vipākacitta since it can experience both pleasant objects and unpleasant objects. As regards vipākacitta, kusala vipākacitta experiences only a pleasant object and akusala vipākacitta experiences only an unpleasant object.

When the five-sense-door adverting-consciousness arises, it knows that an object impinges on the eyesense, or on one of the other senses, and then it falls away. It is succeeded by seeing-consciousness (or one of the other sense-cognitions), which experiences the same object through the appropriate doorway and then falls away. Seeing-consciousness or one of the other sense-cognitions is succeeded by receiving-consciousness, which receives that object and then falls away. Receiving-consciousness is succeeded by investigating-consciousness, which considers that object and then falls away.

Before seeing-consciousness or one of the other sense-cognitions arises and receives the result of kamma through the relevant doorway, there must be a vīthi-citta that knows that an object impinges on one of the sense-doors and this is the five-sense-door adverting-consciousness. The function of this citta is called adverting, āvajjana; the continuity of bhavanga-cittas is interrupted by this citta and it adverts towards the object which impinges on one of the sense-doors. When it has fallen away, it is succeeded by seeing-consciousness or one of the other sense-cognitions that arises and experiences a sense object through the relevant doorway.

The mind-door adverting-consciousness, mano-dvārāvajjana-citta,[7] is the first vīthi-citta that arises and experiences an object through the mind-door. It is the citta arising before akusala citta, kāmāvacara kusala citta, or in the case of the arahat, kāmāvacara kiriyacitta. The mind-door adverting-consciousness, mano-dvārāvajjana-citta, arises also in a sense-door process, but then it does not perform the function of adverting, but the function of determining the object, votthapana, and it is called after its function votthapana-citta.[8] In that case, it succeeds the investigation-consciousness and it does not experience the object through the mind-door, but through one of the sense-doors.

[7] Mano means mind.

[8] It is the same type as the mind-door adverting-consciousness, accompanied by the same cetasikas, but its function is different.

No matter whether the mind-door adverting-consciousness arises in a sense-door process, succeeding the investigating-consciousness, and performing the function of determining, or whether it is the first citta in a mind-door process which experiences the object through the mind-door, it is succeeded by akusala citta, by kāmāvacara kusala citta or, in the case of the arahat, by kāmāvacara kiriyacitta. The mind-door adverting-consciousness prepares the way for the succeeding citta, which is, in the case of unwise attention, akusala citta, and in the case of wise attention, kusala citta (or kiriyacitta for the arahat), and this depends on the accumulated inclinations. Thus, the mind-door adverting-consciousness arises before akusala citta, kusala citta or kiriyacitta in the processes of cittas experiencing an object through one of the six doorways.

The smile-producing consciousness, hasituppāda-citta, is an ahetuka kiriyacitta that conditions smiling only in the case of the arahat, with regard to the six kinds of objects that can be experienced through six doorways.

24 Types of Kāmāvacara Sobhana Cittas:

The twenty-four types of kāmāvacara sobhana cittas are beautiful cittas of the sense sphere, since they are accompanied by beautiful cetasikas, sobhana cetasikas.

The twenty-four types of sobhana cittas include eight types of kāmāvacara kusala cittas (mahā-kusala cittas), eight types of kāmāvacara vipākacittas (mahā-vipākacittas) and eight types of kāmāvacara kiriyacittas (mahā-kiriyacittas). They are classified as follows:

8 Types of Kāmāvacara Kusala Cittas:

1. Accompanied by pleasant feeling, with wisdom, unprompted (somanassa-sahagataṃ, ñāṇa-sampayuttaṃ, asaṅkhārikam ekaṃ). This type is accompanied by paññā cetasika (amoha) and it has strength, it arises without inducement.

2. Accompanied by pleasant feeling, with wisdom, prompted (somanassa-sahagataṃ, ñāṇa-sampayuttaṃ, sasaṅkhārikam ekaṃ). This type, which arises with paññā is weak, it arises by being dependent on inducement.

3. Accompanied by pleasant feeling, without wisdom, unprompted (somanassa-sahagataṃ, ñāṇa-vippayuttaṃ, asaṅkhārikam ekaṃ).

This type, which arises without paññā, has strength, it arises without inducement.

4. Accompanied by pleasant feeling, without wisdom, prompted (somanassa-sahagataṃ, ñāṇa-vippayuttaṃ, sasaṅkhārikam ekaṃ). This type, which arises without paññā is weak, it arises by being dependent on inducement.

5. Accompanied by indifferent feeling, with wisdom, unprompted (upekkhā-sahagataṃ, ñāṇa-sampayuttaṃ, asaṅkhārikam ekaṃ). This type, which arises with paññā, has strength, it arises without inducement.

6. Accompanied by indifferent feeling, with wisdom, prompted (upekkhā-sahagataṃ, ñāṇa-sampayuttaṃ, sasaṅkhārikam ekaṃ). This type, which arises with paññā is weak, it arises by being dependent on inducement.

7. Accompanied by indifferent feeling, without wisdom, unprompted (upekkhā-sahagataṃ, ñāṇa-vippayuttaṃ, asaṅkhārikam ekaṃ). This type, which arises without paññā, has strength, it arises without inducement.

8. Accompanied by indifferent feeling, without wisdom, prompted (upekkhā-sahagataṃ, ñāṇa-vippayuttaṃ, sasaṅkhārikam ekaṃ). This type, which arises without paññā is weak, it arises by being dependent on inducement.

The cetanā cetasika (volition) that accompanies these eight types of kusala cittas accomplishes kusala kamma consisting of ten bases of meritorious deeds, puñña kiriya vatthu.[9] These are the following:

- Dāna or generosity, kusala accomplished by way of dāna, the giving away of useful things to someone else,

- Sīla or morality, kusala accomplished by way of sīla, abstention from akusala kamma,

[9]As explained by the "Expositor" I, Book I, Part IV, Ch VIII, 157.

- Bhāvanā or mental development, kusala accomplished through the development of samatha and of vipassanā,
- Apacāyana or paying respect, kusala accomplished by paying respect to those who deserve it,
- Veyyāvaca or rendering service, kusala accomplished by applying energy in helping someone else with the tasks that are to be done,
- Pattidāna or sharing of merit, kusala accomplished by letting someone else know of one's kusala so that he can appreciate it,
- Pattanumodana or appreciation, kusala accomplished by the appreciation of someone else's kusala,
- Desanā or teaching, kusala accomplished by the teaching of the Dhamma,
- Savana or listening, kusala accomplished by listening to the Dhamma,
- Diṭṭhujukamma or correction of one's views, kusala accomplished by acquiring right view of realities.

Whenever the citta does not apply itself to one of these ten meritorious deeds, it is not kusala citta.

Kāmāvacara kusala citta applies itself to dāna (including giving, sharing of merit, appreciation of someone else's kusala), to sīla (including morality, paying respect and helping) or to bhāvanā (including mental development, the teaching of the Dhamma, listening to the Dhamma and correction of one's views). Kāmāvacara kusala citta arises in the processes of the five sense-doors and of the mind-door, and therefore it is called mahā-kusala (mahā meaning: great).

When the eight types of kāmāvacara kusala citta arise and accomplish kusala kamma, the accompanying cetanā, volition or intention, is kamma-condition, kamma-paccaya, for the arising of kāmāvacara kusala vipākacitta. There are sixteen types of results in accordance with the kamma that produces them at the appropriate time. These sixteen types of vipākacittas are: eight types of ahetuka kusala vipākacittas and eight types of kāmāvacara sahetuka kusala vipākacittas (mahā-vipākacittas).

8 Types of Kāmāvacara Sahetuka Kusala Vipākacittas (Mahā-Vipākacittas):

1. Accompanied by pleasant feeling, with wisdom, unprompted (somanassa-sahagataṃ, ñāṇa-sampayuttaṃ, asaṅkhārikam ekaṃ).

2. Accompanied by pleasant feeling, with wisdom, prompted (somanassa-sahagataṃ, ñāṇa-sampayuttaṃ, sasaṅkhārikam ekaṃ).

3. Accompanied by pleasant feeling, without wisdom, unprompted (somanassa-sahagataṃ, ñāṇa-vippayuttaṃ, asaṅkhārikam ekaṃ).

4. Accompanied by pleasant feeling, without wisdom, prompted (somanassa-sahagataṃ, ñāṇa-vippayuttaṃ, sasaṅkhārikam ekaṃ).

5. Accompanied by indifferent feeling, with wisdom, unprompted (upekkhā-sahagataṃ, ñāṇa-sampayuttaṃ, asaṅkhārikam ekaṃ).

6. Accompanied by indifferent feeling, with wisdom, prompted (upekkhā-sahagataṃ, ñāṇa-sampayuttaṃ, sasaṅkhārikam ekaṃ).

7. Accompanied by indifferent feeling, without wisdom, unprompted (upekkhā-sahagataṃ, ñāṇa-vippayuttaṃ, asaṅkhārikam ekaṃ).

8. Accompanied by indifferent feeling, without wisdom, prompted (upekkhā-sahagataṃ, ñāṇa-vippayuttaṃ, sasaṅkhārikam ekaṃ).

The eight types of mahā-vipākacittas are accompanied by sobhana cetasikas; they are sahetuka kusala vipākacittas, with sobhana hetus or roots. Thus, they are different from the eight types of ahetuka kusala vipākacittas that are not accompanied by sobhana cetasikas.

The eight types of kāmāvacara sobhana kiriyacittas (mahā-kiriyacittas) are cittas of the arahat who has eradicated all defilements. Kusala citta or akusala citta, which are the cause for the arising of vipākacitta in the future, do not arise anymore for him. After he has attained arahatship, there are for him, instead of sobhana cittas of the jāti (nature) of kusala, sobhana kiriyacittas. Kiriyacittas do not cause the arising of vipākacitta anymore in the future. Thus, the arahat has only vipākacitta, the result of kamma performed in the past before attaining arahatship, and kiriyacitta, which is not kusala citta, the cause for the arising of vipākacitta in the future.

8 Types of Kāmāvacara Sobhana Kiriyacittas (Sahetuka Kiriyacittas or Mahā-Kiriyacittas):

1. Accompanied by pleasant feeling, with wisdom, unprompted (somanassa-sahagataṃ, ñāṇa sampayuttaṃ, asaṅkhārikam ekaṃ).
2. Accompanied by pleasant feeling, with wisdom, prompted (somanassa-sahagataṃ, ñāṇa-sampayuttaṃ, sasaṅkhārikam ekaṃ).
3. Accompanied by pleasant feeling, without wisdom, unprompted (somanassa-sahagataṃ, ñāṇa-vippayuttaṃ, asaṅkhārikam ekaṃ).
4. Accompanied by pleasant feeling, without wisdom, prompted (somanassa-sahagataṃ, ñāṇa-vippayuttaṃ, sasaṅkhārikam ekaṃ).
5. Accompanied by indifferent feeling, with wisdom, unprompted (upekkhā-sahagataṃ, ñāṇa-sampayuttaṃ, asaṅkhārikam ekaṃ).
6. Accompanied by indifferent feeling, with wisdom, prompted (upekkhā-sahagataṃ, ñāṇa-sampayuttaṃ, sasaṅkhārikam ekaṃ).
7. Accompanied by indifferent feeling, without wisdom, unprompted (upekkhā-sahagataṃ, ñāṇa-vippayuttaṃ, asaṅkhārikam ekaṃ).
8. Accompanied by indifferent feeling, without wisdom, prompted (upekkhā-sahagataṃ, ñāṇa-vippayuttaṃ, sasaṅkhārikam ekaṃ).

15 Types of Rūpāvacara Cittas:
The fifteen types of rūpāvacara cittas are five types of rūpāvacara kusala cittas, five types of rūpāvacara vipākacittas and five types of rūpāvacara kiriyacittas. Rūpāvacara citta is of a higher degree than kāmāvacara citta, because it is the citta that has reached freedom from sense objects, by developing kāmāvacara kusala that is calm, samatha. When calm has become more established, different degrees of samādhi, concentration, can be attained. When samādhi is firmly fixed on the meditation subject and it has reached the degree of attainment concentration (appanā samādhi), the citta is rūpāvacara kusala citta (rūpa-jhāna kusala citta), it is free of the sensuous plane of citta.

5 Types of Rūpāvacara Kusala Cittas:

1. Kusala citta of the first jhāna, accompanied by the factors of applied thinking, sustained thinking, rapture, happy feeling and con-

centration (vitakka vicāra pīti sukh'ekaggatā sahitaṃ paṭhamajjhāna kusala-cittaṃ)[10];

2. Kusala citta of the second jhāna, accompanied by sustained thinking, rapture, happy feeling and concentration (vicāra pīti sukh'ekaggatā sahitaṃ dutiyajjhāna kusalacittaṃ);

3. Kusala citta of the third jhāna, accompanied by rapture, happy feeling and concentration (pīti sukh'ekaggatā sahitaṃ tatiyajjhāna kusalacittaṃ);

4. Kusala citta of the fourth jhāna, accompanied by happy feeling and concentration (sukh'ekaggatā sahitaṃ catutthajjhāna kusalacittaṃ);

5. Kusala citta of the fifth jhāna, accompanied by indifferent feeling and concentration (upekkh'ekaggatā sahitaṃ pañcamajjhāna kusala cittaṃ).

The jhānacitta of the first stage is accompanied by five factors, and as higher stages of jhāna are reached, jhāna factors are successively abandoned. However, some people can abandon the two factors of applied thinking and sustained thinking when the second stage is reached, and thus, for them there are only four stages of jhāna. That is why there is a fivefold system and a fourfold system of jhāna. The fifth jhāna of the fivefold system is the same as the fourth jhāna of the fourfold system.

5 Types of Rūpāvacara Vipākacittas:

1. Vipākacitta of the first jhāna, accompanied by the factors of applied thinking, sustained thinking, rapture, happy feeling and concentration (vitakka vicāra pīti sukh'ekaggatā sahitaṃ paṭhamajjhāna vipākacittaṃ);
2. Vipākacitta of the second jhāna, accompanied by sustained thinking, rapture, happy feeling and concentration (vicāra pīti sukh'ekaggatā sahitaṃ dutiyajjhāna vipākacittaṃ);

[10]Sahita means accompanied by. Paṭhama means first. The jhāna factors are explained in the section on Samatha in this book.

3. Vipākacitta of the third jhāna, accompanied by rapture, happy feeling and concentration (pīti sukh'ekaggatā sahitaṃ tatiyajjhāna vipākacittaṃ);
4. Vipākacitta of the fourth jhāna, accompanied by happy feeling and concentration (sukh'ekaggatā sahitaṃ catutthajjhāna vipākacittaṃ);
5. Vipākacitta of the fifth jhāna, accompanied by indifferent feeling and concentration (upekkh'ekaggatā sahitaṃ pañcamajjhāna vipākacittaṃ).

When rūpāvacara kusala citta has become strong, one can achieve "masteries," vasī.[11] Someone with mastery in jhāna has skill in determining the time he enters jhāna, in determining its duration, which means, the time jhānacittas are arising and falling away in an uninterrupted succession, and in determining the time of emerging from jhāna, which means that there is an end to the succession of jhānacittas. If his skill in jhāna does not decline, there is a condition for the arising of kusala jhānacitta before the dying-consciousness.

That jhānacitta is the condition for the arising of vipāka jhānacitta that is the rebirth-consciousness of the next life in a rūpa-brahma plane, in conformity with the degree of that jhāna.

5 Types of Rūpāvacara Kiriyacittas:

1. Kiriyacitta of the first jhāna, accompanied by the factors of applied thinking, sustained thinking, rapture, happy feeling and concentration (vitakka vicāra pīti sukh'ekaggatā sahitaṃ paṭhamajjhāna kiriyacittaṃ);

2. Kiriyacitta of the second jhāna, accompanied by sustained thinking, rapture, happy feeling and concentration (vicāra pīti sukh'ekaggatā sahitaṃ dutiyajjhāna kiriyacittaṃ);

3. Kiriyacitta of the third jhāna, accompanied by rapture, happy feeling and concentration (pīti sukh'ekaggatā sahitaṃ tatiyajjhāna kiriyacittaṃ);

4. Kiriyacitta of the fourth jhāna, accompanied by happy feeling and concentration (sukh'ekaggatā sahitaṃ catutthajjhāna kiriyacittaṃ);

[11] See "Visuddhimagga" XXIII, 27.

5. Kiriyacitta of the fifth jhāna, accompanied by indifferent feeling and concentration (upekkh'ekaggatā sahitaṃ pañcamajjhāna kiriyacittaṃ).

The rūpāvacara kiriyacitta is the citta of the arahat at the moment of attainment concentration, appanā samādhi. The rūpāvacara kiriyacitta does not condition the arising of rūpāvacara vipākacitta.

12 Types of Arūpāvacara Cittas:

The arūpāvacara jhāna-cittas are of the same type as the jhānacitta of the fifth stage, accompanied by the same jhāna-factors, but they do not have a meditation subject dependent on rūpa. Someone who has attained the fifth stage of rūpa-jhāna wishes to abandon the meditation subject of rupa-jhāna which is still dependent on materiality and, thus, close to a sense object. He is inclined to meditate on a subject that is immaterial and infinite. The twelve types of arūpāvacara cittas are: four types of arūpāvacara kusala cittas, four types of arūpāvacara vipākacittas and four types of arūpāvacara kiriyacittas.

4 Types of Arūpāvacara Kusala Cittas:

1. Kusala jhānacitta that has the object of "Infinity of Space" (Ākāsānañcāyatana[12] kusalacittaṃ);

2. Kusala jhānacitta that has the object of "Infinity of Consciousness" (Viññāṇañcāyatana[13] kusalacittaṃ);

3. Kusala jhānacitta that has the object of "Nothingness" (Ākiñcaññāyatana[14] kusalacittaṃ);

4. Kusala jhānacitta that has the object of "Neither Perception nor Non-Perception" (N'eva-saññā-n'āsaññāyatana[15] kusalacittaṃ).

The arūpa-jhānacittas are of the same type of citta as the rūpajhānacitta of the fifth stage and therefore, they are also called arūpa pañcama jhānacitta.[16]

---

[12] Akāsa means: space, ananta means: infinite, and āyatana means: place of origin.
[13] Viññāṇa ananta, which means consciousness is infinite.
[14] Ākiñcañña means: state of having nothing.
[15] Saññā means perception and āsaññā means non-perception. The 'n' stands for 'na', which means 'not'.
[16] Pañcama means fifth.

The first type of arūpa-jhāna kusala citta meditates on the subject of space that is of an extension without limits, which is infinite.

The second type of arūpa-jhāna kusala citta meditates on infinite consciousness; its object is the arūpa-jhānacitta of the first stage experiencing infinite space.

The third type of arūpa-jhāna kusala citta meditates on the subject of "nothing." Someone who has reached this stage knows that this subject is even more refined than that of the second stage of arūpa-jhāna, the citta experiencing infinite space.

The fourth type of arūpa-jhāna kusala citta meditates on the arūpa-jhānacitta of the third stage, which has "nothingness" as subject. Someone who has reached this stage knows that even when the subject is "nothing," there is still citta that dwells on this subject. The jhānacitta of the stage of "neither perception-nor-non-perception," which has as subject the citta experiencing "nothing," is of the highest stage of arūpa -jhāna; it is very subtle and refined. At that moment, it cannot be said that there is perception, nor can it be said that there is no perception.

If someone has acquired "mastery" in arūpa-jhāna and his skill in arūpa-jhāna does not decline, there are conditions for the arising of arūpa-jhāna kusala citta before the dying-consciousness. That jhānacitta is the condition for the arising of arūpa-jhāna vipākacitta that is the rebirth-consciousness of the next life in an arūpa-brahma plane, in conformity with the degree of that jhāna.

4 Types of Arūpāvacara Vipākacittas:

1. Vipāka jhānacitta that has the object of "Infinity of Space" (Ākāsānañcāyatana vipākacittaṃ);
2. Vipāka jhānacitta that has the object of "Infinity of Consciousness" (Viññāṇañcāyatana vipākacittaṃ);
3. Vipāka jhānacitta that has the object of "Nothingness" (Ākiñcaññāyatana vipākacittaṃ);
4. Vipāka jhānacitta that has the object of "Neither Perception nor Non-Perception" (N'eva-saññā-n'āsaññāyatana vipākacittaṃ).

When one of the arūpa-jhāna vipākacittas performs the function of rebirth for someone, he is reborn in one of the arūpa-brahma planes, in conformity with the degree of the arūpa-jhāna vipākacitta. He leads the life of a heavenly being in that arūpa-brahma plane until, when life in that plane has come to an end, he passes away. During the time he is a heavenly being of the arūpa-brahma world, there arises for him no rūpakkhandha, only the four nāmakkhandhas. Thus, he is a being without rūpa.

4 Types of Arūpāvacara Kiriyacittas:

1. Kiriya jhānacitta that has the object of "Infinity of Space" (Ākāsānañcāyatana kiriyacittaṃ);
2. Kiriya jhānacitta that has the object of "Infinity of Consciousness" (Viññāṇañcāyatana kiriyacittaṃ);
3. Kiriya jhānacitta that has the object of "Nothingness" (Ākiñcaññāyatana kiriyacittaṃ);
4. Kiriya jhānacitta that has the object of "Neither Perception nor Non-Perception" (N'eva-saññā-n'āsaññāyatana kiriyacittaṃ).

The arūpāvacara kiriyacitta is the citta of the arahat who has developed samatha to the degree of arūpa-jhāna. After he has realized the four noble Truths at the attainment of arahatship, the arūpāvacara citta that arises is kiriyacitta, it is no longer arūpāvacara kusala citta.

8 Types of Lokuttara Cittas:

Lokuttara cittas directly realize the characteristic of nibbāna. Four types are lokuttara kusala cittas that eradicate defilements and four types are lokuttara vipākacittas arising after defilements have been eradicated.

The eight types of lokuttara cittas are:

1. Path-consciousness of the stream winner, kusala citta (sotāpatti magga-citta);
2. Fruition-consciousness of the stream winner, vipākacitta (sotāpatti phala-citta);
3. Path-consciousness of the once-returner, kusala citta (sakadāgāmī magga-citta);

4. Fruition-consciousness of the once-returner, vipākacitta (sakadāgāmī phala-citta);

5. Path-consciousness of the non-returner, kusala citta (anāgāmī magga-citta);

6. Fruition-consciousness of the non-returner, vipākacitta (anāgāmī phala-citta);

7. Path-consciousness of the arahat, kusala citta (arahatta magga-citta);

8. Fruition-consciousness of the arahat, vipākacitta (arahatta phala-citta).

When kāmāvacara kusala citta (of the sense sphere) accompanied by paññā arises and investigates the characteristics of nāma and rūpa, their characteristics can be realized as they are and clinging to the wrong view of realities can be eliminated. When the different stages of insight-knowledge, vipassanā ñāṇa,[17] have been successively attained, lokuttara citta can arise. Lokuttara magga-citta directly realizes the characteristic of nibbāna and eradicates defilements in accordance with the stage of enlightenment that has been attained.

The lokuttara kusala citta which is the path-consciousness, magga-citta, of the sotāpanna, arises only once in the cycle of birth and death. It performs the function of eradicating the defilements of wrong view, doubt, avarice and envy. Moreover, it eliminates the conditions for akusala kamma of the intensity of leading to an unhappy rebirth.

When the magga-citta of the sotāpanna has fallen away, it is immediately succeeded by the phala-citta, which is lokuttara vipākacitta. The magga-citta of the sotāpanna is kusala kamma that produces result immediately; it conditions the arising of the phala-citta, which is lokuttara vipākacitta, without another citta arising in between. The phala-citta also experiences nibbāna as object, but it is different from the magga-citta: the magga-citta experiences nibbāna and eradicates defilements, whereas the phala-citta receives result, it experiences nibbāna after defilements have been eradicated already.

[17] See the section on Development of Vipassanā.

The magga-citta of the sakadāgāmī arises only once in the cycle of birth and death. It performs the function of eradicating the coarse attachment to visible object, sound, odour, flavour and tangible object. When the magga-citta has fallen away, it is immediately succeeded by the phala-citta, which also experiences nibbāna as object after defilements have been eradicated.

The magga-citta of the anāgāmī arises only once in the cycle of birth and death. It performs the function of eradicating the more refined attachment to the sense objects. When the magga-citta has fallen away, it is immediately succeeded by the phala-citta, which also experiences nibbāna as object after defilements have been eradicated.

The magga-citta of the arahat arises only once in the cycle of birth and death. It performs the function of completely eradicating all the remaining defilements. When the magga-citta has fallen away, it is immediately succeeded by the phala-citta, which also experiences nibbāna as object after all defilements have been completely eradicated.

40 Types of Lokuttara Cittas:

Those who have developed samatha and acquired great skill in jhāna, who are "jhāna lābhī,"[18] can have kāmāvacara citta accompanied by paññā arising in between jhānacittas of any stage; in that case, paññā can investigate the characteristics of nāma and rūpa appearing at that moment. When paññā investigates the characteristics of nāma and rūpa and knows them more clearly, the clinging to the wrong view of self can be eliminated. When lokuttara citta of one of the stages of enlightenment arises, it can have jhāna of one of the stages of jhāna as base or foundation, that is, the jhānacitta that was object of satipaṭṭhāna. In that case, the magga-citta and the phala-citta are lokuttara jhānacittas accompanied by the jhāna-factors of the jhānacitta that was their base, and thus, there are forty lokuttara cittas, classified as follows:

- Magga-citta of the sotāpanna with factors of the first, second, third, fourth and fifth stage of jhāna;[19]
- Phala-citta of the sotāpanna with factors of the first, second, third, fourth and fifth stage of jhāna;

[18] Lābha means gain, acquisition.

[19] This means: accompanied by the jhāna factors of the different stages of jhāna. The object of the lokuttara jhānacitta is not a meditation subject but nibbāna.

- Magga-citta of the sakadāgāmī with factors of the first, second, third, fourth and fifth stage of jhāna;
- Phala-citta of the sakadāgāmī with factors of the first, second, third, fourth and fifth stage of jhāna;
- Magga-citta of the anāgāmī with factors of the first, second, third, fourth and fifth stage of jhāna;
- Phala-citta of the anāgāmī with factors of the first, second, third, fourth and fifth stage of jhāna;
- Magga-citta of the arahat with factors of the first, second, third, fourth and fifth stage of jhāna;
- Phala-citta of the arahat with factors of the first, second, third, fourth and fifth stage of jhāna.

The magga-cittas of the four stages of enlightenment can arise only once in the cycle of birth and death. However, the phala-cittas which are lokuttara jhāna vipākacittas can arise again, provided the person who attained lokuttara jhāna is so skilful in jhāna that there are conditions for the arising of lokuttara jhāna vipākacitta in other processes. The lokuttara jhānacitta that arises in a process other than that during which the magga-citta eradicated defilements, is the lokuttara jhāna vipākacitta (the phala-citta) which is called "fruition attainment," phala samāpatti. During "fruition attainment", lokuttara jhāna vipākacittas arise and fall away in succession without there being other cittas in between.

B

Cetasika

52 Types of Cetasikas

- Aññāsamāna cetasikas:13 types
- Akusala cetasikas: 14 types
- Sobhana cetasikas: 25 types

The aññāsamāna cetasikas are of the same nature (jāti) as the other cetasikas they accompany.[1] When aññāsamāna cetasika accompanies akusala cetasikas, it is also akusala, and when it accompanies sobhana cetasikas it is also sobhana. The aññāsamāna cetasikas can accompany akusala cetasikas as well as sobhana cetasikas.

The thirteen aññāsamāna cetasikas can be classified as two categories: seven universals (sabbacitta sādhāraṇā cetasikas)[2] and six particulars (pakiṇṇakā cetasikas)[3]. The seven universals are cetasikas ac-

[1] Añña means 'other' and samāna means 'common'. When kusala citta is taken into account, akusala citta is taken as other, and vice versa.

[2] Sabbacitta means 'all cittas', and sādhāraṇa means 'common', 'general'.

[3] Pakiṇṇaka means 'miscellaneous'.

companying each type of citta. Every citta that arises has to be accompanied by at least seven cetasikas, the seven universals. The five pairs of sense-cognitions (seeing, hearing, etc. which can be kusala vipāka or akusala vipāka), are only accompanied by the seven universals, not by other cetasikas. Thus, they are accompanied by the smallest number of cetasikas. The other types of citta are accompanied by more than these seven cetasikas, depending on the type of citta concerned.

7 Universals:

1. Contact, phassa cetasika, contacts the object. When phassa cetasika arises and contacts an object, it is a condition for the citta and the other cetasikas arising together with it to perform each their own function with regard to that object. Citta, phassa and the other cetasikas arise, perform each their own function and then fall away very rapidly. When phassa contacts the object, it conditions that object to appear, so that also the other cetasikas can perform their specific functions as they, each in their own way, partake of the object, such as like (lobha) or dislike (dosa) towards the object. Phassa, contact, is food, āhāra, which sustains, which brings its fruit; it is food for the citta and cetasikas that arise together and manifest their specific characteristics while they perform their functions. Therefore, phassa cetasika is nutrition-condition, āhāra-paccaya, for the citta and the other cetasikas arising together with it.[4]

2. Feeling, vedanā cetasika, is the cetasika that feels. When citta arises and cognizes an object, the feeling that arises together with the citta feels with regard to that object. It can be pleasant feeling, unpleasant feeling, bodily pleasant feeling, painful feeling or indifferent feeling. Feeling cetasika accompanies each citta and it is different depending on the type of citta it accompanies. For example, unpleasant feeling accompanies dosa-mūla-citta, and indifferent feeling can accompany moha-mūla-citta or lobha-mūla-citta.

[4]There are four kinds of āhāra-paccaya: edible food, contact, volition and viññāṇa, in this case the rebirth-consciousness. Volition is kamma that produces rebirth, it is "food" for rebirth. Viññāṇa, rebirth-consciousness, sustains the cetasikas and the rūpa arising at rebirth.

3. Remembrance or perception, saññā cetasika, remembers or "marks" the object so that it can be recognized. Saññā cetasika remembers each object that appears; it remembers the different objects appearing one after the other as a "whole," as a story, a concept of beings and people. Saññā remembers pleasant feeling, unpleasant feeling, bodily pleasant and painful feeling and indifferent feeling with regard to each object that appears. Saññā cetasika is an important condition inciting to attachment and clinging in life. It is the same in the case of feeling cetasika: when one, for example, feels happy or glad, one attaches great importance to such feeling, one clings to it and wishes it to continue all the time. Therefore, vedanā cetasika and saññā cetasika are each a separate khandha among the five khandhas. The other fifty cetasikas are saṅkhārakkhandha, the khandha of "formations" or "activities." They condition citta each in their own way, in conformity with their different characteristics.

4. Volition, cetanā cetasika, wills or intends; it is active in fulfilling its own task and in coordinating the tasks of the nāma dhammas arising together with it at that moment. Cetanā cetasika is kamma-condition, kamma-paccaya. Cetanā cetasika accompanying vipākacitta is conascent kamma-condition, sahajāta-kamma-paccaya,[5] it performs its function as cetanā that is vipāka, arising together with vipākacitta and the other cetasikas that are also vipāka[6] and then it falls away. Cetanā cetasika that is kiriya is also conascent kamma-condition. It performs its function as it arises together with kiriyacitta and the other cetasikas that are kiriya cetasikas, and then it falls away. However, akusala cetanā which accompanies akusala citta and accomplishes akusala kamma patha (course of action which is completed) and kusala cetanā

[5]Saha means together, and sahajāta means born at the same time.

[6]Thus, it is different from akusala kamma and kusala kamma that bring their results later on. One usually thinks of kamma as a good or bad deed, but the reality of kamma is actually cetanā cetasika. Cetanā is not only akusala or kusala, but it is also vipāka and kiriya. Cetanā that is vipāka or kiriya merely coordinates the tasks of the citta and cetasikas it accompanies, and thus it is conascent kamma-condition. Cetanā that is akusala or kusala has a double task: it coordinates the tasks of the accompanying nāma dhammas and it "wills" or intends akusala or kusala.

which accompanies kusala citta and accomplishes kusala kamma patha, are, after they have fallen away, "kamma-condition operating from a different moment," nānā-khaṇika kamma-paccaya.[7] This type of kamma produces vipāka citta and cetasikas arising later on. Thus, when akusala cetanā and kusala cetanā that are cause, have fallen away, they can produce results in the form of vipākacitta and cetasikas later on, at a time different from the actual committing of evil and good deeds. That is why they are kamma-condition operating from a different time, nānā-khaṇika kamma-paccaya.

5. One-pointedness or concentration, ekaggatā cetasika, focuses on the object that is experienced. Whatever object citta cognizes, one-pointedness focuses on that object. However, one-pointedness accompanying akusala citta is not of the same strength of concentration as that accompanying kusala citta. When, in the development of samatha, citta knows the same object again and again, for a long time, the characteristic of one-pointedness, which concentrates on the object as it accompanies each citta at those moments, appears as samādhi, concentration, and it can be of different degrees. When ekaggatā that is kusala concentrates on the object, it is right concentration, sammā-samādhi, and it can develop so that it successively reaches higher levels.

6. Life faculty or vitality, jīvitindriya, is the cetasika that sustains the life of the accompanying citta and cetasikas, until they fall away. The nāma-dhammas that arise and subsist just for an extremely short moment still need as condition jīvitindriya cetasika which arises together with them and maintains their life at that moment. Jīvitindriya cetasika is faculty-condition, indriya-paccaya, for the citta and cetasikas it accompanies; it is a "leader"[8] in watching

[7]Nānā is different and khaṇa means time. It produces result later on.

[8]Some nāmas and rūpas are indriya, which means controlling faculty or leader. Indriyas are "leaders," each in their own field. The rūpas that are sense organs are indriyas, they control the relevant sense-cognitions. Citta is an indriya, manindriya, it is the leader in cognizing an object. Nāmas such as feeling or paññā are indriyas, leaders, each in their own field.

over the accompanying dhammas so that they subsist just for a moment before they fall away.

7. Attention or manasikāra, is the cetasika that is attentive to the object, that takes an interest in it. Attention to the object is a condition for the accompanying cetasikas to "think" of or to occupy themselves with the object. They think each in their own way of different subjects and condition a variety of effects in the field of science and worldly knowledge, which is endless. This kind of knowledge is different from knowledge in the field of Dhamma.

The seven universals, the sabbacitta sādhāraṇā cetasikas, are of the same nature or jāti as the citta they accompany. When they accompany kusala citta, they are kusala; when they accompany akusala citta, they are akusala; when they accompany vipākacitta, they are vipāka; when they accompany kiriyacitta, they are kiriya. They are also of the same level of citta they accompany: when they accompany kāmāvacara citta they are kāmāvacara; when they accompany rūpāvacara citta, they are rūpāvacara; when they accompany arūpāvacara citta, they are arūpāvacara; when they accompany lokuttara citta, they are lokuttara.

6 Particulars:

The six particulars are cetasikas that can arise with akusala cetasikas or with sobhana cetasikas. They do not accompany every citta.

1. Applied thinking, vitakka cetasika, touches the object which phassa cetasika contacts. Applied thinking accompanies fifty-five kāmāvacara cittas and eleven jhānacittas of the first stage.[9] It does not arise with the five pairs of sense-cognitions nor does it arise with the jhānacittas of the second stage up to the fifth stage. Applied thinking touches the object, it "thinks" of it in accordance with the citta and cetasikas it accompanies.[10] Applied thinking, which thinks of the object, is like the feet of the world; it causes the world to progress, as it accompanies the citta which cognizes the object.

[9]These jhānacittas are: kusala jhānacitta, vipāka jhānacitta, kiriya jhānacitta of the first stage, and eight lokuttara jhānacittas that are accompanied by the factors of the first stage of jhāna.

[10]The function of vitakka is not the same as what is meant by thinking in conventional sense. Vitakka touches or strikes the object, it leads citta to the object.

2. Sustained thinking, vicāra cetasika, is the cetasika that supports vitakka cetasika. Whatever vitakka thinks of, vicāra cetasika supports vitakka with regard to its thinking. Sustained thinking accompanies sixty-six cittas, namely, forty-four kāmāvacara cittas, eleven jhānacittas of the first stage and eleven jhānacittas of the second stage. Sustained thinking does not accompany the five pairs of sense-cognitions nor does it accompany the jhānacittas of the third stage up to the fifth stage. Whatever citta is accompanied by applied thinking is also accompanied by sustained thinking, except in the case of the eleven jhānacittas of the second stage, which are accompanied by sustained thinking but not by applied thinking.

3. Determination, adhimokkha cetasika, is fixed on the object, it is convinced about it and it does not doubt about it. Determination accompanies eighty-seven types of citta. It does not arise with the five pairs of sense-cognitions, nor does it arise with the type of moha-mūla-citta that is accompanied by doubt, vicikicchā. It cannot arise with moha-mūla-citta accompanied by doubt, since it is convinced about the object and does not doubt about it.

4. Energy, viriya cetasika, is the cetasika which makes an effort, strives, and which consolidates the accompanying dhammas so that they do not regress. Energy accompanies seventy-three types of citta. It does not accompany sixteen ahetuka cittas, namely, the sense-door adverting-consciousness, the five pairs of sense-cognitions, the two types of receiving-consciousness and the three types of investigating-consciousness (santīraṇa citta). These sixteen ahetuka cittas each perform their own function and they do not need energy as a condition.

5. Enthusiasm or rapture, pīti cetasika, is delighted, satisfied and thrilled, and therefore, it can only arise together with pleasant feeling, not with other kinds of feeling. Enthusiasm or rapture arises together with fifty-one types of citta which are accompanied by pleasant feeling, namely, eighteen types of kāmāvacara cittas, eleven types of jhānacitta of the first stage, eleven types of jhānacitta of the second stage and eleven types of jhānacitta of

the third stage. The eleven jhānacittas of the fourth stage (of the fivefold system) are accompanied by pleasant feeling, but not by rapture. This stage of jhānacitta is more refined than the third stage of jhānacitta, which is still accompanied by rapture. At the fourth stage, one can forgo rapture.

6. Zeal or desire-to-act, chanda cetasika, is the cetasika that desires to act. This cetasika accompanies sixty-nine types of citta. It does not accompany twenty types of citta, namely, the eighteen ahetuka cittas, and the two types of moha-mūla-citta. When rootless cittas arise, there is no desire to act. Moha-mūla-citta is accompanied by the root of moha, but since there are no lobha or dosa arising together with it, it is not accompanied by chanda cetasika, which desires to act. Chanda cetasika is the reality that desires to act in conformity with lobha-mūla-citta, dosa-mūla-citta or the other cittas it accompanies.

14 Types of Akusala Cetasikas:

Akusala cetasikas are not wholesome or beautiful. When the citta is accompanied by akusala cetasikas, it is akusala citta. Therefore, akusala cetasikas can only accompany the twelve akusala cittas, they cannot accompany kusala citta, vipākacitta or kiriyacitta. It depends on the type of akusala citta by which akusala cetasikas it is accompanied, but each akusala citta must be accompanied by the four akusala cetasikas of ignorance, moha, shamelessness, ahirika, recklessness, anottappa and restlessness, uddhacca. These four akusala cetasikas are common to all akusala cittas, they are called in Pāli: akusala sādhāraṇā cetasikas. Apart from these four akusala cetasikas, other akusala cetasikas accompany akusala cittas as the case demands.

1. Ignorance, moha cetasika, does not know the characteristics of realities as they really are. Moha cetasika accompanies all twelve akusala cittas.

2. Shamelessness, ahirika cetasika, is not ashamed of akusala dhammas. It accompanies all twelve akusala cittas.

3. Recklessness, anottappa cetasika, is not afraid of the danger of akusala dhammas. It accompanies all twelve akusala cittas.

4. Restlessness, uddhacca cetasika, is the cetasika that is not calm, which is distracted with regard to the object that is experienced. It accompanies all twelve akusala cittas.

5. Attachment, lobha cetasika, is the cetasika that clings, that desires the object. It accompanies the eight types of lobha-mūla-citta.

6. Wrong view, diṭṭhi cetasika, is wrong view of realities. It conditions clinging to the ways of wrong practice that is not the right cause leading to the right result. It conditions someone to cling to superstitious beliefs or to be excited about auspicious signs. Whenever someone has wrong view and strives after the wrong practice of the Dhamma through body, speech or mind, there is diṭṭhi cetasika, which can arise with four types of lobha-mūla-citta, those which are diṭṭhigata sampayutta (accompanied by diṭṭhi). When the magga-citta of the sotāpanna arises which realizes the four noble Truths, diṭṭhi cetasika is completely eradicated so that it does not arise again. Thus, the sotāpanna does not have anymore the four types of lobha-mūla-citta accompanied by diṭṭhi.

7. Conceit, māna cetasika, arises when one finds oneself important, when one is proud. It can arise only with the four types of lobha-mūla-citta that are without wrong view, diṭṭhi, but it does not always accompany these types. Sometimes lobha-mūla-cittas without wrong view are accompanied by conceit and sometimes they are not. Only when the four noble Truths have been realized at the stage of arahatship, conceit is completely eradicated so that it does not arise again.

8. Aversion, dosa cetasika, is the cetasika that is coarse; it is the reality that injures or harms, that is anxious or irritated. It accompanies the two types of dosa-mūla-citta. When the four noble Truths have been realized at the third stage of enlightenment, the stage of the non-returner, anāgāmī, dosa is completely eradicated. Thus, the sotāpanna can be sad and sorrowful, because he still has the two types of dosa-mūla-citta.

9. Envy, issā cetasika, is the cetasika that is jealous of someone else's prosperity, his material possessions, his wealth or his good quali-

ties. Envy can arise with the two types of dosa-mūla-citta, but it does not invariably accompany them. Sometimes dosa-mūla-citta is accompanied by envy, sometimes it is not. When the magga-citta of the sotāpanna realizes the four noble Truths, envy is completely eradicated. Thus, the ariyans do not have envy anymore.

10. Stinginess or avarice, macchariya cetasika, arises when someone is stingy with regard to his own property, when he does not want to share it with someone else, and does not want someone else to receive benefit from it. Avarice arises together with the two types of dosa-mūla-citta, it does not accompany lobha-mūla-citta. When avarice arises, there is anxiety and unhappiness with the citta, and therefore, it could not arise with lobha-mūla-citta that is accompanied by indifferent feeling or by pleasant feeling. Avarice is always accompanied by unpleasant feeling. Dosa-mūla-citta is sometimes accompanied by avarice, sometimes not. Avarice is completely eradicated when the magga-citta of the sotāpanna arises and realizes the four noble Truths. Thus, the ariyans do not have avarice anymore. As regards the lay follower who is ariyan but not yet arahat,[11] he has not given up all his possessions, because he still has lobha cetasika. However, he has no avarice, since it was eradicated at the stage of enlightenment of the sotāpanna. He follows the right Path and when there is a proper occasion, he can generously give away things to others.

11. Worry or regret, kukkucca cetasika, is the cetasika that is anxiety and regret about the akusala that has been committed and the kusala that has been omitted. It can arise with the two types of dosa-mūla-citta. Dosa-mūla-citta is sometimes accompanied by regret and sometimes not. Regret has been completely eradicated by the magga-citta of the anāgāmī.

12. Sloth, thīna cetasika, is the cetasika which causes the citta to be listless, to lack energy for kusala. It can arise with the five types of akusala cittas which are prompted, sasaṅkhārika, thus with the four lobha mūla-cittas which are sasaṅkharika and with one type

[11] He is called "learner," sekha, because he still must train himself and practise, so that all defilements can be eradicated. The arahat is a non-learner, asekha.

of dosa-mūla-citta, the type which is sasaṅkhārika. The akusala cittas that are sasaṅkhārika are sometimes accompanied by sloth, sometimes not.

13. Torpor, middha cetasika, is the cetasika that causes the accompanying cetasikas to be inert and drowsy. It can arise with the five types of akusala cittas that are sasaṅkhārika, just as in the case of sloth. Sloth and torpor always arise together, they cannot be separated. Sloth and torpor are eradicated by the magga-citta of the arahat.

14. Doubt, vicikicchā cetasika, is doubt about the characteristics of nāma and rūpa, about the four noble Truths, about the Buddha, the Dhamma and the Sangha. It arises with one type of moha-mūla-citta, the type that is vicikicchā sampayutta, accompanied by doubt. Doubt is completely eradicated by the magga-citta of the sotāpanna.

For the convenience of memorizing, the akusala cetasikas can be classified in the following categories:

- Mocātuka, the quartet[12] of moha and three other cetasikas that are the akusala cetasikas common to all akusala cittas, the akusala sādhāraṇā cetasikas. These are: moha, ahirika, anottappa and uddhacca.

- Lotika, the triad[13] of lobha and two other cetasikas that can arise together with lobha. This triad is: lobha, diṭṭhi, wrong view, and māna, conceit. Diṭṭhi and māna arise with lobha cetasika, but diṭṭhi and māna cannot arise at the same time. When there is lobha-mūla-citta with diṭṭhi (diṭṭhigata sampayutta), it is not accompanied by māna. Māna can accompany the four types of lobha-mūla-citta without diṭṭhi (diṭṭhigata vippayutta), but it does not always accompany these cittas. Sometimes māna accompanies lobha-mūla-citta without diṭṭhi and sometimes not.

[12] Cātu means four.

[13] Ti means three.

- Docātuka, the quartet of dosa cetasika and three other cetasikas that can arise together with dosa. This quartet is: dosa, issā (jealousy), macchariya (avarice), and kukkucca (regret). Issā, macchariya and kukkucca can accompany the two types of dosa-mūla-citta, but these three cetasikas do not arise at the same time and they do not always accompany dosa-mūla-citta. Sometimes they accompany dosa-mūla-citta, sometimes they don't.

- Thīduka, the dyad[14] of thīna, sloth, and middha, torpor. These two cetasikas always arise together, they cannot be separated. They can accompany the five types of akusala cittas that are sasaṇkhārika, but they do not always accompany these cittas.

- Vicikicchā, doubt, has not been classified in a specific category. Thirteen akusala cetasikas are classified in four categories, and thus, together with vicikicchā there are fourteen akusala cetasikas in all.

25 Types of Sobhana Cetasikas:

Sobhana cetasikas are cetasikas that are beautiful, wholesome. When the citta is accompanied by sobhana cetasikas the citta is sobhana, beautiful. Akusala cetasikas are quite different from sobhana cetasikas and they can arise only with the twelve types of akusala cittas. Sobhana cetasikas accompany kusala citta, sahetuka kusala vipākacitta or sobhana kiriyacitta. Sobhana cetasikas accompany kāmāvacara kusala citta (of the sense sphere, mahā-kusala citta), rūpāvacara kusala citta, arūpāvacara kusala citta, lokuttara kusala citta; they accompany kāmāvacara sahetuka vipāka (accompanied by sobhana hetus, mahā-vipāka), rūpāvacara vipākacitta, arūpāvacara vipākacitta, lokuttara vipākacitta; they accompany kāmāvacara sahetuka kiriyacitta (mahā-kiriyacitta), rūpāvacara kiriyacitta and arūpāvacara kiriyacitta.

There are different types of sobhana cetasikas accompanying sobhana cittas: nineteen types accompany each type of sobhana citta and six types do not.

Nineteen sobhana cetasikas are common to all sobhana cittas, the sobhana sādhāraṇa cetasikas. With regard to the cetasikas that do not accompany each sobhana citta, they are the following six types:

[14] Duka means pair, dyad.

- Abstinences, virati cetasikas, of which there are three types, accompanying sixteen types of citta: eight mahā-kusala cittas and eight lokuttara cittas (or forty types).[15]

- Illimitables, appamaññā cetasikas, among which two types (compassion and sympathetic joy) can accompany eight types of mahā-kusala citta, eight types of mahā-kiriyacitta, four types of rūpāvacara kusala citta (not those of the fifth stage of jhāna), four types of rūpāvacara vipākacitta and four types of rūpāvacara kiriyacitta.[16]

- Wisdom, paññā cetasika, which accompanies forty-seven cittas: twelve types of kāmāvacara cittas called ñāṇa sampayutta, accompanied by paññā; twenty-seven types of mahaggata cittas (jhānacittas), which are fifteen types of rūpāvacara cittas and twelve types of arūpāvacara cittas; and the eight types of lokuttara cittas.

19 Types of Sobhana Sādhāraṇā Cetasikas:

1. Confidence or faith, saddhā cetasika, is the cetasika that is pure. It is compared with a purifying gem, which makes turbid water clean and pure. When confidence arises, akusala dhammas, which are compared with mud, subside, they cannot arise. Thus, confidence, saddhā, is the reality that is confidence in kusala dhammas.

2. Mindfulness, sati cetasika, is the cetasika that is mindful, non-forgetful of kusala dhammas. When akusala arises in our daily life, there is no sati that is mindful of dāna, sīla or bhāvanā (mental development). Kusala citta can arise and apply itself to dāna, sīla or bhāvanā when there is sati cetasika, which is mindful, non-forgetful of these ways of kusala.

[15]This will be explained further on.

[16]The two illimitables, which do not arise with every sobhana citta, are compassion, karuṇā, and sympathetic joy, muditā. There are four illimitables or sublime states in all. The other two are loving-kindness, mettā, which is adosa cetasika, and equanimity, upekkhā, which is tatramajjhattatā cetasika, and these two cetasikas are classified among the sobhana cetasikas common to all sobhana cittas. As will be explained later on, the four illimitables can be developed in samatha as the subjects of calm that are the brahma-vihāras, divine abidings. They are called illimitables or boundless states, because when jhāna has been attained, they can be extended to an illimitable number of beings.

3. Moral shame, hiri cetasika, is the cetasika that is ashamed of and shrinks back from akusala dhammas. When kusala citta arises, there is shame of akusala dhammas. The characteristic of shame is compared to the shrinking back from dirt.

4. Fear of blame, ottappa cetasika, is the cetasika that fears the danger of akusala dhammas. Whenever akusala dhamma, even of a slight degree, arises, there is no fear of the danger of that dhamma. The characteristic of fear of blame is compared to fear of touching a lump of hot iron.

5. Non-attachment, alobha cetasika, is the cetasika that does not cling to the object, which is detached from it. When there is delight in and clinging to an object, the ways of kusala of dāna, sīla or bhāvanā cannot arise. Each kind of kusala citta that arises must have alobha cetasika as root, hetu. The characteristic of non-attachment is compared to a water drop, which does not cling to the petal of a lotus.

6. Non-aversion, adosa cetasika, is the cetasika that is not angry, coarse or harsh. It has the characteristic of friendliness, and it is also called mettā (mitto meaning friend), because it extends benevolence to all beings.

7. Equanimity, tatramajjhattatā cetasika, is mental balance, evenmindedness, impartiality. It is neutrality (upekkhā) towards the object that is experienced. There are ten kinds of Equanimity, Upekkhā:[17]

    - Sixfold Upekkhā, chaḷaṅga upekkhā, which is tatramajjhattatā cetasika. This is the evenmindedness or neutrality of the arahat towards the objects appearing through the six doors.

[17] Upekkhā can stand not only for tatramajjhattatā cetasika but also for indifferent feeling, upekkhā vedanā, for paññā cetasika or for viriya cetasika, and this depends on the context. See "Visuddhimagga" IV, 156-166, where the different aspects of equanimity have been explained.

- Equanimity of one of the brahma-vihāras,[18] brahma-vihārupekkhā. This is tatramajjhattatā cetasika which is even-mindedness towards beings.
- Equanimity that is one of the enlightenment factors, bhojjhangupekkhā. This is tatramajjhattatā cetasika, which is among the enlightenment factors leading to the realization of the four noble Truths.
- Equanimity of effort, viriyupekkhā. This is viriya cetasika, which is right effort, neither over strenuous nor lax in mental development.
- Equanimity as to conditioned realities, saṅkhārupekkhā. This is paññā cetasika which is neutral as it penetrates the three characteristics of impermanence, dukkha and anattā of conditioned realities, saṅkhāra dhammas.
- Equanimity of feeling, vedanupekkhā. This is vedanā cetasika, which is indifferent feeling, feeling that is neither unhappy nor happy.
- Equanimity in vipassanā, vipassanupekkhā. This is paññā cetasika which is neutral as it investigates the object that arises because of its appropriate conditions.
- Equanimity of tatramajjhattatā cetasika, tatramajjhattupekkhā. This is tatramajjhattatā cetasika, which effects mental balance, which is devoid of deficiency or excess.
- Equanimity of jhāna, jhānupekkhā. This is tatramajjhattatā cetasika in the development of jhāna, which abandons interest in the dhammas distracting from calm and mental steadiness. This kind of upekkhā arises with the jhānacitta of the third stage (of the fourfold system) and it abandons the jhāna-factor rapture, pīti.
- Purifying equanimity, parisuddhupekkhā. This is tatramajjhattatā cetasika arising with the jhānacitta of the fourth stage (of the fourfold system). It is the condition for calm

[18]The other three are mettā, loving-kindness, karuṇā, compassion and muditā, sympathetic joy.

and purification of all that opposes calm. At this stage there are no more jhāna-factors to be abandoned.

8. Tranquility of body, kāya-passaddhi.[19] This is the cetasika that is calm, not restless, and it conditions the accompanying cetasikas to be calm and not restless.

9. Tranquility of citta, citta-passaddhi. This is the cetasika that conditions the citta it accompanies to be calm. There is no calm when one clings to being alone, to silence, to being in the forest, to freedom from agitation. Then there is lobha-mūla-citta. There is no true calm, freedom from akusala, when one does not apply oneself to dāna, sīla or bhāvanā. Bhāvanā includes samatha, the development of calm by paññā as well as vipassanā, the development of insight wisdom, which knows the true nature of the characteristics of the realities that appear. Tranquility of body and tranquility of citta are cetasikas that are opposed to restlessness, uddhacca cetasika.

10. Lightness of body, kāya-lahutā. This is the cetasika that is light, buoyant, and it conditions the accompanying cetasikas to be light, to be without the sluggishness of akusala.

11. Lightness of citta, citta-lahutā. This is the cetasika that conditions the citta it accompanies to be light, without heaviness. Lightness of body and lightness of citta are opposed to sloth and torpor, thīna cetasika and middha cetasika.

12. Pliancy of body, kāya-mudutā. This is the cetasika that is smooth and pliant. It conditions the accompanying cetasikas to be without rigidity and coarseness.

13. Pliancy of citta, citta-mudutā. This cetasika conditions the citta it accompanies to be smooth, without rigidity. Pliancy of body and pliancy of citta are opposed to wrong view, diṭṭhi cetasika, and conceit, māna cetasika.

---

[19] Body stands here for the "mental body," the cetasikas.

14. Wieldiness of body, kāya-kammaññatā. This is the cetasika that is necessary for the workableness of the sobhana dhammas. It conditions the accompanying cetasikas to be suitable for their functioning as sobhana dhammas.

15. Wieldiness of citta, citta-kammaññatā. This is the cetasika which conditions the citta it accompanies to be suitable in its functioning as sobhana dhamma. Wieldiness of body and wieldiness of citta are opposed to the akusala dhammas which cause citta to be unwieldy with regard to sobhana dhammas.[20]

16. Proficiency of body, kāya-pāguññatā. This is the cetasika that is skilful and it conditions the accompanying cetasikas to be skilful and efficient with regard to the dhammas which are wholesome and beautiful.

17. Proficiency of citta, citta-pāguññatā. This is the cetasika that conditions the citta it accompanies to be skilful with regard to the dhammas which are wholesome and beautiful. Proficiency of body and proficiency of citta are the cetasikas that are opposed to diffidence, lack of confidence in wholesomeness.

18. Uprightness of body, kāya-ujukatā. This is the cetasika that is upright, and it conditions the accompanying cetasikas to be resolute, without crookedness and sincere in the application of wholesomeness.

19. Uprightness of citta, citta-ujukatā. This is the cetasika that conditions the citta it accompanies to be resolute and sincere in the application of wholesomeness. Uprightness of body and uprightness of citta are opposed to deception and craftiness, which cause the citta to be crooked, insincere.

The aforementioned nineteen types of sobhana cetasikas accompany each type of sobhana citta. They do not accompany the twelve types of akusala cittas and the eighteen types of ahetuka cittas, thus, thirty types of citta. Sobhana cittas are either dvihetuka, accompanied by two hetus (alobha and adosa) or tihetuka, accompanied by three hetus

[20]They are opposed to the hindrances such as sensuous desire and hate.

(alobha, adosa and amoha or paññā); there are no sobhana cittas with only one hetu. Whereas akusala cittas are not tihetuka, they can only be ekahetuka, accompanied by one hetu (moha) or dvihetuka, and in that case they are accompanied by moha and lobha or by moha and dosa.

Apart from the nineteen sobhana sadhāraṇā cetasikas, the cetasikas common to all sobhana cittas, there are six sobhana cetasikas that do not accompany each sobhana citta. Among them are the three abstinences, which have as function abstaining from akusala. There is the following classification of the six sobhana cetasikas that do not accompany each sobhana citta:

- Right speech, sammā-vāca, the cetasika that has the function of abstaining from the four kinds of unwholesome speech, from lying (musāvādo), rough speech (pharusavācā), slandering (pisuṇavācā), and idle talk (samphappalāpo). When there is abstention from wrong speech, the cetasika that is right speech abstains from wrong speech.

- Right action, sammā-kammanta, is the cetasika that abstains from the three kinds of wrong action, from killing (pāṇātipāto), stealing (adinnādānaṃ), and sexual misconduct (kāmesu micchācāro). When there is abstention from these three kinds of unwholesome bodily action, the cetasika that is right action performs the function of abstaining from unwholesome bodily action.

- Right livelihood, sammā-ājīva, is the cetasika that abstains from wrong livelihood (micchā-ājīva), namely: the three kinds of unwholesome bodily action and the four kinds of unwholesome speech pertaining to one's livelihood. When there is abstention from wrong livelihood, the cetasika that is right livelihood performs the function of abstaining from wrong livelihood.

Furthermore, there are two "illimitables," appamaññā cetasikas, classified among the six sobhana cetasikas that do not accompany each sobhana citta. They have beings and people as object and they do not arise with mahā-vipākacitta, the rūpāvacara cittas of the fifth stage of jhāna, arūpāvacara cittas and lokuttara cittas. They are classified as follows:

- Compassion, karuṇā cetasika, the cetasika that has compassion for beings who are suffering. It has non-harming as manifestation.
- Sympathetic joy, muditā cetasika, the cetasika that rejoices in the happiness of another being, and it is opposed to jealousy, issā.

There is one more cetasika among the six that do not accompany each sobhana citta:

- Paññā cetasika, the cetasika that is right view, right understanding of the characteristics of dhammas and right understanding of cause and result with regard to realities.

The nineteen sobhana sādhāraṇā cetasikas accompany all sobhana cittas, including kusala citta, vipākacitta and kiriyacitta. They accompany kāmāvacara cittas, rūpāvacara cittas, arūpāvacara cittas and lokuttara cittas.

Six sobhana cetasikas do not accompany each sobhana citta, and there are the following distinctions to be made:

The three abstinences, virati cetasikas, may sometimes accompany eight mahā-kusala cittas and they always accompany the eight lokuttara cittas (or the forty lokuttara cittas with jhāna factors). The abstinences do not accompany each mahā-kusala citta. Only when mahā-kusala citta is abstaining of a particular kind of akusala kamma is it accompanied by the relevant virati cetasika. The three abstinences cannot accompany mahā-kusala citta all at the same time. However, when lokuttara citta arises, all three abstinences accompany the citta at the same time. When the magga-citta arises, the three abstinences perform their function as path-factor while the conditions for wrong conduct are cut off, in accordance with the stage of enlightenment that is attained. They also accompany the phala-cittas. Thus, the eight (or forty) lokuttara cittas must be accompanied by all three abstinences.

The abstinences do not accompany mahā-kiriyacitta, because the arahat has completely eradicated all defilements and there is no need any more for abstention from akusala.

The abstinences do not accompany mahā-vipākacitta. They arise one at a time with mahā-kusala citta at the actual moment of abstaining from akusala. Mahā-vipākacitta, which is the result of mahā-kusala, is not accompanied by the abstinences, it does not perform the function of abstaining from akusala.

Mahā-vipāka (kusala vipāka of the sense-sphere) is different from rūpāvacara vipāka, arūpāvacara vipāka and lokuttara vipāka, vipākacittas with the same types of cetasikas as the kamma that produced them. Rūpāvacara kusala citta is kamma-condition, kamma-paccaya, for rūpāvacara vipākacitta, its result, and this has the same types of cetasikas and it also experiences the same object as the rūpāvacara kusala citta that produced it. They are compared to a body and its reflection, since they are similar. It is the same in the case of arūpāvacara kusala citta and vipākacitta, and lokuttara kusala citta and vipākacitta. However, the mahā-kusala citta and its result, the mahā-vipākacitta, are not accompanied by the same cetasikas. Thus, the mahā-vipākacitta that is the result of the mahā-kusala citta abstaining from akusala, is not accompanied by one of the abstinences.

The abstinences do not accompany rūpāvacara citta and arūpāvacara citta, because at the moment of mahaggata citta (jhānacitta), there is no kamma through body or speech and thus there would be no need to abstain.

As regards the two illimitables of compassion and sympathetic joy, classified among the six sobhana cetasikas that do not accompany each sobhana citta, these do not arise together. They arise one at a time when citta has as object beings or persons, who experience suffering (in which case that being is the object of compassion) or happiness (in which case that being is the object of sympathetic joy). The illimitables do not accompany mahā-vipākacitta, for the same reason as in the case of the abstinences. They can accompany, one at a time, mahā-kusala citta and mahā-kiriyacitta that have beings or persons as object.

Compassion and sympathetic joy are among the four "divine abidings," brahma-vihāras, subjects of calm developed in samatha: the development of loving-kindness, mettā, which is adosa cetasika; the development of compassion, karuṇā, which is karuṇā cetasika; the development of sympathetic joy, muditā, which is muditā cetasika; the development of equanimity, upekkhā, which is tatramajjhattatā cetasika. Samatha can be developed with one of the brahma-viharas as subject. When mahā-kusala citta is accompanied by loving-kindness, compassion or sympathetic joy, calm can become strong and steady, to the degree of access concentration (upacāra samādhi, which is close to absorption in the object), and absorption concentration which accompanies the jhānacitta of the first stage. If calm is developed further, the jhānacitta of the second stage, the third stage and the fourth stage can successively be attained. With the development of loving-kindness, compassion and sympathetic joy four stages of rūpa-jhāna (of the fivefold system) can be attained, not the fifth stage. The jhānacittas of the four lower stages are accompanied by pleasant feeling, but the jhānacitta of the fifth stage cannot be accompanied by pleasant feeling, only by indifferent feeling. Therefore, only the brahma-vihāra of equanimity can be the object of the jhānacitta that has been developed to the fifth stage of jhāna. Loving-kindness, compassion and sympathetic joy can be the meditation subjects of the jhānacitta of the four lower stages whereas equanimity is the meditation subject of the jhānacitta of the fifth stage.

The two illimitables of compassion and sympathetic joy do not accompany arūpāvacara citta, because this type of citta does not have beings and persons as object. Neither do they accompany lokuttara citta because this has nibbāna as object.

Paññā cetasika arises with all kāmāvacara cittas that are ñāṇa-sampayutta, accompanied by paññā. It arises also with rūpāvacara cittas, arūpāvacara cittas and lokuttara cittas, which cannot arise without paññā.

Thus, we see that kāmāvacara kusala citta is always accompanied by the sobhana sādhāraṇā cetasikas. Sometimes it is accompanied by one of the abstinences when it abstains from akusala, sometimes it is accompanied by one of the two illimitables of compassion and sympathetic joy, and sometimes it is accompanied by paññā cetasika. When one develops samatha or vipassanā, there is mahā-kusala citta ñāṇa-sampayutta, accompanied by paññā cetasika.

C
Rūpa

28 Types of Rūpa

Rūpa is the paramattha dhamma that does not know anything. Rūpa is sankhata dhamma, conditioned dhamma, dhamma that arises and falls away. There must be the appropriate conditions for the arising of rūpa. The derived rūpas, upādāya rūpas, arise in dependence on the four Great Elements, the mahā-bhūta rūpas. However, there must be causes for the arising of both the derived rūpas and the four Great Elements, and these are the dhammas that are the origination factors of all rūpas that arise. Rūpas could not arise without these origination factors. There are four origination factors, samuṭṭhāna, which cause the arising of rūpas in the body, namely: kamma, citta, temperature (utu) and nutrition (āhāra).

Rūpas which originate from kamma are called kammaja rūpas.[1]

Rūpas which originate from citta are called cittaja rūpas.

Rūpas which originate from temperature are called utuja rūpas.

[1] Ja means arisen, derived from janati, to produce. Kammaja means originated from or produced by kamma.

Rūpas which originate from nutrition are called āhāraja rūpas.

Kammaja Rūpa

Rūpas that originate from kamma do not originate from the other three factors. There are nine kinds of kammaja rūpas:

1. Eyesense, cakkhuppasāda rūpa,
2. Earsense, sotappasāda rūpa,
3. Smelling-sense, ghānappasāda rūpa,
4. Tasting-sense, jivhāppasāda rūpa,
5. Bodysense, kāyappasāda rūpa,
6. Femininity, itthibhāva rūpa,
7. Masculinity, purisabhāva rūpa,
8. Heart-base, hadaya rūpa,
9. Life faculty, jīvitindriya rūpa.

What seems to be alive but does not originate from akusala kamma or kusala kamma, such as different kinds of vegetation, does not have kammaja rūpa.

Some people do not have all kammaja rūpas. They lack eyesense, earsense, smelling-sense, tasting-sense, bodysense, femininity or masculinity. However, for living beings in the planes where there are five khandhas (nāma and rūpa), there must be heart-base, hadaya rūpa, a base where citta arises, and there must be life faculty, jīvitindriya rūpa. Jīvitindriya rūpa arises in each group of rūpas, kalāpa, originated from kamma.

For beings of the brahma plane who are without consciousness, asañña satta,[2] there is only rūpa, not nāma. So long as they are asañña satta brahmas, citta and cetasika do not arise. There is for them only the kalāpa, group of rūpas, with life faculty. They do not have the rūpas that are the senses, sex or heart-base.

---

[2] Asañña, literally, without perception or memory; satta means being.

The nine types of kammaja rūpas are derived rūpas, upādāya rūpas, which have to arise together with the eight inseparable rūpas, avinibbhoga rūpas.[3] There are the following groups or kalāpas originated from kamma:

1. The decad of the eyesense, cakkhudasaka[4] kalāpa, consisting of the eight inseparable rūpas, eyesense and life faculty.
2. The decad of earsense, sotadasaka kalāpa, consisting of the eight inseparable rūpas, earsense and life faculty.
3. The decad of smelling-sense, ghānadasaka kalāpa, consisting of the eight inseparable rūpas, smelling-sense and life faculty.
4. The decad of tasting-sense, jivhādasaka kalāpa, consisting of the eight inseparable rūpas, tasting-sense and life faculty.
5. The decad of bodysense, kāyadasaka kalāpa, consisting of the eight inseparable rūpas, bodysense and life faculty.
6. The decad of femininity, itthibhāvadasaka kalāpa, consisting of the eight inseparable rūpas, femininity and life faculty.
7. The decad of masculinity, purisabhāvadasaka kalāpa, consisting of the eight inseparable rūpas, masculinity and life faculty.
8. The decad of heart-base, hadayadasaka kalāpa, consisting of the eight inseparable rūpas, heart-base and life faculty.
9. The vital nonad, jīvitanavaka[5] kalāpa, consisting of the eight inseparable rūpas and life faculty.

Groups of rūpa originated from kamma arise at the arising moment, the uppāda khaṇa, of the rebirth-consciousness, paṭisandhi-citta, in accordance with the plane of existence where one is born. Kamma produces rūpa at the three moments of each citta, namely, at the arising

[3] In each group of rūpas there are the four Great Elements of Earth (solidity), Water (cohesion), Fire (temperature) and Wind (motion or pressure), and in addition the rupas of colour, odour, flavour and nutritive essence. These are the eight inseparable rūpas.

[4] Dasaka means decad.

[5] Navaka means nonad.

moment, uppāda khaṇa, the moment of presence, tiṭṭhi khaṇa, and the moment of falling away, bhanga khaṇa.[6] Kamma ceases to produce rūpa shortly before death, that is to say, from the seventeenth moment of citta reckoned backward from the dying-consciousness. Thus, all kammajarūpa falls away together with the dying-consciousness, cuti-citta, at the end of a lifespan.[7]

For those who are born by way of the womb, in the human plane of existence, there are three kalāpas of kammajarūpa, groups of rūpa originated from kamma, arising together with the rebirth-consciousness. These three kalāpas are: the decad of heart-base, the decad of bodysense and the decad of sex. As the newborn being develops, the kalāpas that are the decads of the eyesense, the earsense, the smelling-sense and the tasting-sense arise at the appropriate time.

For those who have a spontaneous birth (opapātika), without the instrumentality of parents,[8] namely, heavenly beings (devas), petas (ghosts), demons (asurakāyas) and beings born in hell planes, there are immediately all seven decads of kammajarūpa . Thus, they have a complete body with the decads of heart-base, bodysense and sex, and in addition the decads of eyesense, earsense, smelling-sense and tasting-sense. However, it may happen that kamma does not condition the arising of specific rūpas, and then these rūpas are lacking at the time of birth (paṭisandhi kāla) as well as in the course of life (pavatti kāla).

For those who have a spontaneous birth in a rūpa-brahma plane, there are only four kalāpas of kammaja rūpa: the decads of heart-base, eyesense, earsense and the vital nonad (the kalāpa with life faculty). There are no smelling-sense, tasting-sense, bodysense and sex. This is the result of the subduing of clinging to sense objects by the strength of the jhānacitta that conditioned birth as a being in a rūpa-brahma plane.

For those who are asañña satta brahmas, who have only rūpa, not nāma, there is one kalāpa of kammaja rūpas, the vital nonad. Someone who is born as an asañña satta brahma has developed the fifth stage

[6]Each moment of citta can be divided into three infinitesimally short moments: the moment of arising, of presence and of falling away.

[7]Rūpa lasts as long as seventeen moments of citta.

[8]Living beings can be born in four different ways: there are egg-born beings, womb-born beings, moisture-born beings and beings who have a spontaneous birth.

of jhāna and abandoned attachment to nāma. He has seen the danger of nāma, because so long as there is nāma, one may be involved in defilements; therefore he wished to be without nāma. If someone's skill in the jhāna of the fifth stage does not decline and kusala jhānacitta of the fifth stage arises shortly before the dying-consciousness, and he turns away from nāma dhamma, the jhānacitta conditions rebirth with only rūpa (rūpa paṭisandhi) in the brahma-plane of the asañña satta, where he will be for five hundred kappas. Since nāma dhamma does not arise, he cannot move at all. In whatever posture he died before his rebirth as asaññā satta, in that posture he is reborn until he passes away from that plane. Then, kusala kamma can condition the arising of rebirth-consciousness and kammajarūpa in a happy sensuous plane. So long as defilements have not been eradicated, one will go around in the cycle of defilements, of kamma and of vipāka.

Cittaja Rūpa

There are six kalāpas of rūpa originated from citta:

1. The pure octad, suddhatthaka[9] kalāpa, a group of eight rūpas consisting of only the eight inseparable rūpas (avinibbhoga rūpas). Cittajarūpa which is a pure octad is produced at the arising moment (uppāda khaṇa) of the first bhavanga-citta, and also after that, throughout life, it is produced at the arising moment of citta. However, the five pairs of sense-cognitions do not produce any rūpa, they are too weak to produce rūpa.

2. The nonad of bodily intimation, kāya-viññatti, a kalāpa of nine rūpas, which are the eight inseparable rūpas and bodily intimation. The citta that by means of rūpa conveys a specific meaning produces at its arising moment this kalāpa.

3. The decad of speech intimation, vāci-viññatti, a kalāpa of ten rūpas, which are the eight inseparable rūpas, speech intimation and sound, sadda rūpa. The citta that originates speech sound produces at its arising moment this kalāpa.

4. The undecad of lightness, lahutā, a kalāpa of eleven rūpas which are the eight inseparable rūpas and the three vikāra rūpas, the

[9] Suddha means pure, and attha means eight.

rūpas of changeability, namely: lightness, lahutā, plasticity, mudutā, and wieldiness, kammaññatā. The citta that wants to assume different postures produces at its arising moment this kalāpa.

5. The dodecad of bodily intimation and lightness, a kalāpa of twelve rūpas, which are the eight inseparable rūpas, the three vikāra rūpas, and bodily intimation. The citta that wants by way of bodily expression or different gestures to convey a specific meaning produces at its arising moment this kalāpa.

6. The tridecad of speech intimation, sound and lightness, a kalāpa of thirteen rūpas which are the eight inseparable rūpas, the three vikāra rūpas, speech intimation and sound. The citta that wants the utterance of a specific sound produces at its arising moment this kalāpa. That sound arises in dependence on the vikāra rūpas at the rūpa which is the base of that sound.[10]

Each kalāpa of cittajarūpa is produced by citta at its arising moment (uppāda khaṇa), not at the moment of its presence (tiṭṭhi khaṇa) nor at the moment of its falling away (bhanga khaṇa).

There are sixteen cittas in all that do not produce cittajarūpa : four types of arūpa-jhāna vipākacittas, the rebirth-consciousness, the five pairs of sense-cognitions, and the dying-consciousness of the arahat.

The four types of arūpa-jhāna vipākacittas do not produce any rūpa, because they are the results of arūpa-jhāna kusala citta that sees the disadvantage of rūpa, the dhamma bound up with defilements. Someone who sees the danger and disadvantage of rūpa develops arūpa-jhāna kusala, which does not have an object, connected with materiality. When the arūpa-jhāna vipākacitta performs the function of rebirth in one of the arūpa-jhāna planes, there is no condition at all for the arising of any rūpa.

The rebirth-consciousness does not produce cittajarūpa , because it is the first citta in a plane of existence and therefore, it does not have enough strength for the origination of cittajarūpa .

[10]Speech intimation is an asabhāva rūpa, a rūpa without a distinct nature or characteristic. A certain change in the rūpas produced by citta conditions the impact between the sound base and the element of solidity produced by citta.

The dying-consciousness of the arahat does not produce rūpa because it is the last citta of the cycle of birth and death, and thus, there are no longer conditions for the arising of rūpa.

Utuja Rūpa There are four kalāpas of rūpa that originate from utu, temperature, which is the element of heat:

1. The pure octad, which is a kalāpa consisting of only the eight inseparable rūpas. As we have seen, kamma produces in a living being rūpa from the moment the rebirth-consciousness arises; it produces rūpa at all three moments of citta: at its arising moment, at the moment of its presence and at the moment of its falling away. At the moment of presence (ṭiṭṭhi khaṇa) of the rebirth-consciousness, utu, that is the element of heat, present in the kalāpa of rūpas produced by kamma at the arising moment of the rebirth-consciousness, can in its turn produce new rūpas. Utu that is present, after it has arisen, originates a pure octad, the eight inseparable rūpas, and from that moment on utu originates at the moment of its presence other rūpas.[11]

2. The sound nonad, which is a kalāpa of nine rūpas: the eight inseparable rūpas and sound. If sound does not originate from citta, in the case of speech intimation, sound originates from temperature, such as the sound of traffic, or of a waterfall.

3. The undecad of lightness, which is a kalāpa of eleven rūpas: the eight inseparable rūpas and the three vikāra rūpas. Temperature is one of the factors that causes rūpa to be light, soft and workable. If utu is not balanced, that is, the right temperature, there will be sickness. Even if citta intends to originate rūpa in order to move the limbs, it cannot do so if there are no vikāra rūpas conditioned by the right temperature.

4. The dodecad of sound and lightness, which is a kalāpa consisting of twelve rūpas: the eight inseparable rūpas, the three vikāra

[11]Temperature, utu, and nutrition, āhāra, can produce other rūpas only at the moments of their presence, not at their arising moment. Rūpa is too weak at its arising moment to produce another rūpa. Compared with the duration of citta, rūpa lasts 17 moments of citta. After its arising moment, it exists 15 more moments, and then there is the moment of its falling away.

rūpas and sound. When there is sound by snapping the fingers or applauding, there are the vikāra rūpas arising together with sound.

Āhāraja Rūpa

Āhāraja rūpa is rūpa originated from ojā rūpa, nutritive essence present in food consisting of morsels that can be swallowed (kabaliṅkāra[12] āhāra). The kalāpas of āhāraja rūpa arise only in the body of living beings. There are two kalāpas of āhāraja rūpa:

1. The pure octad, consisting of only the eight inseparable rūpas.

2. The undecad with lightness, lahutā, a kalāpa of eleven rūpas, which are the eight inseparable rūpas and the three vikāra rūpas. Apart from citta and temperature that produce the three vikāra rūpas, also nutrition produces these rūpas. Even if utu, which originates the vikāra rūpas, is of the right temperature, but food is lacking, the vikāra rūpas do not have enough strength to enable someone to move his limbs with ease and swiftness.

Āhāraja rūpa can arise when the nutritive essence present in morsel food has been absorbed, and at the moment of its presence ojā rūpa can produce other rūpas.[13]

Summary of the Rūpas originating from one of the four factors:

The 8 inseparable rūpas originate from the 4 factors: some kalāpas originate from kamma, some from citta, some from temperature and some from nutrition.

The 5 pasāda rūpas, senses, originate from kamma.

The 2 bhāva-rūpas, sex, originate from kamma.

The heart-base, hadaya rūpa, originates from kamma.

The life faculty, jīvitindriya rūpa, originates from kamma.

The 3 vikāra rūpas, rūpas of changeability, originate from 3 factors: some kalāpas originate from citta, some from temperature and some from nutrition.

---

[12]Kabala means morsel.

[13]Thus, not at the moment of its arising, since it is then weak. It must have arisen already and then it can produce other rūpas.

The 2 rūpas that are intimation, viññatti rūpas, originate only from citta.

Sound, sadda rūpa, can originate from 2 factors: some kalāpas originate from citta and some from temperature.

Pariccheda rūpa or space (akāsa), which delimits kalāpas, originates from 4 factors: it originates from kamma when it separates kalāpas originated from kamma; in the same way it originates from citta, from temperature or from nutrition when it separates the kalāpas originated from citta, temperature or nutrition.

The 4 lakkhaṇa rūpas (origination, continuity, decay and falling away, characteristics inherent in all rūpas) do not originate from any of the 4 factors, because they are only characteristics of the 18 sabhāva rūpas.[14]

Classifications

The 28 rūpas can be classified according to different methods.

They can be classified as having their own distinct characteristic or as being without them:

- 18 sabhāva rūpas, rūpas with their own distinct characteristics: the 8 inseparable rūpas, the 5 pasāda rūpas, the 2 bhāva rūpas (sex), the heart-base, the life faculty and sound.
- 10 asabhāva rūpas, rūpas without their own distinct nature or characteristic: the 3 vikāra rūpas, the 2 viññatti rūpas, the pariccheda rūpa and the 4 lakkhaṇa rūpas.

Rūpas can be classified as internal or personal, ajjhattika, and external, bāhira:

- Ajjhattika rūpas, internal rūpas, which are the 5 pasāda rūpas.
- Bāhira rūpas, external rūpas, which are the other 23 rūpas.

Rūpas can be classified as vatthu, base, and avatthu, non-base:

- 6 vatthu rūpas, the bases where citta arises, namely, 5 pasāda rūpas and the heart-base.

[14]Sabhāva rūpa is rūpa with its own distinct nature and characteristic.

- Avatthu rūpas are the other 22 rūpas.

Rūpas can be classified as dvāra rūpas, doorways, and advāra rūpas, non-doorways:

- Dvāra rūpas are the 5 pasāda rūpas, the doorways through which a sense object is received, and 2 rūpas that can be the doorways for kamma, namely, kāya-viññatti rūpa, body intimation, and vaci-viññatti rūpa, speech intimation.

- Advāra rūpas are the other 21 rūpas.

Rūpas can be classified as indriya rūpas, faculties, and anindriya rūpas, non-faculties:

- 8 indriya rūpas, rūpas which are "leaders," with a controlling power each with regard to their own task, in their own field. They are 5 pasāda rūpas, 2 rūpas that are sex, bhāva rūpas, and jīvitindriya rūpa, life faculty.

- Anindriya rūpas are the 20 other rūpas.

Rūpas can be classified as oḷārika, coarse and sukhuma, subtle:

- 12 oḷārika rūpas. They are: the 7 visaya rūpas, rūpas that are the objects experienced through the senses[15], and the 5 pasāda rūpas.

- 16 sukhuma rūpas are the other 16 rūpas.

Rūpas can be classified as santike, near, and dūre, far:

- rūpas, which are santike, near, can be considered, understood and penetrated, namely, the 5 pasāda rūpas and the 7 objects, visaya rūpas;

- rūpas that are dūre, far, are difficult to penetrate, namely, the other 16 rūpas.

[15]There are 7 sense objects, because through the bodysense the 3 objects of solidity, temperature and motion can be experienced. Visaya means object.

Rūpas can be classified as impinging on each other, sappaṭigha[16] rūpas, and as not impinging and not being impinged on, asappaṭigha rūpas:

- 12 sappaṭigha rūpas, namely the 5 pasāda rūpas that are impinged on by the objects, and the 7 visaya rūpas, the objects that impinge.
- 16 asappaṭigha rūpas, the other 16 rūpas that do not impinge and are not impinged on.

Rūpas can be classified as being impinged on by external objects, gocaraggāhika rūpas[17] and as not being impinged on by external objects, agocaraggāhika rūpas:

- 5 gocāraggāhika rūpas that can be impinged on by external objects, namely, the 5 pasāda rūpas.
- 23 agocāraggāhika rūpas, the other 23 rūpas that cannot be impinged on by any object.

Rūpas can be classified as avinibbhoga rūpas, inseparable rūpas, and vinibbhoga rūpas, separable rūpas:

- 8 avinibbhoga rūpas, rūpas that cannot be separated.
- 20 vinibbhoga rūpas, rūpas that can be separated, namely the other 20 rūpas.

---

[16] Sa, meaning: with, and paṭigha, meaning: impingement.
[17] Gocara means field, object and gāhika means taker.

D

Questions about the Appendices

1. Is every citta that is not accompanied by the hetus of alobha, adosa and amoha, akusala citta?
2. In which way are asobhana citta and akusala citta different?
3. How many asobhana cittas are there? Which are they?
4. What type of citta performs the function of determining, votthapana?
5. Of which jāti is the five-sense-door adverting-consciousness, pañcadvārāvajjana-citta?
6. When sound impinges on the earsense, what is the first citta which experiences that sound?
7. Which type of citta precedes the hasituppāda citta (smile-producing citta of the arahat)?

8. Is the mind-door adverting-consciousness, mano-dvārāvajjana-citta, the mind-door?

9. How many functions has the mano-dvārāvajjana-citta? In how many doorway processes does it arise? Which objects does it experience?

10. Which paramattha dhamma is hetu, root?

11. Which khandha is hetu?

12. Is nibbāna hetu or na-hetu (not root)? Is it ahetuka or sahetuka?

13. What are the dhammas that are na-hetu and not saṅkhārakkhandha?

14. How many hetus are saṅkhārakkhandha?

15. The paramattha dhammas that are hetus are included in which khandha?

16. Is lokuttara citta asaṅkhata dhamma, unconditioned dhamma?

17. Kusala dhamma is included in which khandha?

18. Avyākata dhamma, indeterminate dhamma (neither kusala nor akusala) is included in which khandha?

19. Is there a khandha that is not avyākata dhamma?

20. Is there avyākata dhamma that is not khandha?

21. Is there kusala dhamma that is not khandha?

22. Which jāti is the akusala citta arising in the arūpa-brahma plane?

23. Of which plane, bhūmi, is vedanā cetasika?

24. Is nibbāna feeling? Explain your answer.

25. Which cetasikas are not accompanied by vedanā cetasika?

26. Of which plane of citta is there only one jāti?

27. Of which plane of citta are there two jātis?

28. Of which plane of citta are there 3 jātis?

29. Does the rūpa originated by moha-mūla-citta (cittajarūpa) arise because of hetu-paccaya, root-condition?

30. Is moha cetasika arising with moha-mūla-citta sahetuka, accompanied by hetu?

E

Pāli Glossary

abhaya dāna the giving of freedom from fear.

abhāya freedom from fear or danger.

Abhidhamma the higher teachings of Buddhism, teachings on ultimate realities.

Abhidhammattha Sangaha an Encyclopedia of the Abhidhamma, written by Anuruddha between the 8th and the 12th century A.D.

abhijjā covetousness.

abhiññā supernormal powers.

abhisaṅkhāra kammic activity giving preponderance in the conditioning of rebirth.

adhimāna over-estimating conceit.

adhimokkha determination or resolution.

adhipatis "forerunners" of the arising of the ariyan eightfold Path.

aditthāna determination.

adosa non aversion.

adukkhamasukha neutral feeling.

āhāra-paccaya nutriment-condition.

ahetuka cittas not accompanied by "beautiful roots" or unwholesome roots.

ahetuka kiriyacitta inoperative citta without root.

ahetuka-ditthi The view that here are no causes (in happening).

ahirika shamelessness.

ājīva-duccarita virati abstinence from wrong livelihood.

ākāsānañcāyatana sphere of boundless space, the meditation subject of the first immaterial jhānacitta.

akiriya-ditthi The view that there is no such thing as kamma.

akusala citta unwholesome consciousness.

akusala kamma a bad deed.

akusala unwholesome, unskilful.

alobha non attachment, generosity.

alobha non attachment, generosity.

āmisa dāna the giving of material things.

amoha wisdom or understanding.

an-aññātaññassāmī 't'indriya I-shall-come-to-know-the-unknown" faculty, arising at the moment of the magga-citta of the sotāpanna.

anāgāmī non returner, person who has reached the third stage of enlightenment, he has no aversion (dosa).

ānanda the chief attendant of the Buddha.

anantara-paccaya proximity-condition.

anantarika kamma heinous crimes.

anattā not self.

anicca impermanence.

Aññamañña-paccaya mutuality-condition.

aññasamānācetasikas Añña means "other" and samānā means "common", the same. The aññasamānās which arise together are of the same jāti as the citta they accompany and they all change, become "other", as they accompany a citta of a different jāti. Akusala is "other" than kusala and kusala is "other" than akusala.

aññātāvindriya The final knower faculty, arising at the moment of the phala-citta of the arahat.

aññindriya The faculty of final knowledge , which arises at the moment of the phala-citta, fruition-consciousness, of the sotāpanna, and also accompanies the magga-citta and the phala-citta of the sakadāgāmī and of the anāgāmī and the magga-citta of the arahat.

anottappa recklessness.

anudhamma in conformity with the Dhamma.

anuloma conformity or adaptation.

anumodhanā thanksgiving, appreciation of someone else's kusala.

anupādisesa nibbāna final nibbāna, without the khandhas (aggregates or groups of existence) remaining, at the death of an arahat.

anusayas latent tendency or proclivity.

apo-dhātu element of water or cohesion.

appanā absorption.

arahat noble person who has attained the fourth and last stage of enlightenment.

ārammaṇa object which is known by consciousness.

ariyan noble person who has attained enlightenment.

arūpa-bhūmi plane of arūpa citta.

arūpa-brahma plane plane of existence attained as a result of arūpa-jhāna. There are no sense impressions, no rūpa experienced in this realm.

arūpa-jhāna immaterial absorption.

arūpāvacara citta arūpa jhāna citta, consciousness of immaterial jhāna.

asaññā-satta plane plane where there is only rūpa, not nāma.

asaṅkhārika unprompted, not induced, either by oneself or by someone else.

asaṅkhata dhamma unconditioned reality, nibbāna.

asappurisa a bad man.

āsavas influxes or intoxicants, group of defilements.

āsevana-paccaya repetition-condition.

asobhana not beautiful, not accompanied by beautiful roots.

asubha foul.

asura demon, being of one of the unhappy planes of existence.

atīta-bhavanga past life-continuum, arising and falling away shortly before the start of a process of cittas experiencing an object through one of the sense-doors.

attavādupādāna clinging to personality belief.

Atthasālinī The Expositor, a commentary to the first book of the Abhidhamma Piṭaka.

atthi-paccaya presence-condition.

āvajjana adverting of consciousness to the object which has impinged on one of the six doors.

Avigata-paccaya non-disappearance-condition.

avihiósa the thought of non-harming.

avijjā ignorance.

avijjāsava the canker of ignorance.

avijjogha the flood of ignorance.

avyāpāda the thought of non-malevolence.

ayoniso manasikāra unwise attention to an object.

balas powers, strengths.

bhaṅga khaṇa dissolution moment of citta.

bhava-taṇhā craving for existence.

bhāvanā mental development, comprising the development of calm and the development of insight.

bhavanga calana vibrating bhavanga arising shortly before a process of cittas experiencing an object through one of the six doors.

bhavanga-citta life-continuum.

bhavangupaccheda arrest bhavanga, last bhavanga-citta before a process of cittas starts.

bhavogha the flood of desire for rebirth.

bhikkhu monk.

bhikkhunī nun.

bhūmi existence or plane of citta.

bodhisatta a being destined to become a Buddha.

bojjhangas factors of enlightenment.

Brahma heavenly being born in the Brahma world, as a result of the attainment of jhāna.

brahma-vihāras the four divine abidings, meditation subjects which are: loving kindness, compassion, sympathetic joy, equanimity.

brahmavihāra-upekkhā equanimity, one of the "divine abidings".

Buddha a fully enlightened person who has discovered the truth all by himself, without the aid of a teacher.

Buddhaghosa the greatest of Commentators on the Tipiṭaka, author of the Visuddhimagga in 5 A.D.

cakkhu eye.

cakkhu-dhātu eye element.

cakkhu-dvāra eyedoor.

cakkhu-dvārāvajjana-citta eye-door-adverting-consciousness.

cakkhu-samphassa eye contact.

cakkhu-vatthu eye-base.

cakkhu-viññāṇa seeing-consciousness.

cakkhuppasāda rūpa rūpa which is the organ of eyesense, capable of receiving visible object.

cakkhuppasāda-rūpa eye-sense.

cetanā volition.

chanda "wish to do".

citta consciousness the reality which knows or cognizes an object.

citta-kammaññatā wieldiness of citta.

citta-lahutā lightness of citta.

citta-mudutā pliancy of citta.

citta-pāguññatā proficiency of citta.

citta-passaddhi tranquillity of mind.

citta-ujukatā uprightness of citta.

citta consciousness, the reality which knows or cognizes an object.

cuti dying.

cuti-citta dying-consciousness.

dāna generosity, giving.

dassana-kicca function of seeing.

deva heavenly being.

dhamma reality, truth, the teachings.

dhamma-dhātu element of dhammas, realities, comprising cetasikas, subtle rūpas, nibbāna.

dhamma-vicaya investigation of Dhamma.

Dhammanudhamma paṭipatti the practice of the Dhamma in conformity with the Dhamma (anudhamma).

dhammārammaṇa all objects other than the sense objects which can be experienced through the five sense-doors, thus, objects which can be experienced only through the mind-door.

Dhammasangaṇi the first book of the Abhidhamma Piṭaka.

dhammavicaya investigation of the Dhamma.

Dhātukathā Discussion on the Elements, the third book of the Abhidhamma.

diṭṭhāsava canker of wrong view.

diṭṭhi wrong view, distorted view of realities.

diṭṭhigata sampayutta accompanied by wrong view.

diṭṭhigata-vippayutta attachment which is dissociated from wrong view.

diṭṭhogha the flood of wrong view.

diṭṭhupādāna clinging to wrong view.

domanassa unpleasant feeling.

dosa aversion or ill will.

dosa-mūla-citta citta (consciousness) rooted in aversion.

dukkha suffering, unsatisfactoriness of conditioned realities.

dukkha vedanā painful feeling or unpleasant feeling.

dvāra doorway through which an object is experienced, the five sense-doors or the mind door.

dvi-pañca-viññāṇa the five pairs of sense-cognitions, which are seeing, hearing, smelling, tasting and body-consciousness. Of each pair one is kusala vipāka and one akusala vipāka.

ekaggatā concentration, one-pointedness, a cetasika which has the function to focus on one object.

ganthas bonds, a group of defilements.

ghāna-dhātu nose element.

ghāna-viññāṇa smelling-consciousness.

ghānappasāda rūpa** rūpa which is the organ of smelling sense, capable of receiving odour.

Ghāyana-kicca function of smelling.

gotrabhū change of lineage, the last citta of the sense-sphere before jhāna, absorption, is attained, or enlightenment is attained.

hadaya-vatthu heart-base, rūpa which is the plane of origin of the cittas other than the sense-cognitions.

hasituppāda-citta smile producing consciousness of an arahat.

hetu root, which conditions citta to be "beautiful" or unwholesome.

hiri moral shame.

hiriyati scruples.

idaṃ-saccābhinivesa kāyagantha the bodily tie of dogmatism.

idaṃ-saccābhinivesa the tie of dogmatism.

iddhipādas four "Roads to Success".

indriya faculty. Some are rūpas such as the sense organs, some are nāmas such as feeling. Five 'spiritual faculties' are wholesome faculties which should be cultivated, namely: confidence, energy, awareness, concentration and wisdom.

indriya-paccaya faculty-condition.

indriya faculty.

issā envy.

jāti birth, nature, class (of cittas).

javana impulsion, running through the object.

javana-citta cittas which 'run through the object', kusala citta or akusala citta in the case of non-arahats.

jhāna absorption which can be attained through the development of calm.

jhāna factors cetasikas which have to be cultivated for the attainment of jhāna: vitakka, vicāra, pīti, sukha, samādhi.

jhāna-cittas absorption consciousness attained through the development of calm.

jhāna-paccaya jhāna-condition.

jhāna absorption which can be attained through the development of calm.

jinhā-dhātu tongue element.

jinhāppasāda rūpa rūpa which is the organ of tasting sense, capable of receiving flavour.

jivhā-viññāṇa tasting-consciousness.

jīvitindriya life-faculty or vitality.

kalyāṇa-mitta good friend in Dhamma.

kāma-bhūmi sensuous plane of existence.

kāma-sobhana cittas beautiful cittas of the sense sphere.

kāma-taṇhā sensuous craving.

kāma-vitakka thought of sense-pleasures.

kāma sensual enjoyment or the five sense objects.

kāmacchandha sensuous desire.

kāmāvacara cittas cittas of the sense sphere.

kāmāvacara sobhana cittas beautiful cittas of the sense sphere.

kamma intention or volition; deed motivated by volition.

kamma patha course of action performed through body, speech or mind which can be wholesome or unwholesome.

kamma-paccaya kamma-condition.

Kammassakatāñāṇa understanding of the specific nature of kamma as 'one's own'.

kāmogha the flood of sensuous desire.

kāmupādāna sensuous clinging.

karuṇā compassion.

kasiṇa disk, used as an object for the development of calm.

kāya body. It can also stand for the 'mental body', the cetasikas.

kāya dhātu the element of bodysense.

kāya-duccarita virati abstinence from wrong action.

kāya-ujukatā uprightness of cetasika.

kāya-viññatti bodily intimation, such as gestures, facial expression, etc.

kāya-viññāṇa body-consciousness.

kāyappasāda rūpa bodysense, the rūpa which is capable of receiving tangible object. It is all over the body, inside or outside.

khandhas aggregates of conditioned realities classified as five groups: physical phenomena, feelings, perception or remembrance, activities or formations (cetasikas other than feeling or perception), consciousness.

khanti patience.

kicca function.

kilesa defilements.

kiriya citta inoperative citta, neither cause nor result.

kukkucca regret or worry.

kusala citta wholesome consciousness.

kusala kamma a good deed.

kusala wholesome, skilful.

lakkhaṇaṃ characteristic, specific or generic attribute.

lobha attachment, greed.

lobha-mūla-citta consciousness rooted in attachment.

lokiya citta citta which is mundane, not experiencing nibbāna.

lokuttara citta supramundane citta which experiences nibbāna.

lokuttara dhammas the unconditioned dhamma which is nibbāna and the cittas which experience nibbāna.

macchariya stinginess.

magga path (eightfold Path).

magga-citta path consciousness, supramundane citta which experiences nibbāna and eradicates defilements.

magga-paccaya path-condition.

mahākiriyacitta inoperative sense-sphere citta of the arahat, accompanied by "beautiful" roots.

mahāvipākacitta citta of the sense sphere which is result, accompanied by "beautiful" roots.

mahā-bhūta-rūpas the rūpas which are the four great elements of "earth" or solidity, "water" or cohesion, "fire" or temperature, and "wind" or motion.

mahā-kusalacitta wholesome citta of the sense sphere.

mahā-satipaṭṭhāna four applications of mindfulness, see satipaṭṭhāna.

mahā-vipassanā "principal insight".

manasikāra attention.

manāyatana mind-base.

mano-dhātu mind-element, comprising the five-sense-door adverting-consciousness, and the two types of receiving-consciousness.

mano-dvāra-vīthi-cittas cittas arising in a mind-door process.

mano-dvārāvajjana-citta mind-door-adverting-consciousness.

mano-viññāna-dhātu mind-consciousness element, comprising all cittas other than the sense-cognitions (seeing, etc.) and mind-element.

mano mind, citta, consciousness.

māra "the evil one"—all that leads to dukkha.

mettā loving kindness.

micchā-diṭṭhi wrong view.

micchā-samādhi wrong concentration.

middha torpor or languor.

moha ignorance.

moha-mūla-cittas cittas rooted in ignorance.

muditā sympathetic joy.

n'eva-saññā-n'āsaññāyatana sphere of neither perception nor non-perception, the meditation subject of the fourth immaterial jhāna.

nāma kkhandha group of all mental phenomena.

nāma mental phenomena,including those which are conditioned and also the unconditioned nāma which is nibbāna.

nāma mental phenomena,including those which are conditioned and also the unconditioned nāma which is nibbāna.

nāma-rūpa pariccheda-ñāṇa first stage of insight, insight knowledge of the distinction between mental phenomena and physical phenomena.

natthi-paccaya absence-condition.

natthika diṭṭhi wrong view of annihilation, assumption that there is no result of kamma.

ñāṇa sampayutta accompanied by paññā; ñāṇa means paññā.

ñāṇa vippayutta unaccompanied by paññā.

ñāṇa wisdom, insight.

nekkhamma thought of renunciation.

nibbāna unconditioned reality, the reality which does not arise and fall away. The destruction of lust, hatred and delusion. The deathless. The end of suffering.

nimitta mental image one can acquire of a meditation subject in tranquil meditation.

nirodha-samāpatti attainment of cessation of consciousness.

nissaya-paccaya dependence-condition.

nīvaraṇa hindrances, a group of defilements.

oghas group of defilements, the floods.

oḷārika rūpas gross rūpas (sense objects and sense organs).

ojā the rūpa which is nutrition.

ottappa fear of blame.

paccaya-pariggaha-ñāṇa discerning the Conditions of Nāma and Rūpa.

paccayas conditions.

Pacceka Buddha silent Buddha, an enlightened one who has found the truth by himself but does not proclaim Dhamma to the world.

pacchājāta-paccaya postnascence-condition.

paccupaṭṭhāna manifestation, appearance or effect.

padaṭṭhānaṃ proximate cause.

paṭibhāganimitta counterpart image, more perfected mental image of a meditation subject, acquired in tranquil meditation.

paṭicca sammuppada 'Dependent Origination', the conditional origination of phenomena.

paṭigha aversion or ill will.

Paṭṭhāna Conditional Relations, one of the seven books of the Abhidhamma.

paṭisandhi citta rebirth consciousness.

paṭisandhi rebirth.

pakiṇṇakā the particulars.

Pāli the language of the Buddhist teachings.

pañcadvārāvajjana-citta five-sense-door-adverting-consciousness.

pañcaviññāṇa (or dvi-pañcaviññāṇa), the sense cognitions (seeing etc.) of which there five pairs.

paññā wisdom or understanding.

paññatti concepts, conventional terms.

paramattha dhamma truth in the absolute sense: mental and physical phenomena, each with their own characteristic.

Paramattha Mañjūsā a commentary to the Visuddhimagga.

pāramīs the ten perfections, generosity, dāna, morality, sīla, renunciation, nekkhamma, wisdom, paññā, energy, viriya, patience, khanti, truthfulness, sacca, determination, adiṭṭhāna, loving-kindness, mettā, equanimity, upekkhā.

parikamma preparatory consciousness, the first javanacitta arising in the process during which absorption or enlightenment is attained.

pasāda-rūpas rūpas which are capable of receiving sense-objects such as visible object, sound, taste, etc.

passaddhi calm.

patisanthāro courtesy.

peta ghost.

phala-citta fruition consciousness experiencing nibbāna. It is result of magga-citta, path-consciosness.

phassa contact.

phoṭṭhabbārammaṇa tangible object, experienced through bodysense.

phusana kicca function of experiencing tangible object.

pīti joy, rapture, enthusiasm.

Puggalapaññatti Designation of Human Types, the fourth book of the Abhidhamma.

puñña-kiriya-vatthus "ten bases of meritorious deeds".

purejāta-paccaya prenascence-condition.

puthujjana "worldling", a person who has not attained enlightenment.

rāga greed.

Rāhula the Buddha's son.

rasa function or achievement.

rasārammaṇa object of flavour.

rūpa physical phenomena, realities which do not experience anything.

rūpa-brahma plane or rūpa-bhūmi fine material realm of existence attained as a result of rūpa-jhāna.

rūpa-jhāna fine material absorption, developed with a meditation subject which is still dependant on materiality.

rūpa-jīvitindriya a kind of rūpa produced by kamma and it maintains the life of the other rūpas it arises together with rūpa-khandha aggregate or group of all physical phenomena (rūpas).

rūpa-khandha aggregate or group of all physical phenomena (rūpas).

rūpārammaṇa visible object.

rūpāvacara citta type of jhāna citta.

rūpāvacara cittas ūpa-jhānacittas, consciosness of the fine-material sphere.

sa-upādi-sesa nibbāna arahatship with the khandhas remaining, thus not final nibbāna at death of an arahat.

sabbacitta-sādhāranā the seven cetasikas which have to arise with every citta.

sadda dāna the gift of sounds (should be understood by way of the sounds of drums, etc.).

saddārammaṇa sound.

saddhā confidence.

sahagata accompanied by.

sahajāta-paccaya conascence-condition.

sahetuka accompanied by roots.

sakadāgāmī once-returner, a noble person who has attained the second stage of enlightenment.

sakkāya diṭṭhi wrong view of personality, wrong view about the khandhas.

samādhi concentration or one-pointedness, ekaggatā cetasika.

samādhi concentration or one-pointedness, ekaggatā cetasika.

samādhi-bhāvanā the development of concentration.

samanantara-paccaya contiguity-condition.

samañña lakkhaṇa general characteristics common to all conditioned realities.

samatha the development of calm.

sambojjhanga seven factors of enlightenment.

sammā right.

sammā-diṭṭhi right understanding.

sammā-samādhi right concentration.

sammā-sambuddha a universal Buddha, a fully enlightened person who has discovered the truth all by himself, without the aid of a teacher and who can proclaim the Truth to others beings.

sammā-saṅkappa right thinking of the eightfold Path.

sammā-sati right mindfulness.

sammā-vāyāma right mindfulness of the eightfold Path.

sampaṭicchana-citta receiving-consciousness.

sampajañña discrimination, comprehension.

sampayutta associated with.

sampayutta dhammas associated dhammas, citta and cetasika which arise together.

sampayutta-paccaya association-condition.

Sangha community of monks and nuns. As one of the triple Gems it means the community of those people who have attained enlightenment.

sankhata or saṅkhāra dhamma conditioned dhamma.

saññā memory, remembrance or "perception".

saññā-kkhandha memory classified as one of the five khandhas.

santīraṇa-citta investigating-consciousness.

saṅkāra dhamma conditioned dhamma.

saṅkhāra-kkhandha all cetasikas (mental factors) except feeling and memory.

saṅkhāradhamma conditioned realities.

saósāra the cycle of birth and death.

saóvega a sense of spiritual urgency.

sappurisa good man.

Sāriputta The First chief disciple of the Buddha.

sasaṅkhārika prompted, induced, instigated, either by oneself or someone else.

sati awareness, non-forgetfulness, awareness of reality by direct experience.

satipaṭṭhāna applicatioms of mindfulness. It can mean the cetasika sati which is aware of realities or the objects of mindfulness which are classified as four applications of mindfulness: Body, Feeling Citta, Dhamma. Or it can mean the development of direct understanding of realities through awareness.

satipaṭṭhāna sutta Middle Length Sayings 1, number 10, also Dīgha Nikāya, dialogues 11, no. 22;.

savana-kicca function of hearing.

sāyana-kicca function of tasting.

saṃyojanas The Fetters, a group of defilements.

sīla morality in action or speech, virtue.

sīlabbata-parāmāsā wrong practice.

sīlabbatupādāna wrong practice, which is clinging to certain rules ("rites and rituals") in one's practice.

sobhana (citta and cetasika) beautiful, accompanied by beautiful roots.

sobhana hetus beautiful roots.

sobhana kiriyacittas kiriyacittas accompanied by sobhana (beautiful) roots.

sobhana kiriyacittas kiriyacittas accompanied by sobhana (beautiful) roots.

somanassa happy feeling.

sota-dhātu element of earsense.

sota-dvāra-vīthi-cittas ear-door process cittas.

sota-dvārāvajjana-citta ear-door-adverting-consciousness.

sotāpanna person who has attained the first stage of enlightenment, and who has eradicated wrong view of realities.

soto-viññāṇa hearing-consciousness.

sukha happy, pleasant.

sukha-vedanā pleasant feeling.

sukhuma subtle.

sutta part of the scriptures containing dialogues at different places on different occasions.

suttanta a sutta text.

tadālambana retention or registering, last citta of a complete process of the sense-sphere.

tadārammaṇa-cittas registering-consciousness.

tadārammaṇa as above.

taruṇa vipassanā "tender insight".

Tathāgata literally "thus gone", epithet of the Buddha.

tatramajjhattatā equanimity or evenmindedness.

tejo-dhātu element of fire or heat.

Theravāda Buddhism 'Doctrine of the Elders', the oldest tradition of Buddhism.

thīna sloth.

tiṭṭhi khaṇa the moment of its presence, or static moment of citta.

Tipiṭaka the teachings of the Buddha.

titthi khaṇa static moment of citta.

Udāna Verses of Uplift from the Minor Anthologies.

uddhacca restlessness.

uddhambhāgiya-saṃyojana five higher fetters which tie beings to the higher planes of existance the rūpa-brahma planes and the arūpa-brahma planes.

ujupatipanno the straight, true and proper way.

upacāra access or proximatory consciousness, the second javana-citta in the process in which absorption or enlightenment is attained.

upacāra-samādhi access-concentration.

upādā-rūpa "derived rūpas" the rūpas other than the four Great Elements.

upādāna clinging.

upādānakkhandhas khandhas of clinging.

upanissaya-paccaya decisive support-condition.

upekkhā indifferent feeling. It can stand for evenmindedness or equanimity and then it is not feeling.

Uposatha Uposatha days are days of fasting or vigil; uposatha is observed on the days of full-moon and new-moon, and sometimes also on the days of the first and last moon-quarter. In Buddhist countries there is a tradition for lay-followers to visit temples and to observe eight precepts on these days.

uppāda khaṇa the arising moment of citta.

vaci-duccarita virati abstinence from wrong speech.

vacīviññatti the rūpa which is speech intimation.

vāsanā disagreeable habits accumulated in the past that can only be eradicated by a Buddha. Even arahats who have eradicated all defilements may still have a way of speech or action that is not agreeable to others.

vatthu base, physical base of citta.

vāyo-dhātu element of wind or motion.

vedanā feeling.

vedanā-kkhandha group of all feelings.

Vibhaṅga "Book of Analysis", one of the seven books of the Abhidhamma.

vibhava-taṇhā craving for non-existence.

vicāra sustained thinking or discursive thinking.

vicikicchā doubt.

vigata-paccaya disappearance-condition.

vihiósā-vitakka thought of harming.

vinaya Book of Discipline for the monks.

viññāṇa consciousness, citta.

viññāṇa-dhātu element of consciousness, comprising all cittas.

viññāṇa-kkhandha all cittas (consciousness).

viññāṇañcāyatana sphere of boundless consciousness, meditation subject for the second stage of immaterial jhāna.

vipāka-paccaya vipāka-condition.

vipākacitta citta which is the result of a wholesome deed (kusala kamma) or an unwholesome deed (akusala kamma). It can arise as rebirth-consciousness, or during life as the experience of pleasant or unpleasant objects through the senses, such as seeing, hearing, etc.

vipallāsas perversions. Three kinds: saññā perversion of perception, citta of thought, diṭṭhi of views.

vipassanāñāṇa moment of insight knowledge.

vipassanā wisdom which sees realities as they are.

vippayutta-paccaya dissociation-condition.

vippayutta dissociated from.

viriya energy.

visaṇkāra dhamma unconditioned dhamma (reality).

Visuddhimagga an encyclopaedia of the Buddha's teaching, written by Buddhaghosa in the fifth century A.D.

vitakka applied thinking.

vīthi-cittas cittas arising in a process.

vīthimutta-cittas process freed cittas, cittas which do not arise within a process.

votthapana-citta determining consciousness.

vyāpāda ill-will.

vyāpāda-vitakka thought of malevolence.

Yamaka the Book of Pairs, the sixth book of the Abhidhamma.

yoghas The yokes, a group of defilements.

F

Books written by Nina van Gorkom

- *The Buddha's Path* An Introduction to the doctrine of Theravada Buddhism for those who have no previous knowledge. The four noble Truths - suffering - the origin of suffering - the cessation of suffering - and the way leading to the end of suffering - are explained as a philosophy and a practical guide which can be followed in today's world.

- *Introduction to the Buddhist Scriptures* An Introduction to the Buddhist scriptures with the aim to encourage the reader to study the texts themselves. The book has a particular emphasis to help with the development of right understanding of all phenomena of life, at the present moment. It is a follow-up to Nina van Gorkom 's book "The Buddha's Path".

- *Letters on Vipassana* A compilation of letters discussing the development of vipassanā, the understanding of the present moment, in daily life. Contains over 40 quotes from the original scriptures and commentaries.

- *Buddhism in Daily Life* A general introduction to the main ideas of Theravada Buddhism.The purpose of this book is to help the reader gain insight into the Buddhist scriptures and the way in which the teachings can be used to benefit both ourselves and others in everyday life.

- *Abhidhamma in Daily Life* is an exposition of absolute realities in detail. Abhidhamma means higher doctrine and the book's purpose is to encourage the right application of Buddhism in order to eradicate wrong view and eventually all defilements.

- *Cetasikas* Cetasika means 'belonging to the mind'. It is a mental factor which accompanies consciousness (citta) and experiences an object. There are 52 cetasikas. This book gives an outline of each of these 52 cetasikas and shows the relationship they have with each other.

- *The Buddhist Teaching on Physical Phenomena* A general introduction to physical phenomena and the way they are related to each other and to mental phenomena. The purpose of this book is to show that the study of both mental phenomena and physical phenomena is indispensable for the development of the eightfold Path.

- *The Conditionality of Life* By Nina van Gorkom This book is an introduction to the seventh book of the Abhidhamma, that deals with the conditionality of life. It explains the deep underlying motives for all actions through body, speech and mind and shows that these are dependent on conditions and cannot be controlled by a 'self'. This book is suitable for those who have already made a study of the Buddha's teachings.

F.1 Books translated by Nina van Gorkom

- *The Perfections Leading to Enlightenment* by Sujin Boriharnwanaket. The Perfections is a study of the ten good qualities: generosity, morality, renunciation, wisdom, energy, patience, truthfulness, determination, loving-kindness, and equanimity.